Liberalism, Education and Schooling

ST ANDREWS STUDIES IN
PHILOSOPHY AND PUBLIC AFFAIRS

Founding and General Editor:
John Haldane, University of St Andrews

Values, Education and the Human World
edited by John Haldane

Philosophy and its Public Role
edited by William Aiken and John Haldane

Relativism and the Foundations of Liberalism
by Graham Long

Human Life, Action and Ethics:
Essays by G.E.M. Anscombe
edited by Mary Geach and Luke Gormally

The Institution of Intellectual Values:
Realism and Idealism in Higher Education
by Gordon Graham

Life, Liberty and the Pursuit of Utility
by Anthony Kenny and Charles Kenny

Distributing Healthcare:
Principles, Practices and Politics
edited by Niall Maclean

Liberalism, Education and Schooling:
Essays by T.H. Mclaughlin
edited by David Carr, Mark Halstead and Richard Pring

The Landscape of Humanity: Art, Culture & Society
by Anthony O'Hear

Faith in a Hard Ground:
Essays on Religion, Philosophy and Ethics by G.E.M. Anscombe
edited by Mary Geach and Luke Gormally

Subjectivity and Being Somebody
by Grant Gillett

Liberalism, Education and Schooling

Essays by T.H. McLaughlin

Edited by David Carr,
Mark Halstead and Richard Pring

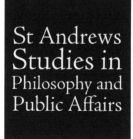

St Andrews
Studies in
Philosophy and
Public Affairs

IMPRINT ACADEMIC

Published in the UK by Imprint Academic
PO Box 200, Exeter EX5 5YX, UK

Published in the USA by Imprint Academic
Philosophy Documentation Center
PO Box 7147, Charlottesville, VA 22906-7147, USA

ISBN 9781845401443 (hbk)
ISBN 9781845401139 (pbk)

A CIP catalogue record for this book is available from the
British Library and US Library of Congress

Cover Photograph:
St Salvator's Quadrangle, St Andrews by Peter Adamson
from the University of St Andrews collection

Contents

Professor
Terence H. McLaughlin
(1949–2006)

As the editors explain in the following introduction to this collection of essays by the late Terence McLaughlin, he was a well known, greatly liked and much respected figure within philosophy of education in Great Britain. He also lectured and published further afield and his work is widely referred to in the literature on moral and religious education in the context of a liberal society. Terry McLaughlin's early death was a loss to his many friends and to the subject, and I am grateful to David Carr, Mark Halstead and Richard Pring for their work in gathering, selecting, ordering and introducing this set of essays. Terry McLaughlin had spoken of bringing together some of his writings either in the form of a collection, or integrated into a monograph, but in the event he died before achieving this. The present volume does not try to guess at what the content of that book might have been, but is instead a selection made by fellow scholars of high distinction judging what is of particular interest and enduring relevance in McLaughlin's academic writings on educational topics.

It is testimony both to the affection felt for Terry McLaughlin and to the high estimation of his work that three leaders in the field of educational studies in Britain have come together to collaborate on this project. David Carr is Professor of Philosophy of Education in the University of Edinburgh; Mark Halstead is Professor of Education, and Head of the Department of Community & International Education at the University of Huddersfield; and Richard Pring is Emeritus Professor of Educational Studies in the University of Oxford and Lead Director of the Nuffield Review of 14–19 Education and Training in England and Wales. I am particularly grateful to

Professor Carr for leading this project and for the considerable time he has given to it; also for the privilege of having the opportunity to publish this material in *St Andrews Studies in Philosophy and Public Affairs*. Thanks are due also to Silvia Jonas and to Anthony Freeman for assistance in the preparation of the text.

John Haldane

General Editor

Acknowledgements

The following chapters originated as essays in journals or books. The editors of this collection are grateful to the publishers and editors of these original sources for permission to reprint those essays in the present volume: publications, publishers and copyright holders are indicated in the following list corresponding to the present chapter order.

1. 'Philosophy and Educational Policy: Possibilities, Tensions and Tasks' *Journal of Educational Policy* Vol 15 No 4, 2000. pp 441-457. © 2000 Taylor & Francis Ltd.

2. 'Education, Philosophy and the Comparative Perspective' *Comparative Education* Vol 40 No 4, 2004. pp 471-483. © 2004 Taylor & Francis Ltd.

3. 'Education of the Whole Child?' in Ron Best (Ed) *Education, Spirituality and the Whole Child* (London, Cassell, 1996) pp. 9-19. © Continuum.

4. 'Beyond the Reflective Teacher' *Educational Philosophy and Theory* Vol 31 No 1, 1999, pp 9-25 © Philosophy of Education Society of Australasia.

5. 'National Identity and the Aims of Education' *Socialiniai Mokslai: Edukologija*, Vol. 5, No. 1, 1996, pp. 7-14. © T.H. McLaughlin.

6. 'School Choice and Public Education in a Liberal Democratic Society', *American Journal of Education* Vol 111, No 4, 2005, pp 442-463. © The University of Chicago.

7. 'Citizenship, Diversity and Education: a philosophical perspective' *Journal of Moral Education* Vol 21 No 3, 1992, pp 235-250. © 1992 Taylor & Francis Ltd.

8. 'The Burdens and Dilemmas of Common Schooling' in Kevin McDonough and Walter Feinberg (Eds) *Citizenship and Education in Liberal-Democratic Societies. Teaching for Cosmopolitan Values and Collective Identities* (Oxford, University Press, 2003) pp 121-156. © T.H. McLaughlin.

9. 'The Ethics of Separate Schools' in Mal Leicester and Monica Taylor (Eds) *Ethics, Ethnicity and Education* (London, Kogan Page, 1992) pp 114-136. © Cengage Learning.

10. 'Distinctiveness and the Catholic School: Balanced Judgement and the Temptations of Commonality' in James C Conroy (Ed) *Catholic Education: Inside-Out Outside-In* (Dublin, Veritas, 1999) pp 65-87. © T.H. McLaughlin.

11. 'Philosophy, Values and Schooling: Principles and Predicaments of Teacher Example' in William Aiken and John Haldane (eds) *Philosophy and its Public Role. Essays in Ethics, Politics, Society and Culture* . St Andrews Studies in Philosophy and Public Affairs (Exeter, UK and Charlottesville, USA, Imprint Academic, 2004) pp 69-83. © Imprint Academic.

12. 'Education, Spirituality and the Common School' in David Carr and John Haldane (Eds) *Spirituality, Philosophy and Education* (London, RoutledgeFalmer, 2003) pp 185-199. © T.H. McLaughlin.

13. 'Sex Education, Moral Controversy and the Common School' in Michael J. Reiss and Shaikh Abdul Mabud (Eds) *Sex, Education and Religion* (Cambridge: The Islamic Academy, 1998) pp 186-224. © The Islamic Academy.

14. 'Wittgenstein, Education and Religion' *Studies in Philosophy and Education* Vol 14 Nos 2-3, 1995, pp 295-311. © Kluwer Academic publishers.

15. 'Israel Scheffler on Religion, Reason and Education, *Studies in Philosophy and Education*, Vol 16, Nos 1-2, 1997, pp 201-223. © Kluwer Academic publishers.

David Carr, Mark Halstead & Richard Pring

Introduction

By the time of his premature death in 2006, Professor Terry McLaughlin of the University of London Institute of Education, Fellow of St Edmund's College Cambridge and formerly senior lecturer in the University of Cambridge Department of Education, was one of the most widely regarded and influential philosophers of education of his generation. Indeed, Terry McLaughlin was deeply respected and admired by friends, colleagues and students, and all were alike devastated by his untimely demise. At the same time, none of this widespread respect and affection was bought at the price of any academic or intellectual compromise. Professor McLaughlin was a scholar of the highest intellectual integrity who was aware that the interests of clarity and truth could not be served without serious critical confrontation with confusion and falsehood. Intellectually he was as tough-minded as they come and did not suffer folly at all gladly – though the patience and charity he showed towards any and all victims of folly and confusion was apparently inexhaustible. At all events, in the course of an all too short career, his contribution to the clarification of some of the deepest and most vexed conceptual issues of contemporary professional educational policy and practice may be considered significant and lasting. The present editors therefore hope that this collection of fifteen of McLaughlin's finest and most influential essays may serve to indicate – without need for further advocacy – something of the valuable academic legacy of a scholar of impressive ability and intellect, absolute integrity and matchless decency, kindness and generosity.

In this short introduction to Terry McLaughlin's work, however, we should perhaps say a little about the personal circumstances that shaped that work. Terry was born in 1949 into a working class family and like other children of his generation and social background he had to undergo the trauma of the British '11+' examination under a deeply divisive selective education system established in the wake of the 1944 Education Act, and—like may other working class children of his generation—he failed this notoriously unequal test. The fact that the 11+ and the selective system of educational provision that it entrained was unjust was by the nineteen sixties widely recognized by educational professionals and policy makers, and over the course of that decade this system was largely (although never entirely) dismantled in favour of a more egalitarian 'comprehensive' system of secondary education. It is possible that Terry McLaughlin's lifelong professional commitment to an ideal of common schooling reflected the deep agreement of one gifted 11+ survivor with the broadly egalitarian drift of comprehensive education. Terry McLaughlin's own educational experiences would have left him in no doubt of the social and moral damage that a selective system could do in foreclosing any and all possible avenues of personal, social and professional development and advancement for large numbers of able as well as less able or privileged young people. But not even the casual reader of McLaughlin could fail to appreciate his reservations about common schooling—or, at any rate, his recognition of the dangers inherent in any aspiration to a common educational experience for all that might ride roughshod over individually significant differences. In particular, as a religious believer, McLaughlin was clearly aware that any thoroughgoing liberal ideal of common schooling would inevitably have to avoid any and all complicity with what he also took to be humanly significant differences of religious, moral and spiritual perspective and nurture. From this viewpoint, Terry McLaughlin was also irresistibly, if not paradoxically, drawn to the moral and spiritual benefits of separate faith schooling. Indeed, to a great extent, his work may be seen as a lifelong struggle to reconcile what he regarded as educationally valuable about both forms of schooling.

At all events, after attending a secondary modern school for five years, Terry McLaughlin transferred to a grammar school for 'A' level studies. He considered a number of occupations or vocations before deciding to undertake a BEd course at Trent Park College of Education in Barnet, specializing in educational drama. The next eight years were taken up with school teaching in Hertfordshire and Bedfordshire, combined with study and part-time teaching at the University of London Institute of Education. It was as a postgraduate student at the London Institute that he came under the influence of Professor Richard Peters who encouraged his interest in philosophy and in the professional application of philosophical analysis to educational issues and problems. It was with the encouragement and support of Richard Peters that he was in 1979 appointed lecturer in Education in the University of Cambridge Department of Education, a post that he held for twenty-four years. It should also not here go unsaid that he was actually appointed by Peters' erstwhile colleague Professor Paul Hirst who remained one of McLaughlin's most supportive friends and colleagues during his Cambridge career. During these years, Terry McLaughlin established a strong local and international reputation as one of the foremost philosophers of education of the day. Locally, he was a pivotal figure in the Philosophy of Education Society of Great Britain, serving successively as Secretary, Vice-Chair and Chair, as well as Assistant Editor of the *Journal of Philosophy of Education* (in addition to his membership of the editorial boards of several other educational journals), and — as local coordinator of the Cambridge branch of the Philosophy of Education Society of Great Britain — he organised and hosted numerous conferences at St Edmunds College of which he was a Fellow. He was also a tireless international ambassador for Philosophy of Education, giving papers in more than 25 countries, and his contribution was particularly significant in Lithuania where he was awarded an honorary doctorate by Kaunas University for his services in rebuilding educational scholarship in that country. His appointment in 2003 to the prestigious London University Institute of Education Chair of Philosophy of Education — a position previously occupied by such distinguished figures as Louis Arnaud Reid, and R. S. Peters — was widely approved throughout the world of educational philosophy. In view of this, his untimely death on March 31 2006 from acute leukaemia at Addenbrooke's Hospital Cambridge, was greeted as a terrible shock and with a sense of profound loss by his numerous friends, students and colleagues.

As already indicated, it was at the University of London Institute of Education — first on the MA programme and then as a PhD student of Ray Elliott and (later) John White — that Terry McLaughlin came under the influence of Professor Richard Peters and of others in the philosophical group that Peters had gathered around him. There can also be little doubt that Terry McLaughlin's encounter with the new London approach to philosophy of education was for him a matter of deep and lasting intellectual conversion. That approach, of which Richard Peters was the principal British pioneer, was of course unashamedly analytical. Drawing on the work of such mid-twentieth century British Oxbridge philosophers as

Wittgenstein, Ryle and Austin, Peters and his followers ushered in a radically new dawn of theorizing about education that was different from anything that had previously been entertained in professional teacher education and training. To begin with, Peters rejected the 'doctrines of the great educators' approach to educational philosophy, common up until that time in the British colleges of education, that consisted in largely amateurish and uncritical introductions to past educational ideas or ideologies of the likes of Plato, Rousseau and Dewey. For the new analytical breed of educational philosopher, the value of philosophy lay not in the study of past philosophers or 'philosophies' — although it was not denied that teachers and other educationalists might stand to learn much from a critical examination of past ideas — but in the practical grasp of professionally useful techniques for the critical analysis of received theoretical and practical discourse regarding education and schooling. Indeed, though they conceded that teachers qua professionals were likely to benefit from exposure to a variety of forms of educationally relevant knowledge and enquiry, the new conceptual analysts held — in view of the epistemically dubious and/or ethically contested nature of much official and professional educational discourse (not to mention the conceptually confused educational theory on which teachers were often invited to draw) — that some capacity for rigorous conceptual appraisal of familiar educational usage was indispensable to professional educational competence. Peters himself set exemplary standards of such analysis with regard to a wide range of basic educational concepts — not least by showing how educational theorists and policy makers had often been unclear about the fundamental point of education, confusing it with such other concepts as training, socialization and even therapy. But this general defense of the professional value of philosophical expertise was also part and parcel of a larger attempt to improve the academic quality and status of professional teacher education. The project of raising teacher education to the status of an all graduate profession grounded in the rigorous study of specialist taught disciplines of philosophy, history, psychology and sociology of education was very much the brain-child of London based philosophy of education, and BEd degrees based on this general pattern soon became the standard fare of the colleges of education.

The Peters 'revolution' in philosophy of education is of course now more than forty years in the past and there has been much new water under the philosophical bridge since that time. To be sure, perhaps the most significant trend in latter day philosophy of education has been a general drift away from the analytical paradigm that Peters pioneered towards what are sometimes referred to as 'post-analytical' approaches, drawing on other traditions of philosophy. Ironically, many of these rival traditions draw upon continental European currents of thought — associated with such movements as Phenomenology, Existentialism, Marxism, Structuralism, Post-Structuralism and Postmodernism, and with such names as Kierkegaard, Nietzsche, Husserl, Heidegger, Derrida, Lyotard, Foucault and Levinas — that were (or would have been) regarded as unhelpful by Peters and his colleagues in mainstream analytical philosophy. However, despite the extraordinary range of his reading and his great intellectual open-mindedness and hospitality to any and all new ideas, Terry McLaughlin remained committed to a broadly analytical conception of philosophy in general and educational philosophy in particular. Like Peters, he saw no good reason to depart from a tried and tested philosophical approach to philosophical questions that he also clearly recognized as one of the greatest of modern intellectual achievements. Although he was very aware that the work of Richard Peters had opened up even more vexed problems than it had solved, he was no less persuaded by Peters' faith in the power of objective rational thought for clarity of understanding and by his mentor's commitment to careful conceptual analysis as a key tool in achieving such clarity. Hence, no less than Peters (and, arguably, in a time-honoured tradition going all the way back to Socrates), McLaughlin keenly appreciated the need for any acceptable perspective on educational practice to be firmly supported by coherent and valid argument and he was second to none in his honest and rigorous pursuit of such argument.

Thus, from his first work on parental rights and the pastoral curriculum, through his explorations of ideas of open-mindedness, values, citizenship, sex and religious education and cultural identity, to his later investigations of school ethos, spiritual education and school inspection, he tirelessly sought to expose the confusions and fallacies into which educational discourse and argument could readily fall without due attention to fine distinctions between different senses of common educational and other terms. There can also be no doubt, as this extremely truncated list of McLaughlin topics is sufficient to show, that Terry McLaughlin's reflections and investigations ranged widely and that it is difficult to think of any educational topic of major theoretical or public concern on which he did not have something important to say. That said, at least in the published work, there was also a certain evident unity in this broad diversity of interest. Hence, although McLaughlin was not greatly drawn to the 'post-analytical' trends of more recent educational philosophy, it is probably fair to say that he was at one with latter day emphases in the broadly political or public policy thrust of his work. For although the early post-war pioneers of analytical philosophy of education had tended to regard (primarily) ethics and epistemology as the principal points of departure for educational reflection (and some early analytical philosophers of education had actually claimed that the key questions of education, curriculum and learning were largely apolitical) it is evident that later work inclined towards a more political, if not politicized, view of educational enquiry, policy and practice. Although Terry McLaughlin would certainly have been somewhat sceptical of this as a general trend — and would certainly not have regarded any and all educational questions as exclusively or narrowly political — it would nevertheless appear that this latter day educational philosophical shift towards questions of public policy chimed greatly with his own interests. Thus for example, although he was deeply interested in questions about religious education, and although the interest of early analytical philosophers would formerly have focused on questions of the educational meaning of religious discourse, Terry McLaughlin's own published work on religion and religious education generally concentrated on more recent educational philosophical concerns with the (political) pros and cons of faith schooling.

Indeed, the issue of faith schooling was for Terry McLaughlin but one particularly significant dimension of a more fundamental and pressing question for open yet culturally pluralist societies about how to reconcile a broadly common liberal form of state schooling — one that does not unduly foreclose life options for young people by forcing them into inherited social, religious or vocational pathways — with different and diverse patterns of nurture that might still be regarded as morally, spiritually and educationally sustaining or nourishing. It was this central issue that tied together what might otherwise appear to be bewilderingly diverse McLaughlin interests in rather disconnected topics and themes. On the one hand, it would be hard to exaggerate McLaughlin's commitment to the fundamental values and virtues of liberal democracy and he was the author of many robust and spirited defences of open-mindedness, critical rationality and individual autonomy. On the other hand, however, he was profoundly appreciative of the respects in which over-emphasis on the secular dimensions of liberalism might paradoxically serve to undermine such autonomy by precluding the exposure of young people to alternative (religious or other) perspectives. Hence, starting with the question of parental rights, Terry McLaughlin's concern was precisely with the question of how far the state or state education might be justified in imposing a particular framework of (perhaps liberal) values on the children of religious or other parents who might not share such values.

It was much the same general problem that was more particularized in the context of his various rich explorations of sex, spiritual, moral, citizenship and religious education. Given that sex, morality and religion are inherently implicated in deeply contested questions of human value, how might children and young people in a culturally pluralist society be meaningfully and positively educated in such matters—not least in common state schools or curricula in which parents might feel that common teaching of such topics falls short of or neglects the more substantial values to which they may be committed? Certainly, given the philosophical complexity of such issues, Terry McLaughlin was keenly aware of their significant ethical and epistemic dimensions: that, for example, to defend a parent's right to bring up their child in a particular way is not the same as saying that such upbringing is right, good or true. From this viewpoint, the political philosopher's defense of a right is neither the philosophical beginning nor the end of the matter. Nevertheless, as someone committed to liberal democracy no less than to a particular faith perspective, Terry McLaughlin appreciated that state imposed (particularly secular) common education could be no less restrictive or coercive of individual liberty than other kinds of formation, and he clearly perceived the importance for a flourishing democracy of a voice for all educational stakeholders.

In this light, the central concern to which Terry McLaughlin returned time and again from a variety of directions was that of how to provide a common public education that might serve to promote maximum possible individual liberty of thought and development without subverting or silencing voices at some odds with the conventional (perhaps secular) moral and intellectual mainstream of public life. To this end, in the course of two decades of serious and painstaking effort, Terry McLaughlin produced an impressive corpus of academically and professionally important work identifying many of the key distinctions that have since come to be regarded as central to the field. This was also sheer hard toil and McLaughlin always found it to be so. His uncompromising struggles with these issues, all too often pursued well into the night and early morning — were well known to his friends, colleagues and other close associates. Much difficulty in this respect was caused by his unswerving intellectual integrity and academic perfectionism. He was known to be the bane of editors of essay collections to which he was frequently invited to contribute who would anxiously have to await McLaughlin submissions well beyond stated deadlines. Moreover, the problem was sometimes not so much (as is often the case with many dilatory contributors) that the essays had not yet been produced, but rather that McLaughlin was reluctant to part with papers already written: for, whereas others would call it a day and let things go, McLaughlin could always see that there was more work to be done no matter what the cost. Whatever the downside of Terry McLaughlin's perfectionism, however, a happier outcome is clearly to be observed in the strikingly perspicuous and well-turned character of the essays reprinted in this collection or published elsewhere. For the present editors, one of the greatest pleasures in assembling this collection has been the opportunity to re-read his clear and elegant work. Indeed, it would be hard to find a better literary and philosophical model for future generations of educational philosophers than that provided by the essays presented in this collection and elsewhere.

That said, the generally high quality of Terry McLaughlin's published output also presented no small editorial obstacle. Faced with the task of selecting a relatively small cross-section of his wide-ranging work for this necessarily limited collection, it was clear that some hard choices lay ahead. In view of this, indeed, it is inevitable that this collection will have failed to include the McLaughlin favourites of all. Hence, given that we finally had to decide against including some strong essays — which might well occasion some understandable disappointment — it is probably important to say something here about our ultimately rather severe criteria for inclusion and exclusion. First, of course, there were fairly basic judgements of relative quality. Any writer, even one of Terry McLaughlin's consistently high quality output, will produce better and worse essays. Secondly, however, it was seen to be important that included pieces together offered a fairly representative view of the broad range of his work. In this light, it was also clear that many of Terry McLaughlin's papers did frequently interrelate and overlap in rich and interesting, but — for present purposes — potentially redundant ways. Thus, for example, while keen to include McLaughlin pieces on both sex and spiritual education, we were aware of three fine pieces — one on sex education, another on spiritual education and a third on the spiritual dimension of sex education. In this instance, it seemed presently best to keep the first two and to reject the third. In cases where there were two fine papers on the same theme — as in the case of the probably most influential McLaughlin papers on citizenship — we finally selected the one (first appearing in *Journal of Moral Education*) that we judged to be of greater lasting influence. Yet a third criterion, however, was that McLaughlin papers should be as far as possible self-standing. From this viewpoint, like many philosophers, McLaughlin devoted a fair measure of book and journal space to critical evaluations of, or responses to, the views of his philosophical contemporaries. Some of these — such as his 1984 essay on parental rights and religious upbringing — are (as we all agreed) impressive McLaughlin fare. All the same, given that it is often not easy to make full sense of many of these replies and critiques apart from the articles to which they are responding, we thought it better to choose more 'self-standing' pieces.

A rather more difficult issue was that of collaborations. Perhaps more than most educational philosophers, Terry McLaughlin often worked and published in collaboration with colleagues in the field — including with all three present editors. Apart from the fact that to leave out any and all McLaughlin collaborations might be not to give a very full or complete picture of his scholarly activities, it was also clear that many of these collaborations were highly successful ventures that produced reputable work. In the end, however, the editors decided against including collaborations. To begin with, it seemed anyway hardly appropriate to include collaborations in which present editors were involved. Moreover, since we could not possibly include all collaborations, any decisions in favour of this or that one might also be taken as a (perhaps adverse) judgement on those not selected — and hence as a possible slight on the work of co-authors thereby excluded. Thus, at the risk of failing to give some exposure to this dimension of Terry McLaughlin's work, it seemed best to add a general 'no-collaboration' rule to others already indicated. At any rate, once these 'no-collaborations', 'stand-alone' and other rules were adopted, the contents of the present collection more or less selected themselves. Hence, despite much interesting discussion between present editors on the merits of this or that individual McLaughlin piece, there was substantial final agreement that the fifteen pieces finally selected provided good coverage of the quality and breadth of his work. So although we cannot possibly expect to have included the personal McLaughlin favourites of everyone, we hope it may still be widely agreed that the present selection provides a representative cross-section of Terry McLaughlin's finest work.

One could not conclude this short introduction to Terry McLaughlin's life and work without some comment on his personal as well as professional character and influence. On this matter, it is difficult to find the right tone of personal detachment for a context such as the present one. However, as Terry McLaughlin was a man of sober judgement and some personal reserve, we can be sure he would have appreciated some restraint and certainly not have welcomed anything too excessive. All the same, we feel the need to convey something of the profound personal impact that Terry McLaughlin had on those with whom he came in contact. Perhaps first and foremost, he was that all too rare creature — a person of deep Christian faith and conviction who succeeded in living up to the true moral and spiritual principles and commitments of that faith. Although he worked his way up from the ranks to one of the highest positions in his field in a contemporary climate in which academic promotion is often driven by personal ambition, it was abundantly evident that Terry McLaughlin did not have a careerist bone in his body, and was quite untouched by vanity or material acquisitiveness. The professional ideals he perfectly exemplified were those of personally unsparing service to others — though for Terry McLaughlin this was always a matter of joyous self-giving, not at all of grudging duty. In this respect, he was extraordinarily mindful of the needs of others and generous to a fault with his time and attention. But, lest this should make him appear unfit for the company of mere mortals, it is also impossible to forget not only the extraordinary good humour, but also the no less wicked wit of Terry McLaughlin. He was invariably the life and soul of the party — and, indeed, was the founder of an internationally renowned tradition of Saturday night parties at the annual Philosophy of Education conferences in Oxford. Always taking the needs of others seriously, he was nevertheless far from taking himself or the world too seriously, and his sense of humour and rich repertoire of Les Dawson jokes was legendary. From this viewpoint, the light and joy with which Terry McLaughlin touched the lives of so many of us is also his lasting legacy.

Philosophy, Educational Policy and Practice

Terry McLaughlin will be remembered most for the philosophical insights he brought to such contested issues as the debate between common schools and faith schools, the question of parental choice of schooling, spiritual and moral values in school, and the relationship between religion and education — and these topics rightly form the focus of attention of sections II and III of this volume. But it seems appropriate to start with a broader view of his output. As a philosopher of education, McLaughlin was concerned with many aspects of education: bringing clarity to educational practices such character education and school inspection; articulating a critical response to educational goals such as the development of national identity or civic virtues like tolerance and open-mindedness; and providing a critical discussion of policy initiatives like citizenship. He also spent time evaluating the work of other philosophers of education (particularly those like John Wilson and Paul Hirst who belonged to the generation before his own). At a deeper level, he was concerned to investigate the kind of contribution that philosophy can make to thinking about educational policy and practice, and the relationship between philosophy of education and other sub-disciplines such as comparative education. A fuller indication of the range of McLaughlin's writings can be gained from the list of his publications contained in Appendix One.

It is the role of philosophy in facilitating reflection on educational policy and practice that provides the theme of the present section. In the important opening essay, McLaughlin locates his own position within the field of philosophy of education, and then proceeds to explore some of the reflective and critical resources that philosophy can bring to bear on educational policy. He positions himself between two extremes in philosophy of education: on the one hand, there is the narrowly defined analytical approach with its emphasis on the clarification of educational concepts, and on the other, traditions of philosophising influenced by postmodernism. The middle path which McLaughlin himself espouses is still broadly analytical, but demonstrates a willingness at the same time to engage with directly practical matters and develop substantive arguments in favour of particular ethical, cultural and political positions on education. What this kind of philosophical approach can contribute to educational policy includes things like the probing of assumptions, the clarification of underlying values, the testing of coherence, the development of a clear and effective vision and the justification of educational decisions.

Similar arguments are put forward in the paper 'Education, Philosophy and the Comparative Perspective', where McLaughlin urges more dialogue between philosophers and those working in the field of comparative education. He suggests that the latter will benefit from philosophers' ability to clarify concepts, to bring critical scrutiny to educational theories, aims, policies and practices, and to provide rational justifications for particular positions and views, while philosophers in turn cannot evaluate a policy or justify a particular vision of education without paying attention to different traditions and the historical and geopolitical context which comparative education provides.

The third article in this section problematises the commonly used terminology of 'educating the whole child'. McLaughlin begins by distinguishing two possible interpretations of the term 'whole' (the first implying that we should aim at broad and balanced development, the second that we should aim at the development of the integrated personality). But any transmission of a comprehensive or holistic view of life is suspect in the context of the common school, which should adopt a stance of critical openness towards different worldviews, rather than attempt to influence children towards any comprehensive framework of beliefs and values.

The fourth article subjects another currently fashionable notion — that of the teacher as 'reflective practitioner' — to similar critical scrutiny. McLaughlin argues that in spite of the concept's intuitive appeal, we need to look beyond the slogan itself and assess its adequacy as an account of teaching and teacher training. In particular, he encourages us to consider how 'reflection' is to be understood, where its value lies precisely, and what the model implies for teacher training. He concludes that teachers need a much broader range of moral, intellectual and personal qualities than the phrase 'the reflective teacher' suggests.

The final article, written in the context of educational developments in post-communist Lithuania, examines whether forming a national identity is a justifiable aim for education. Taking as a starting point the traditional liberal suspicion of the use of education for unduly particular formation and influence (while at the same time recognising that liberal education cannot altogether avoid shaping particular identities), McLaughlin proceeds with some clarification of the concept and value of nationalism and concludes that contextual considerations must play a significant part in any attempt to justify promoting national identity through education. Such considerations include whether national identity has been forcibly suppressed in the past, whether it is currently under threat, and whether it takes a form that is compatible with pluralism and other democratic values.

Mark Halstead

Chapter 1

Philosophy and Educational Policy

Possibilities, tensions and tasks

Educational policy in its various aspects is shaped and determined by many complex interrelated factors and influences. Included among these are factors and influences of a broadly philosophical kind, although the truth that educational policy cannot be based on philosophical considerations alone is too obvious to require emphasis. In this essay, I shall explore the role which philosophy can and should play in relation to educational policy. I shall argue that philosophy has a potentially important contribution to make to educational policy, but that there are some underexplored complexities, which require exploration if the resources of philosophy are to be fruitfully brought to bear in this context. These complexities can be usefully approached in terms of 'possibilities', 'tensions' and 'tasks'. Informed analysis, debate, research and professional experiment in relation to educational policy are vital if policies are to be coherent, justifiable and effective. These reflective and critical resources which should be brought to bear on educational policy are very wide ranging in character. They include *inter alia* insights and perspectives derived from disciplines of enquiry such as history, sociology and psychology, from the various traditions of empirical research and from the practical pedagogic and educational experience of colleagues working in schools. Philosophy constitutes one element of these reflective and critical resources. The context and 'climate' of educational policy making varies from time to time in the extent to which these reflective and critical resources are acknowledged and drawn upon in policy development, implementation and evaluation. In times when these resources are neglected by educational policy makers and treated with indifference or even hostility, the resources will be applied 'at a distance' in commentary and critique.[1] At other times, a different context and 'climate' of educational policy making will prevail, and efforts will be made to draw the resources closer to educational policy making itself.

In common with other elements of these reflective and critical resources, philosophers at present tend to feel that their confirmation is being 'drawn closer' to the process of educational policy making after a long period at a distance. In support of this feeling on the part of philosophers one can point, for example, to the recent wide ranging consultation by the QCA, as a preliminary to its review of the school curriculum for the millennium, on the sorts of educational aims which this curriculum should embody. This consultation has not only addressed fundamental philosophical questions, but has also involved the direct participation of philosophers (Aldrich and White 1998). Further, many recent policy debates and initiatives, such as those related to the National Forum for Values in Education and the Community (see Talbot and Tate 1997) and to education for citizenship (see Qualifications and Curriculum Authority 1998) have not only faced up to philosophical issues implicit in their areas of concern, but have also invited philosophical influence and participation. Philosophers therefore tend to feel, with whatever degree of justification, that at present they have a particularly good opportunity not only to influence and contribute to educational policy from a distance but also more closely. Be this as it may, it is timely to focus attention on the nature of the contribution which philosophy can and should make to educational policy making, and to explore the possibilities, tensions and tasks which arise.

The essay has six sections. In the first section I make a number of general points about the nature of educational policy. The second section considers some preliminary considerations relating to the relationship between philosophy and educational policy. In the following section I offer some reflections about the nature of philosophy itself. The possibilities, tensions and tasks relating to the contribution of philosophy to educational policy are considered in the fourth, fifth and sixth sections respectively.

The Nature of Educational Policy

It is helpful at the outset of our discussion to make a number of preliminary points about educational policy and policy making, which

---

[1]   See, for example, Hartnett and Naish 1986.

are relevant to the contribution which philosophy might make to them. Four preliminary points are of particular significance here.

First, what is an educational policy? In answer to this question, some writers stress the relationship between educational policies and politics, power and control (Codd 1995: 1–2). Prunty (quoted in Codd 1995: 1) defines educational policy making as 'an exercise of power and control directed towards the attainment or preservation of some preferred arrangement of schools and society'. Codd himself argues that 'educational policies are sets of political decisions which involve the exercise of power in order to preserve or alter the nature of educational institutions or practices' (ibid.). Prunty and Codd seem to imply that educational policies can be formulated only by those who exercise power and control and who are involved in politics in this sense. Is it not the case, however, that educational policies can be formulated by many bodies and agencies, including those who do not (either temporarily or otherwise) enjoy the exercise of relevant forms of power and control but seek merely to influence educational arrangements indirectly through (say) appeal to the electorate, lobbying of various kinds or the stimulation of general debate and discussion? The kinds of bodies and agencies one thinks of here include political parties in opposition, subject and teacher associations, 'think tanks' of various kinds and the like. A more sensitive characterization of the relationship between educational policy making on the one hand and politics, power and control on the other seems therefore to be required. What is central to the notion of an educational policy is that it is a detailed prescription for action aimed at the preservation or alteration of educational institutions or practices. However, an educational policy, and the related notion of 'educational policy making' can be used in either (i) power and control related or (ii) 'influence aspirant' senses and contexts.

Second, educational policies originate at different levels and contexts in the educational system and from a number of different agents and agencies ranging from national to school (and even to classroom level). There are different 'languages' of policy debate, which can be roughly labelled as 'official', 'professional', 'research' and 'popular' (McLaughlin 1999a: 37–38).

Third, educational policies differ with respect to the scope of their content and application. One way of expressing these differences is to invoke various kinds of continuum on which policies can be located. One such continuum involves generality and specificity. At one end of this continuum are policies of a very general kind involving matters such as the aims of education and the structure of the educational system, whilst at the other end are very specific policies relating (say) to strategies for the teaching of particular topics within specific subjects. Another (related) continuum can be described as involving 'depth' and 'surface' characteristics. The 'depth' end of this continuum involves educational policies with clear philosophical implications and ramifications. Many current policies concerned with the general area of 'values education' fall into this category. At the 'surface' end of this continuum are educational policies, which are less apt for philosophical reflection. It is important not to assume, however, that 'generality' is uniquely associated with 'depth' and 'specificity' with 'surface' characteristics. General policies may not be suitable for philosophical reflection and specific policies may be rich in philosophical implication.

Fourth, it is useful to note the distinction between different (though interrelated) aspects of educational policy and policy making: (i) the process of educational policy making; (ii) the policy itself, and (iii) the application and evaluation of the policy.

These four preliminary points have significance for the role which philosophy might play in relation to educational policy and policy making. Taken as a whole, the points caution against treating 'educational policy' in an unanalysed way if one is seeking to achieve a sensitive characterization of the contribution which philosophy might make to it. Considered individually, each point contains an insight worth nothing. The first point urges alertness to the influence which power and control might have on proffered philosophical contributions to educational policy; the second point raises awareness of the different levels and contexts where such philosophical contributions might be made; the third point reminds us that not all educational policies are equally apt for philosophical illumination and urges us to reflect on how we might distinguish between those policies which do and those which do not properly invite philosophical attention, and the fourth point brings into focus the different aspects and dimensions of educational policy and policy making which philosophers might seek to contribute to.

Philosophy and Educational Policy: Some Preliminary Considerations

The claim that philosophy is one of the reflective and critical resources, which should be brought to bear on educational policy if policies are to be coherent, justifiable and effective invites attention to the precise nature of the contribution which philosophy might make in these matters.

At the outset, it is important to emphasize that the contribution which philosophy can offer is a modest one. This is for at least two reasons. First, philosophy is only one of the 'reflective and critical resources' relevant to educational policy. Secondly, reflection and criticism may be necessary for educational policy but it is not sufficient for its coherence, justifiability and effectiveness: the wide-ranging contingencies of circumstance and practice are highly salient and decisive. The modesty of philosophy must extend both to an acknowledgement that its contribution to educational policy is a partial one, and to an acceptance that its contribution must be offered in relationship and dialogue with other reflective and critical resources and with the contingencies of circumstance and practice. It should be noted that the contribution which philosophy may make to educational policy need not necessarily be a 'purely' philosophical one, but can (and sometimes should) be linked to, and form part of, reflective and critical contributions of a wider kind.[2]

One starting point for our investigation of the contribution which philosophy might make to educational policy is Amelie Oksenberg Rorty's remark:

> Fruitful and responsible discussions of educational policy inevitably move to the larger philosophic questions that prompt and inform them. (Oksenberg Rorty 1998a:1)

As it stands, this remark requires qualification in a number of ways. First, the remark should clearly not be interpreted descriptively, as referring to what actually happens in discussions of educational policy, but normatively, as indicating what should characterize discussions of this kind. Even interpreted in this way, however, as requiring that all policy discussion should move on to philosophical questions, the remark is not obviously true, in, for example, the case of educational policies with merely 'surface' characteristics. Second, it is not clear that all educational policies are 'prompted and informed' by philosophic questions. Educational policies with merely 'surface' characteristics are again a case in point here. Further, it is not clear that 'prompting' is the most accurate way of characterizing the relationship between philosophy and educational policy. Many policy discussions are prompted by severely practical considerations. Oksenberg Rorty goes on claim that educational pol-

---

[2]   For this point in relation to philosophy and educational research see, for example, Bridges 1997, 1998a.See also Soltis 1988: 8–9.

icy is blind without the guidance of philosophy (1998a: 2). This too seems overstated, in this case with respect to the necessary modesty which I have urged on the role of philosophy in these matters. The remark ignores the contribution, which other reflective and critical resources might make to educational policy including those arising from practical pedagogic and educational experience. The remark also underplays the continuity of philosophical reasoning and reflection with common sense. We all have some capacity to discriminate between sound and unsound reasoning, and to discern the need for clarity and justification.

A more well-grounded approach to discerning the proper contribution of philosophy with respect to educational policy is to focus upon the embeddedness of philosophical considerations in (many) educational policies. Many educational policies contain (to a greater or lesser extent) assumptions, concepts, beliefs, values and commitments which, if not themselves of a directly philosophical kind, are apt for philosophical attention. These elements permeate many educational policies, even if they do not amount to 'a philosophy of education' (cf. Carr 1995 §3), and are not articulated but remain implicit, embryonic and perhaps confused. These philosophically significant elements relate not merely to the 'content' of particular educational policies but also to broader matters relating to education and educational policy in general. The illumination which philosophy can bring is therefore wide ranging. For example, Israel Scheffler in his essay 'The Education of Policy Makers' (Scheffler 1991 section 10) brings into focus why policy making cannot be reduced to merely technical considerations. Policy is made, he argues, in the context of '… multiple human activities, experiences , purposes, and needs' (p. 104) and so broad human understanding is required together with a grasp of matters of value and of the 'normative space' created by policy decisions.

The force of this point is that philosophical considerations do not need to be artificially brought to bear on educational policy. Such considerations are already implicit (and operative) within much policy. This is readily seen, for example in policy-sensitive notions such as 'evidence based teaching'[3] and 'the knowledge-creating school.'[4] Given that education is inherently value-laden, why is (educative) teaching seen as 'based in' rather than 'informed by' evidence? Why is the (educative) school seen as creating knowledge rather than

---

[3]   See Hargreaves 1996, 1997, Hammersley 1997.

[4]   Hargreaves 1999.

(say) insight and commitment? The choice is therefore whether to make philosophical considerations in educational policy explicit and to aim systematically at achieving clarity and justification in relation to them, or to leave the elements unexamined and undisturbed. A choice to take the road of explicitness and systematic attention brings into focus the distinctive contribution of the philosopher, whose watchwords are clarity, perspective, warrant and vision.

Many philosophers have self-consciously sought to influence educational policy. One thinks here of major philosophers such as Plato and Dewey among others, and, in Britain, T. H. Green and the idealist philosophers of the late nineteenth century (on Green and the idealist philosophers see Gordon and White 1979). Amelie Oksenberg Rorty has recently outlined the practical effects on education of the thought of a number of philosophers, and the aspiration of much of this thought to have educational effects of this kind (Oksenberg Rorty 1998b §1. cf. Almond 1995: 3–4). Interestingly, she further argues that 'philosophy rings hollow' without attention to its 'educational import' (Oksenberg Rorty 1998a: 2). A desire to inform practical policies of various kinds can be traced back to the origins of philosophy (See Warren 1992). In addition to direct influence, philosophy contributes to, and influences, educational policy indirectly through the general intellectual and cultural climate:[5] secularism, pluralism, relativism, equality and the salience of market forces all have their philosophical progenitors.

All this is not to suggest, however, that the value of philosophizing about education should be judged solely in terms of its contribution to educational practice in general, and to educational policy in particular. There is some wisdom in R K Elliott's insistence that 'Philosophy did not free itself from domestic service to theology in order to become, in the sphere of education, little better than the odd-job man of pedagogy' (Elliott 1986: 66). Harvey Siegel calls into question the suggestion that philosophers of education have a duty to attend to practical matters (Siegel 1988, cf. Soltis 1988). Nor is hesitation about interaction with the practical domain on the part of philosophers solely to related to a concern with the value of the disinterested pursuit of truth for its own sake. Peters, for example, expresses doubts whether adequate and imaginative 'down to earth' work of a

---

[5]   On the influence of Hegel, Fichte and Kant on the British idealist philosophers of the late nineteenth century who influenced education, see Gordon and White 1979.

philosophical kind can be done unless the 'treatment' ' ... springs from a coherent and explicit philosophical position' (Peters 1983: 55).

The Nature of Philosophy

Any attempt to gain a closer understanding of the distinctive contribution which philosophy can make to educational policy requires attention to how 'philosophy' is being understood. Philosophy, after all, is no one thing and different conceptions of philosophy give rise to potentially different conceptions of the contribution, which it can and should make to educational policy.

One prominent kind of philosophizing about education during the last forty years is locatable within the analytic tradition, associated with the pioneering work of Richard Peters and Israel Scheffler in the 1960s, and continued in a substantial body of work subsequently. The development of this tradition, specifically in the form of the discipline of 'philosophy of education', has been well charted in an extensive literature, as has the related methodological issues and disputes to which this development has given rise.[6]

'Analysis' has been described as ' ... the elucidation of the meaning of any concept, idea or unit of thought that we employ in seeking to understand ourselves and our world, by reducing it, breaking it down, into more basic concepts that constitute it and thereby showing its relationship to a network of other concepts or discovering what the concept denotes' (Hirst and White 1998a: 2). Analysis in this sense is concerned not merely with the meaning of beliefs, but also with their justification and truth (ibid.). The 'connective' character of analysis in this sense is worthy of emphasis: the investigation of ' ... how one concept is connected — often in complex and ragged-ended ways — in a web of other concepts with which it is logically related' (White and White 1997: 2).

Whilst there are common elements across all phases of the analytic tradition in philosophy of education it is possible to distinguish roughly an earlier and a later phase (mirrored by comparable trends in philosophy generally), the earlier phase subscribing to certain preoccupations and methodological commitments which have

---

[6] See, for example, Peters 1966 Introduction, Wilson 1979, Feinberg 1983 § 6, Peters 1983, Jonathan 1985, Cooper 1986, Elliott 1986, Hirst 1986, 1993a, 1998, White 1987a, 1987b, 1995, Soltis 1988, Evers 1993, Carr 1995 esp. Introduction, Kohli 1995 Part 1, White and White 1997, Carr 1998, Haydon 1998, Hirst and White 1998a, 1998b Part I.

come to be less prominent from the perspective of the broader focus and concerns of the later phase.

In the early period, the analytical approach was applied to the clarification of concepts distinctive to education (such as education itself, teaching, development and indoctrination), and the delineation of philosophically interesting connections between them; a critique of currently influential educational theories (such as child-centredness) in terms of the philosophically problematic concepts and claims they contained, and the application of philosophical analyses of educationally relevant concepts (such as knowledge, belief and emotion) and, more generally, of the resources of epistemology, philosophical psychology, ethics and social philosophy to educational concerns (Peters 1966 Introduction , White and White 1997: 6–7).

In retrospect, this earlier period has come to be seen as rather narrow in the character and focus of its concerns and methodology. For example, this is apparent in relation to the 'second-order' character of philosophical activity, which was emphasized. On this view, the task of the philosopher is not to provide an answer to any specific questions about (say) the aims and values of education, much less to provide high-level 'directives for living'. Rather that task is seen in terms of the clarification of concepts, an exploration of the grounds of knowledge, the elucidation of presuppositions and the development of criteria for justification.

This earlier tradition in analytic philosophy of education was subjected to a range of extensive criticisms. The criticisms included *inter alia*: that its approach was inattentive to the history of philosophy, and in particular to the history of concepts; that it aspired to a spurious value-neutrality with respect to its analyses and commitments; that it was uncritical about its own assumptions and values (including the view of human nature which it presupposed); that it espoused an untenable rationalism; that its approach was inherently conservative politically, socially and educationally; that it confined itself illicitly to 'second-order' clarification rather than the development of substantive arguments; that it read too much into what can be legitimately derived from a mere analysis of concepts, espousing an illicit 'essentialism' with respect to their meaning; that it implied that ordinary language use provides an unassailable court of appeal in determining meaning; that it illicitly claimed a universal significance and value for certain ideals and values independent of all cultural and social contexts, and that it was of little use in relation to the determination and improvement of educational policy and practice.[7]

Whilst some of these lines of criticism are not without justification, it is important to be alert to the dangers of overstatement and even misunderstanding (see, for example, Hirst 1986). The claim that the approach sought to be value-neutral, for example, is only one example of the sort of misunderstanding which was evident in some quarters (ibid. pp. 17–18).

Dissatisfaction with this early analytic tradition was apparent even among those who retained allegiance to the analytic tradition in a broader sense. For example, writing in 1982, John White reported his frustration with the confinement of the role of philosophy to mere clarification. Rather than simply confine himself to clarifying the concept of an aim, he developed a substantive argument outlining what the aims of education should actually be (White 1982: x–xi). For White, a concern for clarity had led merely to 'conceptual joustings' (ibid. p. 6). Peters himself came to recognise the limitations of the 'early period', and drew attention to such shortcomings as the pedestrian, narrow, piecemeal, abstract and isolated character of much analysis and a failure to attend to the social and historical background and the view of human nature which analysis presupposes (Peters 1983). Peters' own recommendations for the future of the subject included a need to 'loosen up the analytic approach' (ibid. p. 53)

It is important to note that this 'earlier' period in the analytic tradition in philosophy of education was not disconnected from educational policy. Peters himself edited two collections of philosophical papers which directly aspired to illuminate policy concerns (Peters 1969,1976) and much of the work which was undertaken in this period did, and was intended to have, policy implications.[8] John Wilson, for example, engaged in a sustained and sophisticated attempt to bring a detailed philosophical characterization of morality and the moral educated person to bear upon educational policy and practice (see, for example, Wilson *et al.* 1967, Wilson 1990, McLaughlin and Halstead 2000).[9] Hirst's 'forms of knowledge' thesis influenced certain policy documents on the curriculum, although not in ways which betrayed a clear understanding of the thesis

---

[7]   On these criticisms see the references outlined in section 2.

[8]   On this matter see White 1987a: 157–158. For a further example see White 1973.

[9]   For Wilson's account of philosophical methodology see, for example, Wilson 1979, 1986.

which Hirst was actually arguing (Hirst 1974 §3, cf. 1993b). However, this 'earlier' period had its limitations with respect to its aptness for application to educational policy. One difficulty here was its
emphasis on matters of 'second-order' clarification. As John White
pointed out, those who are practically engaged in education are
interested less in what the concept of an aim might be than in what
the aims of education should be (White 1982: 6). 'Second-order'
pre-occupations could lead to philosophers being perceived as ones
who 'stand on the touch-line and jeer when the work is done'. (Peters
1983: 53). These difficulties were eased with the emergence of the
greater breadth of focus and concern characteristic of the 'later'
phase in the analytic tradition.

This 'later' phase, whilst retaining a commitment to a broadly analytic approach (in the sense that 'connective analysis' remains central), has been characterized by a broadening of approaches,
concerns and sensitivities, and a move towards the more normative
and practical concerns of 'applied philosophy.' The elements which
are part of this development include a willingness to move beyond
'second-order' clarificatory concerns to develop substantive arguments in favour of particular positions; a lessening of concern for
technicality; a willingness to engage with directly practical matters;
a concern with 'thicker' and more substantive concepts such as those
related to 'well being' and the virtues; a concern to articulate the
nature of the person, of human flourishing and of the place of reason
in human life; a greater attention to the cultural and political frameworks within which concepts and educational practices are located;
a central concern with ethics and political philosophy and a questioning of philosophical beliefs and forms of argument associated
with the enlightenment. Specific substantive concerns in this later
period include the articulation of educational aims, values, processes and entitlement in a liberal democratic society (in which the
development of the rationally autonomous individual and the liberal democratic citizen have figured prominently) (White 1987a,
1995, White and White 1997, Hirst and White 1998a: 10–11). These
developments have been influenced by, and have drawn upon,
developments and trends in philosophy more generally, including
neo-Aristotelian ethics, political philosophy and work on human
well being.

It is not difficult to see how this 'later' phase in the analytic tradition is more amenable to application to educational policy concerns
than its earlier counterpart, with its freeing of the philosopher to

make a less technical and a more flexible, substantive and tangibly constructive contribution to debate.

Although it is difficult to pin down the 'methodology' of the analytic tradition as a whole with any precision, a number of salient features can be safely identified. This tradition, with its characteristic emphases upon matters of meaning and justification, employs a recognizable style of argumentation. This form of argumentation is characterized by (amongst other things) the clarification of analysis of concepts, premises and assumptions, the consideration of counter-examples, the detection and elimination of defects of reasoning of various kinds, the drawing of important distinctions, a particular spirit of criticism and the structured development of argument. Central to the analytic tradition is an exploration of the conceptual schemes embedded in our everyday language in a form of analysis which is 'connective' in the sense indicated earlier, involving the elucidation of philosophically interesting connections and relationships between concepts. This, of course, does not imply that philosophers in the analytic tradition are interested only in language. What is at stake are our understandings, beliefs and values and these have transparent significance for human life generally. The analytic approach to philosophy of education is suspicious of unduly general statements and claims. It seeks a more fine-grained and detailed argument and debate in which attention to questions of meaning and justification act as an antidote to undue generality. The approach therefore tends to begin its work not from general statements or theories but from specific questions and problems, seeking their illumination, where appropriate, from the resources of broader philosophical argument.

In the present discussion, the analytic tradition in philosophy of education will be used as a point of illustration and reference throughout. It is important, however, not to overlook other traditions of philosophizing which are relevant to, and are brought to bear upon, education, such as those influenced by postmodernism. Although an extended treatment of these other traditions is impossible here, some attempt will be made to assess their significance for educational policy later in this essay.

Philosophy and Educational Policy: Possibilities

In exploring the possibilities which exist with regard to the relationship between philosophy and educational policy, it is useful to bear in mind parallel questions about the relationship between philoso-

phy and educational research.[10] With regard to the relationship
between philosophy and educational policy, a number of different
but related modes and levels of relationship can be discerned.[11]

One respect in which the modes of relationship between philosophy and educational policy can be traced is in terms of a 'distance/
proximity' continuum relating to the location of philosophizing
vis-à-vis the policy-making process. At one end of this continuum is
philosophizing conducted at some remove from policy making in
universities and similar locations and yielding fruit in lectures, seminars, articles, books and other publications. Some of this work may
be explicitly focused on educational policy.[12] This work, including
its less obviously policy-focused elements, is available as resources
for educational policy makers, although, as indicated at the outset,
the context and 'climate' of educational policy making varies from
time to time in the extent to which resources such as these are
acknowledged and drawn upon. The effect which these resources
have had on educational policy and educational policy makers,
whilst difficult to judge, should not, however, be underestimated.[13]
An obvious issue which arises here is the way in which these
resources can be best mediated to policy makers. One response to
this issue is to move philosophizing further along the continuum
and closer to policy making itself. An interesting current development at the 'mid-point' of the continuum is an initiative of the Philosophy of Education Society of Great Britain in producing a series of
policy focused 'IMPACT' pamphlets offering a philosophical treatment of contemporary policy issues which are launched in symposia
involving policy makers and commentators as participants and
respondents. At the time of writing four pamphlets have been produced: on assessment (Davis 1999), performance related pay for
teachers (Luntley 2000), equality and selective schooling (Brighouse
2000) and post-16 training policy (Winch 2000). Other pamphlets in
preparation are dealing with topics such as the aims of the new

[10] On these matters see, for example, Bridges 1997, 1998a, 1998b, Wilson 1998.

[11] cf. Soltis 1988: 10–12. For US literature on the relationship between philosophy
and educational administration see, for example: Strike, Haller and Soltis 1988,
Haller and Strike 1997.

[12] For some US work of this kind which might be unfamiliar to British readers see
Strike 1981 (on the application of moral theory to desegregation) and Strike 1995
(on the application of discourse ethics to school restructuring).

[13] On this matter, John White writes 'Over the last two or three decades
philosophers have heard on various grapevines that their writings find their way
on to the bookshelves of HMI, local government officers, civil servants and even
ministers at the Department of Education' (White 2000: vii).

National Curriculum, citizenship education and sex education. Also at the 'mid-point' of this 'distance' continuum are seminars and discussions of various kinds organized between philosophers and policy makers aimed at a sharing of perspectives and views. Seminars of these kinds have taken place on a number of policy-sensitive issues over the years such as spiritual and moral development and the aims of the new National Curriculum. At end of the continuum closest to policy making is the more direct involvement of philosophers in educational policy making itself through (say) membership of committees of enquiry. There are a number of examples here including Paul Hirst's membership of the Swann Committee (Great Britain Parliament House of Commons 1985), Bernard Crick's role as Chair of the Advisory Group which produced recommendations relating to citizenship education (Qualifications and Curriculum Authority 1998) and several other instances of philosophers working as members of policy-related groups at all levels including school level (cf. Elliott 1994). Morwenna Griffiths has placed particular emphasis on philosophers and teachers working together closely (Griffiths 1997, 1999).

Another element of the mode of the relationship between philosophy and educational policy concerns the differing aspects of the policy making process on which philosophy might be brought to bear. Ham and Hill (quoted in Codd 1995: 2–3) draw a distinction between 'analysis for policy' and 'analysis of policy' 'Analysis for policy' contributes to the formulation of policy and takes two forms: 'policy advocacy' (which involves the making of specific policy recommendations) and 'information for policy' (which provides policy makers with 'information and data' relevant to policy formulation or revision). Philosophers can contribute to both, although in their case the 'information for policy' will take the form of offering (say) conceptual clarification. 'Analysis of policy', according to Ham and Hill, can also take two forms, 'analysis of policy determination and effects' (which examines the processes and outcomes of policy) and 'analysis of policy content' which examines 'the values, assumptions and social theories underpinning the policy process' (Codd 1995: 3). Presumably, philosophers have a more obvious contribution to make to the latter, although they are not without a role in relation to the former, given Scheffler's point about the 'normative space' created by policy decisions.

Relevant to the mode of relationship between philosophy and educational policy is an important micropolitical issue about which communities of educationists should properly be engaged in philosophical work on the one hand and educational policy work on the other. Many of the points which Bridges makes about regrettable gaps which he sees between philosophers of education and educational researchers have application in the world of educational policy as well (Bridges 1997, 1998a). It seems clear that policies of increasing collaboration between philosophers and educational policy makers should lead to an appropriate overlap of responsibilities and expertise here.

The notion of levels of relationship between philosophy and educational policy refers to the differing degrees of specificity with which philosophy can be focused on educational policy. At one end of a continuum here is work of a very general kind which may be concerned (say) with fundamental philosophical questions such as the aims of education, the nature and justification of moral education and an articulation and justification of principles such as equality of educational opportunity. Work of this generality is not without significance to policy makers, not least in providing a general background or 'framework' for their work. It is at this level that philosophers can offer a 'vision' to guide educational policy (cf. Pring 1995a, 1995b, Bridges 1998a: 69–71, Fielding 1999: 179-180). At a mid-point of this 'generality/ specificity' continuum is work which engages in more detail in the critical assessment of practically significant educational assumptions and theories. At the most specific end of the continuum are analyses and discussions of current educational policies such as those offered by the IMPACT pamphlets and by philosophical journalism.[14] It is at these more specific levels of engagement that the role of the philosopher in articulating and probing concepts, values, assumptions and implications of particular policies comes particularly into play.

Before proceeding, it is useful to re-emphasize the complex interrelatedness of the differing modes and levels of relationship between philosophy and educational policy which have been delineated.

Philosophy and Educational Policy: Tensions

Any sustained exploration of the relationship between philosophy and educational policy will uncover a number of tensions in the relationship. Some of these tensions arise from contingent factors such

---

[14]   For related distinctions see White 1987b.

as the prevailing educational policy making 'climate' of the day (see, for example, Pring 1995a).

In what follows, however, I shall be focusing attention on tensions which are more intrinsic to the relationship between philosophy and educational policy making because they arise from the very nature of the two partners involved.

Philosophy on the one hand and educational policy making on the other do not share the same aims, values, interests and priorities. One overly simple way of stating the differences here is to claim that educational policy, unlike philosophy, is not aimed at the elucidation of (say) truth or goodness but at the resolution of practical issues and problems. However, care is needed not to put this point in a way that presents educational policy making as a wholly technical exercise, without concern for values. The more precise and accurate point to be made here is that the concerns of educational policy are primarily practical (often including evaluative as well as technical matters) rather than theoretical.[15] As Scheffler puts it, the attitude of the policy maker is practical rather than 'reminiscent' or 'speculative' (Scheffler 1991: 112).

One consequence of this is that there is a general tension in policy making between decision on the one hand and discussion and criticism on the other (cf. Scheffler 1991: 115—116). Given practical constraints on decision such as time, policy makers can often engage only in a limited and practically focused amount of discussion and criticism. This has particular significance for the contribution which philosophy might make to educational policy. The nature of philosophy gives rise to tensions with the imperatives of limited and practically focused discussion and criticism in several ways. Philosophy is attracted to the non-instrumental exploration of complexity. The intrusion of philosophical considerations to a policy-making process may therefore not make decision making in relation to educational policy easier or even clearer, and may make it more difficult and opaque. Philosophy may seek to offer clarity and vision, but even where this is achieved it may serve to illuminate complexities, sharpen dilemmas, undermine grounds for practical compromise and encourage further discussion and argument rather than decision. As Scheffler has pointed out—'self-consciousness'—'… increases the burden of choice and enlarges the perception of uncer-

---

[15] There are grounds for arguing that educational policy making should best be seen as kind of praxis on the same general grounds that Wilfred Carr adduces with respect to educational research (see Carr 1997).

tainty', making the 'pervasive drive' to 'simplify', 'objectivify' and 'reduce' fully understandable (Scheffler 1991: 107). Nor is clarity an unambigous good in policy making. Vagueness and ambiguity may have a lubricative and constructive effect here, as in other aspects of education (cf., McLaughlin 1994: 458–460). Whilst points of this kind have significance for all the modes and levels of philosophical involvement with educational policy referred to in the last section, they have particular significance for philosophers closely involved in the policy-making process.

A related source of tension between philosophy and educational policy making arises from the question of the extent to which philosophical considerations can be properly made to 'bite' upon educational practice. An example of this tension can be drawn from the work of John Wilson in relation to moral education, which was referred to earlier. One of Wilson's central preoccupations is to offer a 'mapping' of the domain of moral education in which conceptual questions such as 'What is to count as morality, moral education and the morally educated person' are central (Wilson 1990: 21ff, 1996: 90). Wilson claims that a clear answer to questions such as these, in the form of a 'map' or 'taxonomy,' must be brought to bear upon, and in a sense, control, teaching, research and policy making in moral education if these activities are not to be misconceived and irrelevant. It is not enough, for Wilson, to speak in vague or general ways about what it is to be morally educated. We need to identify a precise set of qualities, attributes, skills, abilities and other features which are relevant to the area of the 'moral' and necessary for one who is going to take the area seriously (Wilson 1990: part 3), and this conceptualization must be brought to bear on the work of teachers and policy makers. Whilst the ambition of applying a taxonomy of this kind to policy making seems intuitively plausible, it gives rise to a general problem I shall describe as 'taxonomic bite', where the difficulties which arise are not merely practical, but have a philosophical flavour to them. Complex questions arise in relation to extent to which policy makers and others can be expected to secure and apply an appropriate grasp of the taxonomy both in its general and specific aspects. It is important for policy makers to achieve a correct understanding of philosophical arguments. The misunderstandings in relation to Hirst's 'forms of knowledge' thesis have already been noted. Wilson may, however, have over-estimated the accessibility of his taxonomy to teachers and policy makers, at least at the level of the detailed understanding, which he seeks on their part. Further, any taxonomy of this kind is going to contain significantly contro-versial elements and the extent to which any such proposal could achieve acceptance for the purposes Wilson seeks is open to dispute. Too much debate about the taxonomy would under-mine its action-guiding function. Further, as John White rightly points out, our work in moral education cannot wait upon a definitive answer to the question of which theoretical account of morality is the correct one (White 1990: 36–40).[16]

The problem of 'taxonomic bite' is related to a general uncertainty about the precise way in which philosophy can be brought to bear upon educational policy, which sustains the tensions, which have been noted. As Brenda Almond points out with reference to the notion of 'applied philosophy' – '... philosophy is the most abstract of enquiries, perhaps even best defined as the investigation of prob-lems that cannot be solved by empirical enquiry, while applied sug-gests a direct relationship with the world of facts that is belied by this understanding of philosophy' (Almond 1987: 2). What, then, is the precise role of the philosopher in a practical activity like policy mak-ing? For a range of reasons, the contribution of philosophy cannot be seen in terms of an 'expert' offering substantive conclusions or rec-ommendations (on the general limitation of the notion of the philos-opher as 'expert' with respect to practical questions see, for example, D'Agostino 1998). The notion of philosophy as offering a set of con-clusions in search of application is deeply misconceived. On the other hand, as indicated earlier, a preoccupation with second-order clarification is similarly problematic. As Brenda Almond rightly insists, professionals are ' ... understandably, unable to hold their hand indefinitely from the plough while a perfect conceptual analy-sis of farming is sought' (Almond 1987: 10). David Bridges sees such an approach as neglecting the more substantive role which philoso-phy might have in providing guidance, patronizing to the ability of non-philosophers to achieve clarity about language and concepts and over-confident about the possibility and coherence of achieving the sort of clarity about the meaning of concepts which is being sought (Bridges 1997: 181–182).

It seems clear that the role of the philosopher as merely a critic is likely to exacerbate the sorts of tensions, which have been indicated. This gives rise to the question of the extent to which philosophers committed to a broadly 'postmodern' tradition in philosophy of education are able to respond to the need to offer more to the policy

---

[16]   cf. McLaughlin 1999a: 39–40.

making process than de-construction and problematization. An answer to this question requires a judicious understanding of the 'postmodern' tradition[17] in its relation to education.[18] Despite the origin of Lyotard's Education and the Postmodern Condition in a response to educational policy questions, it is perhaps unclear what a postmodern policy could be. The stimulative and provocative role of 'postmodernism' in relation to (say) matters of power, and the role of this tradition as a problematizing gadfly is prominent. Whilst the positive theses of 'postmodernism' are not devoid of educational implication (see, for example, Blake *et al.* 1998b) the extent to which a 'postmodern' perspective is compatible with easing the identified tensions is a matter for further reflection and exploration.

A further source of tension between philosophy and educational policy arising from the contrasting natures of the two activities may arise from the disinterestedness which is at the heart of philosophical enquiry, and which may be at odds with the aspiration of some policy makers to seek philosophical contributions under the aspect of providing legitimation for views arrived at on other grounds.

In addition, tensions may arise because of the 'positioning' of the philosopher with respect to the policy-making process, where this refers not merely to physical location but also to appropriateness of motive, commitment and solidarity. Griffiths captures something of what is at stake here in her criticism of philosophers who arrive in the manner of a 'raiding party' '... using education as one more example where their insights can be applied' (Griffiths 1997: 198).

Philosophy and Educational Policy: Tasks

If philosophy is to make a fruitful contribution to educational policy making, a number of tasks (both for philosophers and educational policy makers) emerge from the foregoing discussion.

Many of the points raised earlier give rise to readily specifiable tasks. Whilst philosophy needs to adopt a properly modest approach to the contribution it can make to educational policy, educational policy makers must acknowledge the extent to which the 'content' of their work, and the context in which it is undertaken, is saturated with assumptions, concepts, beliefs, values and commitments which, if not themselves of a philosophical kind, are apt for philosophical attention. Awareness of the differing modes and

---

[17]   For complexities in the use of the term 'postmodern' see Blake et al. 1998a.

[18]   On this see, for example, Beck 1994, Kohli (1995) Part 1, Wain 1995, Burbules 1996, Blake 1996, Blake et al. 1998a. cf. Carr 1998.

levels of relationship between philosophy and educational policy in its different aspects stimulates reflection on practical questions about the precise contexts in which dialogue between philosophers and policy makers can best be promoted, and about the precise kind of philosophical work, which is likely to promote this dialogue. One of the tasks here is surely that of transforming the general political climate so that it is amenable to, and supportive of, dialogue of this kind (on such an amenable and supportive climate in the case of the Irish Republic see Hogan 1995).

Some of the most interesting tasks, however, arise in relation to the tensions between philosophy and educational policy making, which were raised in the last section. Many of the tensions arise with particular significance for philosophers closely and directly involved in policy-making processes themselves. Here considerable practical judgement is called for on the part of philosophers.

In relation to tensions arising from the imperatives of limited and practically focused decision, philosophers must be able to make sensitive and sound judgements in relation to the following sorts of questions: How much philosophical illumination is needed by this policy making process? What kind of philosophical illumination is needed and in relation to which matters? When should forbearance of philosophical influence be exercised in the interests of the imperatives of consensus and decision? When should a conceptualisation or mode of presentation which is sub-optimal philosophically be accepted or even promoted for these kinds of interest?[19] How should a balance be struck between criticism and critique on the one hand and positive argument on the other? How much 'taxonomic bite' is it reasonable and practicable to expect in relation to policy matters, and how are 'best possible' solutions to be achieved?

The need for this kind of practical judgement on the part of philosophical participants in policy making processes, which needs to take account, amongst other things, of the particular 'language' of policy making (McLaughlin 1999a) which is being spoken and the complex empirical realities which intrude, is underscored by the realisation that philosophical contributions to such processes cannot take the form of the crude application of philosophical theories. DeMarco, for example, illuminates the limitations of attempts to apply abstract ethical principles to practical situations. The difficulties which arise here include the inherent abstractness of the princi-

[19] On the prevalence of 'lists' and rhetoric in educational policy documents see Blake at al. 1998 § 12.

ples in the face of inherent contextual complexity of the practical domain.

Demarco's own preference is for a 'middle level' position between '... the excessive vagueness of moral principles and the provincialism of contextual judgements' (DeMarco 1997: 292). Much of the wide ranging general discussion of the proper relationship between theory and practice, and the need for teachers to possess a kind of pedagogic phronesis or practical judgement (McLaughlin 1999b) apply also to the relationship between philosophy and educational policy making. Robin Barrow illuminates the capacity at stake here in terms of a practical form of 'philosophical competence' which headteachers of schools require (Barrow 1976).[20] Perhaps the most important task for philosophers in these matters is to ensure not only that their abstract philosophical judgement is well formed, but also that they are well formed in philosophical and educational judgement of a practical kind.

Conclusions

In this essay, I have sought to explore the role which philosophy can and should play in relation to educational policy.

Properly conceived, that role requires attention to a number of tasks, not the least of which concerns the role that philosophers must play in practical policy making contexts if the fruitfulness of this contribution is to be achieved.

Acknowledgements

I am very grateful to David Bridges, Richard Smith and Paul Standish for helpful discussion of points discussed in this article and to Michael Fielding for his patient encouragement.

---

[20] On some related points relating to judgements of this general kind see White 1987a: 159–160.

Chapter 2

Education, Philosophy and the Comparative Perspective

Introduction

Although philosophy is, in one way and another, implicated in much of the work of comparative education, and comparative educationists themselves have not been inattentive to philosophical considerations, the role of philosophy in comparative education has not been brought into clear focus. One expression of this lack of focus is that relationships between the disciplines of 'philosophy of education' and 'comparative education' are relatively undeveloped: educational studies remain afflicted by 'compartmentalization'. Regardless of the current state of relationship between formally structured educational disciplines, however, philosophical and comparative approaches to the study of education should be in an informed, sensitive and critical dialogue with each other. This article attempts to analyse the proper relationship between philosophy and a comparative approach to the study of education with reference to a range of needs, difficulties and opportunities. The article has three sections, dealing with 'needs', 'difficulties' and 'opportunities', respectively.

Education, Philosophy and the Comparative Perspective: Needs

In this section I shall articulate and defend two claims: (i) that philosophy needs a comparative dimension (in the context of education as elsewhere); (ii) that comparative education needs a philosophical dimension. Progress in relation to both claims requires attention to how 'philosophy' and 'comparative' in relation to education are to be properly understood.

Simon Blackburn describes philosophy as concerned with the exploration of the structure of our thought in its application to particular kinds of questions about ourselves (e.g. What am I? What is consciousness? Do I have free will?), the world (e.g. Why is there something and not nothing? Does it make sense to think that the future might influence the past?) and about ourselves and the world (e.g. How can we be sure that the world is really like we take it to be? What is knowledge and how much of it do we have?) (Blackburn, 1999, pp. 2–3). The particularity (and peculiarity) of these kinds of questions consists in their non-empirical character and in their resisting simple procedures and criteria for pursuit and resolution. Questions of this kind arise from a form of fundamental critical self-reflection that extends to the 'scaffolding of our thought' (Blackburn, 1999, pp. 3–4).

One difficulty in offering a general account of the nature of philosophy is that any account is offered from, and is perhaps biased in favour of, a particular tradition of philosophy. Blackburn's (1999) description of philosophy as 'doing conceptual engineering' (p. 2) and his dismissal of the proponents of certain schools of philosophical thought as 'conceptual engineers who cannot draw a plan, let alone design a structure' (Blackburn, 1999, p. 13) indicates his allegiance to a broadly analytic approach to philosophy. The analytical approach is averse to a conception of philosophy contained in the notion of 'a philosophy' where 'a philosophy' is seen as offering 'an account on the grand scale of the nature of reality, the place of human beings within it, and the implications of all this for how people should comport themselves in the world and towards one another' (Cooper, 2003a, p. 2). The traditional African beliefs referred to in the article by Bridges, Asgedom and Kenaw in this Special Issue is an example of a philosophy in this sense.

An aversion to a conception of philosophy of this kind is captured in Richard Peters' early denial that philosophy (and philosophy of education) should be seen as offering 'high level directives' (Peters, 1966, p. 15; however, cf. Elliott, 1986). Any reference to *'philosophies of education in comparative perspective'* involves the notion of 'philosophy' in the *'a* philosophy' sense. As David Cooper (2003a) observes, ' "Philosophy", as the name of a very general intellectual activity, does not have a plural, no more than does "music" ' (p. 2).

The reality and significance of contrasting, and partly competing, traditions in philosophy is of clear importance for the concerns of this article, and this matter will be returned to in due course. For our present purposes, however, it is useful to illustrate what is involved in a philosophical approach to education by reference to a particular example of such an approach drawn from the broadly analytical tradition which has been prominent in Anglo-American philosophy of education since the 1960s and which has been interpreted in an increasingly broad way in recent years (on the question of increasing breadth of interpretation see, for example, White & White, 2001). From the perspective of this tradition, a philosophical approach to education can be described as including interrelated and overlapping tasks of the following kinds (the categorization of tasks here draws in part upon White, 1987; Burbules & Warnick, 2004).

(1) Analysing an educationally significant term or concept, showing its multiple uses and meanings, for the purpose of clarification. Terms and concepts apt for clarification in this way include (for example) 'creativity', 'citizenship', 'active learning' and 'learning how to learn'. Clarity may not be a sufficient virtue in educational discourse, but (properly understood) it is a necessary one. 'Analysis' has been described as

> the elucidation of the meaning of any concept, idea or unit of thought that we employ in seeking to understand ourselves and our world, by reducing it, breaking it down, into more basic concepts that constitute it and thereby showing its relationship to a network of other concepts or discovering what the concept denotes. (Hirst & White, 1998b, p. 2)

Analysis here should not be seen as uncovering an essential or 'correct' meaning of a term or concept in a putatively value-free way but can include persuasive definition for the purposes of particular arguments and lines of enquiry. The 'connective' nature of this kind of analysis, as involving an investigation of 'how one concept is connected — often in complex and ragged-ended ways — in a web of other concepts with which it is logically related' (White & White, 2001, p. 14) is particularly worthy of note.

(2) Deploying the clarity achieved in (1) in a philosophical critical evaluation of an educationally significant term or concept, identifying hidden assumptions, internal contradictions or ambiguities in uses of the term and/or a disclosure of potential or actual partisan or controversial effects which the term has in professional and popular discourses. The notion of

'critical evaluation' here indicates that philosophers are interested not only in *clarity* but also in justification. For example, once 'creativity' has been clarified, the question of the senses, if any, in which 'creativity' should figure as an educational aim claims the attention of the philosopher. Analytic philosophers should not therefore be seen merely as 'poor relations of dictionary compilers' (White & White, 2001, p. 16).

(3)   Extending (2) into a philosophical critical evaluation of educational or educationally significant practices, policies, aims, purposes, functions, theories and theorists, doctrines, schools of thought and 'visions'.

(4)   Developing positive arguments and proposals regarding the matters referred to in (3) including the philosophical articulation and justification of fundamental educational aims, values and processes. It is here that the move away from a preoccupation with 'second order' to substantive concerns, which has characterized analytical philosophy of education in the last 25 years or so, can be most clearly seen.

The analytical tradition in philosophy and philosophy of education has been described as unified not by shared doctrines but by a range of characteristic methods. It is, however, difficult to pin down the 'methodology' of the analytical tradition of philosophy of education as a whole with any precision, although a number of salient features can be safely identified. This tradition, with its characteristic emphases upon matters of meaning and justification, employs a recognizable style of argumentation, characterized by (amongst other things) the clarification and analysis of concepts, premises and assumptions, the consideration of counter-examples, the detection and elimination of defects of reasoning of various kinds, the drawing of important distinctions (for example, between conceptual, normative and empirical questions), the use of 'thought experiments', a particular spirit of criticism and the structured development of argument. The analytical approach to philosophy of education is suspicious of unduly general statements and claims. It seeks a more fine-grained and detailed argument and debate in which attention to questions of meaning and justification act as an antidote to undue generality. The approach therefore tends to begin its work not from general statements or theories but from specific questions and problems, seeking their illumination, where appropriate, from the resources of broader philosophical argument. (On the analytical tradition in philosophy of education see, for example, Peters, 1966,

Introduction, 1983; Wilson, 1979; Cooper, 1986; Elliott, 1986; Hirst, 1986, 1993, 1998; White, 1987, 1995, 2003; Soltis, 1988; Evers, 1993; Kohli, 1995, Part 1; Haydon, 1998; Hirst & White, 1998a, Part 1, 1998b; McLaughlin, 2000; Heyting *et al.*, 2001; White & White, 2001; Curren, 2003; Curren *et al.*, 2003.)

Although the respects in which education in general has philosophical needs cannot be pursued in detail here, it is clear that much educational thinking, policy and practice is not only apt for philosophical attention but requires it. There is, of course, no suggestion that philosophy alone can fully illuminate, let alone resolve, educational questions. Philosophical reflection in education must be conducted in a close relationship with other disciplines of enquiry and with the insights and imperatives of educational policy and practice (on these matters see, for example, McLaughlin, 2000).

Although the notion of a 'comparative' perspective on education has yet to be brought fully into focus, it is possible to see at this stage how a philosophical perspective on education, properly understood, requires a comparative dimension. This can be illustrated by each of the features of the analytical approach that have been identified. In relation to (1), the analysis of an educationally significant term or concept, what counts as an educationally significant term or concept is (partly) related to matters of place and time: terms and concepts have a context and a history. Philosophizing about education cannot properly take place in a vacuum, including a societal, geopolitical and historical vacuum. If philosophical analysis of educationally significant terms and concepts is to be sufficiently informed and fruitful a comparative dimension is necessary, at least for any extended philosophical analysis. (On the need for a comparative perspective in philosophizing in general see, for example, Smart, 2000; Cooper, 2003a. On a historical dimension to philosophical perspectives on education, see, for example, Oksenberg Rorty, 1998b.) With regard to (2), a philosophical critical evaluation of an educationally significant term or concept, the kinds of criteria invoked for the justificatory judgements being made require assessment and endorsement in the light of appropriately fundamental scrutiny, and this properly involves consideration of the kinds of alternative criteria which a comparative perspective makes available for consideration. Similarly, in relation to (3), a philosophical critical evaluation of educational practices, principles and the like, a comparative dimension is an important resource in the enrichment of the range of possibilities and justificatory arguments open to view. This applies also to (4), the development of positive proposals in relation to the matters referred to in (3). The need for a comparative dimension to philosophy understood in analytical terms is inherent in the philosophical slogan 'Not all your questions answered, but all your answers questioned'. The proper pursuit of philosophy should lead to the problematization of the tradition within which it is conducted and in this, as in other matters, a comparative dimension to philosophizing is important and necessary.

Having attempted to illuminate the nature of a philosophical approach to the study of education by reference to one prominent approach, how can a comparative approach to the study of education best be understood? This is a matter that has been the focus of a good deal of debate in the discipline in recent years (see, for example, Crossley & Jarvis, 2000, 2001). An exploration of the notion of 'comparison' affords one way of illuminating matters here in a very general way for the purposes of the present discussion. 'Comparison' invites attention to: (a) *what is being compared with what* (e.g. teachers, schools, teaching methods and educational systems in differing cultural, national and regional contexts); (b) *the evaluative basis of comparison* (e.g. the norms and principles being invoked in making comparisons); (c) *the reasons and motives underlying the comparisons being made* (e.g. disinterested scholarly enquiry, a search for insights, etc., to be applied from one context to another); (d) *the methods used in making comparisons* (e.g. methods based on natural science, social science, hermeneutic traditions, etc.). The comparative study of education stands in need of a philosophical dimension in relation to each of these four aspects.

In relation to (a), what is being compared with what, the need for a philosophical dimension emerges in relation to at least two matters. The first arises from the general point that many aspects of educational thinking, policy and practice are not only apt for philosophical attention, but require it. Since most of the subject matter for comparison in comparative education is educational in character, a philosophical dimension to the task of comparison is needed simply as a result of the general need of education for philosophical illumination. A philosophical dimension is clearly needed in relation to the ambition of comparative education to develop 'an increasingly sophisticated theoretical framework in which to describe and analyse educational phenomena' (Phillips, 2000, p. 298). The kinds of themes that comparative educationists often address in their theorization are rich in philosophical implication: globalization (see, for example, Crossley & Jarvis, 2000), post-colonialism (see, for example, Crossley & Tikly, 2004), indigenous education (see, for example, May & Aikman, 2003), democracy (see, for example, Davies *et al.*, 2002) and citizenship (see, for example, Ichilov, 1988), as well as regionally based focuses of attention. The second matter in relation to which a philosophical dimension emerges is the illumination of the contexts in which the educational phenomena are located. These contexts include many aspects (cultural, anthropological, political, religious, etc.) that invite and require philosophical attention as part of the range of approaches and strategies needed to bring a given context into focus.

In relation to (b), the evaluative basis of comparison, the presence of the notion of 'evaluation' (with its implication of norms and principles) indicates a role for philosophy in matters of clarification and justification. Here, as elsewhere, the role of philosophy is a contributory one: appropriate forms of empirical enquiry have a place in the investigation of factual aspects of the identification of 'like with like'. In relation to (c), the reasons and motives underlying the comparisons being made, philosophical considerations illuminate reasons and motives such as 'a pragmatic science of educational borrowing' and a 'reading of the world', discussed by Robert Cowen (2000). The latter, seen as involving wide-ranging cultural, historical and political interpretation, is ripe for philosophical illumination. With regard to (d), the methods used in comparison, Robin Alexander notes that comparativists write as much about the purposes and processes of comparing as they do about the out-comes, needing to be cautioned against 'methodolatry': a preoccupation with methods to the exclusion of actually doing research (Alexander, 2001, p. 513). According to Ninnes and Burnett (2003), comparative education has been, despite 'pleas for coherence of focus and method', characterized by 'eclecticism' in that it incorporates 'a range of theories and methods from the social sciences and intersects a range of sub-fields including sociology of education, educational planning, anthropology and education, economics of education and education and development' (p. 279).

Be this as it may, philosophical considerations arise in relation to the articulation and defence of the research methodologies used in comparative education (see, for example, Martin, 2003; Ninnes & Burnett, 2003) and some comparative educationists have addressed these philosophical considerations directly (see, for example, Ninnes & Burnett, 2003). Patricia Broadfoot draws attention to the 'deep methodological divide' between qualitative methods and those of a more quantitative kind associated with a natural science paradigm, which has characterized comparative education (2000, p. 360). She calls for a more critical, theoretically informed, social science perspective in comparative education, involving a greater self-critical awareness, particularly in relation to the value-laden nature of problems, methods and conclusions (Broadfoot, 2000). She insists in particular that 'Comparative educationists … need themselves to be willing to engage in fundamental debates about values; about the nature "of the good life" and about the role of education and learning in relation to this' (Broadfoot, 2000, p. 370). More precisely, she argues, comparative-education has a responsibility to carry debate forward beyond 'means' alone to 'ends'.

Education, Philosophy and the Comparative Perspective: Difficulties

If it is accepted that a philosophical approach to education and a comparative approach to education need each other in the ways that have been suggested, the difficulties involved in achieving the various forms of integrated understanding come into focus. Interdisciplinary research in general faces a wide range of well-recognised difficulties. A number of specific difficulties stand in the way of the achievement of the kind of collaborative understanding to which reference has been made. Four interrelated difficulties will be considered here.

The first difficulty arises from the important point that any attempt to philosophize about an educational context must be conducted in the light of a thorough understanding of the context itself in all its aspects, including non-philosophical aspects. This task involves the wide-ranging and complex general difficulties in achieving an adequately broad and deep understanding of educational realities and their 'background conditions' in given contexts (Grant, 2000) of which comparative educationists have long been aware. Detailed contextually illuminative work of many different kinds is indispensable as a background to philosophical work both inside and outside a particular context (for recent work of these kinds on some of the contexts discussed in this Special Issue see, for example, Green, 2000; Tomiak, 2000; Cave, 2001; Harber, 2002; Jones, 2002; Yamashita & Williams, 2002). An adequate understanding of philosophizing about education in the context of Eastern Europe, for example, requires an understanding *inter alia* of the various non-philosophical factors which conditioned the expression of ideas in the Soviet period and the various adjustments and compromises on the part of thinkers which this required (see the contribution by Godori, Juceviciene & Kodelja in this Special Issue).

A second difficulty relates to the aspiration to *relate* philosophical reflection to the educational (and other) realities of a given context. Some forms of philosophical reflection are extremely general (as in, for example, reflection concerned with the determination of fundamental and general educational aims) and these kinds of reflection may not seek a direct relationship to educational practice and policy-making. Whilst this kind of reflection has its place, it needs to guard against the danger that it might descend into underdetermined and untethered rhetoric, which is both educationally irrelevant and philosophically suspect. Philosophical reflection which is related to, and grounded in, educational realities is often more adequate both educationally and philosophically. Little progress can be made in a philosophical discussion of citizenship education in contemporary China, for example, without attention to the reform of the history curriculum in the post-Mao period (on this matter see Jones, 2002). Oksenberg Rorty (1998a) reminds us that, even though European and Anglo-American countries share some general educational aims, 'their distinctive political and religious histories, and their different socio-economic conditions, set them quite distinctive moral and educational problems' (p. 10). Since solutions to (many) educational questions cannot be general, let alone philosophically general, philosophical reflection about these questions must be related to, grounded in and vary in the light of local considerations of various kinds. The task of exploring the relationship between philosophical reflection and educational realities in given contexts is, however, an extremely complex one. In part, this is because of the complexities involved in the general relationship between philosophy and educational policy-making and practice (on these complexities see, for example, McLaughlin, 2000). For example, philosophical conceptions and principles can neither be simply read off from nor applied to educational realities. Philosophical influence on educational policy-making and practice is often exercised through the pedagogical *phronesis* (or practical judgement) of educational policy-makers, teachers and educational leaders. The general complexities to which reference has been made here are magnified in any attempt to explore the relationship between philosophy and educational policy-making and practice in comparative contexts.

The third difficulty relates to the task of achieving an adequate *understanding* of philosophizing about education across different contexts. One general aspect of difficulty here is practical in character, and this has been addressed in the first two difficulties outlined above. Attention will be focused here, however, on philosophical aspects of difficulty. A good starting point for the achievement of relevant forms of understanding is (perspicuous) *description* of various kinds. However, whilst a description of a philosophical tradition or of the development of philosophizing about education in a given context is necessary for understanding, it is not sufficient (for such descriptions see, in addition to contributions to this Special Issue, the account of philosophy of education in Spain offered by Jover, 2001). One prominent aspect of difficulty concerns the question of understanding *across philosophical traditions*. The analytical tradition of philosophy and philosophy of education, which was given as an example at the outset of this article, is manifestly not immune from criticism, most notably by the continental traditions of philosophizing to which Paul Standish makes reference in his contribution to this Special Issue. Detailed educational visions derived from a philosophy in the sense indicated earlier (namely, overall and wide-ranging philosophical visions and systems) invite engagement with a particularly complex exegetical and interpretive task calling for considerable sensitivity and judgement. (For resources for this kind of task see, for example, Deutsch & Bontekoe, 1997. Specifically in relation to the traditions of thought represented in this Special Issue, see, Albertini, 1997; Deutsch & Bontekoe, 1997, Chs 7-15, 32-40, 43, 45; Masolo, 1997; Weiming, 1997; Cooper, 2003a, Ch. 3, 6, 9. On the relationship between indigenous peoples and western philosophies see, for example, Marshall, 2000.) The understanding of Confucian, Buddhist and Islamic philosophy, for example, presents a particular challenge to western thinkers, not least because of the intricate relationship of these traditions with a whole way of life. One danger confronting western thinkers is that of 'orientalism' inherent in the categorization of non-western philosophies of education in the light of an assumption that all philosophical traditions that are not defined as western constitute an identifiable 'something' simply by virtue of their being non-western (Deutsch, 1997, p. xii). Deutsch also usefully draws attention to another danger in our imagining that the thought of another culture 'has a clear unity and simplicity in contrast to the multifarious character of one's own' (1997, p. xiii). In fact, he insists, many of these 'alternative traditions' are characterized by depth, range, diversity and contention. There is no such thing, therefore, as a Chinese, Japanese or African philosophy (or philosophy of education) *per se*. A related danger is that of 'primordialism', where a particular group identity and its underlying philosophical articulation is seen as a timeless or eternal 'given'. A related problem is the definition of what can count as 'philosophy' (see the paper by Bridges, Asgedom and Kenaw in this issue). A further danger in seeking to understand 'philosophies' is that of deducing educational implications from them in an over-simple way. This danger is illustrated by MacIntyre (1998) in his observation that whilst it is possible to 'fabricate a collage' out of relevant elements of the philosophy of Thomas Aquinas and describe it as his 'philosophy of education', this would be a travesty (p. 96). In these and other matters it is useful to approach the task of understanding 'philosophies' and their educational implications by starting from the educational realities that they mandate (for such an approach see, for example, Halbertal & Halbertal, 1998; MacIntyre, 1998; Mottahedeh, 1998).

The fourth difficulty relates to the task of *engaging in dialogue* with philosophizing about education across different contexts and the related implied task of *making judgements* about the validity or adequacy of the perspectives and arguments encountered. It is important to note that differing philosophical perspectives and traditions do not necessarily stand in a relationship of mere juxtaposition to each other but in relationships of potential and actual disagreement and conflict. Deutsch (1997) insists that

> one's primary concern in the exploration of other traditions ought not to be that of simply finding more of oneself and what is familiar to one, but of learning about other possibilities of philosophical experience that can be opened up to one through cross-cultural encounter. (p. xiii)

Deutsch's claim leads to the thought that one may be a better philosopher and philosopher of education for having embraced a comparative perspective. The greatest difficulty that arises for educationalists from western liberal culture in embracing a comparative perspective is that of being genuinely open to alternative conceptions, values and forms of argument that may conflict with western liberal conceptions, forms of argument and values in significant ways (see particularly the contribution of Mark Halstead to this Special Issue). One difficulty here is the prevalence of notions such as 'postmodernism' that seem to call into question in different ways the evaluative project itself (on postmodernism see, for example, Cooper, 2003b). The notion of 'western liberal conceptions and values' is not, of course, transparent and unproblematic, although an unanalysed general sense of the notion can be invoked for the purposes of the present discussion (for further discussion see White, 2003). The practical and normative pervasiveness of these liberal 'conceptions, forms of argument and values' across the world is manifest, especially given the presence of democracy as one of its central elements (for the pervasiveness of liberal values in the case of Japan see, for example, Feinberg, 1993). One general phenomenon worthy of note here is that of traditional forms of philosophizing being put under intense philosophical (as well as societal and political) pressure by liberal and democratic influences. Tu Weiming (1997) describes how the western Enlightenment tradition gave rise to 'the most devastating disputation that the Chinese mind has ever encountered' (p. 22). Local forms of philosophizing, with their distinctive conceptions, values and forms of argument, face assessment from the putatively 'universal' standpoint of western liberalism (see the contributions by Penny Enslin & Kai Horsthemke and by Bridges, Asgedom & Kenaw in this Special Issue) and many contexts seek adaptation to western norms (see the contributions by Godon, Juceviciene & Kodelja and by Naiko Saito & Yasuo Imai). The major challenge for western scholars here is not only that of reinterpreting local forms of thought and practice in the light of western perspectives in an appropriate and defensible way (on liberal democratic educational aims and values in comparative perspective see Bridges, 1997), but also that of being sufficiently open to the genuine insights contained in local forms of thought. This is important not least because liberal conceptions, forms of thought and values are not unproblematic as they stand, but require enrichment and amendment from other sources. The inadequacies of western liberalism with respect to securing a basis for contra-individualistic motivation and for communal needs and imperatives are, for example, widely felt. Openness to the genuine insights contained in local forms of thought requires considerable resources of sensitivity and imagination which extends beyond the philosophical. It should not, of course, be assumed that the challenges of dialogue and evaluation are confined to encounters with 'philosophies' such as Confucianism, Buddhism and Islam. There is plenty of scope for the exercise of sensitivity and imagination in the encounter between the analytical and the continental traditions in philosophy and philosophy of education (on this encounter see, for example, Blake *et al.*, 1998).

The difficulties indicated here are substantial ones, not least the philosophical ones that have been identified. Any suggestion that the significant progress in relation to the difficulties is impossible, however, would seem to call into question the very possibility of a comparative study of education of any ambition and significance.

Education, Philosophy and the Comparative Perspective: Opportunities

What opportunities arise from an acceptance of the claim that a philosophical approach and a comparative approach to the study of education need each other? There is much scope here for a detailed discussion of possibilities. At the very least it would be a good thing if philosophizing about education became more sensitive to comparative insights and concerns and comparative education became more sensitive to insights and concerns of a philosophical kind. However, the need for sustained and sensitive interdisciplinary co-operation emerges clearly from the foregoing discussion. Here, flexibility is important: for example, philosophical aspects of research should not be seen as solely the province of 'philosophers' or 'philosophers of education'.

Dialogue with the unfamiliar is perhaps a key feature of the comparative approach to education. The suggestion here is that philosophers and comparativists in education are unjustifiably unfamiliar with each other's work and that dialogue between them should both enhance their work and indicate real opportunities for collaborative pursuit of their mutual and overlapping research interests.

Acknowledgement

I am grateful to Robert Cowen for his advice and assistance in relation to the writing of this article.

Chapter 3

Education of the Whole Child?

The claim that we should 'educate the whole child' is familiar to us from many educational contexts and debates. In common with claims such as 'we should teach children and not subjects' and 'process is more important than content', it sounds intuitively plausible and appealing. Claims of these kinds are often brandished as rhetorical slogans in educational discussion and debate, where they can serve several functions. The important truths the slogans are alleged to contain can make a seemingly decisive contribution to a developing argument, and can sometimes bring discussion to an end by appearing to transcend or resolve matters of dispute. However, since the meaning, let alone the truth, of such slogans is unclear they are better seen as contributing suggestively rather than decisively to educational argument and as opening up educational discussion rather than closing it down.

What is meant by the, claim that we should 'educate the whole child' and in what sense is it true? In this essay I shall suggest that, while the claim expresses a number of significant educational truths, it is not unproblematic. In particular, I shall claim that there are important respects in which we should not educate 'the whole child'. This conclusion has important implications for education in relation to 'spirituality' and 'spiritual development', and should lead us to approach these matters with caution.

Education and Wholeness

A critical analysis of the term 'education of the whole child' can usefully begin with attention to what is meant by 'whole' in this context. It is capable of at least two interpretations, which I shall refer to as the comprehensiveness' and the 'integration' interpretations respectively.

Wholeness as comprehensiveness

On this first interpretation, 'whole' is opposed to 'narrow' or 'restricted' and can be read as an appeal for education to focus upon a wide range of aspects of the child, and not merely (say) intellectual development or academic formation. It calls for education to have 'broad', 'rounded' or 'balanced' influence.

In evaluating such claims it is important at the outset to call into question a tendency to see the different 'aspects of the child' as sharply distinct from each other, as in the drawing of crude contrasts between the 'intellectual' and the 'emotional' and between the 'cognitive' and the 'affective'. Such distinctions, including the well-established tripartite categorization of domains of the person into the 'cognitive', 'affective' and 'conative', are untenable in any very rigorous form, and require more nuanced re-statement. All the dimensions of a person are logically as well as psychologically related to each other. A person's beliefs, for example, are logically tied in complex ways to (*inter alia*) his or her attitudes, emotions, virtues and motivations. One way of putting this point is to draw attention to the 'cognitive core' of all aspects of mind and of all human capacities. Emotions, for example, are partly constituted by forms of cognition in which situations are seen under various aspects. To feel fear is to see a situation as threatening, to feel guilt is to see it as involving undischarged obligations and responsibilities, and so on. A proper understanding of a person, therefore, requires a 'holistic' perspective in at least the sense that involves a rejection of the sorts of the sharp distinctions and dichotomies which have been mentioned.

One implication which might be thought to follow from this point is that education is therefore inherently holistic in its effects. To introduce a child to a subject of study is to open up not only possibilities for cognitive or intellectual development but also for the development of new attitudes, emotions, feelings and motivations. Any educational influence, therefore, can transform the whole person. The qualification 'can' is important here, however, because whilst 'holistic' implications are implicit within education, they do not necessarily follow and, if desired, need to be deliberately aimed at. So although there is some substance in the descriptive claim that education *is* as a matter of fact, of the whole child, the prescriptive claim that education *should* be of this kind is not redundant.

What is involved in the claim that education *should* aim at 'wholeness' in the 'comprehensiveness' sense? Whilst we might not accept the early claim of R. S. Peters that 'education is of the whole man' expresses (although imprecisely) a 'conceptual truth' about education (Peters, 1966, p. 32), an aversion to narrowness and restrictedness in educational aims and processes is widely felt. Such narrowness or restrictedness can take many forms, relating to the goals of education, its subject matter and its methods. Educational goals, for example, can be limited to the achievement of basic literacy and numeracy, to narrowly-conceived vocational preparation or to specialized academic training. The 'subject matter' of education may be conceived in a way which excludes or underemphasizes significant elements of knowledge and understanding or kinds of development, and educational methods may concentrate on (say) memorization to the exclusion of critical questioning and other strategies more likely to bring about genuine engagement and understanding.

It is easier to criticize such narrow or restricted conceptions of educational aims and processes than to provide a positive account of an appropriately broad conception. Notions such as 'breadth' and 'balance' in themselves are of limited help here since they are uninformative about the nature and justification of the evaluative judgements they imply (Dearden, 1984, chapter 5). The elements of personhood and learning in relation to which 'breadth' and 'balance' are to be sought, and the criteria which tell us what constitutes 'breadth' and 'balance' all need to be specified and justified. This cannot be done satisfactorily without giving attention to fundamental educational aims, values and purposes.

Without entering in detail into these matters, it is possible to identify a central issue which arises in relation to the claim that education is of persons (Langford, 1985, chapter 7) and that it should exert wide-ranging or 'holistic' influence upon them (on this, see, for example, Bonnett, 1994). Underlying this general claim is the question 'What sort of person does education seek to develop?' The complexity of the judgements of value involved in this question comes readily into focus. In part, this complexity is inherent in questions of this kind, but it is enhanced by the 'value diversity' and 'pluralism' characteristic of liberal democratic societies, which will be discussed in more detail later. In our lack of agreement about what constitutes human good or perfection we are suspicious of claims to wide-ranging educational influence upon the child. This central issue concerning the notion of 'education of the whole child' — the value basis on which we can construct a vision of 'holistic' educational influence —

comes still further into focus in relation to the second interpretation of the term.

Wholeness as integration

On this second interpretation, 'whole' is opposed to 'fragmented' and can be read as an appeal for education to ensure that the different aspects of the child be 'integrated' in some way. Education here seeks 'coherence' for the person.

Leaving aside the complex philosophical difficulties which arise in relation to the notion of personal identity (on these see, for example, Parfit, 1984, Part 3), it can be plausibly argued that since the concept of a person is one of a 'complete existent' it brings with it the notion of 'wholeness' in the sense of 'unitariness' (Langford, 1979, pp. 68-70). What is involved in the 'unity' of a person is complex. One aspect of it is the notion of a person having, or striving towards, a unity of 'purpose and outlook' (Langford, 1979, p. 70) in which, through the governing of conflicts by a stable system of priorities, the person's life becomes, or at least aims towards, a harmony and a wholeness in the 'integration' sense. Mary Midgley claims that this desire to integrate is related to some of our most basic wishes, capacities and needs. She writes: 'People have a natural wish and capacity to integrate themselves, a natural horror of being totally fragmented, which makes possible a constant series of bargains and sacrifices to shape their lives' (Midgley, 1980, p. 190). A continuing preoccupation with the significance of 'wholeness' in the 'integratedness' sense is a feature of Midgley's latest book *The Ethical Primate* (1994).

The notion of a person 'integrating' his or her life in this way gives rise in an even sharper way to the value questions mentioned in the last section. What is the nature of the 'coherence' which is aimed at? 'Coherence' in itself merely suggests the notion of elements fitting together according to some principle. But what the principle, or principles, in question should be remains to be settled (Dearden, 1984, chapter 5). Some of the principles which persons might invoke in relation to their achievement of 'coherence' are 'architectonic' in the sense that they relate to the fundamental structuring elements of a person's overall view of life. Examples of such 'architectonic' principles are those relating to religious belief or unbelief. A position on these matters can shape in a basic way individuals' views of themselves and their lives, and provide central principles for 'integration'. Whilst value questions arise in relation to all aspects of 'integration', 'architectonic' principles illustrate sharply the concerns expressed at the end of the last section about the evaluative basis on which we can approach such matters educationally. One of the features of liberal democratic societies, and their associated cultural and philosophical developments, is absence of agreement about 'thick' or substantial views of human good. We lack a shared view of 'the meaning of life' and, therefore, about what 'architectonic' principles are appropriate for the achievement by persons of 'integration' and 'coherence'. Indeed, we lack a shared conception of what, in detail, 'integration' and 'coherence' mean in relation to the human person. What value-basis can education therefore appeal to in relation to these matters, and to 'education of the whole child' generally?

The significance of these questions can be illustrated by reference to the work of an educationalist particularly noted for his preoccupation with the notion of 'wholeness', Friedrich Froebel.

Froebel and Education of the Whole Child

The educational thought of Friedrich Froebel is particularly interesting for our purposes, because he placed great emphasis not only on 'wholeness' in the aims and methods of education but also on the need for 'the spiritual' to be cultivated in children. Froebel is not much studied these days, and there has been a long-standing tendency to abstract his methodological principles from the wider framework of his thought, together with its religious and metaphysical assumptions. Close attention to Froebel's overall view does, however, illustrate some of the evaluative concerns expressed earlier in relation to the notion of 'holistic' educational influence.

Froebel placed great emphasis on 'unity' in his educational theory, differing in this respect from Pestalozzi (see Bantock, 1984, pp. 80–90). At the heart of Froebel's theory was a teleological (or purpose-directed) conception of the universe and of human beings, involving an 'inner law' binding all into a unity with God. Froebel writes:

> An eternal law pervades and governs all things. The basis of this all-controlling law is an all-pervading, living, self-conscious and therefore eternal Unity. This unity is God. God is the source of all things. Each thing exists only because the divine spirit lives in it and this divine spirit is its essence. The destiny of everything is to reveal its essence, that is, the divine spirit dwelling in it. (Quoted in Bantock, 1984, p. 81)

For Froebel, the 'wholeness' or 'unity' of the educational process is related to, and characterized in terms of, this particular metaphysical theory which, in its affirmation of the 'wholeness' of reality, has affinities to idealism. (On idealism and its educational significance see Gordon and White, 1979.)

The centrality to Froebel's thought of religious concepts and claims is clear, as is the importance of specifically religious teaching and formation to his theories of educational practice (Hamilton, 1952). Froebel writes: 'By education ... the divine essence of man should be unfolded, brought out, lifted into consciousness, and man himself raised into free, conscious obedience to the divine principle that lives in him, and to a free representation of this principle in his life' (Froebel, 1888, pp. 4-5. See also chapters V and VI, pp. 237-48.) Froebel's account of educational 'wholeness' and 'unity', as incorporated, for example, into the Froebellian 'gifts', is inseparable from his religious views. The aim of instruction, claims Froebel, is 'to bring the scholar to insight into the unity of all things, into the fact that all things have their being and life in God, so that in due time he may be able to act and live in accordance with this insight' (p. 128). Froebel's overall framework of thought also needs to be brought to bear if we are to grasp his distinctive interpretation of the claim that we should attend to the 'universal cultivation of the spiritual' in our children (p. 328). For Froebel, the religious sentiment manifests the unity of all things.

Although Froebel expresses his overall metaphysical theory in an imprecise and somewhat 'mystical' way, its religious elements are sufficiently prominent to give rise to serious doubts about the acceptability of the theory as a basis for 'holistic' educational influence in the common schools of a liberal democratic society. This is because, in such societies, we are confronted by the wide-ranging and deep-seated disagreement about values which was alluded to earlier. Froebel's religious assumptions are now seen as highly controversial. Referring to the key concept in his overall theory, Froebel claims: 'a quietly observant human mind, a thoughtful, clear human intellect, has never failed, and will never fail, to recognize this Unity' (1888, p. 1). Froebel is surely wrong about this, at least as far as his own interpretation of 'unity' is concerned, and his view is now likely to be seen as only one of a number of rival overall views of life as a whole which require critical understanding and assessment. To base 'holistic' educational influence on Froebel's theory in its fullness is to invite accusations of metaphysical, if not religious, indoctrination.

Values, Pluralism and Holistic Educational Influence

The central issue which arises in respect to the notion of 'education of the whole child', whether in the 'comprehensiveness' or 'integration' sense, is therefore the difficulty of establishing, especially in the context of the pluralism of a liberal democratic society, an acceptable evaluative basis for holistic' educational influence (on this see, for example, Standish, 1995).

This is not to suggest that such societies are completely lacking in value agreement, or that education based on liberal democratic principles is without any value foundation. However, what is distinctive about the 'liberal democratic' approach to values, in its typical articulation in the philosophical theory of liberalism, is the self-conscious attention paid to the scope of influence and validity of particular value judgements. In this approach, the values which can be insisted upon for all are precisely seen as applying to part, not the whole, of life, and imply a principled forbearance of influence on the part of education.

In liberal democratic societies we are confronted by people holding many different, and often incompatible, views of life as a whole. Catholics, Jews and Muslims live alongside atheists and agnostics. Their differing 'holistic perspectives', articulated by contrasting 'architectonic principles', give varying accounts of human nature and flourishing, and of what constitutes 'integration' in the shape of a whole human life. Education based on such 'holistic' views can specify in some detail the sort of person it seeks to produce. Examples of such 'holistic' educational influence include certain forms of religious schooling, which seek to form (say) Christian or Islamic persons in a substantial way. Froebel's educational recommendations, though more general, can be seen as similarly 'holistic'.

From a 'liberal democratic' philosophical perspective, however, there is no objectively conclusive way of determining which, if any, of these 'holistic' views of life — or 'thick' theories of the good — is correct. They are deeply, and perhaps permanently, controversial. The differences of belief and value involved are tenacious and fundamental. Therefore such 'thick' views cannot be permitted to impose their particular vision on all citizens in the public domain through the use of political power. For example, from the point of view of some 'thick' theories of the good, remarriage after divorce is morally unacceptable because, since marriage is morally indissoluble and divorce has only legal and not moral force, the couple in question are living in a state of permanent adultery. Such a view is significantly controversial in the sense that a number of different perspectives on these matters exist 'within the moral pale'. The view cannot, therefore, be imposed on all citizens through the civil law on divorce. On similar grounds, the education offered in the common schools of a liberal democratic society cannot be based on 'thick' theories of the good.

From a liberal democratic perspective, such 'thick' theories, and the patterns of life which they generate, are matters for individual and family assessment, judgement and response. Many such theories are reasonable and morally worthy but lack the objective grounding to be imposed on all. They should, however, be seen as part of a range of options from which people might construct their lives. Whilst such 'thick' theories cannot form the basis of common schooling, they can underpin forms of distinctive schooling chosen by parents as part of the exercise of their moral rights over their children's upbringing and education (McLaughlin, 1994a).

In contrast to the diversity and pluralism associated with 'holistic' or 'thick' theories of the good, the liberal democratic perspective seeks to establish consensus and unanimity concerning basic or 'public' values. In virtue of their fundamentality or inescapability, such values are seen as binding on all persons. Frequently embodied in law and expressed in terms of rights, they include such matters as basic social morality and a range of fundamental democratic principles such as freedom of speech, justice and personal autonomy. The theory of the good underpinning such values is described in the philosophical theory of liberalism as 'thin' not because of the insubstantiality or unimportance of the values involved, but because of the attempt to articulate them in terms which all people of goodwill can accept regardless of the fuller theory of the good which they hold. 'Public' values do not presuppose some particular metaphysical theory of the self, or of the nature of human destiny Atheists and Catholics differ profoundly on these wider matters, but can share common ground in condemning cruelty and supporting a democratic way of life, even if their overall frameworks of belief given them distinctive perspectives on them. Such 'public' values do not cover the whole of life, but only its 'political' aspects. They form an important part of the value foundation of common forms of education based on liberal democratic principles.

These principles generate a two-fold educational task for common schools which can be expressed roughly as follows. On the one hand, education must 'transmit' the basic or 'public' values, principles and procedures, and secure appropriate forms of respect for, and allegiance to, them. On these matters, the school seeks to achieve a strong, substantial influence on the beliefs of pupils and their wider development as persons. It is unhesitant, for example, in promoting the values of basic social morality and democratic 'civic virtue' more generally. On the side of values associated with 'thick' theories of the good, on the other hand, the school exercises a principled forbearance of influence. It seeks not to shape either the beliefs or the personal qualities of pupils in the light of such theories. Instead, the school encourages pupils to come to their own reflective decisions about the matters at stake, and promotes appropriate forms of understanding, open-mindedness and tolerance.

Much more needs to be said in relation to the articulation of this general perspective and the many problems associated with it (see McLaughlin, 1995a; 1995b). However, regardless of the various philosophical difficulties to which it gives rise, it is recognizable, at least in outline, as a widely-held view of the value basis of education in a liberal democratic society.

From this perspective, the respects in which we should not 'educate the whole child' come into focus. At least in common schools, no substantial 'holistic' view of life should be transmitted to pupils, nor should they be shaped 'as whole persons' in the light of any such theory. Rather, schools should open up views of this kind for critical assessment and exploration. Schools should therefore be suspicious of aiming at 'wholeness' for pupils in the 'integration' sense unless the character of the 'integration' is seen in terms of the pupils' own fashioning of the shape of their lives. With regard to wholeness' in the 'comprehensiveness' sense similar worries arise. A school might argue that it was merely exercising 'open' and non-indoctrinatory influence across a range of aspects of the child's life. One issue which such a claim needs to confront is the question of the rights of Parents in relation to those of teachers. It is not clear that, without further argument, teachers have a right to exercise influence of whatever kind across all aspects of a child's life.

Spiritual Development and Education of the Whole Child

In the light of the discussion above, it is clear why talk of promoting the 'spiritual development' of pupils in schools as part of the 'education of the whole child' is problematic.

Central to evaluating the issues here is clarity about what is meant by 'spiritual development'. General questions of value in recent educational debate and policy-making have often not been handled in a clear, systematic and sustained way. As is widely recognized, the structure and implementation of our recent educational reforms have not been governed by any clear and defensible overall vision, and questions of value were not squarely addressed at the outset. The reforms are widely regarded, even by those not wholly opposed to their general thrust, as pragmatic and piecemeal. A lack of clarity and critical attention to fundamental issues has also characterized the emergence of the area of 'spiritual development' and the other areas of development associated with it. The initiative is widely seen as a belated attempt to enrich the educational reforms with an explicit value dimension, in which the immensely complex issues at stake in the meaning, let alone inspection, of spiritual development were ignored or glossed over. The straightforward question, 'What is meant by "spiritual development"?' by itself fully reveals this complexity. In these circumstances, one can only have the greatest sympathy for OFSTED in its attempts to make sense of the area and to fulfil its obligations with respect to it. The extent and openness of the consultation process which OFSTED has engaged in has been refreshing, and its discussion paper issued in February 1994 (Office for Standards in Education, 1994) asks the right sorts of questions about the area, and provides a focus for philosophical debate (J. White, 1994).

It is important that the debate about spiritual development in schools be located within an overall view of educational aims and purposes: a 'vision' of the educational enterprise as a whole. Without this it will be hard to achieve the coherence sought for the area and for education itself (McLaughlin, 1994b). 'Spiritual development' also needs to be considered in close relationship to other areas of the work of the school, such as 'education for citizenship' (P. White, 1994).

The obscurity of what is meant by 'spiritual development' (see Hull, 1996) makes it difficult to assess in relation to the sorts of general principles outlined above. An interpretation of the term which insists upon a close connection with religious development (see, for example, Carr, 1995) gives rise to worries about undue influence arising from the presupposition of a 'thick' view of human good, as do views of educational influence on the matters at stake which are explicitly secular (see, for example, White, 1995). What seems necessary for compatibility with the values outlined earlier is a view of 'spiritual development' which is significantly 'open' in the sense that it leaves room for critical exploration of the relevant issues by pupils and does not presuppose any significantly controversial assumptions of the sort indicated. One major difficulty here concerns a specification of what could be meant by 'development' in relation to these matters.

The fact that 'spiritual development' is now part of the formal inspection criteria for schools makes it difficult to ignore these issues or to employ 'edu-babble' (imprecise and platitudinous rhetoric) in relation to them; two strategies commonly used in the past.

'Spiritual development' focuses attention in a strong way on the 'holistic' aspects of education. As we have seen, the notion that we should 'educate the whole child' is not as straightforward as it appears, and there are important senses in which, in the light of the values discussed earlier, we should not attempt this. However, one outcome of the debate about 'spiritual development' in schools may be to focus renewed critical attention upon these values themselves and the liberal democratic educational principles discussed in the last section.

One of the major lines of criticism in general of the philosophical theory of liberalism which has emerged in recent years from a broadly 'communitarian' direction is that its values, and the political community which it generates, lacks the substantiality needed to enable persons to achieve defensible and necessary forms of affiliation and commitment to a 'larger moral ecology' beyond their own individual, and indeed individualistic, concerns. Such a 'moral ecology' embodies a social ethos, a consensus on the common good and notions of loyalty and responsibility to the community as a whole as well as a framework of wider beliefs and values providing (at least to some extent) a culture of 'narrative coherence' as well as 'freedom' for lives. The liberal view, it is claimed, leads to individualism in its various forms, and a tendency for individual choice and self-definition to be based on arbitrary preference or self-interest, rather than a view of life which is more coherent and other-regarding. In addition, attention is drawn to the corrosive effects of private economic pursuits and consumerism on the notion of a caring public ethos, the negative effects of an undue separation of public and private realms and so on (on these matters see, for example, Mulhall and Swift, 1992).

These critiques, amounting to a call for the recovery of a more 'holistic' perspective, are also applicable to liberal educational principles. Is the attempt to confine the value basis of the common school to values which are in some sense not 'significantly controversial' counter-intuitive and damaging? Is the influence of the common school as a result undesirably thin? Does the attempt to exercise a principled forbearance of influence lead to a weakening of the power and coherence of the value influence of the school? Must not a greater substantiality – a 'holistic' vision of life and of society – be supplied to the common school and to education itself?

The wide-ranging debate needed for a proper evaluation of the claim that spiritual development' should be seen as part of the process of 'education of the whole child' in common schools raises questions which touch upon some of the central issues relating to the value basis of education in liberal democratic societies.

Chapter 4

Beyond the Reflective Teacher

In its recent survey of initial teacher training courses in England and Wales, the Modes of Teacher Education Project investigated whether courses were based upon an 'agreed model of the teacher' as part of their 'underlying philosophy'. Of the course leaders who answered 'yes' to this question, the vast majority across all phases and courses described this model as that of the 'reflective practitioner' (Whitty *et al.*, 1992, pp. 297–299). This finding should not surprise us, for the concept of the 'reflective practitioner' – and more generally 'the reflective teacher' – is not only currently widely fashionable, but also has a strong intuitive appeal.

This appeal is easy to understand. Who, after all, would want to champion the unreflective practitioner? However, for some time it has been widely recognised that, in common with other educational nostrums, 'the reflective practitioner' is often used as a vague slogan rather than as a concept whose meaning and implications are well thought through and worked out. Such slogans are not without their educational and political value (on the use of the language of 'the reflective practitioner' as a rallying cry to oppose a number of recent developments and trends in the reform of teacher training see Furlong, 1992, pp. 176–177). But, given our current ambition to achieve a much more precise understanding of the concepts and processes involved in teaching and teacher training, the notion of 'the reflective practitioner' cannot escape careful analysis.

In this article I shall suggest that we need to move 'beyond the reflective teacher' in two ways. First, we need to move beyond the slogan of the reflective teacher to explore in more detail what the concept involves and the extent of its adequacy as an account both of teaching and of the demands of teacher training. Second, we need to go beyond the concept itself to acknowledge its incompleteness and its need to be supplemented by, and situated within, a richer account of the nature and requirements of teaching and teacher training. The article has three sections. In the first section I outline briefly the nature of the appeal of the notion of the 'reflective practitioner'. In the second, I pose and explore some critical questions relating to the notion. These concern the nature of reflection, the grounds on which reflection might be thought to be valuable in teaching and the extent to which developmental considerations relating to it can be discerned. In the final section I address the question of the respects in which we need to go beyond the concept of 'reflection' in our understanding of teaching and teacher training.

The Appeal of 'The Reflective Practitioner'

The wide popularity and appeal of the concept of 'the reflective practitioner' is not best explained in terms of a subscription to the details of any specific and well-worked out model of the notion, such as that famously offered by Donald Schon (Schon, 1983, 1987). A number of competing models and conceptions of 'the reflective practitioner' exist, varying in the meaning which they give to the terminology they use and in the nature of the theoretical articulation of the notion which they offer (on this see, for example, Calderhead, 1989; Zeichner, 1994). The preoccupation with 'reflection' in the wide-ranging research tradition into teacher thinking and action, for example, involves a number of varying conceptions of how 'reflective practice' is to be understood (for recent collections of papers on these matters see Tabachnich & Zeichner, 1991; Russell & Munby 1992; Calderhead & Gates 1993; Carlgren *et al.* 1994). Zeichner comments 'Underlying the apparent similarity among those who embrace the slogans of reflective practice are vast differences in perspectives about teaching, learning, schooling and the social order ... Everyone, no matter what his or her ideological orientation, has jumped on the bandwagon ... furthering some version of reflective teaching practice' (Zeichner, 1994, pp. 9–10).

The intuitive general appeal of 'the reflective practitioner' to teachers and teacher educators is two-fold. First, in stressing the significance of 'reflection', the notion captures an aversion to, or suspicion of, a range of attitudes, arguments and policies which seek in different ways to diminish the importance, scope and sophistication of professional thoughtfulness, judgement and autonomy. The targets aimed at here are varied. They include the various narrow and minimalist accounts of teaching and teacher training which have emerged in contemporary debates from the pens of populist writers, certain provisions of policy in the recent reform of teacher training which may reduce opportunities for students to develop critical capacity and perspective, and the perceived threat to the reflective practice of teaching arising from an emphasis on 'skills' and 'competences' (on skills see, for example, Smith, 1987, and on competences, Elliott, 1991; Furlong & Maynard, 1995, ch. 2). The second appealing feature of the notion of 'the reflective practitioner' is the vagueness and elasticity of what is meant by 'reflection'. This enables the slogan to be invoked without involving commitment to any particular view of, or theory about, many underlying and related questions. Thus, for example, those who appear to disagree quite extensively about significant aspects of teacher training make a common appeal to the importance of 'reflection' (see, for example, Elliott, 1993; Hargreaves, 1993). In an area where there is much uncertainty, and a good deal of conceptual and empirical research still to be done, a general inclusive concept with which many can identify has its virtues. However, if progress is to be made in achieving a fuller understanding of the nature and requirements of teaching and teacher training we should heed Zeichner's call for us to pass beyond 'the uncritical celebration' of teacher reflection. 'We need to focus our attention on what kind of reflection teachers are engaging in, on what it is teachers are reflecting about and on how they are going about it' (Zeichner, 1994, p. 18).

'The Reflective Practitioner': Some Critical Questions

The kinds of question invited by the concept of 'the reflective practitioner' (understood henceforth as 'the reflective teacher') are complex and varied.

First, there are questions about how 'reflection' is to be understood. These include queries about the nature of reflection (e.g. how explicit and systematic it is or should be, and how it is related to action) and about its scope and objects (e.g. the matters on which teachers are invited to reflect about).

Second, there are questions about the value of reflection. One way of putting the central question here is to ask whether 'reflection' is valued as an end in itself or as a means to other ends. Given the complexity of means/end relationships in education, however, this way of posing the issue needs to be regarded with caution. It is better put in the following form: is reflection valued simply as a process, or in terms of the quality of the judgements — and possibly action — to which it leads? If reflection is valued because of the quality of judgements achieved or aimed at, attention focuses upon the 'content' of reflection. This raises the question of the criteria that can be invoked for adequate reflective judgement. If reflection is valued because of the action to which it leads, a number of questions arise: does being reflective mean merely thinking about one's teaching or doing something about it? Is a reflective teacher *ipso facto* a good teacher? How, for example, is a weak reflective teacher different from a strong unreflective teacher?

Third, questions arise about the development of reflection. How does an observer recognise a reflective teacher? To what extent can developmental principles for teacher reflection be discerned which can serve to illuminate programmes of teacher training?

This large range of questions (which overlap with, and are partly drawn from, some questions raised by Russell, 1993, p. 144) cannot be addressed fully here. I shall, however, offer some remarks on each of them.

The nature of reflection

Teaching involves a complex amalgam of interrelated kinds of achievement. In general terms, the teacher must have knowledge and understanding of wide-ranging sorts, the ability in the light of that knowledge and understanding to make rational practical judgements about what to do in particular circumstances, skills to carry out what is decided and dispositions (motives and tendencies) to actually do what is judged appropriate (Hirst, 1979). Whilst these kinds of achievement can be isolated in this way for purposes of formal analysis, their essential interrelatedness both practically and logically is obvious. Knowledge and understanding, for example, are involved in practical judgements, skills and dispositions, and are particularly significant in the case of teaching. In specific terms, the sorts of practical tasks and activities in which these kinds of achievement are exercised are extensive and many faceted, as revealed in the many empirical studies of the nature of teaching (e.g. Brown & McIntyre, 1993).

It is frequently claimed or implied that teachers should be *reflective* across all these elements of achievement, task and activity. As suggested earlier, the opposing claim — that teachers should be unreflective about these matters — sounds unappealing. Indeed, the notion of a wholly unreflective teacher is somewhat incoherent. Human agency of any kind involves thought, much of which is tacit and unexamined. The significance of implicit and intuitive elements in human action generally is illuminated by the telling remark of Martin Hollis that if 'rational man' is defined as one who chooses each action by reflecting consciously on what to do next, he would never be able to get to his own front door, immobilised by the decision about which sock to put on first. Given a society of such people, continues Hollis civilization would collapse into paralysis, like some giant centipede told to put its best foot forward first (Hollis, 1977, p. 62).

However, it is hard to conceive of human agency which does not require reflective thought of any kind. At the very least we encounter practical obstacles and challenges of various sorts to our plans and assumptions, which require us to reflect (at least in some sense and to some extent) on them. If this is true of human agency itself, it is still more true in the case of teaching. Forms of reflection arise naturally from the activity of teaching, even if they are confined to lower-level matters of (say) strategy and tactics. Practical judgements requiring reflection (again, in some sense and to some extent) are inescapable in teaching. The positive claim that teachers should be reflective, however, goes beyond these basic points and arises from an acknowledgement of the practical and evaluative complexities inherent in the work of the teacher (McLaughlin, 1994, pp. 152–153) which underscore the need for the sorts of professional thoughtfulness, judgement and autonomy referred to earlier.

However, in what sense should 'reflection' be understood here? On one interpretation, 'reflection' means simply 'thinking'. More specifically, it conjures up notions such as 'pondering', 'considering', 'deliberating', 'meditating' and the like, together with 'critical assessment'. More detailed accounts of the notion take a number of forms. It is helpful to approach these by reference to two continuums along which conceptions of the notion of 'reflection' are located.

The first continuum refers to the *nature* of reflection. Expressed roughly, at one end of this continuum are views of reflection which stress the explicit and the systematic and, at the other end, views which lay emphasis upon the implicit and the intuitive. The matters to which the explicit/systematic or implicit/intuitive are taken to refer to here are both the nature of the reasoning involved and the extent to which it involves a 'standing back' from action.

At the explicit and systematic end of this continuum is a view of reflection which involves 'technical reason'. 'Technical reason' is exhibited in Aristotle's notion of *techne*, an activity of making or production (*poesis*), aimed at a pre-specifiable and durable outcome (a product or state of affairs) which constitutes its purpose (*telos*). Inherent in this activity is 'technical knowledge' which gives the 'expert maker' '... a clear conception of the why and wherefore, the how and with-what of the making process and enables him, through the capacity to offer a rational account of it, to preside over his activity with secure mastery' (Dunne, 1993, p. 9). The limitations of 'technical rationality' as a form of reflection to govern the professional practice of teaching through the application of 'scientific' theory and technique in an instrumental way to solve the problems of practice are widely acknowledged (see, for example, Schön, 1983, ch. 2; Carr & Kemmis, 1986, ch. 2). At the heart of these difficulties is the inappropriateness of conceiving of teaching as a *techne*. Educational ends are neither clear, fixed, unitary nor evaluatively straightforward, and are not achieved (primarily) through technical means/end processes which can be mastered through scientific or technical knowledge and skill.

Also at the explicit and systematic end of this continuum are views of reflection which, whilst not necessarily invoking the notion of 'technical reason', are 'rationalist' in a broader sense, laying a similar stress on the need for reflection to involve the application of theory (in particular the resources and conclusions of the foundation disciplines of education) to the demands and realities of practice. The inadequacy of this account of reflection arises from its faulty conceptualisation of the relationship between rational action and theoretical knowledge. One aspect of this faulty conceptualisation is that the essentially abstract and general character of theoretical knowledge renders impossible its fruitful application to the details of practice in a direct and straightforward way (Hirst, 1983).

The conception of reflective thinking outlined by John Dewey can also be described as 'explicit' and 'systematic' in character. For Dewey, reflection is turning a subject over in the mind and giving it serious and consecutive consideration (Dewey, 1933, p. 3); '... Active, persistent, and careful consideration of any belief or supposed form of knowledge in the light of the grounds that support it and the further conclusions to which it tends' (ibid., p. 9). For Dewey, reflective thinking originates in a state of doubt or perplexity about a given matter, seeks through enquiry to resolve the perplexity, and invites in the process criticism, examination and test (ibid., pp. 12-16). Dewey places a strong emphasis upon scientific modes of thinking and reasoning in his conception of reflectiveness, as seen by his remarks on inference and testing (ibid., ch. 6), and on the structure of reflective thinking with its five phases or aspects, culminating in hypothesis testing (ibid., ch. 7; see also, for example, ch. 11 on systematic method). A number of the features of Dewey's account of reflective thinking invite doubt about its adequacy as a comprehensive account of teacher reflection. Is the sort of reflection engaged in by teachers always so explicit and systematic? Do 'problem solving' and scientific forms of thought have the salience in teacher reflection which Dewey suggests? (on general limitations in Dewey's stress on problem solving in education see Peters, 1977, esp. pp. 112–123).

There are some affinities between Dewey's account of reflective thinking and accounts which stress 'technical reason', although, given the richness and complexity of Dewey's thought, these affinities should not be pushed too far. Nor should Dewey be interpreted as denying the significance of the implicit and the intuitive in human action. (For an overall perspective on Dewey see, for example, Tiles, 1988. For similarities between Dewey's view and that of Schön, cf. Schön, 1987, pp. 26–31.)

At the implicit and intuitive end of the continuum concerning the nature of reflection we encounter Donald Schön, whose arguments about the nature of professional knowledge are by now well known. Schön's rejection of the adequacy of 'technical rationality' as an account of professional knowledge is emphatic. Professional decisions often involve not merely the 'solving' of problems which are already 'given' and well formed, but a process of wrestling with '… messy, indeterminate situations …' (Schön, 1987, p. 4) requiring the 'setting', 'framing', 'construction' (or interpretative determination) of 'problems' in forms of judgement which go beyond the technical. Professionals in these matters are 'world makers' (ibid., p. 36). In addition, the cases and situations confronting the practitioner often involve uniqueness, uncertainty and value-conflict, and therefore cannot be dealt with by the application of routinisable and pre-specifiable procedures and strategies. For Schön, it is in these 'indeterminate zones of practice' that the distinctiveness and importance of professional competence is to be found.

In giving his own account of professional competence in these matters, Schön is wary of using terms such as 'wisdom' and 'intuition', which are in his view apt to be used as 'junk categories' attaching names to phenomena that elude conventional strategies of explanation' (ibid., p. 13). As is well known, his approach is to analyse carefully the 'core of artistry' which is inherent in professional practice. Artistry is an exercise of intelligence and a kind of knowing, revealed in arts such as problem framing, implementation and improvisation. Much of this artistry, along with our everyday competences of recognition, judgement and skill is tacit in character '[it does] ... not depend on our being able to describe what we know how to do or even to entertain in conscious thought the knowledge our actions reveal' (ibid., p. 22). What is involved is 'knowledge in action', contained in, and revealed by, intelligent action itself.

Schön notes that it is possible through observation and reflection on our actions to attempt a description of our tacit knowledge (ibid., pp. 25–26). He takes such reflection to be occasioned by situations of surprise, when our knowing-in-action is insufficient for the unexpected (although Schön does not want to be tied to too restrictive an account of what may stimulate reflection: ibid., p. 29). Schön distinguishes between reflection on action (which is retrospective in character, whether it takes place immediately after the action or much later) and reflection in action, where the reflection can make a difference to what we are doing and therefore has immediate significance for practice. 'Reflection in action' takes a professional form in the shape of 'reflection in practice'. Central to Schön's account of professional competence, it has the crucial function of questioning the 'assumptional structure' of knowing in action (ibid., p. 28) but is often tacit and closely integrated into smooth performance, as in Schön's examples of the cellist sight-reading an unfamiliar piece and the jazz musicians improvising together (ibid., pp. 29–30). At the heart of matters here is a '... reflective conversation with the materials of a situation' (ibid., p. 31). Further stages of reflection involve reflection upon our reflection-in-action so as to produce a verbal description of it, and then reflection upon the description which emerges (ibid., p. 31), so as to facilitate a reflective grasp of practice which is ever widening.

Although the details of Schön's account cannot be pursued further at this point (see, for example, Schön, 1983, chs 5, 6, 9), it is important to note its similarity — at least in some respects — to the activity which Aristotle contrasted with *techne: praxis. Praxis* involves the engagement of persons in activity with others which is non-instrumental in that it is not intended to realise goods 'external' to the persons involved but rather excellences characteristic of a worthwhile form of life. Joseph Dunne's helpful illumination of this notion also brings into focus elements of it on which Schön is silent:

> As an activity that both involved one with other people and at the same time was a realisation of one's self, *praxis* engaged one more

intimately, or afforded one less detachment, than the *poesis* over which one exercised an uncompromised sovereignty. And for this reason — that it, e.g., brought one's emotions so much more into play and both formed and revealed one's character — as well as because of its bringing one into situations that were very much more heterogeneous and contingent than the reliably circum-scribed situations of *poesis*, praxis required for its regulation a kind of knowledge that was more personal and experiential, more supple and less formulable, than the knowledge conferred by *techne*. (Dunne, 1993, p. 10)

This knowledge is described by Aristotle as *phronesis* (or practical wisdom), a major 'ordering agency' in our lives more generally. On a view such as this the sort of reflective thinking that is appropriate for teachers is that harmonious with, and arising out of, *phronesis*, and appropriate for the person who possesses it — the *phronimos*. Whilst Schön's discussion of the nature of professional knowledge reso-nates with the sort of knowledge characteristic of '*phronesis*', his account stops short of a full discussion of the qualities of character and 'personhood' which arise in the Aristotelian perspective. This perspective, and the extent to which it can be appealed to as the basis for a fuller understanding of the nature of teacher reflection, will be returned to later.

Different views of reflection emerging along the continuum we have been considering are associated with different views both of the theory/practice relationship (in general and as it bears upon the promotion of reflection) and of the proper demands of teacher train-ing and development. With regard to the relationship between the-ory and practice, 'technical rationality' and 'Rationalist' approaches can lend support to crude 'theory into practice' accounts of this rela-tionship, with reflection seen as served by exposure to theory appro-priate for 'application'. In contrast, a view such as that of Schön illuminates, and lends support to, accounts which see the role of the-ory as implicit within, and contributing in different ways to the reflective critique of, the common sense or practical knowledge of teachers (Hirst, 1983, 1990a; Griffiths & Tann, 1992). The Aristotelian account is associated with a complex and well-articulated account of the theory/practice relationship (on this see, for example, Carr, 1995a, ch. 4 and Dunne, 1993, esp. Pt 2). With regard to the demands of teacher training, views at the implicit and intuitive end of the con-tinuum underscore the importance of practical experience and train-ing in the preparation of teachers. Crucial for Schön is the notion of a 'reflective practicum' (ibid., pp. 36–40, chs 7, 10, Pt 4) in which the artistry needed to function in the 'indeterminate zones of practice', and, in particular, proficiency in reflection-in-action is developed. Schön's substantial examples of reflective practice in the two books referred to do not include teaching, and the analogies and disanalogies between the examples he does give and teaching are instructive (for an application of Schön's theories to teacher training see, for example, Furlong *et al.*, 1988, esp. ch. 4). Different views of reflection are also related to differing conceptions of the extent to which teachers should be properly seen as 'researchers' (on this general matter see, for example, Rudduck & Hopkins, 1985; Schön, 1983, pp. 307–325. On action research see, for example, Carr, 1995a, ch. 7. For a critique of the concept of 'the teacher as researcher' see Kemmis, 1995).

The second continuum along which views of reflection can be located refers to the *scope* and *objects* of reflection: the matters on which teachers are invited to, or expected to, reflect about. Schön points out that the objects of reflection of a practitioner can be very wide, including '... the tacit norms and appreciations which underlie a judgement... the strategies and theories implicit in a pattern of behaviour ... the feeling for a situation which has led to a particular course of action ... the way in which he has framed the problem he is trying to solve ... the role he has constructed for himself within a larger institutional context' (Schön, 1983, p. 62). One way of describing the continuum on which the scope and objects of reflection are located is in terms of a concern at one end of the continuum for specific and proximate matters and a concern at the other for matters which are general and contextual.

At the specific and proximate end of the continuum are objects of reflection which relate in a close way to the 'present and particular' concerns of the teacher, especially within the classroom. Included here are the myriad interactions and judgements in the classroom in all their complexity, which relate in a concrete way to the various forms of achievement being aimed at for pupils and to the ways in which they can be realised. At the general and contextual end of the continuum are reflections about matters relating to the educational enterprise viewed from a broader and less immediate perspective. Matters for consideration here include the overall aims and purposes of the educational enterprise, the nature of 'ability', the functions and effects of processes of teaching and schooling and the significance of wider influences on the educational system as a whole, which in turn involve questions of a philosophical, psychological, social and political kind. Schön draws attention to the dangers arising from reflection which is limited in scope (Schön, 1983, ch. 9), and brings out the value of, and need for, research into matters (such as 'frames', 'overarching theories' and the like) which help to illuminate these broader matters (Schön, 1983, pp. 307–325). A concern that teacher reflection should range over the full range of this continuum, and not be confined to the specific and proximate is expressed in the various accounts which have emerged of 'levels' of reflection (e.g. McIntyre, 1993, pp. 44-47; Griffiths & Tann, 1992, pp. 76–80; for a related discussion on 'levels of training' see Furlong *et al.* 1988, pp. 129–132). The extent to which students in initial training for teaching can, and should, engage in reflection at the general and contextual end of the continuum is a matter of significance.

The two continua which have been identified, the first concerning the nature of reflection and the second, its scope and objects, are related to each other in a complex way. Differing objects of reflection invite differing forms of reflection. Attention is needed to these differences. Discussions of the ideal of 'the reflective teacher' often equate 'reflection' with 'reflection on one's own experience of practice' (e.g. Griffiths & Tann, 1992, p. 71; McIntyre, 1993, pp. 42–43). This seems too limited, since abstract theoretical matters are also properly objects of reflection. It is useful here, however, to make a distinction between the sources of reflection relevant to teaching and its goal. It might be claimed that, since what is at issue is the reflective teacher, the goal of teacher reflection must be related in some way to practice. This is the force of (for example) Griffiths and Tann's claim that reflection must help students to form their 'personal theories of action' (Griffiths & Tann, 1992, p. 71). We need to be cautious, however, about putting this point too strongly. Too tight a connection between 'reflection' and 'relationship to practice' might inhibit necessary forms of general and contextual reflection. Be that as it may, however, it is clear that the sources of relevant reflection should not be confined to experience of practice. McIntyre, for example, notes that novice teachers need ideas from 'external sources'. Since novices have to reflect upon these theories, McIntyre's claim that reflection is a less significant form of learning for novice teachers than for experienced professionals sounds odd (ibid., pp. 43-44). The oddness here arises from McIntyre's stipulative definition of 'reflection' as 'reflection upon practice'. This underscores the need in discussions of reflection to be alert to the stipulative definitions of the term which may be in use.

The concept of 'reflection' in teaching therefore involves a wide range of conceptions of the nature of reflection and of its scope and objects. These conceptions are not necessarily in opposition to each other but emphasise different aspects of the nature of reflection. Often an appeal to the notion of the 'reflective teacher' as the underlying rationale of a course of teacher training can silence debate by achieving a ready consensus. Far from closing down such a debate, however, such an appeal, properly understood, should open it up — across a wide range of relevant matters.

The value of reflection

Discussions of 'reflection' (of whatever sort) in teaching often seem to suggest that reflection is *per se* a good thing. But is this the case, and, if so, why?

One question which arises is whether a reflective teacher is *ipso facto* a good teacher. What counts as 'good teaching' is, of course, not a straightforward matter (on this see, for example, Brown and McIntyre, 1993, ch. 2, 3). However, on any view of what 'good teaching' amounts to, reflection is not a sufficient condition of it. Teaching involves more than reflection. We would think little of a teacher who was rich in the capacity to reflect (in whatever sense) but who was unable to establish appropriate relationships with pupils, or was disinclined to invite them to engage in any work. Whether reflection is a necessary ingredient in good teaching depends in part upon the sort of reflection that is being referred to and in part on how 'good teaching' is being understood. As mentioned earlier, reflection in some minimal sense is inescapable in teaching. Some of the forms of reflection discussed by Schön seem to be partially constitutive of good teaching in any recognisable sense of the term. Reflection-in-action, for example, is very tightly related to anything that might be regarded as effective classroom performance. And since *phronesis* is understood precisely as uniting good judgement and action, it also seems to be partially constitutive of good teaching. Whether reflection on matters at the general and contextual end of the continuum identified earlier is necessary for good teaching is a more complex matter. It is certainly possible to conceive of teachers who are capable of performing at a certain level of competence without being in possession of a broader perspective on their work arising from reflection on the sort of general and contextual matters we have been referring to. One way of making a strong connection between such wider reflective understanding and good teaching is to *define* a good teacher as one who possesses it. Another is to claim that such wider understandings are implicit in adequate reflection-in-action and in *phronesis*.

Empirical researchers may be tempted to investigate whether such wider understandings do, for the most part, enhance practice, especially when specific attempts are made to achieve such an enhancement. The difficulties in researching such a matter are, however, extensive. They include problems in establishing the nature and extent of the understanding possessed by a given individual, as well as the multifarious problems involved in judging its impact on practice. These arise not least from the fact that many of the influences on pupils arising from teachers with an expanded outlook of the sort in question are very subtle in nature, and involve aspects of the personhood of the teacher.

Discussion of the value of teacher reflection involves the question of the quality of reflection. There is a generic — or 'process' — sense of reflection, where reflection itself is seen as a good thing, without reference either to what is reflected upon or to the quality of the reflection. However, it is important to insist that reflections can be more or less adequate, accurate, insightful, relevant and so forth. McIntyre rightly draws attention to the limits of emphasising (as in notions such as reflecting or theorising) the 'process' rather than the 'content' aspects of these notions (McIntyre, 1993, pp. 39–41, 47–52). (This suspicion of 'process talk' in relation to reflection also arises with respect to mentoring, where there are increasing calls for greater attention to its 'content'; e.g. Furlong & Maynard, 1995, ch. 4.) Flawed reflections may take various forms. Apart from misunderstandings, mistakes and the like, the wrong kind of reflection for particular purposes can be engaged in, as where a teacher employs a faulty 'rationalist' model of reflection to 'apply' theory in some crude way to practice. Inadequacy in reflection can also arise from its narrowness of focus and scope. Flawed reflections (of whatever kind) can inhibit good practice in a number of ways that can be readily imagined. It is important to note, however, that it is not just inadequate reflections which might inhibit good practice. There are a number of respects in which reflection in general can do so, even when there is no inadequacy in the reflection itself. (I leave to one side here the possibility that reflection might be defined in such a way that its adequacy is connected to its positive influence upon practice.) It is important to take heed of Calderhead's point that, in some circumstances, reflection can debilitate, lessening a teachers capacity for action (Calderhead, 1989, p. 45). It is also important to recognise the potentially conflictual and destabilising character of reflective practice on schools inadequately prepared for it (Schön, 1983, pp. 334–336). In addition, it should be noted that reflection can undermine as well as enhance the development of practical skills. Schön's discussion of the senses in which reflection might interfere with action is rather incomplete (Schön, 1983, pp. 275–281). He concedes, however, that there are some situations where reflection-in-action does inhibit performance (the example of the golf player encouraged to change his grip on his club is a relevant case). Such points call for teacher trainers to balance carefully the promotion of reflection with the other demands and priorities of training and professional development (cf. Day, 1993).

The recognition that the adequacy of reflection requires assessment is exhibited by a number of writers. For Dewey, the adequacy of reflection is crucial. Reflection commences, claims Dewey, when we begin to inquire into the reliability, the worth, of any particular indication; when we try to test its value and see what guarantee there is that the existing data really point to the idea that is suggested in such as way as to justify acceptance of the latter (Dewey, 1933, p. 11). For Dewey reflection implies belief on evidence (ibid., pp. 11–12). Hirst lays particular emphasis on the significance of critical assessment and justification. Despite his continuing critique of 'rationalism' (Hirst, 1993), Hirst retains his belief that educational theory is '… primarily the domain which seeks to develop rational principles for educational practice' (Hirst, 1983, p. 5), albeit principles which are 'practical' in character. For Hirst a crucial question is whether the 'theory' implicit in human action and in teaching is 'any good'. 'Are its concepts adequate to capture the complexities of the situations concerned? Is what is believed about these situations true? Are the judgements that are made justifiable on rational grounds?' (Hirst, 1990a, p. 74). For Hirst, the notion of a domain of rationally developing general principles of professional practice is necessary to the intelligibility of the notions of professionalism and professional development (Hirst, 1990b, p. 156. For his related criticisms of the Oxford Internship scheme for its inattention to the significance of justified principles and of what is required for students to be helped to make adequate reflective judgements see pp. 151–159). From such a point of view, an invitation to simply 'reflect' without attention to the ways in which adequacy in reflection can be secured is idle and, indeed, damaging to educational practice. The notion of an appropriate form of criticism is also inherent within the notion of the Aristotelian notion of '*phronesis*' (see Carr, 1995a, ch. 4) and forms part of the grounds on which Carr insists that interpretative research cannot rest content with merely describing what practitioners say about their practice (Carr, 1995a, chs 5, 8).

If the importance of the critique of reflective judgement is insisted upon, however, crucial questions arise about the basis on which criteria can be specified relevant to judgements of adequacy. What is to count as 'adequate' reflection and on what grounds? The inherent difficulty of such questions is amplified by the heterogeneous character of 'reflection'. Schön draws attention to the difficulty of speaking of truth and effectiveness in relation to the value-laden character of many professions, especially across frames of reference. The capacity for frame reflection is therefore important (Schön, 1987, p. 218), as seen for example in Schön's discussion of the field of psychoanalysis, where fundamental interpretative disputes are particularly significant (Schön, 1987, ch. 9). The difficulty in specifying criteria for judgement in such situations is revealed in Schön's discussion elsewhere of the emergence of 'professional pluralism' — 'Competing views of professional practice ... of the professional role, the central values of the profession, the relevant knowledge and skills ...' (Schön, 1983, p. 17). The task of '... choosing among competing paradigms of practice' (Schön, 1983, p. 19) is therefore a complex one.

The difficulties involved in specifying a basis on which adequate criticism of reflective practice can be conducted are illustrated by Gilroy's claim that Schön has failed to provide an epistemology of practice. For Gilroy, such an epistemology is unattainable: the search for an explanation of a particular practice ends when one points to the practice, to the game as it is played, and states. 'This is just how we do it' (Gilroy, 1993, p. 139). Difficulties of this kind are exacerbated by the phenomenon of postmodernism, with its own form of radical questioning of the very possibility of general standards of judgement. Margaret Wilkin, for example, argues that a postmodern perspective renders highly problematic the project of rationally criticising and enriching the practical judgements of student teachers. What could such a project mean in the absence of even the possibility of general standards or norms in relation to which the relevant judgements can be made? (Wilkin, 1993).

Such questions raise fundamental philosophical issues about the evaluative basis of education itself. This debate cannot be pursued here (on an attempt to render compatible an acceptance of certain theses of postmodernism with enlightenment ideals see, for example, Carr, 1995a, esp. ch. 9, 1995b). For the present discussion, however, it is important to note that teacher trainers cannot sidestep this debate by invoking the concept of 'the reflective teacher' and seeking to deflect questions about the adequacy of reflective judgement by appealing to reflection as a 'process'.

The development of reflection

One of the most prominent features of recent discussion of teacher training is a search for developmental principles for the development of reflection. A number of recent discussions of teacher training either offer models for training programmes based on a number of principles from various sources (e.g. Benton, 1990; Furlong et al., 1988) or a critical analysis of such principles themselves (e.g. Elliot, 1993; Eraut, 1994; Hargreaves, 1993; Hirst, 1990b; La Boskey, 1994; McIntyre, 1990).

Whilst these models and principles offer differing accounts of the varying stages or elements of training, they do not offer very detailed developmental principles relating to reflection. Nor is it clear from the foregoing that such developmental principles could ever easily emerge. This is for a number of reasons. First, as we have seen, 'reflection' is no one thing. Calderhead indicates how conceptions of reflective teaching differ with respect to the process, content, preconditions and product of reflection (Calderhead, 1989, p. 44) and of its implications for teacher education (ibid., p. 45). It is therefore hard to specify what reflection itself means, quite apart from what its development might consist in. Second, it is no easy matter to identify the achievement by individuals of the relevant forms of reflection. This might be thought to be easier in the case of reflection-in-action although even here it is not easier to identify the specifically reflective aspects of successful practice.

Calderhead's complaint that, as yet, models of teacher reflection have been inadequately tested empirically (ibid., pp. 45–46) does not address directly this fundamental difficulty. Finally, since what is at stake here is 'development' and not merely 'change' the sorts of complex questions about the evaluation of reflection return here with renewed force.

Beyond Reflection

As we have seen, the difficulties involved in giving a clear account of what is involved in the notion of 'the reflective teacher' are extensive, and the agenda of issues and problems which have emerged require attention if the notion is to function in a meaningful way in relation to teaching and teacher training.

In the final section of this paper, I shall focus attention beyond the notion of reflection to the broader moral, intellectual and personal qualities — qualities of mind and dispositions of character and personhood — that should characterise the teacher. The suggestion here is that we need to recognise the significance of the teacher as a certain sort of person, and that this should be acknowledged in the demands of teacher training. This is important not only in relation to resolving some of the issues which have emerged in relation to 're-flection' but as a worthy emphasis in its own right.

Discussions of the concept of 'the reflective teacher' are apt to treat the notion in a way which abstracts 'reflection' from the broader personal qualities of the teacher. Certainly, reflection involves a number of related attitudes and virtues (see, for example Dewey, 1933, pp. 28–34). But attention needs to be focused on more wide-ranging human qualities.

The sorts of qualities needed by teachers in the task of teaching as a whole are illustrated by William Hare's discussion of the need for teachers to possess appropriate forms of humility, courage, impartiality, open-mindedness, empathy, enthusiasm, judgement and imagination (Hare, 1993). These particular qualities are not presented by Hare as exhaustive, and we can readily envisage additions to them, such as patience, self-knowledge, warmth and humour (see also John Wilson's attempt to outline 'the qualities of an educator': Wilson, 1993, ch. 5 esp. pp. 130-142). It is important to note the respects in which teaching involves these broader aspects of personhood. Smith and Aired, for example, insist that, in relation to pupils, the teacher is one who brings his or her whole being as a person to bear (Smith and Aired, 1993, p. 106), and whose qualities are rooted in the kind of person he or she is rather than in abilities which are possessed (ibid., p. 112). This point is related to the insistence by Michael Oakeshott that certain forms of learning can only be brought about by the example of the teacher (see, for example Oakeshott, 1989, esp. pp. 60–62).

Central to the qualities of a teacher is the form of practical wisdom or *phronesis*, discussed earlier, which contains *inter alia* a broad and rich grasp of the values of the educational enterprise. Dunne comments that practical knowledge is '... a fruit which can grow only in the soil of a person's experience and character' (Dunne, 1993, p. 358). Dunne continues: 'In exposing oneself to the kind of experience and acquiring the kind of character that will yield the requisite knowledge ... [one] ... is at the same time a feeling, expressing, and acting person, and one's knowledge is inseparable from one as such' (ibid., p. 358). Wilfred Carr describes *phronesis* as a comprehensive moral capacity which combines practical knowledge of the good with sound judgement about what, in a particular situation, would constitute an appropriate expression of this' (Carr, 1995a, p. 71). *Phronesis* is an attractive concept with respect to a number of the difficulties which emerged earlier concerning 'reflection'. It offers the prospect of a unified concept of reflection, with practical judgement playing a role in deciding the nature and extent of forms of reflection necessary for particular purposes. It also offers a context for the resolution of the questions of the adequacy of reflective judgement mentioned earlier. Practical wisdom is seen at the heart of the matter, rather than the justification of principles (of whatever kind). Further, the character of *phronesis* is such that it constitutes a fruitful concept which will enable the scope of teacher training to be extended to embrace the sorts of wider human qualities just mentioned.

The suggestion that Aristotelian *phronesis* offers a richer unifying ideal for teaching and teacher training—embracing the attractive features of 'reflection' but remedying its indeterminacy and rootlessness—is worthy of sustained attention. It is worth noting, however, some of the difficulties which the suggestion must address. The central difficulty, to use some words of Dunne is '... the complicity of *phronesis* with an established way of life' (Dunne, 1993, p. 373). *Phronesis* seems to demand established and relatively stable 'communities of practice' (Pendlebury, 1990, 1994). It might be argued that we no longer have the stable communities of educational practice that *phronesis* demands. We no longer, for example, have a stable and rooted sense of the sort of person that a teacher should be and the sort of practice that education is. Another (related) difficulty is the perception that, given the well grounded differences of view about education which are characteristic of modernity and postmodernity, *phronesis* possesses neither a sufficiently robust and sceptical form of reflection to do justice to the genuine demands of fundamental query and criticism nor the resources to defend itself against sceptical and relativist accusations that it is itself only one conception competing against others.

The tension between the demands of 'rootedness' and 'criticism' present in these difficulties are already widely acknowledged in relation to schooling, where it is resolved to some extent by acknowledging the demands of a plurality of different kinds of school, some offering education in the context of a distinctive 'community of commitment' and others in a 'common school'. One outcome of increased attention to the wider human formation for the teacher implied by Aristotelian *phronesis* may be to open up discussion of the value of a plurality of different forms of teacher training, in some of which the relevant Aristotelian 'communities of practice' can be formed and nourished.

In conclusion, it seems clear that we have no choice but to go beyond 'the reflective teacher' as a slogan. Whether we should go beyond 'the reflective teacher' as a concept, either in the Aristotelian direction I have indicated or another, is a matter deserving much future debate.

Acknowledgements

This article was presented as a keynote address to the annual conference of the Philosophy of Education Society of Australasia in Sydney in July 1997. I am grateful to the participants in the conference for criticisms and discussion.

Chapter 5

National Identity and the Aims of Education

The question of whether, and to what extent, education should seek to form a national identity is debated in many societies. Inevitably, the character of the debate takes a different form according to the society in which it takes place. In England and Wales, for example, the sorts of issues which arise in the debate about the educational development of national identity are different from those which arise in the parallel debate in a society such as Lithuania. Each society has its own historical, cultural and political distinctiveness, and this generates a particular perspective from which issues of national identity are viewed.

In this article, I offer a philosophical perspective on some matters of broad principle relating to educational aims and the development of national identity. I am unable to relate my discussion in any detail to the context of Lithuania, but I hope that my remarks might be of interest and relevance to Lithuanian readers.*

There are several ways in which education can aim at the formation of a national identity. An educational institution can form a 'national consciousness' in its students through particular aspects of, and emphases in, its curriculum, through teaching methods and mediums, and through the ethos and organisation of the institution itself. Further, education more broadly can help to shape a national identity in society as a whole through its wide ranging influence upon culture, the media and political life. In this discussion I shall not engage in any detailed exploration of the broader ways in which education can shape national identity, and shall concentrate upon some general points relating to the formation of a 'national consciousness' in students.

---

* The present essay derives from a lecture delivered at Kaunas University in Lithuania, and the text first appeared in *Socialiniai Mokslai* a publication of that university, hence the references to Lithuania. It will be apparent, however, that the points at issue are general ones. — *Editors*.

The article has seven sections. In the first section I shall attempt to situate the discussion by offering some reflections on the broad question of the respective significance of the 'general' and the 'particular' in education, and illustrate how a 'liberal democratic' conception of education is suspicious of unduly particular formation and influence. The thrust of such a view of education is to lead students 'beyond the present and the 'particular'. In the second section, I argue that, whilst a 'liberal democratic' form of education emphasises the formation of a 'general' or 'universal' identity in students, it cannot avoid shaping a 'particular' identity as well. As a first move in the attempt to assess whether a 'national' identity is an appropriate particularistic identity which education should aim at, the third section addresses the meaning of 'nationality'. Claims regarding the value of nationality are explored in the fourth section. In the following section I offer some brief comments on the educational implications of the discussion. In the sixth section, I draw out some implications for nationality, education and the European Union. The concluding section attempts to draw attention to some issues which may be of particular relevance to the Lithuanian context. Needless to say, my treatment of these issues is preliminary and exploratory. Apart from my unfamiliarity with the Lithuanian context, philosophers and philosophers of education have only begun to address the general issues quite recently.

Education and Democracy:
The Shaping of General and Particular Identities

Any conception of education based on liberal democratic principles is suspicious of particularity, especially when the particularity involved concerns the shaping of individuals in ways which presuppose values and commitments which are, from a democratic point of view, significantly controversial.[1] The sort of education attempted in totalitarian societies is seen as objectionable from a democratic perspective on precisely these grounds. In the pre-perestroika Soviet Union, for example, education attempted to shape a particular identity in students based on a significantly controversial theory of the good. This education was designed to bring about the sort of unified, detailed, moral formation contained in the notion of vospitanie. In this process, individuality, criticism and variety were subordinated to Marxist-Leninist theory, which determined the aims and methods of a monolithic and centralised system of schools. These schools,

[1]   For a discussion of related general matters see Taylor (1992).

together with youth organisations and the media, all conspired in a co-ordinated way to develop the ideal communist person, complete with collectivist and atheistic beliefs qualities of character. [2]

In contrast, education based on liberal democratic principles seeks to avoid such a particularistic formation. It might be argued, of course, that a 'liberal democratic' form of education is itself based on a theory of the good which is 'particular' and 'significantly controversial'. Such an education, it might be claimed, also tries to shape a certain sort of person, and to impart a 'particular' individual identity. In reply, a proponent of 'liberal democratic' education will argue that, whilst there is some truth in these objections, education based on democratic principles seeks to reduce particularistic influence to a minimum. Further, the proponent will claim that a liberal democratic form of education is committed to an underlying theory of the good which is maximally hospitable to individual autonomy and to differences of view. Whilst a full articulation[3] and evaluation[4] of a 'liberal democratic' conception of education is beyond the scope of this article its general character can be briefly sketched. The task of education in pluralistic liberal democratic societies is conceptualised in the light of two important realities. First, education of whatever form is inherently value-laden, the values involved being of different kinds. No form of education can be value-free or value-neutral.[5] The question which arises for education is therefore not whether it should be based on, and should transmit, values but which values should be invoked. The second reality is the well-grounded, deep-seated and perhaps ineradicable differences of view about many questions of value which are characteristic of pluralistic liberal democratic societies. This is not to suggest that such societies are entirely bereft of value agreement and consensus. If this were so it would be hard to see how these societies could achieve stability and coherence, much less satisfy the value demands implicit in democracy, such as justice, freedom and democracy. There are, however, large areas of disagreement about

---

[2]   On these matters see, for example, Halstead (1994). For a similar discussion relating to China see Li (1993). For a further example of an educational initiative in a post-communist society involving questions relating to moral education see Lencz (1994).

[3]   For such an articulation see, for example, Gutmann (1987) McLaughlin (1992), (1995a), (1995b).

[4]   For critique of a 'liberal democratic' conception of education see, for example, Dunlop (1996); Kohli (1991)

[5]   On these matters see, for example, McLaughlin (1994)

many questions, most notably about overall views of life as a whole, or 'comprehensive' theories of the good.

In the light of these two realities, public education in pluralistic liberal democratic societies, at least in common schools attended by students from all backgrounds, seeks to base its substantial value influence on principles broadly acceptable to the citizens of society as a whole. This requires that this form of education cannot assume the truth of, or promote, any particular, comprehensive, or all-embracing vision of the good life. Rather, it aims at a complex two-fold influence. On matters which are widely which can be regarded as part of the common or basic values of the society, education seeks to achieve a strong, substantial influence on the beliefs of pupils and their wider development as persons. It is unhesitating, for example, in promoting the values of basic 'social morality' and democratic 'civic virtue' more generally. Involved here is the notion of an ' ... education adequate to serve the life of a free and equal citizen in any modern democracy'[6] which includes the notion of 'education for citizenship'.[7] On matters of disagreement, where scope for a legitimate diversity of view is acknowledged, education seeks to achieve a principled forbearance of influence: it seeks not to shape either the beliefs or the personal qualities of pupils in the light of any substantial or 'comprehensive' conception of the good which is significantly controversial. Instead, public education is either silent about such matters or it encourages pupils to come to their own reflective decisions about them One way of expressing in an overall way the nature of educational influence on this view is that it exerts a complex combination of centripetal (unifying) and centrifugal (diversifying) forces on pupils and on society itself.

Although much more needs to be said in the articulation of this general view and its presumptive relationship with the notion of the common school,[8] it is hopefully clear enough for our purposes.

Education in liberal democratic societies must constantly be alert to the need to articulate and to handle in a fair way for students, differing perspectives on matters of significant controversy, and this gives rise to a number of complexities in the work of the common school.[9]

At the heart of pluralist liberal democratic societies, and the philosophical tradition of liberalism in terms of which they are frequently articulated, is the need within the societies for contrasting demands

[6]   Gutmann (1992) p. 14

[7]   On this see McLaughlin (1992)

[8]   On these matters see, for example, McLaughlin 1995a; 1995b.

[9]   McLaughlin 1995a pp. 244–252

of generality (commonality) and particularity (diversity) to be acknowledged and the familiar tension between them to be properly balanced. Without significant common values, principles and procedures such societies would lack not only stability and coherence, but also the justice required for its members to live together as free and equal democratic citizens. On the other hand, without principled acknowledgement of and provision for, a scope of diversity in belief, practice and value such societies would stand accused of inattention to the legitimate demands of pluralism and difference. The nature of these demands and the relationship between them can be variously expressed in terms of familiar tensions between universalism and particularism, the public and the non-public, and the like. It is in relation to the proper balance that should be struck between these demands that many current in moral and political philosophy are to be and understood.[10] 'Commonality' is especially significant on this view, because it embodies central democratic principles and procedures relating to (for example) personal autonomy, freedom of conscience speech and the range of familiar democratic rights and entitlements. These have a 'general' or 'universal' feel to them in that they are seen as relevant to any democratic society, regardless of the social and cultural context in which it is located. From a democratic point of view it is important to ensure that these general features are not conceived in too particular a way. They should be as free as possible from particular and controversial conceptions of the good.

Therefore, in democratic societies, especially those which are pluralist in character, there is an aversion to basing education on an unduly particular conception of the good, and to shaping an unduly particular identity in students. There is an alertness to the dangers of basing educational influence on a form of communitarian solidarity which requires that ' ... children be educated to accept the singularly correct and comprehensive conception of the good life.[11]

Instead, education is seen as encouraging students to engage in independent critical reflection and to achieve, at least to a significant extent, an appropriate self-directness and personal autonomy. The general or universalistic thrust in the liberal democratic conception of education is well captured in Charles Bailey's insistence that liberal education must 'lead beyond the present and particular, including the incestuous ties of clan and soil'.[12]

---

[10] See, for example, Rawls (1993), Taylor (1992), Milligan & Watts Miller (1992) (Eds.)

[11] Gutmann (1993) p. 3

[12] Bailey (1984) See esp pp. 20–22

Education and the Significance of Particularity

However, education and schooling, however much it might seek to
transcend particularities, cannot escape from them. Education cannot
take place in a vacuum. It is necessarily conducted in particular particular social, political and cultural contexts. The schools of a liberal
democratic society cannot therefore avoid transmitting some norms
which are culturally distinctive in that they selectively favour some
beliefs, practices and values in ways that go beyond what could be
justified from a strictly neutral or 'global' point of view. Amy
Gutmann notes that in the USA local communities have been given
the democratic right to shape their schools in their own cultural
image, within principled liberal democratic constraints.[13] But within
these limits, the shared beliefs and cultural practices which are particular to communities can be transmitted and maintained.

The identity which is developed in students by the educational
process is (to a significant extent) inevitably concrete and particular, shaped by the specifities of the social, political and cultural context in which it takes place. Education may seek to transcend these,
but they cannot be avoided. Education for citizenship, for example,
involves the student coming to understand matters of general democratic principle. But, since there is no abstract 'democratic citizen'
who is not the citizen of a particular place, this process cannot be
wholly general. This point is well summed up in De-Maistre's
remark that - I have seen, in my times, Frenchmen, Italians and Rus-
sians ... but as for Man, I declare I have never met him in my life
...,[14] Education, therefore, must inevitably shape a local as well as a
universal identity. The ingredients of such a local identity are wide
ranging and include such matters as language, literature, custom
and sensibility. The significance of such local ingredients for personal identity, recognition and flourishing have been acknowledged by many writers. Nor can such local identities be seen as
opposed to autonomy and freedom. On the contrary, as Yael Tamir
insists, '... no individual can be context-free, but ... all can be free
within a context'.[15] Indeed, such a context is a prerequisite for
freedom.

Education, therefore, must develop loyalties and commitments in
students which are not merely abstract. This conclusion is supported
by the communitarian critique of liberalism which has emerged in

recent years. This wide ranging critique claims that these values, and the political community which they generate, lacks the substantiality needed to enable persons to achieve defensible and necessary forms of affiliation and commitment to a 'larger moral ecology' beyond their own individual, and indeed individualistic concerns. Such a 'moral ecology' embodies a social ethos, a consensus of the common good and notions of loyalty and responsibility to the community as a whole as well as framework of wider beliefs and values providing (at least to some extent) a culture of 'narrative coherence' as well as of 'freedom' for lives. The liberal view, it is claimed, leads to individualism in its various forms, and a tendency for individual choice and self-definition to be based on arbitrary preference or self-interest, rather than a view of life which is more coherent and other regarding. In addition, attention is drawn to the corrosive effects of private economic pursuits and consumerism on the notion of a caring public ethos, the negative effects of an undue separation of public and private realms and so on[16]

The search for an appropriate form for these wider commitments has suggested a number of candidates for them, including the development of a certain sort of patriotism focused on imaginatively enriched concern for the community as a whole.[17] To what extent, however, should a national identity be sought here?

The Concept of Nationality

'What is involved in the notion of "nationality"'? David Miller, in his recent philosophical defence of nationality, offers an account of it which involves eight interconnected propositions.[18] It is useful to compare Miller's account with that of another recent philosophical defender of nationalism, Yael Tamir. Although the two accounts do not directly address each other, a good deal of agreement between the two can be discerned. There is, however, disagreement about a crucial matter. This can be brought out by outlining the eight propositions which Miller holds to be true of 'nationality', although I shall present them here in a slightly re-ordered form:

---

[16] See McLaughlin (1992)

[17] On these matters, see, for example, Callan (1991) (1994)

[18] Miller (1993)

(I)   National identity may be a constitutive part of personal identity ('may' is important for Miller here, since he does not
        advance the implausible claim that personal identity requires
        a national identity).

(II)   Nations are ethical communities in the sense that 'nationality'
        generates distinctive ethical obligations and expectations.
        We may have, for example, fuller duties to fellow nationals
        than we do to human beings as such.

(III)   National communities are constituted by belief — '... a nationality exists when its members believe that it does'[19] — rather
        than simply by any common at tribute such as race or language. Examples of the shared beliefs at stake here include a
        conviction that its members belong together and that they
        wish to continue their life in common. Both Miller and Tamir
        agree with Benedict Anderson's claim that nations are 'imaginary' in that they are sustained by acts of the individual and
        collective imagination.[20] For Tamir, nations are '... cultural
        communities demarcated by the imaginative power of their
        members.'[21]

(IV)   Members of a nation must, however, share certain distinctive
        traits. These may be varied in character, and include cultural
        features.

(V)   Nations must embody historical continuity, generating depth
        of involvement and obligation in ways not found in more
        transitory groupings.

(VI)   Nations are related to a particular geographical place.

(VII)   Nations are 'active' in the sense that 'they' do things, take
        decisions and so on.

(VIII) Nations must be, at least in aspiration, political communities.
        People who form a national community have a good claim to
        political self-determination, although not necessarily via a
        sovereign state. The actions of nations must include at least
        seeking to control a chunk of the earth's surface.[22]

It seems to me that, although Tamir would want to express some reservations about some of these propositions (particularly their necessity for an account of 'nationality'), it is only in relation to the final
one — the claim that a nation is a political community — that a clear

[19] Miller (1993) p. 6

[20] Anderson (1983)

[21] Tamir (1993) p. 68

[22] Miller (1993) p. 7

point of difference with Miller emerges. For Tamir, a nation does not necessarily have a political dimension, and can be understood solely in cultural terms. For her, a nation is a community bound together by a consciousness, solidarity and a common culture,[23] and she offers a cultural rather than a political interpretation of the right to national self-determination.[24] For Tamir, therefore, the distinction between a nation and other cultural communities is not a clear one. The imprecision of Tamir's account of a nation as (merely) a self-conscious cultural community has been criticised by John White, who argues that her unduly broad account of nationality leads to groupings such as the Amish and the mafia being describable as nations, and to her defence of nationalism amounting in essence to a defence of communitarian insights and an attempt to render them compatible with liberal principles.[25]

Leaving to one side for the moment this point of difference, the two authors share other points of agreement. Both accept, for example, that a nation is not to be identified with a state. A state is a legal and political entity with authority of a specific form (sovereignty), resources of power of various kinds and a well defined territory. Some nations do not have a state, and many modern states, in view of their cultural heterogeneity, cannot be identified with a national society: many states are multi-national in that they contain a number of national communities and cultures.

Another point shared by both authors is that 'nationality' can be disassociated from the negative and indeed often tragic, connotations of 'nationalism'. Helpful here is the distinction drawn by Michael Ignatieff between 'civic' and 'ethnic' nationalism.[26] Civic nationalism is democratic in character, envisaging the nation as a community of equal, rights-bearing citizens, patriotically attached to a shared set of political practices and values. In contrast, ethnic nationalism sees national identity as based on ethnicity rather than citizenship and law. Whilst civic nationalism can be rational, flexible, pluralistic and morally rich, ethnic nationalism is tempted by irrationality, fanaticism and authoritarianism. It is more likely to be 'nationalistic' in John White's definition of the term viz: as implying

---

[23] Tamir (1993) Ch. 3

[24] Tamir (1993) Ch. 3

[25] White (1994)

[26] Ignatieff (1994) pp. 3–6

the inherent superiority of the nation vis a vis others.[27] The distinction between 'civic' and 'ethnic' nationalism illuminated by the distinction which Tamir draws between 'citizenship' and 'nationhood'. Citizenship is a primarily legal concept referring to the relationship between a state and its formal members, embracing such matters as entitlements, rights and liberties. Nationhood involves a sense of membership in an imagined community, and the adoption and practice of a particular imagined cultural and communal identity. In Ignatieff's 'civic' nationalism, 'nationhood' embraces 'citizenship' and does not contradict it.

The Value of Nationality

It is important to note that the various defences of nationality we have been referring to seek to rehabilitate 'civic' rather than 'ethnic' nationality. The defences therefore take the form of arguments providing justification for the 'clothing' of liberal democratic principles and values with nationality, and not their submergence by it.

Tamir, for example, insists upon the 'elective' aspects of personal identity. Our lives should not be determined by history and fate, and significant possibilities for reflective choice should be insisted upon.[28] Tamir's comment that no person can be context-free, but all can be free within a context, was alluded to earlier. Miller holds that nationalism is not necessarily inimical to cultural pluralism. It need not be exclusive. Nor need it be an all-embracing identity, but is compatible with membership of a number of specific cultural groups.[29] John White argues that the notion of British identity and nationality needs to be re-worked to make it acceptable in terms of democratic criteria.[30] A similar concern to render nationality compatible with democracy motivates Penny Enslin's criticism from a femininist perspective of 'nation-building' in the South-African context.[31]

The distinctive benefits claimed for 'nationality' understood in the 'civic' sense, involving such notions as affiliation, attachment, embeddedness, belonging and communal identity and solidarity, resonate with communitarian themes referred to earlier. Miller, Tamir and White all refer to the significance of nationality for the formation of identity. Miller claims that it is a de facto source of the

[27]   White (1995)
[28]   Tamir (1993) Ch. 1
[29]   Miller (1993)
[30]   White (1995)
[31]   Enslin (1993/4)

large scale solidarity which is needed in large societies if social atomisation is to be avoided and collective goods secured. Nations can provide an 'overarching sense of community' of the sort which facilitates this. Since in his view national identity has a flexible, because partly mythic, character, it is capable of accommodating a number of different points of political view.[32]

This line of defence of nationality needs to confront a number of lines of difficulty.[33] Here I shall draw attention to two. First, can the 'communitarian' benefits of nationality be secured when nationality is conceived in 'civic' terms: as contained within, and limited by, a liberal democratic framework? That framework demands inter alia criticism and a provision for pluralism, both inherently corrosive of (for example) affiliation and solidarity. Tamir holds that there is a need for a 'public space ... in which individuals can share a language, memorise their past, cherish their heroes, live a fulfilling national life'[34] and in which the cultural aspects of national life can be given expression. But given an acceptance of pluralism, what 'thickness' and scope of this public space, as distinct from sub-cultural enclave, can be assumed? This first problem sharply re-states the central and general tension inherent in attempts to reconcile communitarian and liberal perspectives, and the search for a defensible form of 'holistic' educational influence which was identified earlier. The second difficulty concerns the precise respect in which 'nationality' is defended here. As we have seen, Tamir gives an explicitly cultural interpretation of the notion. Other defenders face the task of showing quite why political distinctiveness and autonomy (in whatever sense) is associated with the goods they identify.[35] This issue is particularly associated with the matters of 'European' significance which are the concern of this symposium, and which will be returned to in the final section.

Nation, State and Education

The two sorts of difficulty mentioned above surface clearly in relation to the educational implications which follow from the defences of nationality which have been discussed.

---

[32] Miller (1993)

[33] For criticism of the claim that nationalism can be rendered compatible with communitarianism see O'Neil (1994)

[34] Tamir (1993) p. 8

[35] For Ignatieff's claim that the chief value of the nation state lies in the provision of physical security which it affords, see Ignatieff (1994) pp. 7–9

90   *Liberalism, Education and Schooling*

Central to these implications is the distinction between education for citizenship and education for nationality. Tamir argues that a democratic state is justified in compelling education for citizenship for all students, but not education for nationhood. With regard to the latter — room must be made for the cultural and educational autonomy of all national groups'.[36] Since, as indicated earlier, many contemporary nation-states are multi-national, this means that education must make provision for a variety of forms of national formation. Citizenship does not imply cultural assimilation or unification. However, this brings out clearly the difficulty of securing 'thick' communitarian goods in 'civic' nationalism. Cultural fragmentation, or at best a kind of 'thin' public culture, is a foreseeable outcome here, especially in view of the extent of separate educational provision for 'national' formation which Tamir envisages. We are back with the educational dilemmas mentioned earlier.

Another prominent aspect of education for nationality which follows from the views discussed is the significance of a critical dimension. White insists, for example, that pupils in being helped to understand their national identity, must put it into a wide ranging critical perspective.[37] Again, this calls into question its value in achieving the particular benefits of a communitarian kind which were claimed earlier.

Natonality and the European Union

Tamir welcomes the emergence of supra-national groups such as the European Union, and draws attention to the benefits to be gained by nations from their involvement in regional political alliances.[38] She insists, however, on the need for cultural distinctiveness to be protected, and a 'thin' universal culture to be avoided.

In what sense, however, and to what extent, should a broader European identity be shaped in education? This question is clearly significant for Lithuania, as it reaches out towards the EEC. Clearly such a European identity cannot be a 'national' one. Even if Europe eventually became a unified state, it would lack the features of a unified nation. In the light of a number of arguments recently developed by Kevin Williams[39] it can be argued that any other respects in which education might seek to develop a 'European Identity' are in

---

[36]   Tamir (1992) p. 23

[37]   White (1995)

[38]   Tamir (1993) pp. 150–153

[39]   Williams (1993), (1994), (1995)

significant tension with the achievement of communitarian goods, as well as being highly problematic on other grounds.

Williams argues that a 'European' identity is lacking in cultural roots and homogeneity. We have as much, and sometimes more, in common culturally with other nations and national groupings. Arguments for European unity have a primarily economic and strategic rather than a cultural character. Membership of the EEC for Lithuania, for example, will bring economic benefits, and also strategic security. These sorts of arguments, however, do not have sufficient 'depth' to offer us any real sense of what a 'European identity' might mean. Further, these economic and strategic arguments are, in many contexts, highly controversial. Education has a responsibility to encourage critical assessment of the issues at stake, and if it attempts to shape a 'European identity' on the basis of the truth of these arguments it faces not only the problem of lack of 'rootedness' of what is being aimed at but also accusations of indoctrination. Just as an appropriate form of religious education should leave open the question of whether the student should assume a religious identity, so the question of the adoption of a European identity by students should be an open one. Whilst the same point holds true of a national identity, considerations of 'rootedness' favour it as a starting point from which education can proceed. Whilst a critical perspective on national identity must eventually be achieved, a lesser degree of neutrality with respect to it on the part of education is demanded.

If the arguments of Williams hold water they not only question whether the promotion of a 'European identity' by schools can secure communitarian goods, but whether the task should even be attempted.

Conclusion

In this article I have sought to shed some light on the claim that education should promote a national identity. Given the 'civic' character of the recent defences of 'nationality', 'nationalism' and 'national identity' which have recently emerged, it is clear that the salience of liberal democratic values in these defences calls into question claims that any of the communitarian goods invoked in them can be straightforwardly achieved by education, or in any other way. Such communitarian goods are in danger of being eroded by liberal democratic values such as critical questioning, pluralism and personal autonomy. It may, however, be argued that these communitarian goods could be achieved to an extent.

The suggestion that education should develop a 'European identity' runs into similar problems as those which arise in relation to 'national identity', together with the additional difficulty that the notion of a 'European identity' is currently especially intangible and controversial. It is unclear, therefore whether education can defensibly aim at the development in students of a 'European identity' in any sense distinct from inviting students to engage in their own critical reflection on the matters at stake.

In Lithuania, questions of national identity are loccated within a distinctive cultural, historical and political context. The suppression of Lithuanian national identity over many years is undoubtedly an important feature of this context, together with the experience of leading 'double lives' with which this suppression was associated. The claim that education should promote, or at least preserve, Lithuanian national identity is therefore a potent one. Although, as mentioned at the outset, I am unable to explore the significance of my discussion for Lithuania with any degree of confidence, I offer for consideration some questions which might be helpful to those who are well placed to engage in this exploration.

a) What is involved in the notion of a Lithuanian 'national identity'?

b) What features of Lithuanian 'national identity' are valuable and should be particularly promoted in, and preserved by, education and by what means?

c) What features of Lithuanian 'national identity' are less valuable and should be challenged and weakened by education?

d) What if any, are the tensions between Lithuanian 'national identity' and democracy?

e) To what extent is a Lithuanian 'national identity' under threat and from what forces? (e.g. by the homogenising features of global, capitalist culture, and perhaps by attempts to develop a 'democratic mentality' in Lithuanians)

f) What degree of pluralism is present within Lithuanian society (with respect to religion and ethnic origin, for example) and how should education respond to it? Are the worries outlined above about the dangers of 'civic' nationalism for the erosion of communitarian solidarity applicable in Lithuania?

g) To what extent is the promotion and preservation of Lithuanian national identity related to the promotion and preservation of the Lithuanian language? What policies should be adopted in relation to the compulsory use of the Lithuanian language as a medium of educational instruction?

It is not easy to find answers to questions such as these, and this article does not attempt to provide them. My hope, however, is that my discussion will bring the significance of the questions into focus and will help others in their search for answers.[40]

[40] This chapter is based on a lecture given in the Department of Management of Social Systems, Faculty of Administration, Kaunas University of Technology, Lithuania in January 1996. I would like to express my warm thanks to Professor Palmira Juceviciene and to Jolanta Stankeviciute for extending the invitation for my visit and for their hospitality throughout my stay. I would also like to thank all the participants in the lectures and seminars I presented visit for their comments in discussion.

Schooling, Citizenship and Diversity

Terry McLaughlin was committed to liberal values — a point he constantly and thoroughly reaffirmed, as in the paper 'School Choice and Public Education in a Liberal Democratic Society', reproduced here. But, as he also pointed out, 'liberalism' is a contested concept: not all liberals liberally accept other liberals' understanding of liberalism. Distinctions have to be made and different traditions of liberal thought appreciated and argued with. However, he saw the danger of a liberal conception of education so open to alternative views of the life worth living that it lacked any deep moral or spiritual formation. Although those values for McLaughlin were embodied in distinctive traditions, such traditions would need to uphold the sense of togetherness with members of other traditions — a sense of common humanity and commitment to maintenance of common civic values.

Where one stands in this balancing act between: first, the liberal commitment to openness to diversity of views as to what counts as a life worth living (valuing the autonomy of the individual); second, the maintenance of common values that ensure social cohesion and citizenship; and third, the formation of young people within a distinctive tradition of values and beliefs — affects profoundly one's attitude towards the common school as opposed to 'school choice', not least where such choice is driven by parental interests or by a preference for separate faith or other state schooling. Hence, notions of 'choice', 'common school', and 'preparation for citizenship', and questions of the compatibility of common schools and liberal values with separate faith schooling, were matters to which Terry McLaughlin constantly returned.

As Terry McLaughlin argues in his school choice paper, part of the solution to this complex balancing act lies in exposing the considerable complexities inherent in the notion of choice which are rarely attended to by those, parents or politicians, who advocate or appeal to it. It is also fair to say that the hitherto unparalleled precision and care with which McLaughlin unravels that (conceptual, normative and empirical) complexity gives this paper the status of a *locus classicus* for any and all subsequent discussion of 'choice'. Its place in this book is also justified by the difficulty for British readers of getting hold of the American original.

Again, in his 1992 paper, 'Citizenship, Diversity and Education: a Philosophical Perspective', McLaughlin subjects what has since come to be an important British policy initiative (in this case that of the Crick Report on citizenship which was to shape a much heralded change in the national curriculum) to some hard critical scrutiny. McLaughlin clearly shows that, as with many apparently straightforward educational terms, the notion of 'citizenship education' is a deeply contested term, and that the ambiguities and tensions in this notion are also implicated in the 'balancing act' to which we have already referred.

The problems of the balancing act are also apparent in the two papers, 'The Burdens and Dilemmas of Common Schooling' and 'The Ethics of Separate Schools'. The existence or promotion of either 'common schools' and 'separate (faith or other) schools' are in their own ways equally problematic, and may both be opposed or justified on the basis of 'liberal values' — although, as McLaughlin typically shows, the very concept of liberal values is rather more slippery than commonly acknowledged. At all events, whereas the perceived problem of the 'common school' is that it threatens to limit the vision of young learners in pursuit of a narrow view of social cohesion, that of the 'separate school' is that it may entrench socially divisive differences — and it is to this 'dilemma' that McLaughlin succeeds in bringing considerable clarity and light.

These issues are also the concern of the final paper of this section in which McLaughlin asks whether separate Catholic schools can be justified within a liberal tradition and within the state system. This is an important paper — not least in a political climate in which separate faith schools are often held to reinforce inequalities and to subvert the common culture that the state educational system should be promoting. McLaughlin is concerned to question: first, the watering down of what is distinctive in the interest of a superficial commonality; but secondly, at the same time, the emphasis on distinctness at the expense of common values. The main problem that he addresses is therefore that of reconciling: first, the minimalist requirements of liberal education (namely, the pursuit of autonomy for each individual); and second, that of initiation into, and formation within, a particular but contestable conception of 'the good life' — in the interests of some generally acceptable conception of the common good.

Richard Pring

Chapter 6

School Choice and Public Education in a Liberal Democratic Society

Any serious critical engagement with 'school choice' involves matters of considerable complexity. This is so for at least four interrelated reasons. First, school choice is no one thing. There are many different kinds of school choice schemes in many different contexts supported by many different kinds of motive, reason, and justification. Caution is therefore needed to avoid overly general and abstract discussions and judgments about school choice: considerable sensitivity is needed to the features and embodied principles of particular school choice schemes in particular contexts. This feature of complexity can be described as involving complexities of particularity. Seeond, and relatedly, detailed empirical information and assessment are needed if many of the particular features of school choice schemes in particular contexts, especially their predicted effects, are to be brought into focus and judged. Empirical judgments of the kind required are, however, by no means straightforward and give rise to complexities of empirical judgment. Third, while empirical considerations are necessary in the consideration of school choice, they are not sufficient. School choice schemes postulate certain empirical features and outcomes of schemes as desirable and justifiable, and normative matters are therefore involved. The norms relevant to school choice are, however, complex with respect to their interpretation, justification, importance, and priority: complexities of normative judgment therefore arise. Fourth, empirical and normative considerations concerning school choice need to be related to each other since overall judgments here involve an intricate interrelationship of empirical matters and normative matters: this leads to complexities of integrated judgment. The fact that these four complexities interact with each other (as seen in the need to achieve integrated judgment) heightens the difficulty of discussing and judging school choice in a clear and coherent way, as does the need to make many overall judgments under the aspect of practical compromise and with reference to the status quo ante.

Discussion and debate in relation to school choice are susceptible to rhetoric and polarization not only because of neglect of these complexities but also because, as Henry Levin has pointed out, protagonists in the debate tend to view matters 'through the prisms of their own ideologies' (Levin 2001, 4), thereby inhibiting constructive discourse between people of different views. One of the aims of this article is to contribute to the kind of informed, objective, and constructive dialogue about school choice that is much needed.

The article seeks to illuminate some aspects of the complexity involved in serious critical engagement with school choice by addressing from a philosophical perspective some complexities of normative judgment in their relationship to other complexities. Sometimes the efforts of philosophers to illuminate complexity serve only to make it more opaque. Many of the preoccupations of philosophers can also seem to be excessively abstract and disconnected from the practicalities of real life, educational and otherwise. The present discussion docs, however, touch upon accessible considerations that are frequently invoked in general, non-philosophical, discussions about school choice, and the arguments developed do have significant practical implications. The discussion starts from one of the most philosophically significant lines of argument against school choice: that it is possible to specify a substantial conception of public education in a liberal democratic society stipulating a form of 'educational entitlement' that should be seeured for students in the face, if necessary, of parental choice and market forces. Two of the most prominent features of such conceptions are a concern with the development in students of what can be described as 'enriched' forms of personal autonomy and a like concern with enriched forms of democratic citizenship (my use of the term 'enriched' here will be brought into focus in due course). Such features of an educational entitlement are frequently appealed to in judging school choice schemes and in devising forms of regulation and control of schools within such schemes, thereby drawing the boundaries of acceptable school choice. However, this article will attempt to show via a philo-sophical illumination of these features of an educational entitlement that such appeals are not as straightforward as is sometimes claimed. In particular, I will argue that the educational development of enriched forms of personal autonomy and democratic citizenship depends crucially on forms of practical judgment and action (or ped-agogic *phronesis*) by teachers and educational leaders at the levels of the classroom and the ethos and life of schools. The challenge for those appealing to the development of enriched forms of personal autonomy and democratic citizenship as criteria in judging school choice schemes is therefore one of 'capturing' this neglected element of pedagogic phronesis for purposes of judgment, regulation, con-trol, and the drawing of boundaries. The discussion concludes by urging that more sustained attention to this neglected challenge is needed and by indicating some considerations relevant to how it might be met.

School Choice and Public Education: Clearing the Ground

It is appropriate at the outset to offer a general, basic definition of school choice. According to Harry Brighouse, at the heart of the notion of school choice is the provision of systems of schooling 'that officially and directly give substantial weight to the preferences of parents regarding the allocation of their children to schools' (Brighouse 2000, 22-23). Unofficial and indirect forms of parental choice (e.g., via families moving into the catchment areas of favored schools) can, and have, coexisted with schooling systems that do not provide much scope for parental choice in a formal sense. While such unofficial and indirect forms of parental choice are not insignif-icant, what is distinctive of school choice schemes, as Brighouse brings out, is their provision of parental choice in an official and direct way.

The prominence and controversial nature of school choice as an educational policy question in liberal democratic societies arise from the fact that some educational policy makers seek to extend official and direct forms of parental choice into the provision of schooling within the 'public' education system, via, for example, the use of vouchers. Private, fee-paying schools, providing official and direct parental choice in a straightforward way, have long coexisted with public schooling in liberal democratic societies. While the desirabil-ity and justifiability of private schools in these societies are often controversial matters and give rise to many practical and normative issues (see, e.g., Swift 2003), the place of school choice within public schooling systems is particularly contentious and is the focus of concern in the present article.

In the context of public schooling systems, school choice is articulated and defended against alternatives judged as 'direct-choice-deficient' in various ways. The range of grounds of principle and practice on which school choice is advocated against disfavored alternatives is well known (on general arguments in support of school choice schemes, see, e.g., Bridges and Jonathan [2003]; Brighouse [2000, chap. 2]; Rosenblum [2002, 149-50]), although the extent to which these grounds are not all mutually connected, consistent, or supportive needs to be better recognized. It is important to note, however, that just as 'school choice' denotes no one thing, the same is true both of the direct-choice-deficient school systems to which school choice stands opposed and of public schooling systems more generally. Public schooling systems and their underlying rationales are varied. Rosenblum rightly insists, for example, that state or public control of education is an abstraction that needs to be broken down into an array of different legal requirements, funding schemes, and decisions about matters such as curriculum, classroom organization, and the assessment of students made by varied and sometimes competing authorities. There is no one unitary state, public, or government control of education, and there is an inevitable variety in many aspects of public schooling (Rosenblum 2002, 152-53). In a similar vein, John White distinguishes the role of the state in respect of the following separable responsibilities: (a) the determination of the aims and curricula of schooling, (b) the ownership and organization of schools, and (c) the control over admission to schools (White 1994). The shape which public education takes in a particular society is heavily influenced by features of the national context in which it is located. Public education in the United States, for example, is markedly different in a number of respects from public education in England and Wales. These differences are one of the complexities of particularity that the present discussion is unable to pursue. For our present purposes, however, it is important to note that public education in liberal democratic societies is as varied as the school choice schemes that are articulated in contrast to it. In particular, normative conceptions of public education, as well as of public schooling systems, vary in important, if frequently elusive, respects.

The Normative Dimensions of School Choice

The indispensability of a normative dimension to discussion of school choice is seen in Alan Wolfe's insistence that questions relating to school choice 'touch on fundamental questions of our public philosophy: the kind of people we want to be, the requirements for economic and racial equality, the nature of the institutions we wish to see flourish ... our ideas about private and public character ... the nature of the person, citizenship, and the purposes of political life' (Wolfe 2003a, 1–2).

The norms involved here are wide-ranging, embracing political, social, and moral questions among others. An important general point for the purposes of our discussion here is that the issue of what institutional form schooling should take in any society is seeondary to the issue of what the aims and purposes of education in such a society should be taken properly to be. Brighouse is right to criticize the strong tendency in debates about institutional reform for social scientists 'to take the goals of the institutions for granted and to treat questions of reform as merely technical in character' (Brighouse 2000, 3). School choice involves questions about the proper goals of public education in a liberal democratic society (as distinct from impoverished and inadequate goals such as the cost-effective achievement by students of the highest possible median or mean test scores), and the specification of these proper goals involves essentially normative questions that cannot be answered by merely 'looking at' particular educational institutions and their alternatives (ibid.). Further, the meaning, importance, and priority of concepts and ideals central to the school choice debate, such as equality and parental rights, require philosophical articulation and defense, and their meaning and justification cannot be simply assumed (Brighouse 2000, 116).

The normative issues that arise in relation to school choice are apt for consideration by philosophy (for general reviews of such issues, see, e.g., Bridges and Jonathan [2003]; McLaughlin [1994a]). In the light of the complexities of particularity and of integrated judgment alluded to earlier, it is clear that philosophy alone cannot resolve all the issues that arise in relation to school choice, even normative issues. Many other types of consideration are involved, including, inter alia, sociological, cultural, demographic, and practical considerations (on the salience of legal matters in the context of the United States, see, e.g., Wolfe [2003b, chaps. 10–12]). Further, one implication of complexities of integrated judgment is that philosophical and other considerations may not be easily separable from each other (on the continuing presence of many philosophical considerations in apparently pragmatic matters, see, e.g., Gutmann [2002a]). [1]

The critical power of philosophy is partly constituted by its ahistorical and abstract character, notwithstanding its need to attend to the relationship between philosophy and practical contexts and considerations (Brighouse 2000, 1–5). [2] Nevertheless, the precise way in which philosophical reflection should be conducted in relation to educational policy requires careful consideration (on these matters, see, e.g., McLaughlin [2000]). Properly understood, philosophy can help to formulate and answer the more precise questions about school choice that an adequate discussion of the phenomenon requires, such as school choice for what, for whom, and on what grounds?

At the normative heart of school choice is the question of what the proper goals of public education in a liberal democratic society should be taken to be. Before considering the nature of these goals directly, it is important to note that there is an important gap between any specified educational goals (or aims, values, ideals, and the like) and their institutionalization in any particular context. For example, for various reasons it is not possible to derive a commitment to a 'common school' directly and inevitably from a commitment to a conception of common education: the relationship between the two is at best a presumptive one (on these matters, see, e.g., Callan [1997, chap. 7]). In addition, it should be borne in mind that the institution of schooling itself should not be uncritically assumed as the only context in which education takes place (on the growing importance of home schooling and the issues to which it gives rise, see, e.g., Reich [2002]; on the educational significance of civil society in general, see, e.g., Rosenblum [2002]).

---

[1] Gutmann points out that, since interpretations of facts are often as controversial as interpretation of values, a focus on facts rather than values may not resolve disputes among people who disagree on values. Further, she argues, apparently practical matters, such as the requirements for the teaching of literacy, are not independent of philosophical considerations (Gutmann 2002a, 183).

[2] For an articulation of the nature and value of abstract philosophizing in the context of an acknowledgment that philosophy should 'attend to the facts of the world,' see Brighouse (2004a, chap. 2).

Conceptions of Public Education in a Liberal
Democratic Society

A major issue confronting school choice is the extent to which it is, or
can be, compatible with conceptions of public education in a liberal
democratic society: Conceptions of public education are significant
for school choice in that they indicate and stipulate constraints and
limits to which school choice should be subject by specifying an educational entitlement that should not be determined solely by parental choice or the market and that should be seeured for students in
the face, if necessary, of parental objection and market forces. A central precise question in the school choice debate then concerns what
'the state ought to be able to teach even over parental objection'
(Eisgruber 2002, 73). Given the potential personal and civic significance of such educational entitlements, the prima facie moral duty of
extending the entitlements to all children and young people under a
principle of equality emerges. Since few advocates of school choice
deny the importance and justifiability of some constraints and limits
on choice arising from the state (on the general matter of the indispensability of the state with respect to justice, see, e.g., Brighouse
[2000, 161-62]), a central question essentially concerns the nature
and scope of the constraints and limits at issue and the nature and
scope of the corresponding conceptions of public education in play.[3]

Conceptions of public education in a liberal democratic society
embody concerns about matters such as personal autonomy, citizenship, and equality that figure prominently in general educational
and political discourse. Philosophical articulations of such conceptions are the subject of much contemporary philosophical debate. A
range of philosophically articulated conceptions of public education, rooted in philosophical exploration of the values and principles
involved in the notion of a liberal democratic society, can be located
along a continuum of increasing substantiality and demand with
respect to their implications for students, parents, and democratic
society itself. In particular, the conceptions differ with respect to the
way in which they interpret and balance the differing and partly
competing interests and concerns of students, parents, and democratic society and the extent to which the conceptions specify sub-

[3]   Considering the influence of the state, Galston, e.g., writes, 'The state may act to
prevent what amounts to educational abuse and neglect, by means of such
measures as compulsory education statutes and basic standards of education
attainment' (Galston 2002, 100). On the justifiability of complete 'privatization'
with respect to the provision of schooling, see, e.g., Tooley (2003) and Brighouse
(2004b).

stantial and demanding requirements relating to two crucial matters with respect to students: the development of personal autonomy and that of democratic citizenship.

At one end of the continuum are conceptions that I have described elsewhere as imposing 'light' burdens on schooling in view of the relatively minimal nature of the entitlement stipulated (McLaughlin 2003a, esp. 129–31). In such conceptions, there is an emphasis on a contingent 'lowest common denominator' consensus about what all students should learn (literacy and numeracy, what is needed for basic moral and civic formation, and other fundamental matters relating to, among other things, the requirements for making a living, and so forth; see, e.g., Callan [1997, 167–71]). In particular, conceptions of this kind conceive the task of developing the personal autonomy of students and their preparation for democratic citizenship in a restricted way (see, e.g., Galston 1991, chap. 11). With regard to the development of personal autonomy, for instance, it is not seen as part of the role of public education to encourage students to subject (say) the views of life held by their parents and local communities to critical scrutiny by comparison with alternatives. With regard to preparation for democratic citizenship, there is an emphasis on civic socialization rather than on the forms of critical engagement and disposition characteristic of citizenship and its educational requirements more fully conceived. In such conceptions of public education, either the disagreements and controversies characteristic of pluralist, multicultural, and liberal societies are avoided or a strategy of 'accommodating the private' prevails, whereby the public school acknowledges diversity by ensuring that children will be exposed to the level of diversity acceptable to the parents (Brighouse 2000, 174). These conceptions of public education are described by Amy Gutmann as involving 'civic minimalism' in that they insist that 'civic educational requirements imposed by governments must be minimal so that parental control over children's education can be close to comprehensive' (Gutmann 2002b, 23).

Michael W. McConnell can be seen as advocating a minimal view of public education of this kind in virtue of his insistence that, in relation to education, 'beyond the scant essentials, a democratic society can let a thousand flowers bloom. ... The only need is for a modest form of regulation, to weed out those schools that do not make even an attempt to meet ... basic democratic norms' (McConnell 2002, 103). For McConnell, such norms in the context of education relate to 'basic requirements' of 'educational quality' and 'civic responsibility,' together with the provision of funding to ensure adequate educational opportunity for all (88).

It is clear that such conceptions of public education present few principled obstacles to school choice schemes in view of the limited nature of the constraints and limits that they specify and the consequent extensive scope that is open for the exercise of choice. Such conceptions are compatible with a parents-as-determiners view of parental (moral as distinct from legal) educational rights, where the child's educational experience is seen as properly determined to the greatest possible extent by the child's own parents and family (see McLaughlin 1994b). Thus McConnell, for example, argues that families should be permitted 'to choose among a range of educational options, including but not limited to government schools, using their fair share of educational funding to pay for the schooling they choose' (McConnell 2002, 87). There are a variety of different conceptions of light or minimal conceptions of public education (see, e.g., Coons and Sugarman-1978; Galston 1991, chap. 11; 2002, chap. 8; Tooley 1996, 2000, esp. sessions 3 and 4) that require more detailed analysis in a fuller discussion. McConnell's version, for instance, is unusual in being based not on the rights of parents as such but on what is claimed as necessary to the maintenance of a free and equal society in the context of reasonable, but irreconcilable, diversity (McConnell 2002, 88). However, since such conceptions of public education provide few difficulties for school choice, it is appropriate for the purposes or the present discussion to. turn to the fuller conceptions of public education in relation to which such difficulties clearly arise.

Although caution is needed in relation to any claim that 'light' and 'heavy' conceptions of public education can be distinguished from each other with any precision (on this matter, see, e.g., Eisgruber [2002]), fuller conceptions of public education impose heavy (or at least heavier) burdens on schooling because of the much more extensive nature of the educational entitlement stipulated (McLaughlin 2003a, 131-45). A range of differing versions of conceptions of public education that can be described as heavy in this sense has been developed (see, e.g., Brighouse 2000; Callan 1997; Fcinberg 1998; Gutmann 1987; Jonathan 1997; Levinson 1999; Macedo 2000; Macedo and Tamir 2002; McDonough and Feinberg 2003; Nussbaum 1997; Tamir 1995; White 2003). Leaving aside for the moment particular differences, such conceptions in general typically embody a commitment to (i) the development of a significant degree of independent critical reflection and judgment (if not a full-blown notion of personal autonomy) on the part of students that is sensitive to and engaged with matters of diversity and difference and that extends, cither by intention or by consequence, into many aspects of the lives of students and (ii) a development of forms of civic capacity and virtue that extends beyond mere civic socialization in its concern to ensure wide-ranging kinds of critical understanding, sensitivity, disposition, and commitment. Developments (i) and (ii) can be described as 'enriched' in that they embody and specify aims and values that go beyond the more minimal interpretations of these notions involved in 'lighter' conceptions of public education. The significance of the imprecision involved in the attribution of enrichment here will be drawn later.

'Heavier' conceptions of public education are often articulated in terms of the satisfaction of the demands of the public properly understood. For example, Macedo argues that a refusal to recognize distinctively public educational aims runs through many arguments for school reform (Macedo 2003, 53). Similarly, Amy Gutmann argues contra Milton Friedman that schools should not be compared to restaurants because schools serve public purposes as well as private ones and fulfil public obligations to children. How is 'public' being understood here? Macedo characterizes the public obligation of education not in terms of giving people what they want or satisfying their deepest desires or beliefs above all, but rather with providing people 'with a fair measure of basic goods that can be justified from a public point of view … goods that we share as a political society' (2003, 55–56). The educational 'goods' at stake here are frequently articulated in terms of (i) and (ii) above.

In relation to (i), for example, Harry Brighouse argues that 'autonomy facilitating' education should be provided as a matter of justice for all young people. Brighouse suggests that this requirement could involve students studying, for instance, a range of religious, nonreligious, and antireligious ethical views in some 'detail; … the kinds of reasoning deployed within those views; … the attitudes of proponents toward non-believers, heretics, and the seeular world … the diverse ways, including non-reason-based ways, in which seeular and religious thinkers have dealt with moral conflict and religious disagreements, and with tensions in their own views' (Brighouse 2000, 75).

Although (i) and (ii) are frequently linked together, Brighouse is hesitant about (ii) and about the extent to which the goods of education should best be seen as public.[4] (For Brighouse's disagreement with Gutmann on the grounds that she places too much emphasis on the value of democratic participation, see Brighouse [2000, 68, 79–80].)

Gutmann develops a view that can be regarded as including elements of (i) and (ii). She argues that 'citizens should ensure that all children — regardless of their socioeconomic status, gender, race, ethnicity, or religion — receive an education that prepares them for effectively exercising their rights and responsibilities as future citizens' (Gutmann 2002a, 175). Similarly, Nancy Rosenblum characterizes the purposes of public democratic education as involving 'educating future citizens to be free and equal and to relate to one another on terms of mutual respect (along with its practical counterpart — the ability to work together with people different from ourselves); toleration; the ability to be self-supporting; an array of civic competences ranging from basic law-abidingness and the wherewithal to exercise rights to more demanding skills of public deliberation and full-blown civic magnanimity' (Rosenblum 2002, 155).

While it is not denied in heavier conceptions of public education of these kinds that the goods of education have a legitimate private dimension that needs to be balanced against its public one, the potential tension between school choice and such heavier conceptions of public education, with their insistence on the development of enriched forms of personal autonomy and democratic citizenship as part of an educational entitlement to be secured for all students, is clear. The educational (and related) goods in question are seen as owed by justice to all children and young people and as requiring distribution by principles that are sensitive to the demands of equality (Brighouse 2000, 45–46, chaps. 6–9).

Such heavier conceptions of public education are incompatible with the parents-as-determiners view of parents' (moral as distinct from legal) educational rights outlined earlier. As Gutmann insists, 'Parents are not the consumers of education. Children are' (2002a,

[4]   On the notion of education as a public good, see, e.g., Grace (1994). Compare Tooley (1994). For complexities in the general distinction between the public and the private, see, e.g., Geuss (2001). Brighouse opposes what he takes to be a 'deep error' in standard thinking about public schooling: 'The public goods argument treats children as a resource for society, whereas the proper approach treats them as vulnerable wards whose interests must guide society's approach to them' (Brighouse 2000, 45, see also 40–46).

175). The fact that children are not the property of their parents is, for Gutmann, a major reason why schooling should not be seen merely as a private concern of parents (179). The view of parents' educational rights that is most compatible with such conceptions is a view of parents as trustees of their children's educational rights where the central rights in question are seen to be the rights of the children to the sorts of development indicated in (i) and (ii), which are held in trust by parents (McLaughlin 1994b). On this parents-as-trustees view of parents' educational rights, parents do not enjoy any moral rights that are independent of their duties to seeure the educational rights of their children to educational resources for the development of enriched forms of personal autonomy and democratic citizenship. Thus on this view, while parents have (for example) coordinating and monitoring rights over their children's education deriving from their duties with respect to it, they do not have fundamental moral rights to determine the basic character of their children's education, much less to frustrate the exposure of their children to the educational demands of the development of autonomy and democratic citizenship understood in enriched ways.

School Choice and Public Education in a Liberal Democratic Society: The Significance of Pedagogical Judgment

The heavier conceptions of public education in a liberal democratic society that have been outlined in the last seetion, with their emphasis on the development of enriched notions of personal autonomy and democratic citizenship, constitute an important philosophical resource for critically evaluating school choice. Since the central elements of such conceptions are featured, in some form or another, in much general educational and political debate about school choice, the elements are not merely of philosophical interest.

Proponents of heavier conceptions of public education judge school choice in large part according to the extent to which it is compatible with their favored version of such conceptions. Macedo, for example, claims that the most defensible arguments for school choice do not relate to the demands of pluralism of various kinds but to the demands of an equitable public education for all. He argues, 'The most defensible voucher plans are designed and implemented with public purposes in view; they enlist private providers on behalf of public educational aims, rather than sacrificing public educational aims to private choices' (Macedo 2003, 62). Brighouse, while suspicious of the invocation of public good in this context, includes 'autonomy facilitation' as one of the goals that regulation should require of schools in any defensible school choice scheme (Brighouse 2000, 186). Gutmann indicates a willingness to tolerate vouchers under certain conditions linked to her conception of democratic education (see Gutmann 2003).

Considerable attention has been paid by philosophers and others to the justification of such heavier conceptions of public education. The most fundamental issue here is that of providing a convincing justification for such conceptions against claims that lighter conceptions of public education can alone be justified as constraining parental educational choice in a liberal democratic society. Within heavier conceptions, there has also been much debate about the justification of particular versions of 'heaviness' against others. Relevant to these debates at the philosophical level is the question of the extent to which public education in a liberal democratic society should be based on a wide-ranging ethical or comprehensive liberalism or on a more constrained form of liberalism of a political kind (on forms of liberalism and their complex educational implications, see, e.g., Callan [1997, chap. 2]; Gutmann [1995]; Tomasi [2002, 196–97]).

These justificatory debates cannot proceed without extended interpretive work on what the various elements of heavier conceptions of public education, most notably enriched conceptions of personal autonomy and democratic citizenship, can be taken to actually mean and imply (on complexities of interpretation of personal autonomy and democratic citizenship, respectively, that are relevant to questions of justification, see, e.g., O'Neill [2003]; Williams [2003]). In the remainder of this discussion, however, I shall lay justificatory questions to one side and pursue interpretive questions for a different, neglected, reason. The particular question that I shall address is, if one accepts, for the purposes of argument, that some heavier conception of public education is in fact justified, what is involved in bringing the conception to bear on practical judgments about school choice?

I shall argue that both the interpretation and implementation of heavier conceptions of public education require the exercise of pedagogic *phronesis* or practical judgment by teachers and educational leaders at the school and classroom level. My view is summed up in Eisgruber's speculation that 'in a liberal democracy, questions addressed to teachers may be the richest questions about civic education' (2002, 82). Any attempt to bring heavier conceptions of public education to bear upon school choice—and, in particular, upon matters of judgment, regulation, control, and the drawing of boundaries – requires attention to the question of how pedagogic phronesis can be captured for these purposes.

The significance of pedagogic phronesis for heavier conceptions of public education emerges when the interpretive complexities inherent in such conceptions are brought into focus. It will be recalled that heavier conceptions of public education are articulated in the context of extensive evaluative controversy. Stephen Macedo is correct in his observation that such conceptions involve an educational intervention 'in the most private of relationships, for the most sensitive of purposes' (Macedo 2000, 145). It should be remembered, after all, that these conceptions seek to constrain parental choice and to insist upon an educational entitlement in the face, if necessary, of parental objection. The evaluative basis of heavier conceptions of public education therefore invites and requires careful scrutiny. Such conceptions are clearly not value-neutral. As Nancy Rosenblum points out, 'Even minimal public requirements for democratic education will implicitly treat some conscientious positions as mistaken' (Rosenblum 2002, 152). Macedo argues, 'It is important that the values taught in public schools should be publicly defensible; it is impossible that they should be equally attractive to the different worldviews and religious views that people espouse' (Maccdo 2003, 55; on the limitations of the invocation of neutrality as a principle in arguments relating to education from a liberal point of view, see, e.g., De Marneffe [2002]; on the inadequacy of relativistic, postmodern, or communitarian bases for liberalism in general, see, e.g., Brighouse [2000, 3–5]).

If it is accepted that any conception of public education must invoke a particular evaluative basis of a distinctive kind, a central general concern that arises is captured in Rob Reich's insistence that 'the need for a unifying civic education must be carefully balanced against an unjust oppression of the diverse convictions of citizens' (Reich 2003, 436). 'Reasonable pluralism' is an important normative constraint on the influence of public education.[5] A central specific concern that arises is captured in McConnel's question, 'Can com-

---

[5] Relevant to the notion of 'reasonable pluralism' is John Rawls's attempt to illuminate reasonable disagreement between reasonable persons by identifying sources of ineliminable rational disagreement in the notion of 'the burdens of judgment' (Rawls 1993, 54–58). For Rawls, the burdens of judgment indicate 'the many hazards involved in the correct (and conscientious) exercise of our powers of reason and judgment' (56), thereby providing an important basis for the democratic idea of toleration.

mon schools be operated without effectively establishing an official orthodoxy regarding questions of legitimate disagreement?' (McConnell 2002, 97).

In the face of concerns of these kinds, heavier conceptions of public education propose the exercise of forms of subtly judged and balanced educative influence that seek to embody forms of enrichment compatible with normative constraints arising from the demands of reasonable pluralism. The subtlety of the sorts of educative influence that are envisaged here is visible, for instance, in Harry Brighouse's support for 'autonomy facilitating' but not 'autonomy promoting' education (2000, 80–82), in Gutmann's emphasis on the principles of nonrepression and nondiscrimination in the context of an acknowledgment of a degree of legitimate plurality in the educational conditions needed for the development of democratic character (Gutmann 1987), and in accounts of the requirements for the fair handling of controversial issues in citizenship education and elsewhere (see, e.g., McLaughlin 2003b).

The nature and requirements of these forms of educative influence can and should be articulated as fully as possible at the level of principle. However, articulation at the level of principle can go only so far. Practical and contextually sensitive judgments on the part of teachers and educational leaders are clearly needed in the implementation of principles. However, such judgments are not confined to matters of implementation. The process of implementation cannot be seen in terms of the mere practical 'application' of principles that can be articulated at the abstract level with complete clarity and completeness: the principles themselves require interpretation via kinds of practical and contextually significant judgment. It is important to emphasize that the judgments involved at the classroom and school level about matters of interpretation and implementation are essentially practical, not abstract or theoretical, and involve a form of pedagogic practical wisdom or *phronesis* (on the nature of these kinds of judgment in more detail, see, e.g., McLaughlin [1999, 2004a]; Smith [1999]).

Teachers and educational leaders certainly require a good understanding at the level of abstract principle of the kind of educative influence that is proposed in heavier conceptions of public education. In particular, they need to have a firm grasp of the principles relating to the subtlety and balance in educational influence that are required from an acknowledgment of the significance of reasonable pluralism. For example, teachers and educational leaders need to have a good understanding at the level of principle of the educational significance of moral texture and complexity (for one interpretation of these principles and their educational implications, see McLaughlin [2003a]). Teachers and educational leaders need to ensure (for example) that students gain a clear understanding of the nature and scope of reasonable moral disagreement, that students are not subject to unjustifiably homogenizing and assimilative pressures in relation to moral and other matters, and that students are able to negotiate a fit between their own substantive views of human good and the demands of (circumscribed) public moral evaluation. As part of this principled understanding, teachers and educational leaders need a grasp of the distortive hazards associated with certain interpretations of central notions such as 'respect' and 'toleration.' In addition to an understanding of all these matters at the level of abstract principle, however, teachers and educational leaders also need to be able to interpret their meaning and significance at the practical level of particular classrooms and schools. For example, questions relating to matters such as the particular topics that should be judged as significantly controversial in particular classroom and school environments and the range of diverse moral views that should be presented for consideration by students in these environments cannot be resolved solely *in abstracto*. This point is reinforced when the full range of issues of contextual sensitivity (including forms of negotiation and compromise with parents and other parties) are brought clearly into focus. Questions of practical and contextual interpretation by teachers and educational leaders of the kinds of principles under discussion cannot be separated from questions relating to the implementation of these principles. The kinds of educative influence envisaged in heavier conceptions of public education are brought' about (or implemented) via the practical judgment and action of teachers at classroom and school level. At the classroom level this judgment and action is revealed in part by the kinds of questions asked of students in the discussion of controversial topics; the characterization, timing, and prioritization of certain lines of argument presented for consideration; the extent to which neglected perspectives are reinforced at certain times; the encouragement of certain individuals to participate in discussion; and so forth. Eisgruber makes an important point in insisting that no text prescribed for study by students is self-interpreting (Eisgruber 2002, 62): the interpretive role of the teacher is vital. The inherently contextual nature of this kind of educative influence is emphasized by recognition of the important point that the way in which the teacher acts in relation to such matters is highly significant (on the nature and importance of the example of the teacher, see, e.g., McLaughlin [2004a]). At the level of the school, the judgment and action of teachers and educational leaders is revealed in part by decisions and reactions relating to the many elements that make up the ethos of the school.

The importance and significance of the kind of pedagogic *phronesis* that is being referred to here is not, of course, confined to the forms of educative influence associated with heavier conceptions of public education. However, the subtle and controversial nature of heavier forms of public educational influence makes pedagogic *phronesis* particularly important and significant in this context. A wide range of questions clearly arise about how such *phronesis* is best nurtured and developed, in which the notion of 'communities of practice' is an important point of reference (on this notion, see, e.g., McLaughlin [2004b]).

If the importance and significance of pedagogic *phronesis* at the classroom and school level in relation to heavier conceptions of public educational influence are acknowledged, what are the implications of this acknowledgment for the deployment of such conceptions in arguments about school choice? Two general implications are worthy of emphasis here.

First, such an acknowledgment may serve to underline the recognition that there is at best a presumptive relationship between any specified educational goals (including heavier educational goals) and any particular schooling arrangements. The notion that a particular category of kind of school is particularly well placed per se to embody heavier conceptions of public education may therefore come more clearly under a critical spotlight. The 'common school' is often seen as a favored institutional context for the achievement of the goals of heavier conceptions of public education, and it therefore features in many arguments against school choice alternatives. In such arguments, a common school is typically conceived as a school that is open to and intended for all students within a given society regardless of their specific differentiating characteristics and that embodies a conception of common education (McLaughlin 2003a, 122–25). However, an acknowledgment of the importance and significance of pedagogical phronesis at the classroom and school level may focus attention in judging favored environments for the achievement of heavier forms of educational influence away from the category of a kind of school per se to the details of what is happening within particular classrooms and the ethos of particular schooling environments. The force of this point can be seen at two levels. At the level of the contingent performance of particular institutions in particular contexts, it is widely acknowledged that many de jure common schools may not de facto embody the forms of pedagogic *phronesis* that serve the needs of heavier forms of public educational influence. Brighouse observes, for example, that many public high schools in the United States do not embody the liberal ideal of the autonomy-fostering common school whereas many private religious schools do (2005, 85-86). The contingent performance of particular institutions in particular environments is one of the aspects of complexity referred to at the outset of this discussion and leads to the need for hesitation and nuance in the development of arguments relating to school choice. The force of the point about the importance and significance of pedagogic *phronesis* for heavier forms of public educational influence goes deeper, however, than the level of the contingent performance of particular institutions in particular contexts and invites acceptance of the point that there is an ineliminable plurality of different kinds of ways in which heavier forms of public educational influence can be exerted. This line of argument about the impossibility of specifying any one favored way in which this kind of educative influence can be brought to bear extends to claims about the impossibility of specifying any single category of schooling context even in ideal terms as a favored context for heavier forms of public educational influence.

Shelley Burtt, for example, rejects the claim that religious forms of education and schooling embodying and transmitting a comprehensive vision of the good life are necessarily inimical per se to the development of autonomy and democratic citizenship. Burtt calls into question the view that school-based exposure to alternative understandings of the good life, linked to an 'informed consumer' model inviting students to make their own free choices, is necessarily the only way in which education for autonomy can be adequately conducted. The capacity for autonomous thought and action should not, she argues, be 'reduced to a requirement that individuals relate to their ends in the manner held out by the metaphor of the menu' (Burtt 2003, 186). For Burtt, there are considerable resources within 'comprehensive' lives and forms of education, including, one might add, appropriate forms of pedagogic *phronesis*, that can contribute toward the development of both autonomous thought and action and the ability and disposition to reflect upon the justice of the exist-ing social order (for rejection of the claim that religious schools are necessarily divisive, see, e.g., Halstead and McLaughlin [2005]; Glenn [2003]; on the potentially biased nature of the term 'seetarian' as applied, say, to religious schools, see Salomone [2003, 258-59]; on the claim that religiously distinctive schools can serve public purposes, see, e.g., O'Keefe [2003]).

It might be considered, however, that the common school should be seen as enjoying a favored status with respect to the realization of heavier conceptions of public education because it has the unique de jure feature of bringing together students from many different back-grounds with resultant favorable consequences for the development of enriched forms of personal autonomy and democratic citizenship. Amy Gutmann, for instance, insists that 'schools educate not only by what and how they teach but also by whom they teach together in classrooms. ... Association among children of different back-grounds within schools is an important part of the promise of a dem-ocratic education' (Gutmann 2002b, 178). (On the value, including that to nonreligious students, of common schools being religiously mixed in terms of the promotion of civic virtue and individual autonomy, see Levinson and Levinson [2003].)

However, many de jure common schools do not succeed de facto in achieving a balanced intake, which is why the reality of dc facto choice of public schools by the purchase by parents of housing in catchment areas and the consequent importance of the issue of admission policies in a defensible system of common schooling is widely recognized.[6] However, a balanced intake alone is insufficient to realize the aims of heavier conceptions of public education. Acknowledgment of this point and of the related points above leads naturally to the claim that proponents of heavier conceptions of public educative influence should judge school choice schemes not merely by category of school but by the presence or absence of appropriate forms of pedagogic *phronesis*. This claim leads to a seeond implication.

This seeond implication has to do with the difficulty in capturing pedagogic *phronesis* for use in school choice arguments relating to

---

[6]   On the claim that de jure common schools are 'crucibles of community,' Brighouse observes, 'I ... doubt that any neighborhood-based system of schooling has achieved the ideal very well where private schooling is a live option, and where neighborhoods are segregated along class, and often along ethnic, lines' (Brighouse 2000, 191).

such matters as judgment, regulation, control, and the drawing of boundaries. The difficulty arises here from the point that teachers and educational leaders enjoy a good deal of ineliminable autonomy in respect of the detailed and subtle forms of pedagogic *phronesis* that are the object of our attention, and their judgments and actions in these matters are not amenable to detailed assessment, direction, and systematic monitoring and review. Eisgruber is correct in pointing out that the way in which a particular text is taught by a teacher cannot be externally controlled (Eisgrubcr 2002, 77–78). Yet proponents of heavier conceptions of public education need to be able to develop a range of arguments and policy proposals that relate school choice proposals to these heavier conceptions in a number of ways. These arguments and policy proposals involve, inter alia, issues of judgment, regulation, control, and the drawing of boundaries. Judgment is needed of the extent to which any existing or envisaged schooling context docs or is likely to serve and achieve heavier public educational goals. Regulation and control arise as issues because proponents of heavier conceptions of public educational influence seek to ensure that their favored educational goals are actually achieved in given schooling contexts, including schools accepted under school choice schemes but subject to regulation requirements. Proponents of heavier forms of public educational influence in the context of school choice schemes must be able to draw boundaries between acceptable and nonacceptable schools from the point of view of this kind of educational influence. However, in the light of the importance and significance of pedagogic *phronesis* regarding this influence and of the inaccessibility of pedagogic *phronesis* for the development of arguments and policy proposals needed in the context of school choice debates, how can the relevant arguments and policy proposals be confidently developed by proponents of heavier conceptions of public education in relation to school choice?

With regard to matters of judgment, for example, Brighouse notes in some detail the considerable difficulties that arise in relation to any attempt to judge the provision of 'autonomy facilitating' education (which he favors) as distinct from 'autonomy promoting' education (which he regards as overstepping the mark with respect to normative warrant). These difficulties include the complexity of the methods involved in teaching students to be critically evaluative and the difficulties involved in appealing merely to the 'content' of ways of life selected by students in order to assess their autonomy: an appeal to content alone cannot indicate the extent to which any choice was genuinely autonomous (see Brighouse 2000, chap. 4, 80–82, 196–99).

In relation to matters of regulation and control, long-standing difficulties arise about attempts to bring detailed and subtle 'higher level' educational aims to bear on schooling systems and in specifying the requirements involved in such attempts (on these matters, see, e.g., Chubb and Moe [1990, esp. chap. 2]; Eisgruber [2002]; Gutmann [2002a]; McLaughlin [2000]). James Dwyer argues that 'thick regulatory strings' (2002, 340) should be attached to vouchers cashed in private schools in the United States as a condition of their receipt of public funds. However, from the perspective of heavier forms of educative influence, fuller attention is needed to what such regulatory strings require and imply. Gutmann observes that 'there are (almost) always at least two ways of teaching a single value (and many more ways of not doing so). The claim that most liberal democratic values are better taught by classroom practices than by textbooks is probably true, but the extent and limits of public authority over both classroom practices and textbooks stand or fall on the same sorts of arguments. And those arguments … often cannot bypass general principles' (Gutmann 2002a, 189). While this is true, the problem remains for the proponent of heavier forms of educative influence of gaining access to considerations relating to classroom practices for purposes of the development of argument and policy proposals.

It will be recalled that school choice debates focus upon schools as focuses of choice. In the light of the present discussion, this focus is rather too blunt to embrace the full range of concerns that exercise proponents of heavier forms of educative influence. Yet these fuller concerns are not easily brought into focus for purposes of argument and policy proposal in the context of school choice. Since what is at stake in school choice debates from the point of view of proponents of heavier forms of educative influence is seeuring certain educational goods in the face, if necessary, of parental choice, there is a need for these proponents to articulate these educational goods clearly and provide reassurance to parents and others that the forms of subtly judged and balanced educative influence that they propose as ensuring compatibility with the demand of reasonable pluralism are indeed in place, It is also necessary for such proponents to illuminate the relationship between these forms of educative influence and any particular schooling arrangements. Proponents of heavier conceptions of public educational influence face considerable challenges in meeting these needs in the face of the importance and significance (and yet the inaccessibility) of pedagogical *phronesis* at classroom and school level in regard to the educational goods to which they are committed.

It may be objected that there is much that proponents of heavier conceptions of public educational influence can do to contribute to school choice debates without entering into matters of pedagogic *phronesis*, and this is true. It is also true, however, that such matters arise inevitably in relation to these heavier conceptions and require attention if such conceptions are to be brought to bear on matters of school choice in a thorough and convincing way.

It may also be objected that this discussion has focused upon rather areane philosophical considerations relating to school choice while ignoring more immediately tangible considerations that arise in contemporary school choice debate. This is true also. The present discussion has focused self-consciously on a particular set of issues and concerns. The discussion began by drawing attention to the range of complexities inherent in discussions of school choice. In seeking to illuminate from a philosophical perspective some complexities of normative judgment relating to school choice, the discussion may have served to deepen complexity. However, the aim has been to illuminate some considerations relevant to school choice that have significance beyond the philosophical perspective within which they have been considered and that constitute an important set of issues and concerns requiring attention in the school choice debate more generally. Precisely how these issues should be pursued and the concerns that have been raised met requires and repays serious attention both by philosophers and by all those concerned with school choice.[7]

[7]   This article arises from a keynote address given to the conference School Choice: Public Education at a Crossroads held at the University of Calgary, Canada, in May 2002. I would like to thank the organizers of the conference for their invitation, the participants in the conference for stimulating discussion, and Professor Lynn Bosetti in particular for her encouragement and support.

Chapter 7

Citizenship, Diversity and Education

A philosophical perspective

The concept of 'education for citizenship' which is now part of the National Curriculum of schools in England and Wales,[1] gives rise to a number of philosophical questions of interest, importance and complexity.

The sorts of questions and concerns that philosophers of education are likely to raise about this notion can be readily anticipated. For example, attention has been recently drawn to the ambiguities and tensions inherent in the concept of 'citizenship' which are therefore involved in any attempt to educate for citizenship. It has been argued not only that these ambiguities and tensions require clarification and resolution before the educational task can proceed defensibly and effectively, but also that an unduly restrictive conception of that task needs to be avoided.[2]

In this article I shall offer a brief review of these concerns and shall then focus on a number of philosophical problems which are particularly associated with any attempt to educate for citizenship in the context of the diversity of a pluralistic democratic society. Such a society seeks to balance its elements of social and cultural diversity

---

[1]   National Curriculum Council (1990a). See also National Curriculum Council (1990b); Great Britain, Parliament, House of Commons (1990); Batho, G. (1990); Edwards, J. & Fogelman, K. (1991); Fogelman, K. (1991).

[2]   See, for example, Carr, W. (1991a); Wringe, C. (1992). See also Heater, D. (1990) especially Sections 8.2, 9.4.

with those of cohesion,[3] an aspiration which invokes (among other things) a familiar distinction between 'public' and 'private' values and domains. I shall explore some of the specific and neglected demands upon 'education for citizenship' generated by this context. The questions with which I shall deal are not merely of philosophical interest, but are of inescapable significance not only for those involved in the practical task of 'education for citizenship' but for all citizens. The way in which the National Curriculum has been introduced has inhibited reflection and debate about such matters. I shall argue that, for various reasons, it is vital that this reflection debate take place widely among both educators and citizens more generally.

The Concept of Citizenship

It hardly needs stating that the concept of 'citizenship' is complex and contested even when discussion is confined to citizenship in the context of Western democratic societies.[4] Many of the debates about the interpretation and justification of the concept are related to fundamental and long-standing social and political traditions commitments and disputes. This can be seen in the different meanings given to the concept of citizenship by the various main political parties in the United Kingdom in the recent debates concerning it, and the different societal ills for which it is seen as a remedy.[5]

Much of the ambiguity and tension contained within the concept of citizenship can be roughly mapped in terms of minimal and maximal interpretations of the notion. These contrasting interpretations of democratic citizenship, locatable on a continuum rather than in terms of discrete conceptions, and related to underlying political beliefs and to contrasting interpretations of democracy itself,[6] can be briefly illustrated by reference to four features of the concept. The features of citizenship I shall allude to are the *identity* that it is seen as

---

[3] On this conception of society see, for example, Great Britain, Parliament, House of Commons (1985) Ch 1.

[4] For a detailed outline and discussion of the concept of citizenship see Heater, D. (1990). See also Great Britain Parliament House of Commons (1990) especially Section 1; Morrell, F. (1991).

[5] On this matter see, for example, Heater, D. (1990) especially Section 8.2. On the 'Citizen's Charter' presented by the Prime Minister to the British Parliament in July 1991, and contrasting charters produced by the Labour party and the Liberal Democrats, see, for example, Farnham, D. (1992).

[6] On conceptions of democracy see, for example, Carr, W. (1991a), pp. 377–380; Wringe, C. (1992), pp. 30–32.

conferring upon an individual, the *virtues* of the citizen that are required, the extent of the *political involvement* on the part of the individual that is thought to follow, and the *social prerequisites* seen as necessary for effective citizenship.[7]

On 'minimal' views, the identity conferred on an individual by citizenship is seen merely in formal, legal, juridical terms. A citizen is one who has a certain civil status, with its associated rights, within a community of a certain sort based on the rule of law. On maximal views, however, this identity is seen as a richer thing than (say) the possession by a person of a passport, the right to vote and an unreflective 'nationality'. Identity on these fuller views is conceived in social, cultural and psychological terms. Thus, the citizen must have a consciousness of him or her self as a member of a living community with a shared democratic culture involving obligations and responsibilities as well as rights, a sense of the common good, fraternity and so on. This latter, maximal, interpretation of the identity required by a citizen is dynamic rather than static in that it is seen as a matter for continuing debate and redefinition. It also gives rise to the question of the extent to which social disadvantage in its various forms can undermine citizenship, especially when a sense of effective personal agency is seen as a necessary ingredient of what is at stake.

The virtues seen as required by a citizen can also be construed in minimal or maximal terms. On minimal views, for example, loyalties and responsibilities are seen primarily as local and immediate in character. Thus the citizen is one who is law abiding and 'public spirited' in the sense of helping neighbours through voluntary activity. In contrast, on maximal views, citizens are seen as requiring a more extensive focus for their loyalty and responsibility. For example, they are seen as having a responsibility to actively question and extend their local and immediate horizons in the light of more general and universal considerations such as those of justice and to work for the sort of social conditions that will lead to the empowerment of all citizens in the sense referred to above.

This last point is connected to the extent of political involvement and participation which is seen as required by citizenship. On minimal views, there is a degree of suspicion of widespread involvement, and the citizen is seen primarily as a private individual with the task of voting wisely for representatives. In contrast, maximal views favour a more fully participatory approach to democracy.

---

[7]   My discussion here partly follows distinctions made by Heater, D. (1990), Parts 2 & 3.

With regard to the social prerequisites for citizenship, minimal approaches are content to see these simply in terms of the granting of the formal legal status described earlier, whilst its maximalist counterparts insist that, although citizenship is an egalitarian status in theory and intention, social disadvantages of various kinds must be considered if that status in any real and meaningful sense is to be achieved.[8]

Much more nuanced discussion is needed, of course, of the contrasts I have sketched here. For example, it must not be assumed that 'minimal' conceptions are more free than their 'maximal' counterparts of ideological content or significance. It must also be re-emphasised that what is offered here is a continuum of interpretations rather than a set of distinct conceptions (including political ones). For example, it should not be assumed that 'maximalist' interpretations are necessarily hostile to conservative political thought and policy. The interpretation as I have sketched it merely insists that questions relating to substantial identity, to virtues of general focus, to significant participation and to the problem of social disadvantage be seen as relevant to citizenship, not that they be given a particular answer. Acknowledging the oversimplifications involved, the differences between the minimal and the maximal ends of this continuum can be broadly expressed in several kinds of contrast, e.g. Form/Substance; Private/Public; Passive/Active; Closed/Open and the like. Perhaps one of the most salient points of contrast for educational purposes concerns the degree of critical understanding and questioning that is seen as necessary to citizenship. Maximal conceptions require a considerable degree of explicit understanding of democratic principles, values and procedures on the part of the citizen, together with the dispositions and capacities required for participation in democratic citizenship generously conceived.

Education for Citizenship: Some Preliminary Considerations

It is clear that the conflicts of interpretation between minimal and maximal conceptions of citizenship are related directly to parallel conflicts between maximal and minimal interpretations of 'education for citizenship'.

On minimal interpretations, 'education for citizenship' has as its major priority the provision of information (relating, for example, to the legal and constitutional background to the status of citizenship

---

[8]   On the notion of 'social citizenship' see, for example, Marshall, T.H. (1950).

juridically conceived and to the machinery and processes of government and voting) and the development of virtues of local and immediate focus (such as those relating to voluntary activity and basic social morality). There is nothing in interpretations of this kind which require the development in students of their broad critical reflection and understanding informed by a political and a general education of some substance, or virtues and dispositions of the democratic citizen conceptualised in fuller terms.[9] Nor is there a concern to ameliorate the social disadvantages that may inhibit the students from developing into citizens in a significant sense.

There is an echo of such a conception of 'education for citizenship' in William Galston's paper 'Civic Education in the Liberal State'.[10] Galston distinguishes 'Civic Education' from what he calls 'Philosophic Education'. The latter is a form of general liberal education which is committed to the seeking of truth and the promotion of rational inquiry. It is not decisively shaped by specific social and political circumstances and stands in a critical (and potentially corrosive) relationship to them.[11] In contrast, in Galston's 'Civic Education', truth and critical inquiry are subordinated to the aim of forming individuals who can effectively conduct their lives within, and support, their political community.[12] For Galston, the notion of *support* for the political community is a criterion of the adequacy of civic education. Since he considers that, even in liberal democratic societies, rational enquiry can undermine such support, civic education should not in his view embody (for example) a study of history which is fully open and critical but one which is more 'noble' and 'moralising', yielding – '... a pantheon of heroes who confer legitimacy on central institutions and constitute worthy objects of emulation'.[13] Nor, granted that basic requirements of civic deliberation and tolerance are satisfied, is civic education justified in fostering in children critical reflection on beliefs, values and ways of life inherited from parents or cultural communities.[14]

It is easy to see how the minimalist kind of interpretation of 'education for citizenship', which resonates with a number of recent dis-

---

[9]   On such virtues see White, P. (1987, 1989, 1990, 1991a, 1991b).

[10] Galston, W. (1989, 1991).

[11] On the notion of general liberal education see Bailey, C. (1984).

[12] Galston, W. (1989), pp. 89–90.

[13] Galston, W. (1989), p. 91.

[14] Galston, W. (1989), p. 99. Compare Gutmann, A. (1987, 1989). For an assessment of Gutmann's overall position see Sher, G. (1989).

cussions in Britain,[15] is open to a number of important objections. The most notable of these is that it may involve merely an unreflective socialisation into the political and social *status quo*, and is therefore inadequate on educational, as well as on other, grounds.

There is in consequence support in many circles for a more maximalist conception of 'education for citizenship'. As can be seen from the conceptions of citizenship with which it is associated, this requires a much fuller educational programme, in which the development of a broad critical understanding and a much more extensive range of dispositions and virtues in the light of a general liberal and political education are seen as crucial.[16] It also requires the consideration of a more explicit egalitarian thrust in educational arrangements.[17]

Where can the recent guidance from the National Curriculum Council[18] be located in relation to this continuum of maximal and minimal conceptions of 'education for citizenship'?

There are a number of elements in the document which indicate a minimalist interpretation. Thus, for example, in its introduction the document specifies two important ways in which the school can lay the foundation for 'positive, participative citizenship':

i. by helping pupils to acquire and understand essential information;

ii. by providing them with opportunities and incentives to participate in all aspects of school life.[19]

The reference to (mere) 'information' here, and to 'school life' as the context for participation does not encourage a maximalist reading of the intentions of the guidance This is also true of other statements of basic principles which are offered. Thus 'education for citizenship' is defined as developing — '... the knowledge, skills and attitudes necessary for exploring, making informed decisions about and exercis-

[15] See, for example, discussion in Heater, D. (1990), pp. 305–306 of the attitude of recent Education Secretaries to the teaching of history and Cox, C. *et al.* (1986) on parental rights in relation to education.

[16] See, for example, Callan, E. (1991); Carr, W. (1991a); Crick, B. & Porter, A. (1978); Gutmann, A. (1987, 1989); White,]. (1990); White, P. (1983); Wringe, C. (1984, 1992).

[17] See, for example, Fielding, M. (1988).

[18] National Curriculum Council (hereinafter NCC) (1990a).

[19] NCC (1990a), p. 1.

ing responsibilities and rights in a democratic society'[20] and its aims
are seen as: ... to:

> establish the importance of positive, participative citizenship
> and provide the motivation to join in; help pupils to acquire and
> understand the information on which to base the development
> of their skills, values and attitudes towards citizenship.[21]

In addition to underscoring here the significance of 'information',
the document fails at any point to offer any clear definition of how
citizenship is being understood, and has recourse instead to statements of a general and procedural kind about the development of
relevant skills, values and the like. Further, the document refers only
briefly later to the 'conceptual framework' that might be provided
for 'education for citizenship' by core and foundation subjects of the
National Curriculum.[22]

However, other aspects of the document give encouragement to a
maximalist reading. Thus among the 'positive attitudes' that are
stressed are 'independence of thought on social and moral issues'
and 'an active concern for human rights'.[23] ' Moral codes and values
are to be explored and discussed in relation to difference, conflict,
complexity and context.[24] The 'eight essential components' of content outlined in the document include an exploration of 'diversity,
fairness and justice, co-operation and competition, prejudice and
discrimination', 'inequality ... sexism and racism', knowledge of
political systems and processes, an understanding of the 'social,
political and economic contexts' in which decisions about work,
employment and leisure are made and 'different perceptions about
the best forms of provision' for public services.[25]

However, it is impossible to read the document in an unambigu-
ously maximalist way because, in common with the National Curriculum in general, it does not contain a clear and detailed account of its
fundamental aims, values and principles.[26] Most notably, as mentioned earlier, it does not offer a clearly worked out conception of

---

[20] NCC (1990a), p. 2.

[21] NCC (1990a), p. 2.

[22] NCC (1990a), p. 14.

[23] NCC (1990a), p. 4.

[24] NCC (1990a), p. 4.

[25] NCC (1990a), Section 4.

[26] For criticism of the National Curriculum on these grounds see White, J. (1990),
      Ch 1, 8.

'citizenship'. Wilfred Carr[27] is therefore correct in noting that the guidance will need to be interpreted by individual schools, where fundamental disputes are likely to take place. Teachers will engage in an exegesis of the wording of the document, unguided by clear guidance about fundamental principles. Although the document has a maximalist tone, at the very least it fails to provide guidance at the very points when it is most required. For example, what educational implications arise from the need to ensure that pupils realise that—'... distinguishing between right and wrong is not always straightforward'?[28] As is widely recognised, this general problem of interpretation exists also in relation to other aspects of the National Curriculum, where teachers are using the scope within proposals to interpret and implement them in the light of their own aims, values principles. However, Carr is pessimistic about the guidance relating to 'educatio' for citizenship' being implemented in terms I have described as 'maximal', not least because it is located within the context of a set of educational reforms, including the National Curriculum, which he sees as inadequate with regard to the educational requirements of democracy.[29]

Whether or not this view is justified, the problems encountered by any attempt to engage in 'education for citizenship' in any maximalist sense in the context of the diversity of a pluralistic democratic society are often underestimated. In the next section of this paper I shall outline some of the problems of a philosophical character which arise, and which are often neglected in educational (and more general) discussion.

Citizenship and the Educational Demands of Diversity

In order to identify these problems, it is necessary to sketch some central elements of the philosophical background to the notion of a pluralistic democratic society.

There are a number of elements in this background. In what follows, I shall confine my attention to the philosophical theory of liberalism, which illuminates some of the major problems clearly. Central to liberalism is the phenomenon of the existence in society of diversities in belief, practice and value, to which it is seen as a response. Given fundamental disagreement about substantial or 'thick' conceptions of human good or perfection, (for example, religious views

[27] Carr, W. (1991a).

[28] NCC (1990a), p. 4.

[29] See also Carr, W. (1991b).

Liberalism, Education and Schooling

which provide a comprehensive account of human life and how it should be lived), liberalism holds that no such conception can be imposed on citizens of a pluralist society or invoked to characterise and underpin the notion of the public good. What is needed for this purpose is a 'thin' conception of the good, free of significantly controversial assumptions and judgements, which maximises the freedom of citizens to pursue their diverse private conceptions of the good within a framework of justice. An example of an aspect of a 'thin' conception of the good is a commitment to the requirements of basic social morality. The label 'thin' here refers not to the insignificance of such values, but to their independence from substantial, particular, frameworks of belief and value. Although on this view the state must be neutral on matters of private good, it has a non-neutral commitment to the basic principles of justice involved in the notion of the good in public terms, and on the basis of this seeks to achieve a balance between cohesiveness and diversity.[30]

Although much more needs to be said in a full articulation of this general view in the light of the range of criticisms to which it has been subjected,[31] and the need for a detailed treatment to be given of such matters as the complexity of the relationship between public and private values and domains,[32] I trust that its basic outlines are recognisable enough to serve for the purposes of this discussion.

Given this view, a central general task of education (expressed roughly) is to gain the understanding and commitment of students to the various public values, principles, procedures and loyalties (public virtues), whilst encouraging in relation to the diversity characteristic of the private domain, exploration, understanding, debate and critical reflective decisions by individuals. As Eamonn Callan points out[33] education in this context exerts both centripetal (unifying) and centrifugal (diversifying) forces upon society. With regard to its centripetal influence, it must steer a course between two kinds of educational failure: (a) becoming a vehicle for an unacceptable monism or homogeneity of belief, practice and value, and therefore

[30] For an account of this general position in more detail, see, for example, Brown, A. (1986), Ch 3; Gutmann, A. (1989); Kymlicka, W. (1990), Ch 3; Macedo, S. (1990); Mendus, S. (1989), Ch 4; Rawls, J. (1971, 1985, 1987, 1988).

[31] On communitarian critiques of liberalism see, for example, Gutmann, A. (1985); Kymlicka, W. (1989); MacIntyre, A. (1981, 1988, 1990); Sandel, M.J. (1982).

[32] On this matter, see, for example, Benn, S.I. & Gaus, G.F. (1983); Cochran, C.E. (1990); Hampshire, S. (1978); Hannon, P. (1992); Macedo, S. (1990); Pateman, C. (1983).

[33] Callan, E. (1991), pp. 66–68.

being open to charges of indoctrination or illicit moulding, and (b) failing to secure a commitment to the range of public virtues which hold the society as a whole together, and therefore being open to the charge of contributing to its disintegration. Callan is correct in claiming that it is only when we have determined what these public virtues are that we can distinguish in a principled way between legitimate and illegitimate educational forces of a centripetal kind. 'Education for citizenship' is particularly (though not exclusively) concerned with the 'public' virtues, and with the attempt to exert a legitimate centripetal influence.[34] It is important to remember that 'citizenship' and 'education for citizenship' are not abstract notions, but require concrete specification in relation to a particular society. 'Public' virtues are vital to this task of specification since they articulate the character and scope of citizenship. Their identification is therefore crucial to an adequate delineation of 'education for citizenship' in the context of a pluralistic democratic society.

Both minimalist and maximalist interpretations of 'education for citizenship' are controversial. Minimalist interpretations, as noted earlier, are open to accusations of uncritical socialisation, not least into the unexamined political values which they often embody. On the other hand, maximalist interpretations, given the range of controversial questions which they open up, are in danger of presupposing a substantive set of 'public virtues' which may exceed the principled consensus that exists or can be achieved.

What are these 'public' or 'civic' virtues which support a liberal polity and take priority over 'private' commitments in cases of conflict? For Galston, the major criterion to be used in determining these is what is functionally necessary to the needs of the polity's sociopolitical institutions.[35] As we saw earlier, Galston's view about what these needs are has minimalist undertones. Central to the view is Galston's claim that liberal freedom entails the right to live unexamined as well as examined lives. For Galston, to insist upon the 'examined life' as an ideal (and to conduct public education so as to facilitate it) is to go beyond the demands of liberal neutrality. This position sheds light on Galston's suspicion of the role of critical

---

[34] 'Education for citizenship' is concerned with the 'private' domain also since a citizen is one who has the moral awareness and judgement necessary to be able to distinguish between 'public' and 'private' values and domains in particular cases. Given the complexity of the judgements involved, the educational task here is a considerable one.

[35] Galston, W. (1989), p. 100.

reason and his acceptance of the need for – '... parental bulwarks against the corrosive influence of modernist skepticism'.[36]

Galston's conception of the sort of reasoning needed by the citizen is that it should meet '... at least the minimal standards of reasonable public judgement'.[37] One way of interpreting this conception is that it aims at the achievement by citizens of a form of 'autarchy' rather than of 'autonomy'.[38] The rational deliberation and self-determination of the (merely) autarchic person is limited in extent and scope, not extending, for example, as far as calling into question fundamental matters of belief or convention, such as prevailing social and political structures. (Galston holds, for example, that civic deliberation is compatible with unshakable personal commitments).[39] In contrast, the rational deliberation of autonomous persons must extend much further. Thus, they must achieve (at least to a significant extent) a distanced critical perspective on all important matters, and their belief and action must result from principles and policies which they 'have themselves 'ratified' by critical reflection.[40]

Many thinkers in the liberal tradition hold that a commitment to the ideal of personal autonomy in some significant and defensible sense must be seen as part of the 'public virtue' that a liberal democratic society should be concerned with.[41] Although something of a restriction of the neutrality of the state on conceptions of the good is involved here, it is claimed that this restriction is unlike others in that it creates 'openness' for individuals; the opportunity for them to engage in the task of self-appropriation and self-definition distinctive of the liberal ideal. It is clear that if personal autonomy is seen as a crucial element in basic liberal democratic values in this way, considerable implications follow for the character of education in such a society. In particular, more maximalist conceptions of both citizenship and education for citizenship are licensed.

[36] Galston, W. (1989), p. 100.

[37] Galston, W. (1989), p. 99. Compare Gutmann's notion of 'deliberative character' in Gutmann, A. (1987), p. 50–52.

[38] On this distinction see, for example, White, J. 1990, p. 97.

[39] Galston, W. (1989), p. 99.

[40] There is an extensive critical literature on the subject of 'autonomy' and its cognates. For a guide to this see Karjohn, L. (1989). See also Haworth, L. (1986); Young, R. (1986); Dworkin, G. (1988); White, J. (1990).

[41] See, for example, Ackerman, B. (1980); Gutmann, A. (1987, 1989); Kymlicka, W. (1989); Macedo, S. (1990); Raz, J. (1986); White, J. (1990).

The view that the promotion of personal autonomy is part of the basic values of a liberal democracy faces two kinds of challenge, both of which are significant to the task of identifying the common values which are relevant to an adequate conception of 'education for citizenship'.

The first relates to the fundamental defence of the perspective. It depends, among other things, on the possibility of drawing a clear distinction between 'autonomy' (which it sees as a basic good for individuals) and 'autarchy' (which it sees as inadequate). But how is 'autonomy' to be distinguished from 'autarchy'? What sorts and degrees of reflection must be engaged in by the autonomous person, and in relation to which matters? As I have suggested elsewhere, the adequate delineation of what is involved in 'autonomy' as distinct from 'autarchy' is not only a practical, but a theoretical problem of some complexity.[42] This is likely to be reflected in continuing disputes both about the ideal itself and the educational aims and practices which it generates.

If, however, one accepts for the purposes of argument that the development of personal autonomy is in some significant sense a public virtue in a pluralist democratic society, a second challenge comes into focus. What are the other public virtues in relation to which personal autonomy is exercised and which constitute constraints on the individualistic and centrifugal tendencies inherent in it? Without a specification of these it will be impossible to characterise a 'maximal' notion of 'citizenship' and (therefore) 'education for citizenship'. Critical reasoning and independent judgement are strong features of maximalist perspectives on these matters and proponents of such perspectives are right to stress their centrality. But there is an equally important need to delineate the shared values, loyalties and commitments that are required by this view.

This is no easy task. It is connected to wide ranging concerns expressed by many writers about how such common values, and indeed the common good more generally, can be characterised in relation to the liberal democratic conception of a pluralist society.[43] There are certainly general principles derivable from the liberal perspective (concerning such matters as the distinction between public and rate domains, tolerance, respect for persons and the like) which

---

[42] See McLaughlin, T.H. (1992), pp. 125–128.

[43] On the failure of the Swann Report to provide an account of the 'framework of common values' to which it appealed see Haydon, G. (1987a, 1987b); White, J. (1987).

are relevant to articulation of these notions but there is widespread concern that these are too 'thin', abstract, or merely procedural, to constitute common values or the common good in any substantial sense. Many of these concerns have been articulated by critics of a communitarian persuasion who have a general hostility to liberalism,[44] but they are also acknowledged by writers sympathetic to it. There is thus a widespread realisation of the need for liberals to specify an account of the common good which is rich (or 'thick') enough to satisfy the demands of commonality, but which combines respect for the important role of independence and critical reason for individuals and the demands of justice relating to diversity.[45]

Complaints about the lack of 'thickness' or substantiality of the liberal 'public virtues' are of different kinds. Common to most of them is the claim that the liberal notions do not enable persons to achieve defensible and necessary forms of affiliation and commitment to a 'larger moral ecology' beyond their own individual, and indeed individualistic, concerns. Such a 'moral ecology' embodies a social ethos, a consensus of the common good and notions of loyalty and responsibility to the community as a whole as well as a framework of wider beliefs and values providing (at least to some extent) a culture of 'narrative coherence' as well as of 'freedom' for lives. The liberal view, it is claimed, leads to individualism in its various forms and a tendency for individual choice and self-definition to be based on arbitrary preference or self-interest rather than a view of life which is more coherent and other-regarding. In addition, attention is drawn to the corrosive effects of private economic pursuits and consumerism on the notion of a caring public ethos, the negative effects of an undue separation of public and private realms and so on.

Claims such as these are complex and wide ranging. They are not all purely philosophical in character, although they may all be seen as having philosophical roots. A full evaluation of such claims would require an extensive investigation, giving careful attention to the different category of claim. Part of the philosophical task of evaluation would involve, for example, attention to the dangers of over-generality in the claims[46] and an assessment of rejoinders from

---

[44] See footnote 31.

[45] On this matter see, for example, Bellah et al. (1985, 1991); Callan, E. (1991); Hollis, M. (1989, 1992); Mendus, S. (1992); Milligan, D. & Watts Miller, W. (1992); Norman, R. (1992); Watts Miller, W. (1992); Reynolds, C. & Norman, R. (1988); Strike, K. (1991); White, J. (1992).

[46] See Stout, J. (1988).

liberals arguing that the liberal tradition has resources within it to meet challenges of lack of substance and 'thickness'.[47]

It is the absence of agreement about these 'public virtues' and the common good, which gives rise to the various disputes about 'citizenship' and 'education for citizenship' which have been alluded to. With regard to the educational task, this lack of agreement constitutes a challenge to those seeking to justify a 'maximalist' approach, to specify the concrete shape it should take, to defend it against accusations of exercising illicitly centripetal influence and to provide confident answers to questions such as whether education for citizenship can transmit a particular way of life.[48]

What is to be done about the characterisation of 'public virtues' and the common good in the context of a liberal pluralistic democracy? So far I have presented the problems primarily as philosophical ones, arising within the tradition of liberalism and requiring philosophical responses.

It is clear, however, that the problems are also practical ones, inextricably connected with social and political issues and realities in particular societies and requiring concrete attention in these contexts. This is particularly so when it ' remembered that what is at stake is not only the characterisation of these 'public virtues' but also their achievement. Philosophical reflection can make an important contribution to these more practical tasks. However, no actual society either embodies, or can be organised in terms of, purely philosophical principles, and practical reflection and action of various kinds are necessary in order to discern and achieve the 'public virtues' and the common good.

What does this task involve in practical terms? Although this is a highly complex question, it is clear that it is one which must involve society as a whole rather than simply educationists. A wide ranging dialogue and debate is at the heart of what is needed, although this alone is insufficient. There is also a need for important initiatives and changes in society, such as the encouragement of 'intermediate associative structures'[49] and the kinds of institutional reform which will enable wider citizen participation.

---

[47] See, for example, Macedo, S. (1990).

[48] See, for example, Crittenden, B. (1988); Levin, M. (1985); Rich, J. (1985).

[49] Examples of 'intermediate associative structures' include the family, churches and various forms of local civic organisations. These are intermediate between the individual and the larger national society, and the significance of their associative character consists in the fact that they embody substantial views of

Education is seen as having a crucial role in the determination of the common values of a liberal democratic pluralist society, either narrowly in terms of promoting negotiation in relation to values,[50] or more generously, as promoting and preparing persons for dialogue[51] not least through 'education for citizenship' itself. It is clear, however, that more general reflection and agreement about the public virtues and the common good must be *brought to* the educative task as a result of wide ranging debate within society as a whole if 'education for citizenship' is to avoid becoming either ineffectively 'minimalist', or in a 'maximalist' guise, the object of serious controversy of a political, and more general, kind.

The guidance offered by the NCC acknowledges that education for citizenship involves controversiality[52] but does not relate the questions at stake to the more fundamental issues which have been outlined here. There is an important need for there to be a national debate, and as far as possible a degree of agreement, about the 'public virtues' and the common good, and about how 'citizenship' and 'education for citizenship' themselves are to be understood. Part of this involves the achievement of a practical political consensus on the questions at issue. Leaving the controversial matters involved to surface in a rather random way at school level is a recipe either for continuing conflict or for failure to educate for citizenship in a significant sense.

A good example of the sort of issue that requires the kind of wide ranging national debate I refer to emerges from a consultation paper[53] recently issued by Her Majesty's Chief Inspector of Schools in England concerning the framework which is to guide the work of the new 'Registered Inspectors' of schools. One of the statutory functions of these inspectors is to report on the 'spiritual, moral, social and cultural development' of pupils in school (Introduction, Para 1). Reaction is sought to sections in a draft inspection schedule relating to these matters (Section 2, Paras 5.3; 5.4). Predictably enough, both the suggested evaluation criteria and the relevant evidence raise matters of fundamental significance and dispute. Paragraph 5.3, for

---

the world and human good and provide a coherent basis for contra-individualistic motivation and obligation. (See Bellah, R. *et al.*, 1985, 1991).

[50] On this see, for example, Haydon, G. (1986, 1987b); White, J. (1987). For criticisms of the notion see Leicester, M. (1986); Pring, R. (1992).

[51] Bellah, R. *et al.* (1991), Ch. 5.

[52] NCC (1990a), p. 14.

[53] Her Majesty's Chief Inspector of Schools in England (1992).

example, invites inspectors to assess the response of pupils to opportunities to '... exercise responsibility, community and citizenship...'
but neither in the 'suggested evaluation criteria nor the relevant evidence proposed is there any indication of an awareness of the issues
of value complexity which have been the subject of discussion
above. The same is true of the treatment of the spiritual and moral
development of pupils in paragraph 5.4.

Since it deals with such fundamental aspects of the education of
pupils in a liberal democratic society, a consultation of this kind
demands a wide ranging national discussion. This in turn presupposes a climate of debate about educational matters rather different
from the one which has prevailed in recent years. Such a debate is
likely to reveal deep differences of opinion on a number of issues. It
also runs the risk of being conducted at a level of fruitless abstraction. But an effort must be made to achieve general agreement on
both: (i) the public values which should articulate the practice of a
substantial form of 'education for citizenship' and (ii) the broad
character of defensible practical policies and strategies required for
this educative task, including those relating to the handling of controversial issues with pupils. A failure of such an effort in a pluralistic liberal democracy bodes ill for citizenship itself in that context.

Conclusion

In this article, I have argued the following points concerning 'education for citizenship' in the context of the diversity of a liberal democratic society:

a. That the concept of 'citizenship' is complex and contested. It is
    capable of being roughly mapped in terms of a continuum of
    'minimal' and 'maximal' interpretations. This is correspond-
    ingly true of 'education for citizenship'.

b. A major point of contrast between 'minimal' and 'maximal'
    interpretations of 'education for citizenship' is the degree of
    critical understanding and questioning on the part of students
    that is being aimed at and the extent to which a general liberal
    and political education of some substance is seen as implied.

c. Although the recent guidance from the National Curriculum
    Council on 'education for citizenship' is ambiguous in this
    matter there are good arguments for supporting a more 'maxi-
    mal' interpretation of the notion.

d. In the context of the diversity of a liberal pluralist democracy, a
    'maximal' conception of 'education for citizenship' runs the

danger of presupposing a substantial set of 'public virtues' which exceeds the principled consensus on these matters which exists or can be achieved. Since these 'public virtues' articulate the character and scope of citizenship their identification is crucial to an adequate delineation of 'education for citizenship' and a resolution of the matters of controversy which arise. Although philosophical reflection can illuminate what is at stake in relation to the 'public virtues', there is a vital need for a wide ranging national debate about their character and achievement which is not confined to educationalists. Part of this involves practical agreement about defensible strategies and policies for 'educating for citizenship', including those relating to the handling of controversial issues with pupils. Only in this way can 'education for citizenship', and indeed citizenship itself, be given a firm basis.

Acknowledgements

Earlier versions of this article were presented to a meeting of the Scottish branch of the Philosophy of Education Society of Great Britain and to audiences at the Faculty of Education, Simon Fraser University, Burnaby, Canada and the Program for the Study of Cultural Values and Ethics at the University of Illinois at Urbana-Champaign, USA. I am grateful to the participants in all these discussions for their helpful comments and criticisms.

Chapter 8

The Burdens and Dilemmas of Common Schooling

Schools of every kind, place, and time shoulder burdens and face dilemmas. Many of these burdens and dilemmas are universal in that they are inherent in the very activity of schooling and teaching. Every school faces the burden of arousing the interest of students in what it is in their interests to learn, and of ensuring that the learning in question is satisfactorily brought about. Every school also faces dilemmas arising from the relative weight and priority to be given to contrasting and competing demands such as those captured in tensions between reassurance and challenge in the handling of individuals, breadth and depth in determining what is to be learnt, and equality and excellence in the overall aims and ethos of the classroom and school.[1]

Common schools in pluralist, multicultural, liberal democratic societies, however, shoulder burdens and face dilemmas of very specific and demanding kinds. These burdens and dilemmas relate to the particular educational role and mandate which common schools are given in such societies which is in turn related to, and derived from, the complex principles, values, and practices which articulate and underpin societies of this kind. Bhikhu Parekh expresses in a clear way the centrality to these principles, values, and practices of the achievement of a certain kind of balance between unifying and diversifying imperatives and forces: 'Multicultural societies throw up problems that have no parallel in history. They

---

[1] The extent to which such dilemmas are experienced at school level is, of course, dependent in part on the extent to which the dilemmas are resolved by convention or circumstance, or at a higher level within the educational system of which the school is a part.

need to find ways of reconciling the legitimate demands of unity and diversity, achieving political unity without cultural uniformity, being inclusive without being assimilationist, cultivating among their citizens a common sense of belonging while respecting their legitimate cultural differences, and cherishing plural cultural identities without weakening the shared and precious identity of shared citizenship.'[2] Common schools are typically seen as having an important educational role and mandate in relation to these challenges. It is widely argued that a common school, underpinned by an appropriate conception of common education, is the most favored context in which these challenges can be met and liberal democratic educational aims, values, and processes realized.

In this chapter, I shall explore some of the neglected resultant burdens and dilemmas faced by common schools in pluralist, multicultural, and liberal democratic societies. The potential weight and complexity of these burdens and dilemmas is reflected in Stephen Macedo's observation that common schools give rise to questions relating to some of the 'deepest divisions' and 'most intractable conflicts' characterizing the public lives of modern states.[3] The chapter has five sections. Section 1 outlines some general considerations relating to common schooling and a conception of common education, and Section 2 offers a sketch of some general features of such conceptions. In Sections 3 and 4 respectively, some of the burdens and dilemmas of common schooling are explored. Although these burdens and dilemmas are brought into focus by the sort of philosophical reflection and analysis attempted in this chapter, they have a pre-eminently practical character. Neglected questions relating to this important truth will be addressed in Section 5.

1. Common Schooling and a Conception of Common Education

At the most basic level, a 'common school' can be regarded as a school which is open to, and intended for, all students within a given society regardless of their specific differentiating characteristics. Ideals of 'common schooling,' however, normally specify not merely a particular institutional arrangement for schooling but also a 'conception of common education' which the school should embody and

[2]   B. Parekh, Rethinking Multiculturalism: Cultural Diversity and Political Theory (London: Macmillan, 2000), 343.

[3]   S. Macedo, Diversity and Distrust: Civic Education in a Multicultural Democracy (Cambridge: Harvard University Press, 2000), 39.

enact. The notion of a 'conception of common education' prescribes a range of educational outcomes of wide ranging kinds as appropriate and desirable for all members of the society in question.[4] Conceptions of common education, and therefore the role and mandate which is given to the common school, vary across differing societies. In theocratic societies, common schools typically embody the form of religiously based education and formation judged appropriate for all citizens and for the maintenance of favored forms of moral and cultural monism and homogeneity.[5] In the former Soviet Union common schools sought to transmit, and shape students in the light of, a particular view of the good expressed in part in the sort of unified, detailed, moral formation contained in the notion of *vospitanie*. A range of differing philosophical resources can be appealed to in articulating a conception of common education.[6] In the context of the sorts of pluralist, multicultural, and liberal democratic societies which are the focus of the present discussion, however, 'common schools' are seen as a favored context in which to realize a 'conception of common education' based on liberal democratic philosophical and educational ideals and embodying an appropriate balance between the kinds of complex unifying and diversifying imperatives and forces mentioned earlier. This 'conception of common education' is seen as an entitlement for all students and as therefore in tension with the claims of diversity, parental rights, and the mechanisms of the educational marketplace. It generates a series of educational aims and processes which involve not merely the development of relevant forms of knowledge and understanding, but also of forms of sensitivity, disposition, virtue, and commitment.[7]

[4]   Callan, Eamonn, *Creating Citizens: Political Education and Liberal Democracy* (Oxford: Oxford University Press, 1997). 163-6.

[5]   Parekh defines 'moral monism' as the view that . .only one way of life is fully human, true, or the best, and that all others are defective to the extent that they fall short of it', B. Parekh, *Rethinking Multiculturalism: Cultural Diversity and Political Theory*, 16.

[6]   For an Aristotelian perspective on public education, see R. R. Curren, *Aristotle on the Necessity of Public Education* (Lanham: Rowman and Littlefield Publishers, 2000).

[7]   See, for example, Callan, Creating Citizens; A. Gutmann, *Democratic Education* (Princeton: Princeton University Press,1987); W. Feinberg, *Common Schools/Uncommon Identities: National Unity and Cultural Difference* (New Haven and London: Yale University Press, 1998); M. Levinson, *The Demands of Liberal Education* (Oxford: Oxford University Press, 1999); T. H. McLaughlin, 'Liberalism, Education and the Common School', *Journal of Philosophy of*

It is useful to make a number of preliminary general points about the 'common school' and a 'conception of common education' in pluralist, multicultural, and liberal democratic societies. First, 'common schools' are not, and cannot be, 'common' in every respect. Walter Feinberg acknowledges that common schools differ in their material and intellectual resources, in their curriculum and pedagogy, and in their racial, gender, and social class composition and effects.[8] Common schooling, understood as requiring similarity of educational provision, experience, and outcome does not, and cannot, exist. In the United States and in England and Wales, there are marked and widely recognized differences in publicly funded schools related to such factors as location, and in both contexts greater diversification in publicly funded schooling is being urged. What is fundamentally 'common' in common schools is the 'conception of common education' which they seek to embody and certain *de jure* provisions relating to such matters as open admission criteria and a learning environment which is hospitable in different ways to diversity. In addition, the de facto realization of such provisions, albeit imperfectly, is also significant. However, whilst conceptions of common education are compatible with certain kinds of variety in common schooling, both *de jure* and de facto, the unifying and egalitarian elements inherent in such conceptions imply that some differences among common schools are troubling, for example, those have implications for equality of educational opportunity in its various aspects. Parameters within which variety in common schooling should be contained can therefore be derived from most conceptions of common education,[9] as can criteria for the limits of accommoda-

Education, 29(2) (1995), 239-55. Macedo, *Diversity and Distrust*; K. A. Strike, 'On the Construction of Public Speech: Pluralism and Public Reason', *Educational Theory*, 44(1) (1994), 1-26. K. A. Strike, 'Liberalism, Citizenship and the Private Interest in Schooling', *Studies in Philosophy and Education*, 17(4) (1998), 221-9; P. White, *Civic Virtues and Public Schooling: Educating Citizens for a Democratic Society* (New York: Teachers College Press, 1996).

[8]   Feinberg, Common Schools/Uncommon Identities, 2-3.

[9]   See, for example, the discussion of the compatibility of certain recent proposals for school reform in the United States with civic educational ideals in Macedo, *Diversity and Distrust*, ch. 11. On the limits of tolerance with respect to kinds of schooling within a liberal democratic perspective see also, for example, H. Brighouse, *School Choice and Social Justice* (Oxford: University Press, 2000); Callan, *Creating Citizens*, ch. 7; Levinson, *The Demands of Liberal Education*, ch. 5, section 2; R. C. Salomone, *Visions of Schooling: Conscience, Community and Common Education*, (New Haven: Yale University Press, 2000) ch. 8.

tion between conceptions of common education and such aspects of diversity as religious belief.[10]

Second, and relatedly, it is a 'common conception of education' and common schooling per se which is seen as of fundamental value. The 'common school' is regarded as valuable not as an end in itself but to the extent that it is an appropriate context for the realization of the underlying conception of common education. Common schools are widely considered to be particularly favored contexts for this purpose, however, since in bringing together students from many diverse backgrounds in a common institution, common schools constitute an educational environment which is both intimately related to the requirements of conceptions of common education and unobtainable elsewhere.[11] Be this as it may, however, the practical shortcomings of common schools in particular contexts, the impossibility of deriving conclusions for schooling arrangements from philosophical and political premises alone, and complexities inherent in conceptions of common education themselves, mean that the relationship between common schools and a common conception of education is at best a presumptive one.[12] I have argued elsewhere that certain forms of 'non-common' educational provision, such as certain kinds of religious schools, can be compatible with conceptions of common education.[13]

[10] For an expansive account of such limits emphasizing flexibility and inclusion see, for example, J. Spinner-Halev, *Surviving Diversity. Religion and Democratic Citizenship* (Baltimore: The Johns Hopkins University Press, 2000) 135-41. For arguments in support of pluralism in schooling in liberal democratic societies in which common schools are not given pride of place, see F. Schrag, 'Diversity, Schooling and the Liberal State', *Studies in Philosophy and Education*, 17(1) (1998), 29–46; E. J. Thiessen, *In Defence of Religious Schools and Colleges* (Montreal: McGill-Queen's University Press, 2001). See esp. ch. 13.

[11] Of common schools, Macedo writes: 'That the schools bring children from many backgrounds together in a common institution is the whole point' (*Diversity and Distrust*, 232). On the significance of this feature of common schools, see also Spinner-Halev, *Surviving Diversity*, 112-14. On general considerations supporting common schooling, see Callan, *Creating Citizens*, 174-8.

[12] On the relationship between philosophical considerations and educational policy see T. H. McLaughlin, 'Philosophy and Educational Policy: Possibilities, Tensions and Tasks', *Journal of Educational Policy*, 15(4) (2000), 441-57. On complexities concerning the relationship between conceptions of education and schooling arrangements, see Callan, *Creating Citizens*, ch. 7.

[13] T. H. McLaughlin, 'The Ethics of Separate Schools' in M. Leicester and M. J. Taylor (eds), *Ethics, Ethnicity and Education* (London: Kogan Page, 1992). On these matters, see also Callan, *Creating Citizens*, ch. 7; E. Callan, 'Discrimination and Religious Schooling' in W. Kymlicka and W. Norman (eds), *Citizenship in Diverse*

Third, the extent to which a conception of the 'common school' and a 'conception of common education' is explicitly articulated and implemented at the level of policy and practice in any particular pluralist, multicultural, liberal democratic society varies. In the United States the political, legal, and historical context of the 'public school' has given a sharpness of focus to central matters of educational principle and their relationship to practice, even though these matters have been subject to development and require careful interpretation.[14] In England and Wales, there is less sharpness of focus given to matters of educational principle by the political and legal context, in part because of the lack of separation between church and state and a different history of the relationship of publicly funded schooling to religion.[15] Religious education and an act of worship are compulsory in all publicly funded schools to which the sponsoring religious body makes a financial contribution in exchange for control over certain aspects of the life and work of the school, including admissions of students, religious teaching, certain staff appointments, and school ethos.[16] Until relatively recently, educational aims and values have not been explicitly and systematically addressed and articulated at the policy level in England and Wales[17] and insufficient

Societies (Oxford: University Press, 2000); Spinner-Halev, *Surviving Diversity*, 115-23; E. J. Thiessen, *Teaching for Commitment: Liberal Education, Indoctrination and Christian Nurture* (Montreal: McGill-Queen's University Press, 1993); Thiessen (2001). For a discussion of relevant considerations, see Macedo, *Diversity and Distrust*, 234-6, 260-8. For arguments against religious schools see, for example, J. G. Dwyer, *Religious Schools v Children's Rights* (Ithaca: Cornell University Press, 1998).

[14] On the history of the 'public school' in the United States see, for example, Macedo, *Diversity and Distrust*, chs 2-4. On these matters, see also Salomone, *Visions of Schooling*, chs 1-6. For an argument against the claim that state funding to religiously affiliated schools violates US constitutional principles, see Spinner-Halev, *Surviving Diversity*, 120-3.

[15] On this history see, for example, P. Chadwick, *Shifting Alliances: Church and State in English Education* (London: Cassell, 1997).

[16] On proposals to extend the number of faith based schools in the publicly funded schooling sector in England and Wales see, for example, Archbishops Council, *The Way Ahead: Church of England Schools in the New Millennium* (London: Church House Publishing, 2001).

[17] A significant recent initiative in this respect was the consultation process on educational values launched by the former Schools Curriculum and Assessment Authority, which involved the establishment of the National Forum for Values in Education and the Community and culminated in the statement of values included in the new National Curriculum (see School Curriculum and Assessment Authority, *National Forum for Values in Education and the Community: Consultation on Values in Education and the Community* (London: SCAA, 1996), and

attention has been given at this level to specific concerns, such as education for citizenship and the appropriate handling of controversial issues, which are inherent in 'conceptions of common education'.[18] The theoretical articulation of ideals of the 'common school' and a 'conception of common education' at an abstract level is one thing, and the articulation and realization of those ideals at the level of educational policy and practice is another. Meira Levinson is correct in drawing attention to the limitations of purely theoretical reflection about educational ideals and the need to pay attention to contextually sensitive matters of policy and practice if a full understanding of the matters at stake is to be achieved.[19] Before proceeding, it is worth noting that the term 'common school' is not widely or

QCA Department for Education and Employment and Qualifications and Curriculum Authority, *The National Curriculum Handbook for Secondary Teachers in England: Key Stages 3 and 4* (London: DfEE, 1999), 195–7; M. Talbot and N. Tate 'Shared Values in a Pluralist Society?' in R. Smith and P. Standish (eds), *Teaching Right and Wrong: Moral Education in the Balance* (Stoke on Trent: Trentham Books, 1997). For criticisms of this initiative see, for example, J. Beck, *Morality and Citizenship in Education* (London: Cassell, 1998), esp. 85-95; G. Haydon, *Values, Virtues and Violence: Education and the Public Understanding of Morality* (Oxford: Blackwell, 1999), esp. chs 3, 13 and 14; R. Smith, 'Judgement Day' in R. Smith and P. Standish (eds), *Teaching Right and Wrong: Moral Education in the Balance* (Stoke on Trent: Trentham Books, 1997); P. Standish, 'Fabulously Absolute' in R. Smith and P. Standish (eds), *Teaching Right and Wrong: Moral Education in the Balance* (Stoke on Trent: Trentham Books, 1997); J. White, 'Three Proposals and a Rejection' in R. Smith and P. Standish (eds), *Teaching Right and Wrong: Moral Education in the Balance* (Stoke on Trent: Trentham Books, 1997). Most recently, an exercise has been conducted by the Qualifications and Curriculum Authority to determine the overall aims of the school curriculum for the new millennium. This exercise, which has involved the participation of philosophers (see R. Aldrich and J. White, *The National Curriculum Beyond 2000: The QCA and the aims of education* (London, Institute of Education: University of London, 1998)) has yielded for the first time a set of published aims for the National Curriculum (Department for Education and Employment and Qualifications and Curriculum Authority, (1999), 195–7). For concerns about the adequacy of the statement of aims and the extent to which the aims are being brought to bear on the curriculum itself see S. Bramall and J. White, *Will the New National Curriculum Live up to its Aims?* (Impact No. 6, Philosophy of Education Society of Great Britain, 2000).

[18] For recent developments in relation to these matters, see Qualifications and Curriculum Authority, *Education for Citizenship and the Teaching of Democracy in Schools: Final Report of the Advisory Group on Citizenship* (London: QCA, 1998), sect. 10; and Qualifications and Curriculum Authority, *Citizenship at Key Stages 3 and 4: Initial Guidance for Schools* (London: QCA, 2000), Appendix 2. For a philosophical appraisal of recent policy developments relating to citizenship education in England, see T. H. McLaughlin, 'Citizenship Education in England: The Crick Report and Beyond', *Journal of Philosophy of Education*, 34(4) (2000), 541–70.

[19] Levinson, *The Demands of Liberal Education*, 109, see also ch. 4; and Brighouse, *School Choice and Social Justice*, ch. 8.

unproblematically used in either the United States or in England and Wales, although it has a long history in the United States. The 'common school' is exemplified in broad terms in the United States by the 'public school' and in England and Wales by the 'non-voluntary' school in the 'maintained' or publicly funded schooling sector (*viz*: a school which does not have a religious sponsor). The use of the term 'common school' in the present discussion is intended to focus attention upon certain matters of broad principle relating to schooling rather than the details of particular institutional arrangements.

Fourth, the notion of a 'conception of common education', and therefore of the precise role and mandate of the 'common school' within pluralist, multicultural, liberal democratic societies, is the subject of continuing debate and dispute at the theoretical and practical level. Some of these debates and disputes will emerge in the discussion of the burdens and dilemmas of common schools which emerge in this chapter.

2. Common Conceptions of Education: Some General Principles

In approaching the specific burdens and dilemmas faced by common schools in pluralist, multicultural, liberal democratic societies, it is helpful to begin with an outline of the basic framework of principle and value typically employed in the articulation of conceptions of common education for such societies. This basic framework can then be elaborated and sophisticated to enable the burdens and dilemmas to emerge.

A good starting point in the articulation of this framework is the report of the Swann Committee of Inquiry into the Education of Children from Ethnic Minority Groups.[20] The report captures well a number of the central features of such frameworks, including the centrality of a judicious balance of unifying and diversifying imperatives and forces. In the report, a pluralist democratic society is characterized as one which '… values the diversity within it, whilst united by the cohesive force of the common aims, attributes and values which we all share'[21] and which therefore seeks to achieve a balance between '… on the one hand, the maintenance and active

[20] 'Swann Report', Great Britain Parliament House of Commons. *Education for All*, The Report of the Committee of Inquiry into the Education of Children from Ethnic Minority Groups, cmnd 9453 (London: Her Majesty's Stationery Office, 1985).

[21] Ibid., ch. 1, para 6.

support of the essential elements of the cultures and lifestyles of all the ethnic groups within it, and, on the other, the acceptance by all groups of a set of shared values distinctive of the society as a whole.'[22] The vision of the report is therefore one of a society stressing 'diversity within unity',[23] in which a stark dichotomy between assimilation and separatism with respect to minority groups is avoided.[24]

With regard to unifying elements, the report insists that, in a genuinely pluralist society, there must be a '... framework of commonly accepted values, practices and procedures ...'[25] which embodies a common political and legal system and fundamental democratic commitments, such as those relating to freedom and to justice and equality.[26] The framework also acts as a limitation upon the scope of diversity within society. Thus all members of society have an obligation '... to abide by the current laws of the country and to seek to change them only through peaceful and democratic means',[27] and whilst the majority community within a pluralist society cannot be untouched by the presence of minority groups, those minority groups '... cannot in practice preserve all elements of their cultures and lifestyles unchanged and in their entirety ... if they were to wish to do so it would in many cases be impossible for them then to take on the shared values of the wider pluralist society.'[28]

With regard to diversifying elements, the report urges that ethnic minority groups should be allowed and encouraged to maintain their distinct identities within this common framework. They must be free '... within the democratic framework to maintain those elements which they themselves consider to be the most essential to their sense of ethnic identity — whether these take the form of adherence to a particular religious faith or the maintenance of their own

[22] Ibid., ch. 1, para 4.

[23] Ibid., ch. 1, para 6.

[24] Ibid., ch. 1, para 3.

[25] Ibid., ch. 1, para 4.

[26] Ibid., ch. 1, para 2. Thus the framework is seen as generating an obligation for government to ensure '... equal treatment and protection by the law for members of all groups, together with equality of access to education and employment, equal freedom and opportunity to participate fully in social and political life ... equal freedom of cultural expression and equal freedom of conscience for all' (Ibid., ch. 1, para 4).

[27] Ibid.

[28] Ibid.

language for use within the home and their ethnic community — without fear of prejudice or persecution by other groups.'[29] Although the Swann Report is concerned with ethnic diversity, many of its basic principles are relevant also to a number of other aspects of significant diversity.

The educational conclusions which the Swann Report draws capture several of the central elements of the framework of thought relevant to common conceptions of education. The report argues that all children must be educated to '... an understanding of the shared values of our society as a whole as well as to an appreciation of the diversity of lifestyles and cultural, religious, and linguistic backgrounds which make up this society and the wider world.'[30] The insistence of the report that all pupils must be given the 'knowledge and skills' needed not only to contribute to British society but also '... to determine their own individual identities, free from preconceived or imposed stereotypes of their "place" in that society'[31] reflects the centrality to common conceptions of education of the autonomy of the child. Thus the report regards as 'entirely wrong' any attempt to '... impose a predetermined and rigid "cultural identity" on any youngster, thus restricting his or her freedom to decide as far as possible for themselves their own future way of life'.[32]

As I have remarked elsewhere,[33] such a general conception of education involves the exertion of a complex twofold educational influence. On the one hand, education seeks to bring about the commitment of pupils to the shared, or common, values of the society. In the Swann Report, the autonomy of the child is seen as in an important sense non-negotiable, as are the sorts of qualities and dispositions to be developed in all pupils, including flexibility of mind, an ability to engage in 'rational critical' analysis, a global perspective, a willingness to find '... the normality and justice of a variety of points of view' non-threatening and stimulating, and the skills to

[29] Ibid.

[30] Ibid. The report therefore insists that a good education '... must reflect the diversity of British society and ... the contemporary world' (Ibid., ch. 6, para 2.1); and the curriculum for all pupils must be '... permeated by a genuinely pluralist perspective which should inform and influence both the selection of content and the teaching materials used' (Ibid. ch. 6, para 3.1).

[31] Ibid., ch. 6, para 1.4.

[32] Ibid., ch. 6, para 2.5.

[33] T. H. McLaughlin, 'Liberalism, Education and the Common School.'

resolve conflicts positively and constructively.[34] Similarly non-negotiable is the 'genuinely pluralist perspective' that should characterize the content and teaching materials of the curriculum and be brought to bear on 'the hidden curriculum'[35] and the need for an appropriate form of political education.[36] Racism is presented as wrong and all schools are invited to combat it.[37] Such elements of non-negotiability underlie the insistence of the report that all pupils should '... share a common educational experience which prepares them for life in a truly pluralist society.'[38] This leads to a strong emphasis on the value of the common school, and the majority view of the report expresses an opposition to the establishment of separate schools of a religious, or other, kind by ethnic minority groups within the publicly supported school system.[39]

On the other hand, with regard to values which are not shared or common (e.g. those relating to a particular religious faith) the report insists that the common school has no role in bringing about substantive commitments in pupils, as distinct from the development of understanding and critical reflection. With regard to religion, for example, the report holds that it is not the role of the school to encourage in pupils belief in a particular religion: 'It is ... the function of the home and of the religious community to nurture and instruct a child in a particular faith (or not), and the function of the school to assist pupils to understand the nature of religion and to know something of the diversity of belief systems, their significance for individuals and how these bear on the community.'[40] Pupils must therefore be enabled, through an approach to religious education which seeks to illuminate the character of the religious domain rather than to engage in religious nurture, to '... determine (and justify) their own religious position.'[41] This leads the report to call into question the legal requirement that all schools in England and Wales (including common schools) provide an act of collective worship

[34] Swann, ch. 6, para 2.7.

[35] Ibid., ch. 6, para 3; chs 7 and 8.

[36] Ibid., ch. 6 paras 3.7-3.12.

[37] Ibid., ch. 2; ch. 6, para 2.3.

[38] Ibid., ch. 8, II, para 2.11.

[39] Ibid., ch. 8, II. It should be noted that the report allows for separate schools on grounds of gender. On this, see Ibid., chs 8, 11, para 2.15. For the minority-report on separate schools, see Ibid., 515.

[40] Ibid., ch. 8,1, para 2.8.

[41] Ibid., ch. 8, I, para 2.11.

which is broadly Christian in character,[42] and (with the exception of the minority report) to express the attitude to separate religious schools within the publicly supported system which was reported earlier.[43] This general framework of principle and value relating to a pluralist, multicultural, liberal democratic society and the form of common conception of education which is typically related to it is a familiar one in broad outline, as is the range of philosophical assumptions on which such frameworks typically rest. Frameworks such as these are far from being unproblematic, and are open to a number of significant and searching lines of enquiry and criticism. For example, the Swann Report does not address tensions between the unifying and diversifying elements of the framework arising from fundamental or deep-seated conflicts. Further, central features of the report, such as its commitment to the autonomy of the child, clearly invite more extended interpretation and defence. Whilst it is unreasonable to expect a report such as this to engage in such reflection and argumentation, the need for such an engagement in a fuller account of the matters at stake is manifest. Some of lines of enquiry and criticism addressed to general frameworks of the sort articulated in the Swann Report touch upon the fundamental justification of the framework itself. For example, Alasdair MacIntyre claims that, since there exists in liberal societies a number of rival and incompatible accounts of the virtues none of which can establish its superiority by criteria of rational argument which are generally shared and agreed, there can be no shared programme for moral education which is rationally defensible, but only a range of rival and conflicting programmes based on specific standpoints.[44] The present discussion does not pursue these more fundamental challenges to general frameworks such as those developed in the Swann Report and concentrates attention upon the burdens and dilemmas of common schooling which arise within their parameters. These burdens and dilemmas come into clearer focus in exploring in more detail how central elements of such a framework can be variously interpreted.[45]

---

[42] Ibid., ch. 8, I, para 5.3.

[43] Ibid., ch. 8, II.

[44] A. Macintyre, 'How to Seem Virtuous Without Actually Being So' in J. M. Halstead and T. H. McLaughlin (eds), *Education in Morality* (London: Routledge, 1999).

[45] The conclusions of the Swann Report did not have a decisive impact on educational policy and practice in England and Wales. For a recent report, see

3. Conceptions of Common Education and the Common School: Light and Heavy Burdens

The burdens of a conception of common education on the common school can be located on a continuum of 'lightness' to 'heaviness' according to the precise interpretation which is offered of, and emphasis placed upon, central elements in the conception, relating to both its unifying, common, or public aspects and its diversifying, non-common, or non-public aspects. Questions relating to the unifying, common, or public aspects involve issues concerning the nature, status, and grounding of the public values, such as the form and scope of the sort of personal autonomy which is proposed for development and the kind of democratic citizenship which is being aimed at. Questions relating to the diversifying, non-common, or non-public aspects involve issues relating to the nature and extent of the diversity which should be valued, the sense(s) in which it should be valued, and the general question of the role which the common school is invited to play in the 'non-public' domain. The respects in which all these questions are related to underlying philosophical positions such as 'ethical' or 'comprehensive' liberalism on the one hand and 'political' liberalism on the other can be readily discerned.[46]

To put matters roughly, 'light' burdens arise for the common school from conceptions of common education which embody *inter alia* an uncomplicated view of public values and the public domain generally (e.g. one which invokes uncontroversial de facto consensus as a basis for common moral influence), a restricted view of the form and scope of personal autonomy and of democratic citizenship, an uncomplicated view of the nature of diversity and its implications, and a reluctance to extend its educative ambitions into the non-public domain. 'Heavy' burdens arise for the common school from conceptions of common education which embody *inter alia* an account of public values and the public domain which is articulated in terms of (often complex) matters of principle which need to be understood by students, an expansive view of the form and scope of personal autonomy and of democratic citizenship, a view of diversity and its implications which is sensitive to complexity and sub-

Commission On The Future Of Multi-Ethnic Britain, *The Future of Multi-Ethnic Britain* (The Parekh Report, London: Profile Books, 2000).

[46] On such matters see, for example, Callan (1997), ch. 2; A. Gutmann, 'Civic Education and Social Diversity', *Ethics*, 105 (1995), 557–79.

tlety, and an ambition to engage educationally in a significant way with the 'non-public' domain.

At the 'light' end of this continuum, therefore, are conceptions of common education of the sort which Eamonn Callan describes as 'minimalist' because the character of the education is determined merely by a contingent 'lowest common denominator' consensus in society about what all children should learn (e.g. basic literacy, respect for law and order, and the educational prerequisites of economic productivity and competitiveness).[47] Such conceptions generate 'light' burdens for the common school because the disagreements characteristic of pluralist, multicultural, and liberal democratic societies are simply evaded: any personal autonomy aimed at is restrictively conceived, any education for citizenship attempted is seen in minimal terms as little more than low-level civic socialization;[48] and the 'non-public' domain is seen as off-limits.[49] Also at the 'light' end of this continuum is William Galston's well known view of civic education.[50] Galston sees civic education as primarily concerned with supporting and strengthening a particular political community and not with truth seeking and rational enquiry, which are, in Galston's view, in tension with the development of citizens who will embrace the core commitments of a liberal society. Civic education requires a pedagogy which is 'rhetorical' and 'moralizing' rather than rational.[51] Further, Galston insists that civic educational requirements do not extend to an interest in how children think about different ways of life.[52] In Galston's view public education may not '… foster in children skeptical reflection on ways of life inherited from parents or local communities'[53] because promoting a Socratic ideal of self-examination in the public education system of a liberal state both goes beyond what is functionally necessary for its sociopolitical institutions and conflicts with the liberal

[47] Callan, *Creating Citizens*, 169-71.

[48] T. H. McLaughlin, 'Citizenship, Diversity and Education: A Philosophical Perspective', *Journal of Moral Education*, 21(3) (1992), 235–50.

[49] For criticisms of such conceptions, see Callan, *Creating Citizens*, 171–4.

[50] W. A. Galston, Liberal Purposes: Goods, Virtues, and Diversity in the Liberal State (Cambridge: University Press, 1991), ch. 11.

[51] Ibid., 242–4.

[52] Ibid., 251–5.

[53] Ibid., 253. For criticism of Galston's claim that children will become autonomous through other influences see Callan, *Creating Citizens*, 133.

freedom to lead an unexamined life.[54] Galston's view imposes 'light' burdens on the common school because the school has little work to do in achieving a critical and principled understanding of the public domain on the part of students or an engagement by students in a fair and balanced way with issues in the non-public domain.

Also at the end of the continuum which involves 'light' burdens for the common school are conceptions of common education which seek to promote in an unequivocal way *via* education a form of 'ethical' or 'comprehensive' liberalism as a view of the moral life as a whole. In such views, there is no recognition of the significance and demands of normative diversity and the non-public domain;[55] Macedo, in accusing Dewey of a kind of 'civic totalism', sees him as advancing a kind of view of education of this kind.[56] Such conceptions impose relatively 'light' burdens upon common schools because of the straightforward value influence they propose. There is little work for the school to do in, for example, the area of the interface between the 'public' and the 'non-public' and in relation to complexities relating to the latter.

Conceptions of common education which impose 'heavier' burdens on common schools specify the achievement by students of independent critical reflection and judgment (if not a full blown notion of personal autonomy) which is sensitive to, and engaged with, matters of diversity and difference. Conceptions of this general kind vary somewhat in their detailed formulation. To sketch matters roughly, Gurmann and Callan see the demands of civic virtue as requiring a form of autonomous deliberation about matters relating to the common good which include the capacity to evaluate values, commitments, and ways of life. Once developed, however, this capacity cannot be confined to the political realm and its development leads to a form of autonomy which is exercised across wider

[54] For criticisms of Galston see, for example, Callan, *Creating Citizens*, ch. 5; Spinner-Halev, *Surviving Diversity*, 103–4; Brighouse, *School Choice and Social Justice*, ch. 5; Gutmann, 'Civic Education and Social Diversity.' For a defense of Galston's version of democratic liberalism, but a claim that he seriously underestimates the incompatibility of 'deep' diversity with public schooling, see Schrag, 'Diversity and Schooling ...'

[55] Callan describes an education derived from any form of comprehensive liberalism as '... wide in scope, transforming the selves of future citizens in ways that push beyond the sphere of political obligation as they learn to live according to the prescribed comprehensive values ... (and requiring) ... a pedagogy pitted against all sources of diversity at odds with those values' (*Creating Citizens*, 16).

[56] Macedo, Diversity and Distrust, 139–45.

aspects of the life of the person, including those which fall into the 'non-public' domain.[57] Callan's view, for example, embodies a substantial account of the nature and demands of the attitudes, habits, and abilities required by public virtue.[58] In particular, Callan sees 'public virtue' as requiring the development by students of Rawlsian 'reasonableness' involving acceptance of the Rawlsian 'burdens of judgment' (the sources of ineliminable rational disagreement)[59] thereby leading to the development of a grasp of the scope of reasonable diversity and the grounds of freedom of conscience and reasonable toleration. Callan therefore concludes that '... the development of the virtue of justice under pluralism implies the growth of autonomy to a notably sophisticated level.'[60] Callan resists Galston's claim that civic tolerance of deep differences and civic deliberation are compatible with unswerving and unshakable beliefs and commitments relating to one's own way of life[61] and insists that a proper understanding of the Rawlsian 'burdens of judgment' requires them to be actively rather than passively embraced by students and brought to bear by them on matters which extend beyond the political realm to wider conceptions of the good.

In this way, Rawls's attempt to restrict the intentional scope of education to political matters in the light of a 'political' and not an 'ethical' conception of liberalism comes to grief.[62] For Callan, a proper embrace of the 'burdens of judgment', together with the development of other aspects of 'civic virtue', brings a form of ethical liberalism and wide ranging Rawlsian 'reasonableness' in 'through the back door', together with educational influence that, contra Rawls, cannot be confined to the political domain and leave

[57] Gutmann, Democratic Education; Callan, Creating Citizens.

[58] Of these attitudes, habits, and abilities, Callan writes: 'These include a lively interest in the question of what life is truly and not just seemingly good, as well as a willingness both to share one's own answer with others and to heed the many opposing answers they might give; an active commitment to the good of the polity, as well as confidence and competence in judgment regarding how that good should be advanced; a respect for fellow citizens and a sense of common fate with them that goes beyond the tribalisms of ethnicity and religion and is yet alive to the significance these will have in many people's lives' (*Creating Citizens*, 3).

[59] J. Rawls, *Political Liberalism* (New York: Columbia University Press, 1993), 54–8.

[60] Callan, *Creating Citizens*, 68. For a discussion of the scope of the justification of autonomy required by Callan's overall thesis, see chs. 3 and 6.

[61] Galston, *Liberal Purposes*, 253. See especially Callan, *Creating Citizens*, ch. 5.

[62] Gutmann calls into question whether political liberalism is more hospitable to social diversity via civic education than comprehensive liberalism. See Gutmann, 'Civic Education and Social Diversity.'

'non-public' commitments undisturbed.[63] Thus Callan sees education as requiring a sympathetic, critical, and serious engagement
with beliefs, ways of life, and conceptions of the good which are different from, and at odds with, those which the child has inherited
from his or her parents and background culture.[64] For Callan, therefore, '… the education we should want for our children would transform the character of the self in ways that have large consequences
for how they will live beyond the realm of civic responsibility …'[65] It
is important to note, however, that Callan is careful not to characterize his position as advocating a full blown form of autonomy or 'Socratic self-examination', but merely the kind of autonomy necessary
to avoid a state he describes as 'ethical servility.'[66]

Kymlicka holds that autonomy in the sense of a capacity to engage
in rational reflection upon, and possible revision of, our conceptions
of the good life is not in itself one of the basic virtues of liberal citizenship, although it is closely related conceptually and develop-
ment-ally to various civic virtues. However, although autonomy in
this sense is not a direct aim of education for citizenship, it will nevertheless be indirectly promoted by it.[67]

Macedo, although making clear that his account of civic education
is based on a form of 'political liberalism',[68] places great emphasis

---

[63] Callan. *Creating Citizens*, ch. 2.

[64] Callan, *Creating Citizens*, 133. Callan writes, '…the relevant engagement must be
such that the beliefs and values by which others live are entertained not merely as
sources of meaning in their lives; they are instead addressed as potential elements
within the conceptions of the good and the right one will create for oneself as an
adult… to understand ethical diversity in the educationally relevant sense
presupposes some experience of entering imaginatively into ways of life that are
strange, even repugnant, and some developed ability to respond to them with
interpretive charity, even though the sympathy this involves must complement
the tough-mindedness of responsible criticism' (Callan, *Creating Citizens*, 133).
For criticism of Callan's 'moral psychology', see Spinner-Halev, *Surviving
Diversity*, 99–102, 132–3.

[65] Callan, Creating Citizens, 51.

[66] Ibid., ch. 6.

[67] W. Kymlicka, 'Education for Citizenship', in J. M. Halstead and T. H. McLaughlin
(eds), *Education in Morality* (London: Routledge, 1999), 90–3. Here Kymlicka holds
that the promotion of autonomy may be justifiable as part of a person's broader
well-being and education.

[68] Macedo, *Diversity and Distrust*, chs 7 and 9. On forms of political liberalism see, for
example, Ibid., chs 7–9; J. Tomasi, *Liberalism Beyond Justice: Citizens, Society and the
Boundaries of Political Theory* (Princeton and Oxford: Princeton University Press,
2001), ch. 1; Callan, *Creating Citizens*, ch. 2. On the notion of 'reasonable

upon its wide-ranging transformative implications. For Macedo, an excessive deference towards diversity and the 'non-public' domain is unwarranted by liberalism properly understood[69] and by the need to shape diversity in support of the demands of liberal citizenship and a shared public life.[70] According to Macedo, this process requires '... a certain ordering of the soul'[71] and a shaping of our deepest moral commitments so that they are supportive of liberalism.[72] However, this is governed by a restraint which respects the non-public domain and a commitment to a form of autonomy.[73] Similarly, Feinberg insists that the common school is '... an instrument of individual and cultural change ... [which] ... alters the way people think, changes basic moral understandings, and alters commitments and loyalties'[74] yet within a framework of restraint similar to that invoked by Macedo. The complexities of the burdens on the common school arising from positions such as these are illustrated by Macedo's observation that 'Public schools intervene in the most private of relationships, for the most sensitive of purposes'[75] and Feinberg's recognition that the common school is seeking to bring about a standpoint which is '... neither natural nor easy to learn.'[76]

Further along the continuum of burdens for the common school in the direction of 'heaviness' are various views which assign to the common school a significant role in relation to the non-public domain. Jeff Spinner-Halev claims that common schools should become involved in various forms of cooperation with religious schools and homeschoolers and should include, in a fair way in its curriculum and life, religious students and religious perspectives,

disagreement', see, for example, A. Gutmann and D. Thompson, *Democracy and Disagreement* (Cambridge: Harvard University Press, 1996). ch. 1.

[69] Macedo rejects a conception of liberalism as '... a kind of anemic non-judgmentalism, a position that is morally uninspired and uninspiring, incapable of pressing even its own core values in the face of disagreement' (*Diversity and Distrust*, 8).

[70] Ibid., e.g. chs 1 and 9.

[71] Ibid., 30.

[72] Ibid., 164.

[73] Ibid., 236–40. On the relationship between the positions of Macedo and Callan on matters such as the Rawlsian 'burdens of judgment', see S. Macedo, 'Liberal Civic Education and its Limits: A Comment on Eamonn Callan', *Canadian Journal of Education*, 20(3) (1995).

[74] Feinberg, Common Schools/Uncommon Identities, 56–7.

[75] Macedo, Diversity and Distrust, 145.

[76] Feinberg, Common Schools/Uncommon Identities, 239.

trying to accommodate where possible the special needs of religious students.[77] Spinner-Halev accepts that, in general, good citizens should be autonomous in a robust fashion[78] and that common schools should, in general, encourage the virtues of autonomy and liberal autonomy and facilitate appropriate engagement with diversity of ideas.[79] However, Spinner-Halev provides a defence of the legitimacy of, and the need to secure the conditions for choosing, a conservative religious life in a 'community of obedience' within the principles of liberal citizenship and the context of a diverse autonomy-supporting mainstream society. Two claims are central to Spinner-Halev's argument here. The first is that: 'Liberalism aims to enable the life of individuality, but it does not insist that people choose this life. The religious conservative may lead a life of minimal autonomy, a life guided by one main choice. But this life is safely within the confines of liberalism, as long as this life is chosen, people are given a decent education, and are not coerced. Liberalism demands that people choose the sort of life they want to lead, not that they live lives couched in constant choices.'[80] The second claim is that each condition for autonomy (appropriate mental abilities, an adequate range of options, and independence)[81] should not necessarily apply to every community within a liberal society.[82] Spinner-Halev draws attention to the fact that, despite appearances to the contrary, the religious conservative in a liberal society is more likely to be autonomous in significant ways than many people in the mainstream of the society who lead unreflective lives, and that restrictive communities can aid autonomy.[83] Spinner-Halev's proposals relating to the common school are designed to entice religiously conservative parents to send their children to such schools as part of a

[77] Spinner-Halev, *Surviving Diversity*, 110.

[78] On Spinner-Halev's discussion of citizenship in relation to his overall theory, see Spinner-Halev, *Surviving Diversity*, ch. 4.

[79] Ibid., 112-14. Despite his defense of religiously affiliated schools, Spinner-Halev argues that the liberal state should try to 'entice' parents to send their children to common schools by encouraging cooperation between public and private schools (p. 125).

[80] Ibid., 54.

[81] On these conditions, see Ibid., 32.

[82] For Spinner-Halev's arguments relating to the inadequacy of liberal theory with respect to the recognition of points such as these, see Ibid., esp chs 2 and 3.

[83] On the elements of autonomy involved in living a conservative religious life in liberal societies and the respects in which restrictive communities can aid autonomy, see Ibid., chs 2 and 3, respectively.

pragmatic and flexible attitude of inclusion and the maximization of goods. The forms of cooperation which are envisaged, including allowing students from religious affiliated schools in common schools for some part of their curriculum and life,[84] encouraging the teaching of religion in the curriculum of the common school,[85] and providing for the accommodation in different ways of religious views and perspectives within the common school,[86] give rise to a range of potentially complex questions and resultant burdens.

Heavy burdens arise for the common school from Kenneth Strike's argument that the demands of the 'non-public' require greater recognition and salience in the common school than they receive in much contemporary discussion.[87] Strike points to several neglected aspects of 'non-public' educational interests, including the significance of reasonable and coherent comprehensive (or partially comprehensive) theories of the good in the Rawlsian sense as resources for the practical reasoning of students in relation to good lives, together with difficulties in seeing such comprehensive theories as apt for presentation merely as objects of choice for students. To enable students to understand such theories and to achieve 'competence' in them, claims Strike, it is necessary for the common school to acknowledge the significance of initiation and of 'conversational fora' insulated to some extent (and, no doubt, pro tem) from criticism from other, rival, comprehensive doctrines.[88]

The sorts of concerns addressed by Strike are taken up in an extended way by John Tomasi, whose conception of the role of the common school specifies particularly heavy burdens for it.[89] Tomasi claims that civic education should be as much about the 'ethical situatedness' of students as about their political liberation[90] and should attend to the fit between the public and the non-public views which students affirm. This includes not merely discerning how the students own non-public views support public views, but also how

[84]   Ibid., 125–8.

[85]   Ibid., 128–35.

[86]   Ibid., 135–41.

[87]   Strike, 'Liberalism, Citizenship and the Private Interest in Schooling.'

[88]   For a discussion of Strike's arguments relating to these matters, see T. H. McLaughlin, 'Kenneth Strike on 'Liberalism, Citizenship and the Private Interest in Schooling',' *Studies in Philosophy and Education*, 17(4) (1998), 231–41.

[89]   Tomasi, Liberalism Beyond Justice.

[90]   Ibid., 95.

the public norms support their non-public views.[91] For Tomasi, civic education for political liberals '… must address issues that lie deep in the moral worlds of individual citizens.'[92] This view stands in stark contrast to a view such as that of Feinberg, who argues that, if as a result of their education children develop a more questioning attitude, then '… the school has done its job regardless of the accommodations the student makes to her familiar environment.'[93]

Lying behind Tomasi's educational claims is his view that political liberalism should pay more attention to the non-public virtues and personality traits which should characterize citizens in a liberal society and which are not related solely to questions of justice and legitimacy. For Tomasi, '… the normative domain of liberal theory construction is importantly wider than the domain of public, deliberative value'[94] in the context of a liberal polity based on political liberalism which is as welcoming as possible to '… the aims and self-understandings of all politically reasonable citizens.'[95] Tomasi argues that attention needs to be paid to the ways in which citizens construct their lives as a whole in such a society as part of placing issues of human flourishing and well-being at the heart of citizenship.[96]

For Tomasi, citizenship requires the skilful exercise of non-public reason by diverse good souls[97] as part of making a success of a life '… lived on the interface of public and personal identity components',[98] and he therefore sees ethical development in a liberal society as requiring the finding by persons of personal meaning in life across this interface.[99] This is turn requires citizens to deploy 'compass' concepts which are 'thick' and 'identity dependent' and which provide a set of bearings in the background culture of a society enabling citizens to discover what their political autonomy means for them in

[91]   Ibid., 86.

[92]   Ibid., 88.

[93]   Feinberg, Common Schools/Uncommon Identities, 241.

[94]   Ibid., xvi.

[95]   Ibid., 74.

[96]   Tomasi refers to the nature of the person postulated by political liberalism as 'hybridized' in virtue of the presence of differentiated public and non-public normative components (*Liberalism Beyond Justice*, 36).

[97]   Ibid., 71.

[98]   Ibid., 75.

[99]   Ibid., 84.

the light of their fuller conception of their good, and which guide them in the way in which they should exercise their rights. [100]

Tomasi therefore specifies a range of virtues of the liberal citizen which relate to the interface between the public and the non-public domains, and which concern such matters as the ability to achieve an appropriate equipoise between one's political standing and the fuller commitments characteristic of one's fuller non-public life. What this requires of citizens of different kinds varies. Citizens who are religious believers, for example, require dispositions to enable them to resist the commercial and secular nature of modern society.[101] In giving a role for common schools in the development of non-public virtues of this kind, a range of significant consequent burdens come readily into focus.

A range of other burdens arise for common schools from other sources, most notably concerns about the conditions required for the provision of equality of opportunity in its different aspects.[102] Space precludes a consideration of these further burdens at this point. It is time now to turn to a consideration of a range of the dilemmas arising from the burdens which have been identified.

4. Conceptions of Common Education and the Common School: Burdens and Dilemmas

The range of burdens which have been identified in relation to the common school generate a range of corresponding dilemmas. 'Dilemmas' rather than (say) 'problems' best captures the intractability of what is at stake here and the lack of availability of clear unambiguous solutions. The need for common schools to achieve the trust and support of diverse citizens sharpens the force of the dilemmas which such schools face and the need to discover at least 'best possible' resolutions of them.

The dilemmas are felt at a number of levels. At the theoretical level, they pose the sort of quandaries which philosophers of education (and educational theorists more generally) puzzle over and try to clarify and resolve. Educational policy makers are also confronted by some of the dilemmas in that they have implications for such matters as the structure of the educational system and the determination of policy on many relevant matters. However, many of the dilemmas

[100] Ibid., ch. 3.

[101] Ibid., 77.

[102] On the notion of equality in relation to education see, for example, Brighouse, *School Choice and Social Justice*, ch. 61.

are constituted by fine-grained subtleties which require a practical response at the level of the school and classroom by educational leaders and teachers via the exercise of a form of pedagogic *phronesis*. For example, issues relating to the achievement by students of a proper understanding of the nature and scope of such notions as 'respect' and 'toleration,' and to the fair and balanced conduct of controversial issues, can only be dealt with in detail at this level. The practical aspect to these dilemmas will be considered in due course.

In what follows I identify a range of dilemmas arising for common schools from the kinds of burdens identified in Section 3. For convenience, the discussion is divided into matters relating to the public domain, the non-public domain, and the interface between the two, although clearly this categorization is somewhat artificial.

Before proceeding, it should be noted that these burdens and dilemmas arise not only in relation to *what* is taught, but also to the *way* in which it is taught, to *whom* it is being taught, and the general context in which it is being taught. This general point reinforces the significance of the sort of pedagogic *phronesis* to which attention has been drawn.

Burdens and dilemmas relating to the public domain

Common schools based on a rationale which goes beyond the minimalistic yet which does not stipulate unequivocal value influence based on a form of ethical or comprehensive liberalism, bear the burden of ensuring that their students are not merely socialized into the public values but achieve a critical understanding of their nature and scope. As I have argued elsewhere,[103] students in such schools must achieve a grasp of the salience and importance of public values for political purposes, but also come to appreciate the limitations of these values with respect to overall moral evaluation and to life considered more broadly. Such an awareness is implicit in the achievement of the sort of 'moral bilingualism'[104] on the part of students which is often seen as a major aim of the common school, and which involves an appreciation by students that the language of public evaluation is a kind of 'moral pidgin.'[105] One of the major implications of this point is that, whilst accepting that public values have

[103] McLaughlin, 'Liberalism, Education and the Common School', 248–50.

[104] K. A. Strike, 'Ethical Discourse and Pluralism' in K. A. Strike and P. Lance Ternasky (eds), *Ethics for Professionals in Education: Perspectives for Preparation and Practice* (New York: Teachers College Press, 1993).

[105] Strike, 'On the Construction of Public Speech', 19.

potentially transformative implications of the sort which Gutmann, Callan, Macedo, and Feinberg identify, and which cannot therefore leave values in the 'non-public' domain just as they are, the common school must not underplay the role which reasonable moral views in the non-public domain play in overall moral evaluation and in human life more generally. Moral debate in the common school should not therefore be confined to public values and to the exclusive adoption of what Thompson and Gutmann call 'moral economizing.'[106] The common school should not promote a liberal view of life as a whole, nor a secular one.[107] David Archard's privileging of a liberal choice and consent based sexual morality as a basis for sex education in the common school seems to be problematic on precisely these grounds.[108] Nor should deep seated moral disagreement be smoothed away by (say) presenting homosexual practice as morally acceptable by invoking only public values as criteria for judgment and excluding, or failing to bring to bear adequately, reasonable non-public perspectives on the matters at stake.[109] Tomasi's insistence that political liberals must be concerned '... about ways of gently protecting diversity from the pursuit of legitimate public ends'[110] seems justified here, as does his concern that '... by teaching children the detached, rights-based forms of thinking central to public reason, liberal civic education unintentionally encourages those forms of thinking in all domains of reason, including ones where such ways of thinking are transformative beyond

[106] Spinner-Halev, *Surviving Diversity*, 155.

[107] For concerns about common schools along these lines see, for example, Thiessen, *Teaching for Commitment*, ch. 13.

[108] D. Archard, 'How Should We Teach Sex?' *Journal of Philosophy of Education*, 32(3) (1998), 437–49. D. Archard, *Sex Education. Impact* No 7 (Philosophy of Education Society of Great Britain, 2000); cf. T. H. McLaughlin, 'The Moral Basis of Sex Education: Principles and Controversies.' *Sex Education* (forthcoming).

[109] On this matter see, for example, P. White, 'Parents' Rights, Homosexuality and Education', *British Journal of Educational Studies*, 39(4) (1991), 398–408. McLaughlin, 'Liberalism, Education and the Common School.' 248-50; Callan, 'Discrimination and Religious Schooling.' 58–63; J. M. Halstead and K. Lewicka 'Should Homosexuality be Taught as an Acceptable Alternative Lifestyle? A Muslim Perspective', *Cambridge Journal of Education*, 28(1) (1998)', 49–64. J. Beck, 'Should Homosexuality be Taught as an Acceptable Alternative Lifestyle? A Muslim Perspective: A Reply to Halstead and Lewicka', *Cambridge Journal of Education*, 29(1) (1999), 121-30. J. M. Halstead, 'Teaching about Homosexuality: A Response to John Beck', *Cambridge Journal of Education*, 29(1) (1999), 131–6.

[110] Tomasi, Liberalism Beyond Justice, 107.

what the bare attainment of political autonomy requires.'[111] Whilst
common schools cannot aspire to influence which is wholly neutral
across all aspects of diversity, or which is completely fair to every
viewpoint,[112] Tomasi may have a point in arguing that because of
unavoidable 'unintended spillovers' within the classroom, lessons
about public value must include an 'internal corrective.'[113]

A number of burdens arise in relation to achieving for students a
proper understanding of notions in the public domain, such as 'respect.' The common school must encourage 'civic respect' for reasonable differences of view which goes beyond a grudging attitude
of 'live and let live.' Callan captures something of the deeper, more
principled basis underlying civic respect in his invocation of the
Rawlsian 'burdens of judgment' as part of his account of the nature
of public virtue.[114] However, the common school needs to achieve a
fine-grained understanding of 'respect' on the part of its students.
'Civic' respect does not constitute the only form of respect and students should be made aware that what is worthy of 'civic' respect is
not necessarily worthy of respect considered from all points of view.
Further, care must be taken by the common school not to convey the
impression that giving 'respect' requires the necessary approval of
the choices which people make within the limits of their rights.
Macedo points out that such a requirement would be self-defeating
from a liberal point of view, since an important aspect of liberal freedom is allowing people to disagree about important matters.[115] It
may, however, be difficult to avoid a relativistic implication being
drawn from encouragement to give 'respect.' Spinner-Halev identi-

[111] Ibid., 90.

[112] Macedo, *Diversity and Distrust*, ch. 8. Parekh observes that, in a liberal
environment '... the very awareness of other traditions alerts each to its own
contingency and specificity, and subtly alters the manner in which its members
define and relate to it' (Parekh, *Rethinking Multiculturalism*, 220). For an argument
against the value and possibility of 'world view neutrality' in the common school,
see S. Sandsmark, *Is World View Neutral Education Possible and Desirable? A
Christian Response to Liberal Arguments* (Carlisle: Paternoster Press, 2000).

[113] Ibid., 126.

[114] Callan insists that: 'To give the respect due to ethical viewpoints in deep conflict
with our own, we must learn to enter them imaginatively and to understand that
much of the pluralism that permeates our social world is a consequence not of evil
or folly but of the inherent limits of human reason' (*Creating Citizens*, 43).

[115] Macedo, *Diversity and Distrust*, 223. Feinberg argues that students must learn to
respect members of other groups without necessarily understanding them or
agreeing with what they say (*Common Schools/Uncommon Identities*, 212). See also
chs 5-7.

fies a central problem here when he asks: 'How do we teach mutual respect and appreciation for others while avoiding teaching that each way of life is equally acceptable to the others?'[116] What is required of common schools in these matters is the achievement by students of an understanding of significant aspects of moral texture and complexity.[117]

One dilemma which arises from an attempt to encourage a fine-grained understanding of 'respect' on the part of students is that an attempt to achieve 'civic' respect for (say) a particular lifestyle may be undermined by too much emphasis on critical evaluations of the lifestyle to be found at the non-public level. For example, an attempt to overcome blatant forms of ignorant prejudice against, and hatred of, homosexual people may be undermined by the successful illumination of reasonable non-public perspectives which make a distinction between homosexual orientation and practice and hold that the latter is morally unacceptable.[118] From such perspectives, 'civic respect' for homosexual persons, important though it is, is importantly distinguishable from moral acceptance of homosexual practice. However, some students, especially if they are ignorant and prejudiced in relation to homosexual persons, may not find such distinctions easy to grasp and may see them as lending support

---

[116] Spinner-Halev, *Surviving Diversity*, 133.

[117] On the difficulty that acceptance of liberal political values such as mutual respect might come at the price of an enfeebled acceptance of the fuller ethical values held by citizens, see E. Callan, 'Liberal Virtue and Moral Enfeeblement' in D. Carr and J. Steutel (eds), *Virtue Ethics and Moral Education* (London: Routledge, 1999).

[118] For example, in a recent statement of the late Cardinal Hume on the teaching of the Catholic Church on homosexual people, it is insisted that all persons, including those of homosexual orientation, should be treated with dignity, respect, and fairness, that the oppression and contempt which homosexual people have suffered should be combated by the church, and that homophobia and violence against homosexuals in speech and action should be condemned (B. Hume, 'A Note on the Teaching of the Catholic Church Concerning Homosexual People', *Briefing*, 16 (Mar. 1995), 3–5. paras 12, 14, 15). Further, the statement acknowledges that civil legislation relating to the elimination of injustice against homosexual people requires practical judgment and the assessment of social consequences in relation to which Catholics may reach diverse conclusions (Ibid., para 13). These remarks indicate a form of valuing and respect for homosexuality. However, the value and respect which is accorded to homosexuality is restricted in an important way. Drawing a distinction between homosexual orientation and homosexual acts (Ibid., paras 6, 7), the statement reiterates church teaching on the immorality of the latter. Thus, whilst it is suggested that it might be appropriate to acknowledge legal rights of some kind to engage in homosexual acts, it is insisted that '... there can be no moral right to homosexual acts, even though they are no longer held to be criminal in many secular legal systems' (Ibid., para 5 cf. para 12).

to their ignorant and prejudiced civic attitudes. For example, the notion of 'homophobia' is often invoked in the process of establishing civic respect for homosexual persons. However, an illumination of moral texture and complexity is likely to problematize 'homophobia', especially uses of the term which imply that all moral criticism of homosexual practice is ipso facto homophobic. Gary Colwell, for example, argues that the term 'homophobia' is part of a '... rhetorical tactic that has been used with increasing success to prevent the moral discussion of the Tightness or wrongness of homosexual practice from ever taking place.'[119] It is, in his view, a 'fending-off mechanism'[120] which serves to preempt necessary moral debate in a democracy. Such points, legitimate as they may be within the framework of political liberalism, may provide some comfort to those resisting its civic demands. The dilemma of the relative prioritization of 'public' and 'non-public' perspectives also arises in this particular example in judging the appropriare educational response to students who are themselves homosexual. A similar kind of dilemma arises in other aspects of sex education, where the need to protect health and safety may be in conflict with illumination of the fact that, from some non-public perspectives, many 'safe-sex' practices are immoral.

However, the achievement of 'moral bilingualism', and the fine grained (and potentially conflicting) forms of respect and evaluation which it embodies, is an important consequence of taking seriously the claim that we are confronted by serious value conflicts, as distinct from mere differences of view, in a pluralist multicultural liberal democratic society. The sorts of dilemmas to which attention has been drawn are intensified by a realization of the important point that there is no escaping forms of 'moral distress' in serious dialogue about value diversity.[121] Callan sees such distress as involving '... a cluster of emotions that may attend our response to words or actions of others or our own that we see as morally repellent,'[122] a 'discriminating susceptibility' to which he sees as a fundamental aspect of virtue and of moral education in a pluralist multicultural liberal

[119] G. Colwell, 'Turning the Tables with 'Homophobia'', *Journal of Applied Philosophy*, 16(3) (1999), 207-22.

[120] Ibid.

[121] Callan, *Creating Citizens*, ch. 8.

[122] Ibid., 200.

democratic society. In such a society we encounter strangers as well as friends.[123]

Another aspect of the 'public' dimension of conceptions of common education involves the concept of autonomy. Macedo indicates the cen-trality of the notion of personal autonomy to such conceptions in his observation that the common school and its associated educational ideals is based in part on 'distrust' of particular groups regarding the extent to which they can and will promote auton-omy.[124] A crucial issue, however, is how autonomy is to be properly interpreted.[125] Parekh is right to insist that autonomy '… is difficult to define and impossible to measure or demonstrate'[126] and to draw attention to the role of culture in srructuring in a particular way a person's understanding of, and capacity for, autonomy.[127] Dilemmas arise for the common school in the determination of the nature and extent of the kind of autonomy which should be promoted , and the matters in relation to which autonomy is seen as appropriately exercised.

The complexities inherent in such dilemmas are captured in distinctions such as those between 'autonomy' and 'autarchy,'[128] and between 'autonomy promoting' and 'autonomy facilitating' education.[129] One ingredient in judgements here is the extent to which

---

[123] On the complexity of the ethical difficulties, attitudes, and virtues demanded by liberalism, including the role that certain forms of hypocrisy play in sustaining liberal democratic society, see J. Shklar, *Ordinary Vices* (Cambridge: Belknap Press of Harvard University Press, 1984).

[124] Macedo, Diversity and Distrust, 240.

[125] An indication of Macedo's conception of autonomy is given in his reaction to the case of the Amish with respect to exemption from public education: 'All children should have an education that provides them with the ability to make informed and independent decisions about how they want to lead their lives in our modern world. Liberal freedom to choose is the birthright of every child' (Ibid., 207).

[126] Parekh, Rethinking Multiculturalism, 253.

[127] In criticizing the notion of a 'transcultural' and 'culturally untainted' 'power of autonomy', Parekh notes how culture shapes people in many ways. As a result, he argues, a person's capacity for autonomy '… is structured in a particular way, functions within flexible but determinate limits, and defines and assesses options in certain ways' (Ibid., 110). Parekh charges contemporary liberal responses to diversity with absolutizing liberalism by equating 'non-liberal' with 'illiberal' and by failing to distinguish between a universal and a liberal moral minimum in relation to human values (ch. 3). Whilst supporting diversity, Parekh argues that autonomy needs to be given a more nuanced role in the values of a pluralist society (see esp chs 7 and 10).

[128] McLaughlin, 'The Ethics of Separate Schools', 126–7.

[129] Brighouse, School Choice and Social Justice, chs 4 and 5.

autonomy can be confidently expected to be developed outside the school.[130] The position which the common school takes with respect to these matters can be quite significant for the perceived fairness of the overall value influence which it exerts, and to whether, for example, it is promoting a form of ethical or comprehensive liberalism. It seems important for the common school to encourage reflection about the limits of an examined life.[131]

It is also important for the school to confront dilemmas inherent in the complex unifying and diversifying influence which it seeks to exert. In relation to public matters, the school seeks to achieve a strong substantial influence on the beliefs of students and their wider development as persons, whilst in relation to matters in the 'non-public' domain, the school exerts a principled forbearance from influence. The school therefore faces dilemmas inherent in simultaneously trying to bring about, on the one hand, affirmation, and on the other, hesitation and problematization, in the experience of students.[132]

Further dilemmas arise from the fact that abstract philosophical principles alone cannot provide us with a precise uncontroversial answer to the question of which matters should be regarded as public and which as non-public in a particular liberal democratic society.[133] These matters require complex judgement and perhaps negotiation, with attention to the significance of 'default' norms. There is room for considerable debate about matters of cultural salience in the common school, not least because the common school cannot be culturally neutral and must have a cultural content which selectively favors some beliefs, practices, and values in ways that go beyond what could be justified from a strictly neutral point of view.[134]

---

[130] On this matter see, for example, Schrag, 'Diversity and Schooling in the Liberal State'; Spinner-Halev, *Surviving Diversity*.

[131] Macedo, Diversity and Distrust, 245–53.

[132] Galston notes that one danger which needs to be guarded against is not that children will believe in something too deeply, but that they will believe in nothing very deeply at all (Galston, *Liberal Purposes*, 255). For critical comment on this claim, see Callan, *Creating Citizens*, 133. On the complex kinds of education in character and virtue required in the common school, see T. H. McLaughlin and J. M. Halstead 'Education in Character and Virtue' in J. M. Halstead and T. H. McLaughlin (eds), *Education in Morality* (London: Routledge, 1999).

[133] McLaughlin, 'Liberalism, Education and the Common School.' 245–8.

[134] On these matters, see also Parekh, *Rethinking Multiculturalism*, 257–63. Tomasi notes that school classrooms and the wider school community are 'ethically charged' in ways that '... extend far beyond what is politically relevant or

Another source of dilemmas arise in relation to the requirements of ensuring that common schools are communities in a significant sense.[135] The role of ethos and community is manifested in many of the educational tasks of the common school. With regard to ethos and community, one of the central difficulties concerns the extent to which, given its commitment to a principled forbearance from influence in significant matters, the common school can satisfy the demands of substantiveness and determinancy which are constitutive of the notions of ethos and community.

Burdens and dilemmas relating to the non-public domain

Conceptions of common education vary in the extent to which they require the common school to enter into the non-public domain. 'Liberal silence'[136] with respect to this domain is highly problematic for a range of reasons, as is any attempt to exclude non-public perspectives from a discussion of moral issues.[137]

Acceptance of the burden of fairly illuminating aspects of the non-public domain for the purposes of understanding gives rise to a range of dilemmas. Many of these concern religion.[138] As noted earlier, both Spinner-Halev and Tomasi call for a form of teaching religion in common schools in the United States.[139] Such teaching has been adopted in common schools in England and Wales for many years. The form of education at stake here can be described as 'education in religion and spirituality from the outside.'[140] In this form of education, no one religious or spiritual tradition is given normative status. Issues of meaning, truth, and value relating to the religious

required' (*Liberalism Beyond Justice*, 98) and Spinner-Halev draws attention to the limits of the extent to which the common school can avoid transmitting the dominant culture as a default norm (*Surviving Diversity*, 116–17).

[135] K. A. Strike, 'Schools as Communities: Four Metaphors, Three Models and a Dilemma or Two', *Journal of Philosophy of Education*, 34(4) (2000), 617–42.

[136] Strike, 'Ethical Discourse and Pluralism', 178.

[137] McLaughlin, 'Liberalism, Education and the Common School', 250-1. On the difficulty in separating out religious from other considerations in relation to many issues see, for example, Spinner-Halev, *Surviving Diversity*, ch. 6.

[138] On the role of religion in liberal societies see, for example, Ibid., esp ch. 8; see also N. L. Rosenblum (ed.), *Obligations of Citizenship and Demands of Faith: Religious Accommodation in Pluralist Democracies* (Princeton: University Press, 2000).

[139] Spinner-Halev, Surviving Diversity, 128-30; Tomasi, Liberalism Beyond Justice, 89–90.

[140] H. Alexander and T. H. McLaughlin, 'Education in Religion and Spirituality' in N. Blake, P. Smeyers, R. Smith and P. Standish (eds), *The Blackwell Guide to the Philosophy of Education* (Oxford: Blackwell, 2003).

and spiritual domains are seen primarily as matters for exploration, discussion, and critical assessment. Religious and spiritual belief, commitment, and practice on the part of individuals are neither presuppositions nor aims of the enterprise. What is being sought on the part of students are appropriate forms of understanding and autonomous judgment and response. For these reasons, education of this kind can be described as 'from the outside' of particular religious and spiritual traditions.[141] Dilemmas relating to the fair illumination of diversity here include concerns about the appropriate kind of critical enquiry considered appropriate for the domain of religion[142] and the extent to which religious and spiritual understanding can be achieved independently of religious and spiritual practice and forms of life.[143] The danger of superficiality involved in any attempt to exhibit, however sympathetically and imaginatively, a range of religious and spiritual traditions 'from the outside' for consideration has significant philosophical support. There is a danger, as Callan notes, of religious practices being '… celebrated as so many charming ornaments of ethnicity.'[144] Further dangers include the possibility that students may be given the impression that relativism in its various forms is an appropriate (or inevitable) perspective to take toward the possibility and nature of 'truth' in and across the religious and spiritual domains, that differing religions should be seen as apt for choice by individuals simply on criteria relating to individual appeal, that spirituality should be seen under a merely therapeutic aspect, that religion should be seen in reductionist or functionalist terms, and so forth.[145]

The need for the common school to take care in the view of these matters which it transmits to students is reflected in Macedo's obser-

[141] It is important to insist, however, that education of this form cannot remain 'on the outside' in the sense that no attempt is made to understand the religious and spiritual domains from the insider's point of view. Such attempts are necessary if religious and spiritual traditions and ideas are to be properly illuminated for the purposes of understanding and assessment.

[142] On the relationship between religious and secular forms of reasoning, see R. Audi, *Religious Commitment and Secular Reason* (Cambridge: University Press, 2000).

[143] On this matter see, for example, T. H. McLaughlin, 'Wittgenstein, Education and Religion' in P. Smeyers, and J. Marshall (eds), *Philosophy and Education: Accepting Wittgenstein's Challenge* (Dordrecht: Kluwer Academic Publishers, 1995).

[144] Callan, 'Discrimination and Religious Schooling.' 57.

[145] Spinner-Halev insists that while the common school may teach about different beliefs relating to salvation they should not teach that each answer is equally true (*Surviving Diversity*, 128–35).

vation that whilst political liberalism does not assert a 'particular view of the whole truth', this does not mean that 'there is no truth about these large matters.'[146] The pedagogic challenges involved in conveying the relevant distinctions are, however, extensive.

A number of similar difficulties arise in relation to the widely voiced perception that the school should, in relation to a contested moral issue, illuminate a range of alternative perspectives for consideration. To what extent can such an illumination really bring to life the different views at stake (given e.g. their housing in fuller moral traditions) and avoid giving the impression that the alternatives in question are 'exhibits' to be viewed spectatorially or as mere alternatives under (say) a relativistic aspect which does not invite the need for, and possibility of, serious moral evaluation? On what grounds can the range of views at issue be selected? Although it is tempting to think it appropriate that an attempt be made to 'represent' each of a range of views along a spectrum, this approach has its difficulties. Apart from the impossibility of representing *all* views, there is a need to ensure that the differing views are in dialogue with, and not merely juxtaposed against, each other in the interests of promoting a coherent debate and bringing about appropriate forms of understanding. Another problem which arises in relation to a strategy of 'representation' is the phenomenon of diversity within (say) religious traditions. Which 'representation' is to be seen as the correct or most balanced one? Dilemmas such as these are part of a larger range of concerns about what is involved in making a 'deliberative arena' genuinely inclusive.[147]

In addition to dilemmas arising in relation to the fair illumination of diversity, the dilemmas arising from the phenomenon of moral distress which was alluded to in the last section should also be borne in mind.

A particularly interesting question relating to pluralism and multiculturalism concerns the degree of acceptance and tolerance that common schools can consistently extend to features of 'minority' belief and culture which appear to infringe, or to be in significant tension with, a number of the values typically insisted upon as 'common' or 'public' (and therefore importantly non-negotiable).[148]

[146] Macedo, Diversity and Distrust, 197.

[147] On this matter see, for example, Callan, 'Discrimination and Religious Schooling.'

[148] On the attitude which liberal societies should take towards ways of life which are culturally self-contained in different ways, see, for example, Parekh, *Rethinking Multiculturalism*, 170–2.

A useful resource in conceptualizing the range and nature of diversity in a liberal democratic society and the limits of toleration is Tomasi's categorization of four main types of adult citizens as types A–D, according to the extent to which the values of autonomy and individuality govern their lives.[149]

Burdens and dilemmas relating to the interface of the public and the non-public domains

Particularly significant burdens and dilemmas arise for the common school in relation to conceptions of common education which require the common school to engage significantly in the area of the interface of the public and non-public domains. Here there is space only to consider the views of Tomasi, which exemplify this kind of conception in a particularly striking way.

As we saw earlier, Tomasi rejects the view that the liberal virtues can be identified by '… making a list only of those virtues whose need happens to be common to all citizens.'[150] For Tomasi, the good liberal citizen must possess additional virtues enabling her to construct her fuller life within the confines of justice by negotiating the interface of public and non-public normative structures. Tomasi holds that liberal civic education cannot be confined to fitting students for the role they will play as public persons in the light of public reason, but must extend to equipping them to lead their non-public lives in a rewarding way in the light of a relevant form of non-public reason.[151] Thus students must come to have an understanding of the fit between public reason and '… the more local, internal understandings of value particular to the various politically

---

[149] Tomasi, *Liberalism Beyond Justice*, ch. 2. According to Tomasi, A-people give the values of autonomy and individuality a governing role in their lives, affirming ethical or comprehensive liberalism as a world view in their public and non-public lives, and rejecting the authoritativeness of any ethical doctrine based on authority. B-people (which Tomasi takes to be the vast majority of citizens) affirm liberal principles such as freedom and equality in their public lives, but do not affirm general or comprehensive doctrines in their non-public lives, which are characterized by a degree of muddle and variability. C-people affirm liberal principles in their public lives, but some general ethical doctrine based on religious authority in their non-public lives. D-citizens affirm a comprehensive doctrine in both their public and non-public lives and reject liberal principles and public reason, seeking (e.g.) to impose their distinctive beliefs on others politically.

[150] Ibid., 78.

[151] Ibid., 86–7.

reasonable narrative traditions each citizen will inhabit',[152] thereby enabling them to consider the meaning of their rights within the context of their lives considered more fully. The interface of public and non-public norms are therefore at the heart of Tomasi's conception of civic education as concerned not merely with the political liberation of citizens, but also with their eventual 'ethical situatedness.'[153]

What are the implications of this view for the common school? At the outset it is important to note that Tomasi supplies a number of conditions to his educational proposals which reflect the location of his view within the framework of political liberalism. Thus, all students are to be prepared for 'full political autonomy' and all school environments should include a mandatory and non-optional provision designed to ensure that its requirements are met. Further, the consideration by students of their non-public values and commitments is situated within an awareness of this political autonomy and its constituent values and principles. Therefore 'controlling' as distinct from 'compass' concepts are ruled out, as are beliefs (such as those held by Tomasi's 'D' citizens) which are incompatible with public reason and civic virtue. Further, no one view in the non-public domain is to be favored, or given normative status, in the common school.[154]

Within this framework, however, Tomasi calls not only for the teaching of religion in common schools[155] but also for careful attention to the nuances and subtleties inherent in the discussion of controversial matters, an approach which he considers in relation to the case of Mozert v. Hawkins[156] Tomasi is sensitive to the existence of 'informal assimilative pressures' in large common schools[157] and for the need to attempt to 'level the playing field' within the domain of the politically reasonable, however possible. For Tomasi, this means

[152] Ibid., 87.

[153] Ibid., 95. For Tomasi, the central challenge for political liberals in relation to education is '… to devise reintegrative forms of schooling that prepare students to live lives of integrity affirming their own (diverse and incompatible) doctrines as true, even once recognizing a common moral foundation for it in political standing of diverse others.' (Ibid., 96)

[154] On all these matters, see Ibid., ch. 5.

[155] Ibid., 89–90.

[156] Ibid., 91–5. For discussion of *Mozert v. Hawkins* see, for example, S. Burts, 'Religious Parents, Secular Schools: A Liberal Defense of an Illiberal , Institution.' *Review of Politics*, 56 (1994) 51–70; Callan, (1997), ch. 6; Macedo *Diversity and Distrust*, chs 6–8; Spinner-Halev, *Surviving Diversity*, ch. 5.

[157] Ibid., 98.

'... allowing all reasonable reintegrative ideals a more equitable share of influence in classrooms and hallways and on athletic fields'[158] thereby creating an educational environment which is 'ethically charged' in a more 'open' and 'even handed' way. The activities which Tomasi mentions as arising from this perspective include inviting parents into schools to speak of matters of work, family, and religion, and allowing students to express their own non-public views and perspectives[159] in significant contexts, including school ceremonies, where this has not previously been seen as appropriate in the US public school. A central feature of Tomasi's approach is that students should not be disrupted from the ethical worldviews formed within their families beyond '... what an appreciation of their own nascent political autonomy requires ...'[160] Therefore, Tomasi holds that common schools must be 'ethically subservient' to children's (politically reasonable) parents in relation to 'reintegrative questions.'[161]

Tomasi argues that the schools he has in mind are '... vibrant places, full of the color, warmth, and variety found in the society they are to serve.'[162] Tomasi's position stands in need of further interrogation and defence. Does the position assume, for example, that students come to school with non-public 'identities' which are more fully and coherently formed than is in fact typically the case? In the absence of a full consideration of Tomasi's position, however, it is clear that the burdens arising from it for the common school are extensive and highly complex,[163] and they give rise to many dilem-

---

[158] Tomasi, Liberalism Beyond Justice, 99.

[159] Ibid., 27–8.

[160] Ibid., 98.

[161] Ibid., 97. On these matters, see also S. Burn, 'In Defense of Yoder. Parental Authority and the Public Schools' in I. Shapiro and R. Hardin (eds), *Political Order: Nomos* XXXVIII (New York: New York University Press, 1996); Burtt, 'Religious Parents, Secular Schools.'

[162] Tomasi, Liberalism Beyond Justice, 126.

[163] Tomasi sums up the task which each student should take up as part of the liberal social world in the following way: 'Become just, but do so in a way that makes sense of the importance that your own particular history up to now has to you. The great good of social justice is not the only good recognizable from a political liberal perspective. For you, citizenship involves not only the performance of public duties but the way you build your life. We encourage you to build that life, not *in spite of* the ethical background culture of your society; but *through your use* of that background culture and the distinctive forms of communication made available there. We must prepare each of you to excel within the particular kind of social world you are now entering – a world where human lives must be built

mas. The dilemmas which have been identified in the discussion so
far are intensified by the more wide ranging and less predicable
salience of non-public considerations in Tomasi's account of the role
of the common school. Whilst Tomasi invokes principles which
restrict the expression of non-public views that are politically unreasonable, within the domain of politically reasonable non-public
belief and commitment, dilemmas arise relating to the achievement
of appropriate forms of coordination and control with respect to the
presentation of views and the conditions needed for balanced overall value influence.[164] Dilemmas arise also from the role given to parents on Tomasi's view. How should this role be balanced against the
need for respect to be given for the developing autonomy of the
child? The logic of Tomasi's own position would seem to require that
the school take an active part in the achievement by students of an
understanding of the 'fit' between their non-public commitments
and public norms. However, this would seem to involve the school
in a form of 'diagnosis' of the beliefs and perspectives of individual
students.[165] The dilemmas which arise here are extensive and
include questions relating to the objectivity and fairness with which
such 'diagnoses' could be undertaken, the nature of the mandate
which the school can be said to possess with respect to these matters,
and the need to achieve forms of trust on the part of parents and
society generally.

5. Policy, Pedagogy, and Practical Judgment

The role of the common school in addressing the sorts of complex
dilemmas which have been indicated in the previous sections invite
attention at the level of, and pose specific challenges to, educational
policy, pedagogy, and practical judgment. Tomasi rightly insists
that there is an important gap between abstract philosophical and
political principles and their realization in particular practical contexts.[166] Central questions which arise here concern the way in which

across the interface of public and non-public normative structures. It is as political
liberals, therefore, that we respectfully play our part in preparing you all to be
good people. For it is in your capacity to live well that the liberal settlement finds
its mortal point' (Ibid., 99–100).

[164] Macedo acknowledges the historical reality of '...the pretenses and hypocrisy of
claims to public school neutrality with respect to religion and ... morality'
(*Diversity and Distrust*, 42).

[165] For a similar perspective, see B. Ackerman, *Social Justice in the Liberal State* (New
Haven: Yale University Press, 1980), ch. 5. 1

[166] Tomasi, *Liberalism Beyond Justice*, 105–7.

the subtleties and complexities inherent in the dilemmas which have been identified can best be addressed and eased, if not resolved.

At the level of general educational policy making it is important to note the limitations of the extent to which the sort of complex subtleties which have been identified can be embodied clearly and extensively in policy guidelines and documents capable of guiding schools and teachers in relation to the dilemmas in a detailed way. The best that can be hoped for here are statements of general principle.[167] An underlying question here is the extent to which a complex philosophical characterization of an educational principle can be made to 'bite' upon educational practice.[168]

It is important to note that central to the resolution of many of the dilemmas which have been identified is a form of practical judgment on the part of educational leaders and teachers at school level. Callan accepts that reasonable disagreement about matters of timing and sensitivity in pedagogy in controversial matters is likely to be expected under pluralism[169] and this is a major area in relation to which practical judgment needs to be exercised, as are areas potentially inviting appropriate forms of accommodation and compromise.[170] Many of the dilemmas which have emerged in this discussion require resolution at the classroom level via a form of pedagogic phronesis. This kind of judgment is required by, and exercised in relation to, a myriad of questions about *inter alia* what fairness, balance, and objectivity require in the articulation of a particular controversial matter, when weight should be placed in a particular situation upon a civic norm at the expense of non-public considerations which might tend to undermine it, and when to pursue or not to pursue a particular line of argument, perspective, or objection at a particular time in the interests of (say) sensitivity to moral distress. As indicated earlier, the influence exerted by the common school extends far beyond teaching in the classroom to embrace teacher example and the ethos and community of the school. The burdens of the common school demand from teachers

[167] On guidance given to teachers in England and Wales in relation to the teaching of controversial issues in citizenship education, see Qualifications and Curriculum Authority, (1998), sec. 10; also Qualifications and Curriculum Authority, (2000), Appendix 2.

[168] On these matters see, for example, McLaughlin, 'Philosophy and Educational Policy.'

[169] Callan, *Creating Citizens*, 158–9.

[170] Spinner-Halev, *Surviving Diversity*, 135–41.

considerable qualities of attentiveness, skill, commitment, and understanding which are not sufficiently summed up in the notion of the 'reflective teacher.'[171]

What seems clear is that the teacher who can realize the educational mandate of the common school must be a *certain sort of person*, who possesses not merely an abstract understanding of the features of the conception of common education in play (though this is important), but can also exhibit the kind of pedagogic *phronesis* of the sort which has been referred to. The implications of this for teacher formation are extensive.

The ideal of the common school is a complex one which gives rise to a range of significant burdens and dilemmas. These burdens and dilemmas do not in themselves undermine the coherence and importance of the ideal or constitute insuperable obstacles to its realisation in practice. However it is important to note that a realization of the complex ideal of the common school requires considerable understanding, contextualized judgment, and professional skill on the part of teachers, amounting to a form of 'pedagogic *phronesis*.' The conditions required for the development of this capacity repay attention. After all, the task of clarifying and justifying the ideal of the common school is idle in the absence of clear reflection on some of the central conditions required for its realization.

[171] T. H. McLaughlin, 'Beyond the Reflective Teacher.' *Educational Philosophy and Theory*, 31(1) (1999), 9–25.

Chapter 9

The Ethics of Separate Schools

Introduction

The case for 'separate schools' is now the subject of increasing theoretical and practical debate and controversy in which ethical considerations have a significant place.

Much of this debate is located, explicitly or implicitly, within the context of the sort of culturally and racially diverse and pluralistic democratic society outlined in Chapter 1 of the Swann Report (GB, P, H of C, 1985; hereinafter referred to as Swann). At the heart of this view of society is the need for a careful balance to be struck between social and cultural *cohesion* and *diversity*. In this context, separate schools of whatever sort are viewed with considerable suspicion, and there is a widespread view that common schools represent the only ideal, or in some cases acceptable, form of educational environment.

In this chapter I shall argue that opponents of separate schools have a harder case to argue than is commonly supposed, and that greater recognition needs to be given to the demands of diversity in schooling. My intention here is not to engage in a full-scale defence of separate schools, much less an attack upon the common school. My aim is rather to map some of the major contours of the ethical territory on which debates about separate schools are conducted and to draw attention to some neglected and complex features of the terrain which opponents of separate schools often overlook. Exploration of these features should result not only in a renewed appreciation of the force of the concerns underlying demands for separate schools, and a consideration of some new lines of argument in relation to them, but should also have implications for the illumination of a defensible concept of common schooling.

This chapter has two main sections. The first deals with issues concerning separate schools which arise within what I shall loosely refer to as a 'liberal' conception of education, with its commitment to notions such as critical rationality and rational autonomy. Such a view of education is closely associated with the kind of society delineated by Swann, and can be argued to be a central feature of it. In the second section I shall turn to more intractable problems concerning private schools involving educational principles at odds with those of the liberal tradition.

Before proceeding, however, it is important to note that there can be no simple, general treatment of 'The Ethics of Separate Schools'. This is at least for two reasons.

First, the concept of a 'separate school' is complex. 'Separate schools' (proposed or actual) can be of many different kinds. There is a wide range of (explicit and implicit) criteria for separation based on a variety of characteristics of the students attending the school. These include: ability, disability, gender, ethnicity, race, religion, culture, class, and willingness and capacity of the family to pay school fees. These criteria are often related to each other in complex (explicit and implicit) ways. Each case for separation will employ different criteria (or a different mixture and weighting of them) and the ethical considerations will vary accordingly. A further difficulty is that the notion of 'separation' in schooling can only be understood in contrast to what 'separation' is *from*. The alternative to 'separate schools', 'the common school', gives rise to its own problems.

This first point should dispel a temptation to see the question of separate schooling as arising uniquely in relation to the needs and demands of ethnic minorities. Ethnic diversity provides just one focus upon, and dimension to, a matter of more general educational concern.

Although there can be many kinds of separate school, I shall focus somewhat in this chapter on the specific case of religious schools. This is not only because of the prominence of such schools in recent debate, but also because they raise particularly interesting ethical questions which are of significance with regard to ethnicity.

A second factor preventing a simple treatment of our question is that, even if the kind of separate school at stake is more precisely defined, ethical and philosophical considerations alone cannot settle whether, and in what way, such institutions should be established. Many other issues (for example, of a practical, pedagogic, psychological, sociological, political and demographic kind) need to be considered in a full assessment of practical educational policies. Ethical and philosophical reflection must be conducted in relation to this fuller range of complex considerations and not in an abstract way independent of them.[1] It is rash, for example, to condone or condemn certain kinds of separate school solely on grounds of philosophical principle. Much depends on how the institutions actually operate, and what their effects actually are on students and the broader community.

Liberal Education and the Separate School

A good example of the conception of education I have in mind here is contained in Richard Pring's chapter in this volume, 'Education for a Pluralist Society' (see pp 19–30), which resonates with, and can only be fully understood in relation to, the fuller tradition of liberal education of which it is a part.

What is meant by 'liberal education'? Leaving to one side narrow conceptions of the notion,[2] I shall offer as an illustration a broad conception developed by Charles Bailey in his book *Beyond the Present and the Particular: a Theory of Liberal Education* (1984 - hereinafter CB). For Bailey, a general liberal education is characterised by four main features:

1.   Most importantly, it aims at liberating those who receive it. Bailey expresses this in terms of the classic distinction between freedom from and freedom to. What a liberally educated person is freed from, according to Bailey, are the limitations of the 'present and particular' — 'specific and limited

[1]   For a further discussion of this, and related matters, see Hirst (1983).

[2]   I shall therefore be using the term in a broader way than Hirst does in his well known and influential paper, 'Liberal education and the nature of knowledge' and related discussions (Hirst, 1974a, chs 3, 6). Hirst sees liberal education as providing only a part, albeit for him an important part, of the total experience of the child. He claims that in addition to liberal education, but distinct from it, are aspects of education such as specialist education, physical education and the development of moral character. This is because Hirst sees liberal education as the unconstrained development of the mind in rational knowledge. It is concerned solely with crucial (non-instrumental) aspects of the cognitive elements of the achievements of rational autonomous agency, the necessary dispositions and capacities crucial to the child actually functioning as an autonomous person, and the additional knowledge necessary, being supplied from outside it. Hirstian liberal education may provide a necessary basis for these other achievements, but is not itself directly concerned with them. In my view, there are good reasons for rejecting this 'narrow' conception of liberal education in favour of a broader one. (See, for example, Bailey, 1984, pp 79–80; White, J, 1982, p 70).

circumstances of geography, economy, social class and personal encounter and relationship' (CB, p 21). The education of such a person has not sought to 'entrap or confirm' him or her in these circumstances but to 'widen ... horizons, increase ... awareness of choice, reveal ... prejudices and superstitions as such and multiply . . . points of reference and comparison' (CB, p 21). What a liberally educated person is freed for, on Bailey's view, is 'a kind of intellectual and moral autonomy, the capacity to become a free chooser of what is to be believed and what is to be done ... a free chooser of beliefs and actions ... a free moral agent, the kind of entity a fully-fledged human being is supposed to be' (CB, p 21). The precise characterisation and defence of this central notion of 'autonomy' in liberal education has given rise to a great deal of discussion, and I shall return to this issue in due course.

2.   A commitment in learning and teaching to what is fundamental and general.

3.   A concern to 'locate' — activities in ...' aspects of knowledge and understanding which can become ends in themselves ... likely to have intrinsic value rather than only capable of serving as means to other ends' (CB, p 20, emphasis in original).

4.   A concern for involvement with the life of reason, since this is a necessary condition for the individual achieving anything in 1–3 above. For Bailey 'A general liberal education is necessarily ... the development of the rational mind ... simply because nothing else could be so liberating, fundamental or general' (CB, p 20).

Bailey's version of liberal education, with its clear Kantian influences, is, of course, open to a number of lines of query and criticism[3] and is only one of several broad conceptions of liberal education that can be pointed to. Theorists of liberal education differ quite widely in the interpretation and emphasis that they give to elements of the sort outlined by Bailey.[4] It is not necessary here to undertake a

[3]   For comment upon, and criticism of, Bailey's view, see, for example, Gibson, (1986); O'Hear, (1985).

[4]   For example, Bruce Ackerman significantly plays down (ii) and (iii) in his account (Ackerman, 1980, ch 5). John White's view of liberal education is in conflict with Bailey's interpretation of (iii) and (iv). With regard to (iv), White's later writings have tended, without denying the significance of the development of critical reason, to place more emphasis on the shaping of dispositions, virtues and qualities of personhood more generally. (See, for example, White, J, 1982, ch 6; 1990; White and O'Hear, 1991). Relevant also here is Patricia White's work on the nature and educational significance of democratic virtues such as self-esteem,

detailed mapping of the precise positions of the range of philosophers committed to liberal education or to discuss in any detail the epistemological, ethical and political underpinning of the concept.[5] For my purposes in seeking a basic account of liberal education to inform subsequent discussion, it is sufficient to draw attention to a recognisable family of conceptions including:

i.   the aim of developing autonomy;

ii. an emphasis on fundamental and general knowledge;

iii. an aversion to mere instrumentality in determining what is to be learnt; and

iv. a concern for the development of critical reason which, notwithstanding the complex issues (not least of interpretation) to which they give rise, constitute fundamental elements in the basic concept of liberal education.

Such a conception of education can be clearly discerned in the Swann Report.[6]

It must be remembered that presupposed to this conception of education is a related conception of the sort of society in which it is located. Roughly speaking, this is the pluralist democratic society of which Swann speaks, with its balance of diversity and cohesion. I shall have more to say below about the distinctively liberal principles which underpin such a conception.

In exploring the attitude of liberal educators to separate schools it is helpful to begin by illustrating briefly the implications of this conception of education for a particular area of the curriculum — education (as distinct from catechesis)[7] in religion. These implications are contained in many influential discussions of the subject

---

self-respect, courage, friendship, trust, hope and confidence. (White, P, 1987a, 1987b, 1989,1990,1991a, 1991b). Philosophers of education of a more existentialist persuasion, such as Michael Bonnett, whom Bailey considers to be a liberal educator, offer a distinctive interpretation of both (i) and (iv). (See, for example, Bonnett, 1986.) In relation to (iii) a number of liberal educators have attempted to achieve a reconciliation of liberal and vocational aims (Pring, 1985; Wallace, 1986). For Pring's reservations about certain construals of (i) see Pring, 1984, pp 72–5.

[5]   On these matters see, for example, Crittenden (1982), Hirst (1985), White, J (1990).

[6]   See McLaughlin, (1987).

[7]   On the distinction between education and catechesis, see, for example, Hirst (1981).

which, while offering different emphases, share a common view-point.[8]

The central implication of this view is, of course, arising from (i) above, that in education in religion, children must not have their religious commitment (or lack of it) determined in any way, but must be allowed to make their own judgements on the basis of appropriate reasoning and evaluation. Arising from (ii) is a notion that a broad introduction to the religious domain is required, not merely the teaching of one religion, and certainly not as if it were true. The implication of (iii) is that education must not see itself as having the merely instrumental aim of producing religious persons and (iv) gives rise to the insistence that appropriate *reasoning* be involved in the judgements made by individuals, and that education should develop this capacity.[9]

What attitude to separate schools is likely to result from such a conception of education? While there is an important gap between the conception and particular schooling arrangements, it is easy to see that each of its features generates a prima facie suspicion of separate schools in the mind of the liberal educator. These suspicions can be briefly sketched. With regard to (i) a concern for developing the autonomy of the child, can and will separate schools embody this adequately? Bailey, for example, expresses his concern about religious schools which educate and train their pupils into a predetermined set of beliefs and attitudes (CB, pp 227–28). With regard to (ii) can a separate religious school, with its commitment to the truth of a particular religion, meet the requirement that students be given a broad exposure to the religious domain as whole? Related to these concerns is a doubt about whether a separate religious school can foster adequately the kind of reasoning demanded in (iv). With regard to (iii), liberal educators are sensitive to the possibility that separate religious schools will act as agents not of non-instrumental general education but of specific religious formation.

[8]   See, for example, Cox and Cairns (1989), Hirst (1972, 1974a, especially ch 3, p 12, 1974b, 1981, 1984, 1985), Hull (1984), Schools Council (1971), Sealey (1985), Smart (1968), Swann, Ch 8.

[9]   These claims involve related claims about the character and status of the religious domain. These include such claims as: it is possible to engage in reasoning in some form in the area of religion; that no one set of religious claims can be shown to be true; that there is controversially about their status; that important distinctions between the religious and moral domains need to be acknowledged, and so on.

Liberal concerns of this sort about separate schooling are general ones, and extend to many contexts beyond the specific case of religious schooling. They arise in relation to all separate schools whatever their criteria of membership. A liberal educator will be similarly concerned about threats to autonomy, breadth of curriculum, non-instrumental general education and appropriate reasoning capacity arising for other categories of pupil as a result of their being segregated from the mainstream of pupils in a potentially restrictive educational environment. These include the disabled, gifted, girls, working class and ethnic minority pupils in addition to those who are members of particular religious faiths. In these other cases, the sources of restriction may be seen as arising not only or necessarily from the explicit transmission of a particular view of the good life (as in the case of religious schools) but from (say) implicit assumptions about the character and destiny of the group of pupils in the school and the effects of isolation from the majority of pupils on aspiration, self-perception and opportunity.[10] There is an egalitarian thrust in the liberal position in the sense that *all* children are seen as having a right to a liberal and liberating education, and separate schools can be seen as a threat to this.

Yet these concerns about separate schooling are only *prima facie* in character. This is often overlooked in treatments of liberal education. Discussions of the notion, and its associated ideas and difficulties, have tended merely to assume its institutionalisation in one basic form: common 'pluralist' schools. This has provided the main context for discussions of concepts such as objectivity, neutrality, bias and so on.[11]

But is it possible to conceive of considerations which would lead a liberal educator to see separate schools in certain circumstances as consistent with his or her basic educational commitments? A liberal educator might reply to this that while *in principle* separate schools are unacceptable *in practice* they may need to be tolerated. This is because of the gap that exists between educational principles and their actualisation in any given society. In the formulation of practical educational policy, compromise and practical judgement are

[10] These concerns may, of course, arise in relation to religious schools also. See Clara Connolly's chapter in this volume, pp 137–45.

[11] Despite an otherwise comprehensive and wide-ranging approach to the subject, Bailey seems to assume throughout that the 'common school' is the only context in which liberal education can take place, and religious schooling, for example, is characterised in rather a crude way and ruled out (see, for example, CB, pp 227–8). On general issues concerning objectivity, neutrality and bias see Bridges (1986).

necessary, and this may include the acceptance of certain kinds of separate school given practical constraints.[12]

But do liberal educational *principles* licence (certain forms of) separate schooling? There are, of course, a number of levels of principle here, which practical considerations have a role in forming. At the fundamental level are principles concerning the basic aim and character of the liberal educational enterprise, of the sort indicated in (i)–(iv) above. At a subsidiary level are related means principles[13] concerning, say, forms of schooling.

What liberal educational principles might lead to a principled acceptance of (certain sorts of) separate schools? I shall examine four categories of argument, each appealing to a different ground on which distinctive educational provision, including separate schooling, might be claimed. These categories are, of course, not wholly unrelated to each other. (For example, on the common ground that Muslims and Radical Feminists might share in seeking single-sex schools, see Halstead, 1991.) I shall claim that some of the strongest and most neglected arguments for separate schools within the liberal educational tradition are to be found in the final category.

(a) Ethnicity and cultural membership

What significance does membership of an ethnic minority group have from the point of view of liberal education? Bearing in mind the caution that is needed in the use of terms such as 'ethnic minority group' (Swann, p vi), I shall begin by referring generally to 'cultural membership', separating out considerations relating distinctively to ethnicity in due course.[14]

From a liberal point of view, membership of a distinctive cultural community is no ground for claiming that a form of education *radically in conflict* with liberal principles is justified, particularly principles relating to the development of autonomy. This is because the sort of society and community characteristically stressed by liberals

---

[12] An example of this approach is the position of the minority report in Swann on the question of religious schools (Swann, p 515), where such schools are seen as contingently valuable and necessary because Swann's conception of Education for All is not yet a reality, and existing common schools do not yet meet the needs and concerns of minority groups. The minority report concedes that when Education for All is enacted, separate religious schools will be unnecessary (Swann, p 515).

[13] The distinction between ends and means in the educational context needs to be treated with considerable caution. On this, see, for example, Sockett (1973).

[14] On the notion of 'ethnic identity' see Swann, ch 1, para 2.

gives salience to the political, rather than the cultural, community. The political community is the context or framework in which individuals are fellow citizens, governed by the principles of justice. It is articulated by an insistence upon state neutrality in relation to perfectionist or substantial conceptions of the good life, and seeks to sustain a 'culture of freedom' necessary for individuals to pursue their freedom in choice of lives.[15] The cultural community is the context (involving such shared features as language and history) where individuals live their lives in a fuller sense, forming and putting into practice their substantial conceptions of the good life. Although political and cultural communities may be identical, in culturally plural societies they are not, and the issue of 'minority' cultures arises, together with possibilities for conflict.

That liberalism has neglected the significance of cultural community, plurality and the collective rights of minority cultures is a charge developed by Will Kymlicka, (Kymlicka, 1989), who seeks to provide an appropriate treatment of these matters from within a liberal perspective. He criticises Rawls for failing to include cultural membership as a 'primary good' with which justice should be concerned. However, it is important to note that what emerges from this argument is not a defence of cultural membership *per se*. Such membership is only seen as valuable because individuals need a rich and secure cultural structure to serve as a 'context of choice' in which they become aware of meaningful options and develop the capacity seriously to evaluate them (ibid, ch 8). Certain forms of cultural membership are inimical to liberal ideals, given (say) Rawls' claim that an essential precondition for our being able to pursue our essential interest in leading a good life is that we have the freedom to form and revise our beliefs about value. The 'shared ends' of existing com-

[15] For an outline of the liberal position in more detail see, for example, Brown (1986, ch 3); Kymlicka (1990, ch 3); Mendus (1989, ch 4); White, P (1983, chs 1, 2). At the heart of liberalism is a kind of agnosticism, or at least a lack of certainty, about what the good life, in any substantial sense, consists in. In the light of this, Rawls, at any rate in the original version of his theory (Rawls, 1971), invokes a non-perfectionist 'thin' theory of the good, putatively free of significantly controversial assumptions and judgements, to distribute to individuals in a just way 'primary goods' (such as liberties and opportunities). These primary goods, neutral between particular, or substantial, conceptions of the good, enable individuals to pursue, within a framework of justice, many different ways of, and conceptions of, life. (For Rawls' later views, which involve what has been described as a 'communitarian turn' see Rawls, 1985, 1987, 1988. For some specific criticisms of Rawls see Haldane, 1985, 1991a. The explicit commitment of liberalism to the value of autonomy is apparent in Rawls' later work. See also Raz, 1986.)

munity practices therefore come up for assessment against this criterion. For liberals, cultural membership or ethnic identity *as such* has
no moral significance or weight independent of, or in conflict with,
its significance for individuals. Nor can it take precedence over the
values implicit in political membership, most notably the rights of
individuals to full and equal consideration and participation in the
political, economic and cultural spheres without regard to race, sex,
religion, disability, and so on. Kymlicka therefore uncompromis-
ingly defends the right of individuals within minority cultures (ibid,
ch 9). The major educational implication of this view is that membership of a particular cultural community or ethnic group does not in
itself generate educational rights fundamentally at odds with the
liberal tradition.

However, there is clearly room within liberal principles, and
indeed a demand within them, for cultural membership to be *taken
into account* in educational arrangements. The most obvious sense in
which this is so is in relation to disadvantage. This is where ethnic
(and more specifically racial) characteristics assume a particular significance, given their visibility and unalterability and their tendency
to lead to disadvantage to individuals and groups because of phenomena such as racism. These characteristics constitute an important set of unchosen, and therefore morally irrelevant, grounds on
which disadvantage, an inequality in the 'context of choice', can
arise. I shall discuss in (c) below, arguments relating to disadvantage, together with the question of the extent to which *separate schools*
are justified on this kind of ground.

In addition to arguments relating to the countering of disadvantage, ethnic and cultural membership should also be taken into
account in educational provision because of what is involved in educating all children, including children from minority backgrounds,
in a fair and adequate way. This generates, among other things, the
familiar but important principles relating to the aims, curriculum
and practices of the common school contained in Swann's philosophy of *Education for All* (Swann, especially parts II and III).[16]

But can ethnic and cultural membership constitute a ground,
within liberal principles, on which *separate schools* can be justified?
The Swann Report's misgivings about separate schools catering
explicitly to ethnic minority groups encapsulates a mainstream liberal educational response to this proposal. (See Swann; especially ch

---

[16]   For a discussion of central concepts concerning education and cultural diversity
       see Halstead (1988, ch 6–8).

8, section II). A similar range of anxieties is evident in the Commission for Racial Equality document *Schools of Faith* (1990).

However, in (d) below, I develop a line of argument relating to complexities in what is involved in the development of autonomy and liberal citizenship, which may offer a broader perspective on the matter.

(b) The educational rights of parents

The second category of argument yielding a principled ground on which separate schools might be seen as acceptable within a liberal framework of educational values concerns the educational rights of parents, which are often appealed to in the defence of separate schools, and in favour of greater variety of educational provision generally. This category overlaps with (a) but is clearly separable from it.

What attitude to parental rights emerges from the point of view of liberal education?

It seems clear that *unlimited* parental rights are incompatible with such a perspective. Bruce Ackerman, for example, claims that parents have no 'basic right' to determine the education of their children. What is basic here is the right of the *child* to a liberal and liberating education which will provide him or her with the tools for autonomy and self-definition; the opportunity to assess (and perhaps deviate from) parental norms. For Ackerman, such a liberal education is one of the conditions for a liberal political community. Ackerman thus rejects Friedmanite suggestions that schools compete for pupils in the marketplace, with parents having complete freedom of choice of schools via a 'voucher' system. He claims that since parents are likely to spend their vouchers on schools which reinforce their existing values, the plan

> legitimises a series of petty tyrannies in which like-minded parents club together to force-feed their children without restraint. Such an education is a mockery of the liberal ideal. (Ackerman, 1980, p 160).

Ackerman accuses Friedman of being blind to the moral indoctrination of children undertaken by parents - a process which infringes 'the dialogic rights of the powerless'. As I shall indicate below, this basic position is shared by a large number of philosophers committed to liberal educational principles.

It stands in sharp contrast to much recent advocacy of the rights of parents, for example by the Hillgate group in their manifesto, *Whose*

Schools? (Cox *et al*, 1986) and by philosophers such as Antony Flew (Flew, 1987, especially chs 1, 4).

However, the Hillgate Group nowhere *defends* its commitment to parental rights, and nor does it discuss or acknowledge the character and significance of the concept of the autonomy of the child. *Whose Schools?* merely asserts, for example, that 'Children *need* to be instructed in religious doctrine, in accordance with the wishes and the faith of their parents' (Cox *et al*, 1988, p 2, my emphasis). What is the justification for this need claim? An attempt by Anthony O'Hear to provide a philosophical justification for the Hillgate Group's proposals in an article in *The Times Educational Supplement* (O'Hear, 1987) is deficient. O'Hear claims that the proposals 'allow just the sort of genuine flexibility and diversity in education that true liberals ought to cherish', and he welcomes the notion of different kinds of school in each area promoting its own vision of what a good education should be. He supports this view by invoking J S Mill's strictures in *On Liberty* (Mill, 1859) against the necessarily despotic and homogenising character of a general system of state education. But Mill himself inadequately considers both the significance of the autonomy of the child and the possibility that a certain form of general, common, educational provision might promote it. This inadequacy is inherent therefore in O'Hear's Millian defence of the Hillgate Group proposals. The absense of a convincing justification for parental rights is also a feature of Flew's discussion.[17]

The claim that a (certain sort of) non-parentally determined national curriculum is required by liberal education is a strong one. Both Flew and the Hillgate Group see a national curriculum as compatible with their plans. Indeed, the Hillgate Group sees such a curriculum as 'essential'. However, this is conceived very sketchily in terms of a core of 'reading, writing and arithmetic' and 'a settled range of proven subjects', constituting 'a testable and coveted body of knowledge which it is the duty of any educational system to pass on from generation to generation' (Cox *et al*, 1986, p 7). There is no consideration given to the possibility that what might be required in terms of a core or entitlement curriculum for all young people is a

[17] Flew claims that his view of education 'follows as a corollary from a recognition of the most fundamental and universal human rights' (Flew, 1987, p 14), but the rights in question are never analysed, and there is no detailed treatment of the tension and potential conflict between the rights of parents and of children.

richer diet determined by what is needed as preparation for life as a rationally autonomous person in a pluralistic democracy.[18]

Views such as those of the Hillgate Group and Flew seem to invoke a conception of society such as that described by Amy Gutmann in *Democratic Education* as 'the state of families', where educational authority is placed exclusively in the hands of parents (Gutmann, 1987, pp 28–33). The essence of the arguments which Gutmann develops against this conception echoes Ackerman's and is captured by Gutmann in her principle of 'non-repression'; one of the two principled limits to parental and political authority over education which she specifies (see Gutmann, 1987, pp. 44–5).

It is important to note, however, that this denial by liberal educators of unlimited parental rights does not involve a denial of all parental rights, or their unqualified transferral to (say) the state. It involves merely a denial that parents have a right to determine exclusively the educational experience of their children.[19]

The principles of liberal education establish merely in very general terms a tension in the determination of schooling between 'rights of parents' and 'rights of children to liberal education'. This 'principled tension' is visible in the positions of many philosophers sympathetic to liberal education.[20] However, Ackerman himself observes that such a principle does not enable us to determine the particular kind of parental control that is justified within a particular institutional setting (Ackerman, 1980, p 148).[21] Agreement at the level of basic principle is compatible with quite wide-ranging dispute about the scope of parental rights thereby licensed. Leaving

[18] On such a requirement, see, for example, White, J (1990); White and O'Hear (1991); White, P (1988a); Crittenden (1988, ch 5, 7); Peters (1981); Swann, part II.

[19] Gutmann, for example, holds that neither parents nor the state have a right to complete authority over the education of children. Ackerman acknowledges that the child's family will typically exercise continuing powers of 'legitimate control and guidance' over their children and that this will have implications for the rights of professional educators (Ackerman, 1980, ch 5). See also the various educational duties, including duties of coordination and monitoring, which Patricia White lays upon parents (White, 1983, ch 5). For a general treatment of parental choice in education see Johnson (1990).

[20] See, for example, Bishop (1980); Bigelow (1988); Callan (1985); Chamberlin, R (1989); Crittenden (1988); Feinberg (1980); Fisher (1982); Gutmann (1987); Hamm (1982); Henley (1979); Hobson (1984); Walzer (1983); White, J (1990); White, P (1983, 1988a, 1991c); Young (1980).

[21] For an illustration of this general point see Gutmann (1987, ch 3, 5).

aside complexities,[22] and arguments from within the liberal tradition arguing for more wide-ranging parental rights,[23] can an argument for certain sorts of separate school be developed within the principles relating to parental rights adopted by the majority of liberal educators?

One source of such an argument concerns disadvantage, which I shall explore in the next section. In section (d) I shall outline my view that, given a defensible 'core' concept of liberal education, there can be a number of forms of it, including certain kinds of separate school, each compatible with the development in the child of fundamental liberal capacities such as autonomy and liberal citizenship, but approaching that development in different ways. In relation to such alternatives, parents can be conceded, within the principles of liberal education, legitimate rights of choice.

(c) Countering disadvantage

I shall discuss this category of justification for separate schools briefly, since, although it often contains strong arguments, its detailed working out and justification involves mainly practical considerations.

The essence of arguments in this category is that certain kinds of pupils are disadvantaged by their attendance at common schools in virtue of the inability of such schools to overcome obstacles to the satisfaction of their specific needs, including their capacity for achieving the kind of autonomous agency enshrined in the aims of liberal education. Thus girls may be thought to flourish better in a single-sex educational environment because of the negative influence on their attitude and achievement by the behaviour of boys and other aspects of sexism; certain categories of able and disabled pupil may require special provision, and pupils from certain ethnic or racial minorities may be thought to benefit from being removed from common schools in which they meet hostility and a failure to address their distinctive cultural and other needs. It might be thought that, at least in certain circumstances, these measures *could* include the justification of certain sorts of separate school.

[22] One question which can be raised about this 'tension' is whether it is a tension between conflicting rights. It has been argued that the parent has no educational rights which are independent of the child's right to liberal education (see, for example, White, P, 1983, ch 5). If all parental rights are seen as subserving the educational rights of children in this way, then no real tension between rights can arise; the tension is one between conflicting duties.

[23] See, for example, Cohen (1981), Coons and Sugarman (1978).

Arguments of this general sort vary in the extent to which they see the considerations invoked as short term, arising (for example) from the contingent features of existing common schools, or more permanent in character. The detailed justification of arguments of this sort, especially the claim that the need for distinctive provision requires separate *schools*, depends upon fairly extensive empirical argument in the light of powerful countervailing arguments concerning the value of common provision. Such separate schools would, of course, need to satisfy certain conditions relating to the fundamental principles of liberal education, not least those relating to the development of critical rationality and independence.

Liberal principles create room for such a line of argument, because it concerns justice, which is a central liberal ideal. The detailed working out and justification of the argument in particular cases is, however, essentially an empirical task, given an alertness to the value judgements that may be involved in the categorisation of pupils and the delineation of their needs. I turn now to a category of argument in which philosophical considerations have a more direct role to play.

(d) Alternative starting points for autonomy and liberal citizenship

This final category of justification for separate schools may overlap with the others but is not uniquely associated with any one of them. The central claim here, which has a more distinctively philosophical flavour to it, is that there are a number of legitimate educational starting points[24] for the child's journey towards autonomy and liberal citizenship. In relation to these, both ethnic/cultural identity and parental rights have significance.

One such starting point for a child is indeed from the basis of experience in a common school, and the various values to which it is com-

---

[24] Clarification of the notion of a 'starting point' is required here. This might be understood in one of two senses. In a weak sense, it might refer to the beliefs (etc.) that the student actually brings into the classroom from his or her background, previous reflection and so on. These existing beliefs are the 'starting point' for the educational enterprise in that (roughly expressed) it is the 'material' that must be acted upon. There must clearly be a plurality of 'starting points' in this sense, especially since the range of beliefs brought to the class by students in the common school might be very wide. However, I have in mind a stronger sense of 'starting point'. This is where the educational process itself starts off with the presupposition of the truth of (say) a particular religious position which is presented as the 'norm' of belief and practice initially and from which the search for critical independence proceeds.

mitted.[25] However, another possible and legitimate starting point is from the basis of experience of a particular 'world view' or cultural identity; a substantiality of belief, practice and value, as in (say) a certain sort of religious school. Such schools, in relation to which parents can exercise legitimate rights of choice, would not seek to entrap their pupils in a particular vision of the good, but to provide a distinctive starting point from which their search for autonomous agency can proceed.

I have developed elsewhere the view that there are a number of different schooling contexts in which the demands of 'openness' and 'stability' in the conditions required for the development of autonomy can be variously balanced (McLaughlin, 1987)[26] and have indicated a number of the complex conceptual and practical issues to which it gives rise. The argument is parallel to one concerning the rights of parents within a liberal framework of values to give their children certain sorts of religious upbringing.[27]

Although my development of the argument elsewhere refers to the notion of a 'liberal religious school', I see no reason why a similar argument could not be developed in relation to a number of the other kinds of distinctive school that might be advocated.

The motivation for such an argument stems not merely from the need for practical compromise in the formation of educational policy, but from complexities inherent in the basic principles of both liberalism and liberal education. These difficulties are related to the neglect by liberals of cultural aspects of community which was mentioned earlier, but are also associated with more wide-ranging concerns about liberalism. I shall illustrate these by indicating briefly some of the philosophical challenges which have been made to the principles. Points have been made such as the following:

- the danger of invoking an unduly abstract and a-historical conception of autonomy, rationality and the human agent;
- a possible neglect of the rootedness of persons in particular cultural traditions of belief, practice and value and of the significance of involvement and engagement in such traditions for the ability to achieve identity and critical independence;

[25] For an outline of these see, for example, Hirst (1974b; 1981; 1985).

[26] For a similar general point expressed in terms of the need to achieve a balance between distance and proximity to the surrounding world in the development and exercise of autonomy see Mendus (1989, ch 4).

[27] See McLaughlin (1984, 1985, 1990); Callan (1985); Gardner (1988; 1991).

- use of an unreal model of the child as an abstract, rootless chooser, unchanged by choices made;
- the need to encourage initial stable beliefs, reflective commitment and a range of determinate dispositions and virtues in the development of autonomy;
- lack of specification of the character and range of autonomy, and of critical reflection;
- the impossibility of determining a single optimum route to the achievement of autonomy;
- the problem of specifying general criteria for choice and value;
- difficulties in distinguishing between 'public' and 'private' values.
- Such difficulties are elaborated and discussed not only by philosophers of education,[28] but also by philosophers sympathetic to the values and benefits of tradition and by communitarian critics of liberalism.[29]

Difficulties of this sort are seen by some as requiring the rejection of liberalism and liberal education. However, another response is to see them as requiring not abandonment of these notions but their restatement in a more nuanced way.[30] Part of this, I suggest, involves acceptance of the notion of a plurality of legitimate forms of liberal education and schooling. At the very least, the difficulties indicated cast doubt on the suggestion that there is anything straightforward about the conditions in which liberal education can best take place. For example, they indicate the complexities involved in outlining significantly non-controversial ethical and other principles for the conduct of the common school, even within a liberal framework of values. Among the issues here are dangers of superficiality in learning, or disorientation, arising from a 'babel of values' in the common

---

[28] See, for example, Callan (1989); Crittenden (1988); Godfrey (1984); Haydon (1986, 1987b); Jones (1987); Lloyd (1980, 1986); Thiessen (1987); Ward (1983); White, J and P (1986); White, J (1990).

[29] For emphasis on the importance of tradition see, for example, Almond (1990); Bambrough, (1987); Cooper, (1987); Hampshire (1983); Kekes (1988, 1989); Kerr (1986); MacIntyre (1981, 1987, 1988, 1990); Midgley (1980, especially ch 12); Nagel (1979, ch 9); Oakeshott (1962, especially the essays 'Rationalism in polities', 'The tower of Babel', 'Rational conduct', 'On being Conservative'); O'Hear (1981, ch 5, 1985, 1986, 1988); Quinton (1971); Scruton (1980a, 1980b, 1983); Weil (1952). On the communitarian critics of liberalism, see, for example, Gutmann (1985); Sandel (1982); Sacks (1991); Kymlicka (1989, especially ch 4, 8; 1990, ch 6); Macedo (1990); Rasmussen (1990).

[30] See, for example, Kymlicka (1989, especially ch 4, 8); Macedo (1991).

school, and doubts about whether the fairness of such a context can be sufficiently established to enable it to be insisted upon as the only context in which liberal education can take place. There are also concerns about whether the values of the common school can be 'thick' enough to generate a deeply humanising education.[31]

While all these issues require further discussion, the onus lies with liberal educationalists opposed to all forms of separate schooling to show that the difficulties mentioned above can be resolved in such a way that only one starting point and institutional form of liberal education can be specified, and the one I suggest as an alternative for parental choice be ruled out either on grounds of incoherence or incompatibility with the liberal ideal. Part of this task would be to show that philosophical difficulties concerning the significant neutrality of the common school can be overcome.[32]

A crucial question here concerns the sorts of conditions that would need to be satisfied by acceptable separate schools. These conditions relate to the role of the school in achieving a balance between 'openness' and 'stability' in such a way that the development of both autonomy and liberal citizenship are not frustrated. I have attempted to say something about these conditions elsewhere (McLaughlin, 1987, pp 77–83).

A full defence of this notion would require a detailed treatment of such matters. In the case of religious schools, it would need to take account of the wide ranging debate concerning them which has been in progress for some time.[33] Another issue requiring attention concerns the *status* and *funding* of such schools, which is in turn related to the distinction between the state and private provision of education, and the right of parents to pay for the education of their children privately. Given the egalitarian thrust of liberal education principles, this is an issue which is troubling for liberal educators. I cannot, however, pursue it here.[34]

[31] See Strike (1991).

[32] On this see, for example, Crittenden (1988: esp 120-128; 206–218), Callan(1989); McLaughlin (1987: especially 75–77; 1991).

[33] For criticisms of religious schools see, for example, Ball, S (1988); Ball, W and Troyna (1987); Commission for Racial Equality (1990); O'Keeffe (1988c); Socialist Educational Association (1981, 1986); Swann, ch 8.

[34] On the general issue of whether religious schools should be supported by public funds see, for example, Almond (1988); Callan (1988); Crittenden (1988, especially ch 8); Flew (1968); Strike (1982, ch 5). For a broad perspective on issues relating to public and private provision of education see Walford (1990).

It is appropriate to refer to two lines of criticism which relate particularly to issues of ethnicity. Both concern the point that, although there may be some doubt about the precise sense and extent to which liberals generally are committed to a vision of community, there is an undeniable need for society to be held together by communal bonds, commitments, loyalties and the like, which go beyond mere toleration.[35] While a pluralist society must be *diverse*, it must also be *cohesive*, and separate schools may be seen as a significant threat to the achievement of this in at least two ways.

First, separate schools may fail to develop in their students the range of qualities demanded by liberal citizenship. These include an understanding of, and commitment to, the publicly recognised principles of justice together with qualities of understanding, imaginative sympathy and the like.[36] However, schools justified within the liberal framework of values will have as one of their conditions that they engage in an appropriate programme of civic education, not limited (for example) by a lack of critical thrust.[37] The strongest forms of criticism of this claim require justification of the view that there is something inherent in the very notion of separateness which makes the achievement of certain of these objectives very difficult, impossible or incoherent. It is also important to bear in mind that common schools, in virtue of the 'thin' character of the values which underpin them, may have their own difficulties in achieving their civic aims.[38]

The second concern, of particular significance for ethnicity, involves the fear that separate schools may lead to segregation of different ethnic, cultural and racial groups within society, with its attendant evils such as the spread of prejudice and discrimination. While this is a genuine concern, there is insufficient evidence to make a clear judgement about this matter.

It is important to note that considerations relating to all these issues requires a judgement to be made about the *balance* to be drawn between the legitimate demands of diversity and cohesion, openness and stability. A strong case against separate schools requires that balance to be drawn in a very confident way in a situation of considerable complexity.

[35] On this see, for example, Callan (1991); Haldane (1991b); Mendus (1989).

[36] For an outline of the 'democratic virtues' and their educational significance, see White, P (1983, 1987a, 1987b, 1988b, 1989, 1990, 1991a, 1991b).

[37] Compare Galston (1989).

[38] See Strike (1991, p 30).

A major concern about separate schools among liberal educators is that acceptance of them will lead to the establishment of schools of a distinctly illiberal character. I turn now to problems relating to schools of this kind.

Non-Liberal Education and Separate Schools

I have argued in the first section of this chapter that separate schools *of a certain sort* may be compatible, at least in principle, with liberal educational principles. In this second section of the chapter, I shall explore some of the questions concerning separate schools which emanate from, and are associated with, conceptions of education in conflict with the liberal view.

The presence in societies such as Britain of ethnic or religious minorities who do not value the autonomous life poses a major practical and theoretical challenge to liberal education and to liberal democratic theory generally.[39] Our earlier discussion has illustrated how individual autonomy and critical independence are non-negotiable elements of the liberal point of view. Thus liberal philosophers such as Joseph Raz hold that communities not supporting autonomy, even if they are 'morally worthy' in the sense that they do not harm or restrict the freedom of non-members and provide a life for its members which is adequate and satisfying, have a culture inferior to liberal ones. In relation to such cultures, options of coercion, assimilation and (mere) toleration arise (Raz, 1986, pp 423–4). Susan Mendus claims that in such cases liberalism will see toleration not as a good, but as a necessary evil (1989, ch 4). This principled position applies also to non-liberal educational views, proposals and practices. Thus John White insists that in an 'autonomy-supporting' society, *all* children must be protected against true believers who wish to impose on them a non-autonomous conception of the good life' (1990, p 105, emphasis in original). Similarly Pring insists that not every cultural tradition is educationally acceptable. Those which, in various ways, close the mind to reflection and critical enquiry are anti-educational and therefore not to be given equal status.

A host of *practical* difficulties arise for liberals from such views. What is actually done about illiberal cultural traditions and groups? Because of the range of negative effects associated with policies of coercion, caution is invariably urged in relation to them (see, for

[39] On this, see, for example, White, J (1990: pp 24–6; 103–5); Mendus (1989, especially ch 4–6).

example Raz, 1986, p 424).[40] Such caution can be seen also in the educational domain in White's acceptance that 'gentle' methods of persuasion should be adopted, avoiding open conflict between different cultural groups and respecting the integrity of the child's psychological development (White, J, 1990, p 105). Pring, however, rules out negotiation as a means of dealing with such educational disputes, so it is difficult to know how he would proceed in a situation of conflict.

It may be felt, therefore, that this general problem is one to be settled by practical politics, in an untidy process of struggle, compromise and, perhaps, democratic vote.[41] One element in such a process is the political difficulty of conceding separate schools to some cultural groups and not others. It may be thought politically impossible to render explicit the grounds for refusal, which may lead to the surfacing of other profound sources of conflict in a multicultural society.[42]

Leaving political and practical considerations to one side, it is by no means obvious, however, that the issues of *principle* arc clear here. How are the non-liberal cultures at issue to be *identified*? This is not merely a practical matter. The theoretical difficulty with this question for liberals can be illuminted by reference to obscurities concerning the meaning and justification of their central notion of autonomy.

I shall approach this point by looking first at matters of justification. Both White and Raz advance a justification for autonomy which at first sight seems powerful. They both concede that such a justification which applies to human beings in general, those in both 'tradition-directed' and 'non tradition-directed' societies, cannot be provided, but that in a non-tradition directed society, but not necessarily in any other, autonomy is necessary to flourishing.[43] Such a claim is attractive in that it offers the possibility of avoiding controversial fundamental value disputes by appealing to practicality. For

[40] Alternative policies can involve attempts to liberalise such traditions and groups without destroying them (see, for example, Kymlicka, 1990, p 170).

[41] For a celebrated recent example of a pratical conflict see the case of Wisconsin v. Toder in the USA, which concerned the desire of parents from the Old Order Amish community not to send their children to school beyond the age of 14 because of its corrosive effects on their traditional way of life. For the text of the judgements see O'Neill and Ruddick (eds) (1979, pp 280-305). For discussion see, for example, Feinberg (1980).

[42] On such conflicts see, for example, Harris (1982).

[43] See, for example, White, J (1990, pp 25-6, ch 6).

us, claims Raz, 'The value of autonomy is a fact of life. Since we live in a society whose social forms are to a considerable degree based on individual choice ... we can prosper in it only if we can be success-fully autonomous' (1986, p 394).[44] This claim needs, however, to be treated with considerable caution, which becomes clear when ques-tions about the meaning of autonomy are turned to.

What is the *nature* and *extent* of the kind of autonomy that is justi-fied on this view? White appeals to a distinction between *autarchy* and *autonomy* (White, J, 1990, p 97). The rational deliberation and self-determination of the (merely) autarchic person is limited in extent and scope, not extending, for example, as far as calling into question fundamental matters of belief or convention (such as pre-vailing social structures). Thus, one can be autarchic within the con-fines of a tradition-directed society or cultural group. In contrast, the rational deliberation of autonomous persons must extend much fur-ther. They must achieve a distanced critical perspective on all impor-tant matters, and their belief and action must result from principles and policies which they have themselves 'ratified' by critical reflec-tion. A distinction of a similar sort between kinds, levels or degrees of autonomy has been drawn by a number of writers.[45]

The crucial question here is whether the 'practical' justification demonstrates only the value of autarchy,[46] given the under-determined and ambiguous character of the term 'autonomy.[47] Mendus complains that the attempt by liberals to articulate concepts of autonomy and rationality independent of the background or assumptions (relating to, say, metaphysics or the teleology of human nature) invoked by philosophers such as Kant, Locke and Mill makes it impossible to assess and use them. They become vacuous (1989, pp 88–109).

It is clear that every cultural group and tradition will value and embody certain forms of reason and individual thought.[48] Can crite-

---

[44] For a similar argument about the implications of the fact of pluralism for the immunity of holders of traditional views from reflection, see Fitzmaurice (1992).

[45] See, for example, Ward (1983); Barrow (1974, especially 123–4); Phillips (1975).

[46] White concedes that Raz's judgement justifies merely the value of autarchy and not autonomy. For his attempt to support Raz's conclusion with a supplementary argument see White, J (1990, 98–103).

[47] For an annotated bibliography of sources relating to the concept of autonomy and its significance for education see Karjohn (1989, pp 104–10). See also Haworth (1986); Young (1986); Dworkin (1988).

[48] See, for example, MacIntyre (1988, especially ch 17, 18).

ria be outlined to indicate the degree and kind of critical thought that is constitutive of acceptable autonomy? There are a number of difficulties here concerning not only the specification of these criteria (in the light, for example, of problems about the limits of fundamental questioning) but also the correct identification of their absence or presence in the cultural groups and traditions at issue (given, for example, problems of knowledge, understanding and interpretation). Care is needed, for example, in the use of the notion of fundamentalism in relation to certain cultural groups (see CRE, 1990, pp 16-18).[49] This is particularly true in the case of Islam.[50] These problems are carried over into educational proposals made by the various groups.[51] It is also important to remember that potentially illiberal views and proposals should not be uniquely identified with minority cultural groups.

It is difficult to draw a very sharp line in practice between views which fall inside, and those which fall outside, the liberal education tradition. The suggestion here is that it is also difficult to draw such lines in theory.

In the light of this it is appropriate for liberals to regard all proposals for separate schooling as falling *prima facie* within the framework of principles outlined in the previous section of this chapter. This will have a number of benefits. As well as being even handed and a defence against the misunderstanding, misrepresentation and alienation of minority cultures and their educational demands,[52] such an approach offers the best hope for the defensible liberalisation of such proposals and the avoidance of the development and entrenchment of patently illiberal attitudes.

It may well be that certain proposals will be unacceptable. If so, one benefit of this strategy will be to focus discussion on the concrete issues at stake, rather than matters of elusive abstract principle.

An important factor in creating a climate for the discussion of issues of separate schooling which is both just and likely to promote the most satisfactory solutions overall is for liberal educators to acknowledge that, given their complexity, there is a less strong and

---

[49] On the notion of fundamentalism, see, for example, Barr (1977); Sacks (1991: ch 5).

[50] On Islam, critical thought and post-enlightenment culture, see, for example, Akhtar (1990).

[51] On some of the philosophical complexities involved in proposals for Muslim schools, see Halstead (1986).

[52] See, for example, Straw (1989).

direct connection than is sometimes supposed between their educational principles and the notion of the common school.

Acknowledgements

An earlier version of this chapter was presented as a paper to a meeting of the London Branch of the Philosophy of Education Society of Great Britain. I am grateful to the participants in that discussion for helpful comments. I am also grateful to my colleague, Madeleine Arnot, for the benefit of her remarks on an earlier draft of this work. The chapter was completed during my fellowship at the Centre for Philosophy and Public Affairs at the Department of Moral Philosophy at the University of St Andrews. I am very grateful to Dr John Haldane, Director of the Centre, for his offer of the Fellowship and for making my stay so fruitful and congenial.

Chapter 10

Distinctiveness and the Catholic School

Balanced judgement and the temptations of commonality

Introduction

It has recently been observed that in the United Kingdom, the United States of America and Australia there has been a new awakening of interest in, and appreciation of, Catholic schools (February, 1998, p.210). In these and other contexts it is widely agreed that there is much to celebrate in the work and achievements of Catholic schools today, and many grounds for optimism about what these schools can achieve in the future.

In England and Wales, Catholic schools have, in general, received favourable reports in inspections recently conducted by The Office for Standards in Education (OFSTED)[1] and the schools enjoy considerable popularity among parents. Catholic schools in England and Wales have not confined their attention to students who are academically able or otherwise privileged. Many Catholic schools have a particular concern for students from poor and disadvantaged backgrounds and are notably successful in relation to them (Bishops' Conference of England and Wales, 1997a). Further, Catholic schools are increasingly responsive to calls that they be open to the educational demands of a liberal democratic society in terms both of the

[1]   On the performance of Catholic schools in England and Wales in recent OFSTED inspection reports see, for example, Catholic Education Service, 1995, 1996a. For analyses of the reasons for the academic success of Catholic schools in England and Wales see, for example, Morris, 1998a, 1998b, 1998c. Compare Bryk *et al.*, 1993.

common good in general (Catholic Education Service, 1997) and the needs of members of other religious faiths in particular (Bishops' Conference of England and Wales, 1997b).

A broadly similar picture of Catholic schooling can be discerned in the United States. Andrew Greeley, for example, has argued that research evidence relating to Catholic schools in the US over the last forty years has painted a picture of these schools which is over- whelmingly encouraging in many respects. (Greeley, 1998, esp. pp.181–187; cf. Bryk *et al.*, 1993) In Australia, a similarly positive and encouraging vision of Catholic schools emerges (Canavan, 1998).

In all three contexts, and elsewhere, there has been a recent increase in research effort focused on Catholic schools, evidenced by scholarly publications and by the establishment of research centres, projects and journals.

This climate of interest, appreciation, celebration and optimism in relation to Catholic schools is not uncritical. Quite properly, critical questions are raised about a number of pertinent and important issues. Included here are questions about the precise nature and significance of the 'Catholic effect' in the success of the schools, about priorities in the aims and goals of the schools, about the spe- cific institutional and other challenges and dilemmas which arise for Catholic schools in particular contexts and about practical obstacles and requirements needed for the realisation of the different aspects of the work of the schools. In these and other ways, the 'success story' being told about Catholic schools today is placed in a critical perspective.

Of the critical questions which are posed to Catholic schools today, perhaps the most fundamental, and the most difficult, con- cern the distinctiveness of Catholic schools. The inescapable require- ment that Catholic schools have a distinctive character has been reiterated in the recently published document from the Congrega- tion for Catholic Education, The Catholic School on the Threshold of the Third Millennium. The Catholic school, the document reminds us, has 'an ecclesial identity and role' which is '… not a mere adjunct, but is a proper and specific attribute, a distinctive characteristic which penetrates and informs every moment of its educational activity, a fundamental part of its very identity and the focus of its mission' (Congregation for Catholic Education, 1997 §11). The fostering of this 'ecclesial dimension' of the Catholic school, the document continues, '... should be the aim of all those who make up the educating community' (ibid.).[2]

It may be argued that Catholic schools exist in order to transmit the Catholic tradition of faith and life and to educate within it. Catholic schools therefore have, or should have, a distinctive educational responsibility and character which is rooted in the distinctiveness of Catholic education itself. Other schools — for example 'common' schools in a liberal democratic society — are based on a somewhat different conception of education and therefore have a somewhat different educational responsibility and character (McLaughlin, 1996). One central difference between these two kinds of school is that Catholic schools, in contrast to 'common' schools, can base their educational influence on a specific and detailed vision of the meaning of human life and of existence as a whole (Congregation for Catholic Education, op. cit., §10).

These claims about the distinctive character of Catholic schools seem to be obviously true. As general statements of the nature of Catholic schools and Catholic education how could they be denied? How could contradictories of the statements be coherently maintained? Could it be intelligibly argued, for example, that Catholic schools exist in order *not* to transmit the Catholic tradition of faith and life and to educate within it? And what sense can be made of a claim that Catholic schools on the one hand, and the 'common' schools of a liberal democratic society on the other, have — and should have — an identical educational responsibility and character?

However, deeper exploration of these statements reveals a number of complexities, arising both in relation to (a) the claim that the Catholic school exists in order to transmit the Catholic tradition of faith and life and to educate within it, and (b) the claim that Catholic schools on the one hand and common schools on the other are, and should be, based on a somewhat different conception of education and have a somewhat different educational responsibility and character.

With regard to (a) ambiguities and questions arise in relation to two matters. First, how is 'the Catholic tradition of faith and life' to be understood? Many disputes about questions of distinctiveness in relation to Catholic schools have their roots in different interpretations of this tradition. These differing interpretations need not

---

[2] Congregation for Catholic Education 1997 §11. For a sensitive and comprehensive discussion of matters of distinctiveness in relation to Catholic schools see Sullivan, 1998.

necessarily involve fundamental incompatibility and conflict — differences of priority or emphasis may be at stake. Secondly, scope for dispute arises in relation to 'transmit' and 'educate within'. Some disputes here relate to the 'content' of transmission and education and hence, in part, to disputes about the nature of the Catholic tradition of faith and life. Other disputes, however, relate to the notions of 'transmission' and 'education' themselves and to the nature of their practical implications in particular contexts. The concepts of 'transmission' and 'education' are, or can be perceived to be, somewhat in tension with each other, and this tension is apparent, for example, in familiar debates about the appropriate relationship between 'catechesis' and 'religious education' (Astley and Francis, 1994; Gallagher, 1996; Wrenn, 1991). Further, it is clear that the form which 'transmission' and 'education within' should take in given practical circumstances requires institutional and pedagogic interpretation in particular contexts. This interpretation takes place in the complex and partly intuitive practical judgement and wisdom of teachers and educational leaders, and here there is ample room for dispute and differences of view.

With regard to (b) ambiguities and questions arise with regard to the precise account which should be given of the relationship between Catholic schools and 'common' schools. It is important to insist here that Catholic schools on the one hand and 'common schools' on the other are not based on wholly different conceptions of education nor have a wholly different educational responsibility and character. After all, there exists an 'overlapping consensus' (Rawls, 1996, pt lect. 4) between specifically Catholic beliefs and values and the 'public values' of a liberal democratic society, and this consensus extends to many educational beliefs and values also. It is important to emphasise, therefore, that Catholic schools are, and should be, somewhat different from their 'common' counterparts with respect to their educational conceptions, responsibility and character (McLaughlin, op. cit., pp. 145–148).

Notwithstanding these complexities, ambiguities and questions, however, it is possible to re-state, at least in general terms (a) the claim that the Catholic school exists in order to transmit the Catholic tradition of faith and life and to educate within it and (b) the claim that Catholic schools on the one hand and 'common' schools on the other are, and should be, based on a somewhat different conception of education and have a somewhat different educational responsibility and character. It may be argued, therefore, that whilst the meaning and interpretation of the claims clearly require much analysis and debate, the claims themselves are, at least in general terms, indisputable.

Before proceeding, however, it is worth considering a particular challenge to (a) which arises from a claim that there can be a legitimate plurality of different 'models' of Catholic school. From the perspective of this challenge it is argued that, whilst some Catholic schools have the role of transmitting to Catholic students the Catholic tradition of faith and life and educating them within it, other Catholic schools have a different educational role, for example in relation to the provision of certain forms of service to students who are marginalised or disadvantaged or in relation to the encouragement of dialogue with students of other faiths (Bishops' Conference of England and Wales, 1997b, ch.3).[3] In these other models, it is suggested, the Catholic school has a principled role in relation to students who are not Catholics which does not amount to 'transmission' or 'education within' the Catholic tradition of faith and life. However, whatever the merits of the arguments in support of these alternative models of Catholic school, it seems possible to accommodate these arguments within (a). This is because it seems a necessary part of any coherent attempt to show that these 'alternative models' of Catholic school are indeed Catholic schools that it be claimed that they are in fact engaged in *some* sense in transmission and education with respect to the Catholic tradition of faith and life, though in a particular and more diffuse way (for example, through exemplification and witness).

The present chapter therefore assumes that the general claims made in (a) and (b) are true. The task of analysing their meaning and implications is extensive. This chapter will explore a number of questions relating to the appropriate response of teachers and educational leaders in Catholic schools to the significance of the claims. The chapter has three sections. In the first, I indicate the importance of the claims and offer some thoughts about aspects of their practical significance for teachers and educational leaders in Catholic schools. In the next two sections I consider in turn two general issues relevant to an appropriate response to the claims; the question (related to (a)) of what is involved in the achievement of balanced judgement in relation to the claims in the light of 'the Catholic tradition of faith and

[3]   See also Bishops' Conference of England and Wales, 1997b, ch. 3.

life' and the need (related to (b)) to avoid in response to the claims a phenomenon I shall call 'the temptations of commonality'.

Both in the matters selected for discussion, and in the broadly philosophical approach adopted, the present discussion is necessarily partial and incomplete.

The Distinctiveness of Catholic Schools: Importance and Practical Significance

The importance of questions of distinctiveness for Catholic schools is manifest. This importance extends beyond the familiar point that a shared educational vision on the part of teachers and educational leaders in schools is a generally recognised requirement for educational effectiveness. In the case of Catholic schools, questions concerning distinctiveness are implicated in, even if they do not wholly determine, the criteria of what is to count as effectiveness.

Questions of the distinctiveness of Catholic schools can, and should be, explored in an abstract or theoretical way by theologians, bishops, philosophers, sociologists and others viewing education 'from a distance'. The present discussion, however, seeks to explore some aspects of the practical significance of questions of distinctiveness for teachers and educational leaders in Catholic schools. A number of matters are of relevance here.

At the outset, it is important to recognise that a school is not a seminar concerned with the exploration of abstract or theoretical ideas in a detached and disinterested way. A school is engaged in a practical enterprise of great complexity which calls for many forms of practical knowledge and understanding, judgement and wisdom, skill, disposition and commitment on the part of teachers and educational leaders. In the light of this recognition, a number of questions relating to the practical significance of questions of the distinctiveness of Catholic schools come into focus.

First, it is important to recognise that practical questions and demands relating to the distinctiveness of the Catholic school arise in relation to many issues in the school and in many different ways. The pervasive and polymorphous character of these distinctiveness-related questions and demands can be seen by considering the wide range of contexts in the Catholic school in which these questions and demands arise. At the level of the school as an institution these contexts include the writing and publication of statements of aim and mission, the recruitment, appointment, promotion (and perhaps dismissal) of staff, the admission of students, the 'marketing' of the school (perhaps in a competitive environment) and the prioritisation of resources. At the level of the life of the school as a whole, they include matters relating to the ethos and culture of the school in their various aspects (including liturgy and worship). At the level of the curriculum they include questions relating to pedagogy and 'content' in areas such as catechesis and religious education as well as in areas relating to the curriculum as a whole, including 'cross-curricula' elements such as sex education and specific subjects such as English, Mathematics and Science. At the level of the 'management' or leadership of the school they include processes such as school review, target setting, staff appraisal and the like. Indeed, it can be argued that questions and demands of distinctiveness cannot be excluded from any aspect of the life and work of the Catholic school.

Second, the professional qualities and capacities which are needed on the part of teachers and educational leaders in Catholic schools as a response to the many contexts in which questions and demands of distinctiveness arise are themselves wide ranging. These qualities and capacities include an understanding of issues relating to questions of distinctiveness at the level of general principle (derived, say, from scholarly resources, Church documents and professional guidelines and conferences), an ability to judge what is demanded in practical terms as an expression of the demands of distinctiveness in particular contexts (for example, with respect to decisions relating to staff appointments or to aspects of the ethos and culture of the school), the skill to put such judgements into practice (for example, in leading prayer or engaging in certain kinds of pedagogic practice), the disposition to be concerned about matters of distinctiveness and to act in relation to them, and the commitment to pursue these matters in the face of obstacles and difficulties. The complexity of some of the practical judgements involved in these matters scarcely requires emphasis.

It might be argued that the full range of these professional qualities and capacities cannot be expected of all teachers in Catholic schools. Teachers holding certain posts of responsibility, it might be claimed, can be expected to possess a fuller range of these qualities and capacities than other teachers. Further, it might be argued, certain qualities and capacities can be expected only of Catholic teachers — or, more precisely, Catholic teachers with an appropriate kind of religious commitment and practice who are prepared and able to bring this commitment and practice to bear upon their professional responsibilities. Whilst there is some truth in these claims, caution is needed in relation to them. For example, many teachers will testify that some of their colleagues who are not Catholics make a more significant contribution to the distinctiveness of the school than those who are Catholics. Further, and crucially, it is appropriate to ask all teachers in Catholic schools, whatever their level of responsibility within the school and whatever the nature and degree of their religious commitment and practice, to indicate the ways in which they contribute to the distinctiveness of the school, or might be able to do so. Every teacher, it has been argued, can and should make some sort of contribution to this distinctiveness and this contribution should feature in their formal appraisal.[4] A demand of this kind arises from the aspiration of the Catholic school to exercise a kind of holistic influence (McLaughlin, op. cit., pp.14lff; Congregation for Catholic Education, op. cit., §14, 18, 19) from which no teacher can be exempted.

Third, it is important to consider how these professional qualities and capacities demanded of teachers and educational leaders in Catholic schools by the questions and demands of distinctiveness may be best developed. The varied character of the qualities and capacities that have been identified indicate that no simple answer can be given to this question. The promotion of forms of theoretical study on the part of the professionals involved is only part of the story. The qualities and capacities do not involve a crude 'application' of theory to practice by teachers and educational leaders. It has long been realised that the proper role of 'theory' in relation to educational practice cannot be seen in terms of crude 'application'. A more adequate view sees 'theory' as initially developed in practice as part of the 'professional common sense' of teachers and educational leaders, much of which is unreflective and tacit in character. More explicit and systematic 'theory' (including that developed in relation to the distinctiveness of the Catholic school) has a role in gradually sophisticating this understanding in an appropriate way at various stages and contributing to the development of a body of educational practices informed and justified by defensible 'practical theory' (Hirst, 1990). On this view, abstract or theoretical analyses still have an indispensable value and role. I have suggested elsewhere, for example, that the lack of an articulated contemporary Catholic philosophy of education deprives the Catholic educational

[4]   I owe this point to John Sullivan. See Sullivan, 1998, Appendix One.

community of an important resource for dealing with questions of distinctiveness (McLaughlin, op. cit., pp. 138f). Such abstract and theoretical analyses, however, merely have a contributory role in relation to an understanding of and engagement with the practical questions which arise.

Educational practice cannot wait upon the achievement of the sort of clarity required in a philosophical discussion, nor can it proceed in a unduly rationalistic way. Practical experiment, intuition, compromise, 'artistry' and the like are inherent in the very nature of educational practice (McLaughlin, 1994). The sorts of professional qualities and capacities that are being sought are best developed in close relationship with educational practice itself.

It is claimed in some quarters that the sorts of professional qualities and capacities we have been referring to are best conceptualised in terms of the concept of 'the reflective teacher'. Thus, it may be claimed, the questions and demands of distinctiveness will be best addressed if Catholic teachers become 'reflective teachers'. However, despite the insights which are embodied in the concept of the 'reflective teacher', the concept lacks clarity and is apt for use as a vague slogan. An adequate account of the concept requires sustained attention to the meaning and implications of 'reflection' and to its scope and objects. Further, the concept of 'the reflective teacher' seems incomplete. We want and need teachers to have qualities and capacities which extend beyond reflection (McLaughlin, 1999).

The professional qualities and capacities to which we have been referring are better conceptualised in terms of a form of pedagogic practical wisdom or *phronesis* in the Aristotelian sense. Wilfred Carr describes *phronesis* as ' ... a comprehensive moral capacity which combines practical knowledge of the good with sound judgement about what, in a particular situation, would constitute an appropriate expression of this good' (Carr, 1995, p. 71). The full articulation of this notion, and its educational implications, lies beyond the scope of this chapter, and only central suggestive elements of the notion can be indicated here.[5] In *phronesis* practical knowledge of the good is related to intelligent and personally engaged sensitivity to situations, individuals (including oneself) and a tradition of belief and life, in making inherently supple and non-formulable practical

[5] For such articulations see, for example, Carr, 1995, ch.4, Dunne, 1993, esp. pt.2. For an articulation of the notion of practical judgement in the context of moral judgement see, for example, Smith, 1997.

judgements about what constitutes an appropriate expression of the good in a given circumstance.

Sustained attention is needed to the exploration of a distinctively Catholic form of pedagogic *phronesis* which could form the basis of distinctively Catholic forms of teacher education and training at pre- and in-service levels and which could constitute the best way in which the professional qualities and capacities which have been identified might be developed. Here an emphasis would be placed on the development of the teacher in a broad way. Dunne comments that the sort of practical knowledge which is at stake in *phronesis* is '... a fruit which can only grow only in the soil of a person's experience and character' (Dunne, 1993, p. 358). Dunne continues: 'In exposing oneself to the kind of experience and acquiring the kind of character that will yield the requisite knowledge ... [one]... is at the same time a feeling, expressing, and acting person, and one's knowledge is inseparable from one as such' (ibid.). A notion of a Catholic form of pedagogic *phronesis* involves the wide-ranging formation of the teacher in the Catholic tradition of faith and life in general, and the Catholic educational tradition in particular. Such a wide-ranging formation, in which spiritual development has a central place, has some affinities with kinds of formation offered to members of religious orders.

Several of the demands of distinctiveness seem apt for satisfaction by *phronesis*. These include the need for teachers and educational leaders to exercise complex contextualised judgement and to exert influence of relevant kinds through their personhood and example.

The suggestion that a Catholic form of pedagogic phronesis might be explored may encounter a number of objections and difficulties. Joseph Dunne draws our attention to '... the complicity of *phronesis* with an established way of life' (ibid., p.373). In the case of the kind of *phronesis* under discussion, this is the Catholic tradition of faith and life. The difficulty here is whether this tradition, in the circumstances of present-day life, is sufficiently 'established' in the required sense. Further, the notion of 'pedagogic *phronesis* seems to demand flourishing and relatively stable 'communities of practice' (Pendlebury, 1990). It might be argued that we do not, at least in Britain, enjoy a sufficiently robust Catholic form of life and a sufficiently flourishing 'community of practice' among Catholic educators for the notion of a Catholic 'pedagogic *phronesis* to get off the ground. A further difficulty, it might be claimed, is that we lack a sufficient number of Catholic teachers with the relevant commitments. We ought, however, to move towards the implementation of this notion, albeit in a gradual way.

However, in the absence of the specification and enactment of a wide-ranging formation for teachers and educational leaders in Catholic schools of the sort associated with the notion of a Catholic 'pedagogic *phronesis*, it is nevertheless possible for a number of valuable steps to be taken in relation to the development of the professional qualities and capacities which have been discussed, and many of these steps have been taken in England and Wales and elsewhere. Some of these steps include encouraging teachers and educational leaders to go beyond 'edu-babble' (imprecise and platitudinous rhetoric) in their handling of the questions and demands of distinctiveness (McLaughlin, 1996). Further, the understanding by the professionals of the issues at stake can be enhanced by a number of initiatives and practical strategies and requirements. These include publications and statements (Catholic Education Service, 1996b; Catholic Education Service and *Briefing*, 1997), courses of various kinds, professional exercises and policy requirements. Prominent among potential misunderstandings concerning the questions and demands of distinctiveness is the mis-perception that they arise only in relation to a part of the life and work of the Catholic school and in relation to certain members of staff only.

Needless to say it is important to emphasise that the questions and demands of distinctiveness cannot be dealt with teachers and educational leaders in Catholic schools in isolation from other important agents and influences, such as Church authorities and the educational policies of the state. These broader influences require consideration in a fuller account.

The development and exercise of the professional qualities and capacities needed by teachers and educational leaders in Catholic schools relevant to the questions and demands of distinctiveness give rise to many issues. I focus attention in turn below on two of these: the need for teachers and educational leaders to achieve balanced judgement in relation to the Catholic tradition of faith and life and the need for them to avoid what I shall refer to as 'the temptations of commonality'.

Balanced Judgement and the Catholic Tradition of Faith and Life

In his book Travels in Sacred Places, Geoffrey Robinson, Auxiliary Bishop of the Archdiocese of Sydney and Chairman of the Catholic

School Board in that city, recalls a vision of God which is widely seen as having been dominant in the minds of earlier generations of Catholics. This is a vision of an 'angry' God, who frowned on enjoyment and 'this-life', inspired fear and demanded unquestioning obedience to detailed rules. As the Bishop reminds us 'the Catholic Church is famous for its angry God' (1997, p. 6). Whilst acknowledging the need to take a balanced and carefully judged view of the conception of God which was in fact presented to, and experienced by, Catholics in earlier times, the Bishop nevertheless considers that, for many people, the image of an 'angry' God was dominant and overwhelming (ibid., ch. 2).

Such a vision of an 'angry' God is, the Bishop insists, deeply flawed in many respects. It is clearly damaging to the health and growth of individuals psychologically and spiritually and can be mis-used as a device for manipulating people. A vision of an 'angry' God involves a distortion of the Christian message. For good reasons, he notes, contemporary Catholics have reacted against the conception of God as 'angry', and seek to avoid the transmission of such a conception of God to their own children.

In the face of this the Bishop poses an interesting question in relation to this reaction. Has it, he asks, gone to an opposite extreme, and generated a conception of God which is inadequate in other ways? He describes this reactive conception in the following terms: 'This new God is full of love, tenderness, compassion, kindness and warm feelings. This God permanently consoles, never challenges, doesn't forgive because there is no such thing as sin and thus nothing to forgive, and often doesn't even encourage, for encouragement could imply challenge' (ibid., p. 9). Such a vision of God, observes the Bishop, ascribes 'unintelligent love' to God and limits God's response to all human situations to something akin to the giving of a 'big hug'. It is a vision of God which is, in his view, not only unintelligent and limited but also undemanding and unsatisfying. Further, the Bishop implies, this reactive vision of God is false and harmful.

In place of this kind of exaggerated reactive vision of God, the Bishop urges the acceptance of a deeper and more adequate vision, which preserves in a delicate balance the notion both of a God of love and a God of challenge.[6]

Bishop Robinson's discussion serves as an illustration of the indispensability of balanced discernment and judgement in matters of

[6]   See esp. chs. 6,8–11, 28, 30, 33–42, 46–48.

faith, and the need to be alert to the dangers of distorted perception and reaction. In the Catholic tradition of faith and life, as elsewhere, balanced discernment and judgement are essential.

Any attempt to illuminate the notion of 'balanced discernment and judgement' in the Catholic tradition of faith and life involves issues of great complexity. To sketch matters roughly, a first move in any such illumination requires an outline of the clarification of the general features of the tradition in which 'balanced discernment and judgement' is to be exercised.

There have been many attempts to elucidate the central features of the Catholic tradition of faith and life. Richard McBrien offers the following general answers to the question: 'What is Catholicism?'

> Catholicism is a rich and diverse reality. It is a Christian tradition, a way of life, and a community ... it is comprised of faith, theologies, and doctrines and is characterised by specific liturgical, ethical and spiritual orientations and behaviours; at the same time, it is a people, or cluster of peoples, with a particular history. (McBrien, 1994, p.3)

> '... the Catholic Church is a community of persons (the human dimension) who believe in God and shape their lives according to that belief (the religious dimension); who believe in God as tri-une and in Jesus Christ as the Son of God and the redeemer of human kind, and who shape their lives according to that belief (the Christian dimension); who ritually express and celebrate that belief especially in the Eucharist, and who ... recognise the Bishop of Rome to be 'the perpetual and visible source and foundation of the unity of the bishops and of the multitude of the faithful' (the ecclesial dimension). To be Catholic, therefore, is to be a kind of human being, a kind of religious person, and a kind of Christian disciple belonging to a specific eucharistic community of disciples within the worldwide, or ecumenical, Body of Christ, (ibid., p. 1187)

McBrien holds that the distinctiveness of Catholicism consists in a particular and unique configuration of characteristics including the principles (or themes) of sacramentality, mediation and communion, and of tradition, reason, analogy and universality. The task of articulating these characteristics, and Catholicism itself, in detail is clearly an extensive one, in which reference to such resources as the Catechism of the Catholic Church (1994) is important.

The notion of balanced judgement is involved in relation to the Catholic faith and life in a number of ways. First, the notion of balance is inherent in the very nature of Catholicism itself. McBrien emphasises the centrality of the notion of balance to Catholicism by referring to its embracing of 'both/and' rather than 'either/or' approach:

> It is not nature or grace, but graced nature; not reason or faith, but reason illumined by faith; not law or Gospel, but law inspired by the Gospel; not Scripture or tradition, but normative tradition within Scripture; not faith or works, but faith issuing in works and works as expressions of faith; not authority or freedom, but authority in the service of freedom; not unity or diversity, but unity in diversity, (ibid., p. 16)

An emphasis upon the notion of balance in the structure of Catholic faith and life is a central feature of Kevin Nichols' recent book Refracting the Light: Learning the Languages of Faith (1997). Nichols focuses his attention upon four interrelated 'languages of faith': narrative expression or story, doctrine, liturgy and Christian morality. The need for balanced judgement is inherent within each of these 'languages of faith' and between them. With regard to balanced judgement within each 'language', Nichols illustrates how, for example, such judgement is required in relation to the 'language of story' in the discernment of the 'truth' of stories (ibid., pp. 32–41), and is aided by the role of metaphor in unifying diverse elements of faith (ibid., p. 41). Such judgement is required in relation to the 'language of doctrine' in achieving an appropriate understanding of the nature and importance of doctrines, and in ensuring (for example) that they are not on the one hand mistaken for the objects of faith nor on the other hand seen as insignificant for faith or as merely relative or provisional: whilst doctrine develops and is not exhaustive, Nichols maintains, it is nevertheless true (ibid., pp. 56–64). Further, such judgement is required in discerning the 'hierarchy of truths' of the faith. Such judgement is required in relation to the 'language of liturgy' in discerning its distinctive character as a mode of expression of faith (ibid., ch. 3). Balanced judgement is also required in relation to the 'language of morality', in such matters as the achievement of an understanding of the proper relationship between the moral demands of, on the one hand, law, authority, general principle and the avoidance of sin, and on the other of love, conscience, the making of contextually sensitive concrete decisions and the development of virtue.[7] With regard to balanced judgement between the various

[7]   Ibid., pp.110–111; 126–129; ch. 5.

'languages' of faith, Nichols illustrates the mutual interaction, nourishment and correction that exists between them (ibid., p.22).

As well as the notions of balance and balanced judgement being inherent in the very nature of Catholicism itself, these notions are clearly required in the process by which individuals appropriate the tradition of faith and life. One reason for this is that the tradition cannot be conceived as wholly fixed, static and transparent. Nichols points out how a balanced grasp of the different languages of faith in relation to each other is necessary to guard against distortions and narrowness of perception and vision. And since the languages of faith do not have a precise grammar and syntax, being a Catholic is best seen, in Nichols' view, in terms of being the occupant of a house. He writes:

> It is a way of knowing which is oblique and partial. It is not knowledge which we are meant to do up in neat packages and present cockily to others as a set of ultimate facts. We are meant, rather, in humility, to draw others into this way of understanding … It is a house in which we have space to live and breathe, to relate to others, now intimately, now stormily. It is a house in which we are never bored though sometimes afflicted; often also surprised by joy. (ibid., p. 152)

The achievement of 'balanced judgement' in relation to the Catholic tradition of faith and life is clearly important for teachers and educational leaders in Catholic schools in their handling of the questions and demands of distinctiveness. This is for a number of reasons. One reason concerns the need to avoid distortion and bias in the interpretation of the Catholic tradition. This general concern about distortion and bias can be illustrated by reference to the case of catechesis. The General Directory of Catechesis (1997, pt. 2, chs I and II) insists that catechesis involves a normative content to be transmitted in a way which is comprehensive, systematic, structured and approved on behalf of the universal Church, since catechesis is an ecclesial activity. Therefore, catechists must be able to '… "integrate",… [and be]… capable of overcoming "unilateral divergent tendencies"… and … [be] … able to provide a full and complete catechesis. They must know how to link.. .orthodoxy and orthopraxis, ecclesial and social meaning … lest tensions arise between them' (ibid., §238–245).[8] A somewhat similar set of concerns underlies recent attempts to specify in more detail the aims and content of religious

[8]   See also §67, 78f, 282, 284f, 219, 236f, 238–248, 249.

teaching in Catholic schools (Bishops' Conference of England and Wales, 1996a). This concern to do justice to the Catholic tradition of faith and life has application beyond the specific areas of catechesis and religious education to all the aspects of the work of the teacher and educational leader in the Catholic school.

Apart from concerns about distortion and bias, however, a balanced grasp of the Catholic tradition of faith and life is needed by teachers and educational leaders in Catholic schools if their work in relation to distinctiveness is not to be merely superficial. The achievement of 'balanced judgement' in relation to the Catholic tradition of faith and life is not, however, straightforward. It involves the kind of *phronesis* which was outlined earlier, and the sorts of difficulties and obstacles noted in relation to the acquisition of 'pedagogic *phronesis* apply here also. A further difficulty emerges by confronting the question: What is to count as a balanced judgement in relation to the Catholic tradition of faith and life? The notion of 'balance' is, in itself, a purely formal one and is uninformative about what precisely a balance is to consist in with regard to any specific judgement. A significant issue relevant to this matter is dispute and disagreement within the Catholic tradition of faith and life about a number of issues and the phenomenon of lack of unity and cohesion within the Church.[9] The existence of disputes and disagreements of these kinds was indicated earlier as explanatory of many disputes and disagreements with respect to the questions and demands of distinctiveness. On the part of teachers and educational leaders in Catholic schools these disputes and disagreements may require the adoption of approaches and attitudes such as those distinctive of the 'Catholic common ground' project in the United States.[10]

A balanced grasp of the Catholic tradition of faith and life is also important if Catholic teachers and educational leaders are to avoid what I shall call 'the temptations of commonality'.

The Temptations of Commonality

The 'temptations of commonality' can be seen as arising in the form of a reaction to an earlier distorted vision of Catholic education. Just as Catholicism used to be famous for its 'angry God,' so too, it might be argued, it used to be famous for a form of education which

[9]   On this matter in relation to catechesis see, for example, Congregation for the Clergy, 1997, esp. §28.

[10]   'On the Catholic Common Ground Project' see The Tablet, 17 August 1996, p.1085; 7 September 1996, pp.1156–1159. Compare Robinson 1997, ch. 48.

emphasised authority, guilt creation, doctrine, orthodoxy, rigid rules, sanctions and rituals, and the development of a Catholic identity somewhat defensive with respect to the wider world. Such a view of Catholic education, it is claimed, failed to awake a real understanding of and commitment to the faith on the part of young people, and frequently amounted to a form of mere 'sacramentalising of the unevangelised'. Further, it is urged, this form of education was seriously deficient with respect to the attitudes to the wider world which it conveyed. As with the conception of God as 'angry', this view of Catholic education needs to be seen in a clear and fair perspective; caricatures need to be avoided and the true nature and value of earlier emphases appreciated (O'Donoghue, 1997). However, again as with the 'angry God' this model of Catholic education is sufficiently recognisable for its dominance in the experience of earlier generations of Catholics to be acknowledged.

A typical reaction to this model of Catholic education is discernible in a recent piece of research which explored the distinctiveness of a system of Catholic secondary schools run by a religious order. Here the particular details of the research are not at issue, but rather the general picture of Catholic schools which it presents. The research showed that there was much evidence of forms of distinctiveness in the culture and life of the schools which was authentically derived from the charisma of the founder of the order. However, these forms of distinctiveness were mainly concerned with extensions of, or specific emphases relating to, values commonly recognised in society as a whole such as caring, social justice, self-esteem and 'the spiritual quest' broadly conceived. The researcher found that, despite the centrality to the thought of the founder of specifically religious aims and concepts (in particular the importance of catechesis), in the schools there was a lack of clarity about their religious and ecclesial purposes, that these matters lacked clear and consistent expression, that there was considerable ambivalence concerning the spiritual purposes of the schools, that the staff did not see their efforts as aiming at 'traditional Catholic practice' on the part of the students, that the more specifically religious goals of the schools were not strongly subscribed to by the students, that both the students and the staff were 'largely disconnected' from the 'institutional Church' and that parents were sending their children to the schools less and less for specifically religious reasons. What is interesting about this research is that the phenomena identified were seen by staff in the schools not merely as *de facto* states of affairs dictated by practical, and perhaps regrettable, realities, but in some cases as expressions of what Catholic schools today should properly be aiming to achieve.

The concept of the angry God led to the over-reaction of the concept of an unrestrictedly nice God which was equally (though differently) inadequate. Has the concept of the dogmatic Catholic school led to the over-reaction of a Catholic school unduly dominated by variants of common values?

Indeed, the researcher in question raises the issue of whether the schools in his study had, in their emphasis upon variants of 'common' values linked to the charisma of the founder in a sometimes platitudinous way, brought about a diversion of attention away from Jesus and the Gospel.

The attractions of 'commonality' are easy to understand. It is clear, for example, that the Christian message has implications for the world and for engagement with its issues and problems. Further, the Catholic tradition of social teaching can be shown to have telling application in relation to the notion of 'the common good'. It is also true that attention to matters of 'commonality' is needed for purposes of student motivation and engagement. Michael Paul Gallagher, for example, argues that inhibitions or blockages to religious faith experienced by many young people today requires educators to engage in a kind of analysis and critique of contemporary culture, '… helping students to identify the dehumanising factors present in life-styles and assumptions …' (1997, p. 25).

The attractions of commonality become temptations when they prevent due attention being given to the specifically religious concepts and perspectives which a properly balanced perspective on the Catholic tradition of faith and life requires. This is not to suggest that Catholic schools are as a matter of fact succumbing to temptations of these kinds, merely that vigilance is needed with respect to them.

Conclusion

In this chapter I have attempted to illuminate the importance and practical significance of the questions and demands which arise for teachers and educational leaders in Catholic schools relating to the distinctiveness of these schools, and have indicated two issues requiring particular attention. A number of steps can and have been taken in relation to the development of the range of professional qualities and capacities needed by teachers and educational leaders in Catholic schools if they are to deal adequately with these questions and demands. However, it has been suggested that the nature both of the questions and demands and the professional qualities and capacities needed in response to them indicate the need to explore the notion of a distinctively Catholic version of pedagogic phronesis as the most favourable context in which relevant forms of professional formation and development can take place.

Moral, Religious and Values Education

Despite the fact that ethical enquiry formed the very core of McLaughlin's work, and that he was a key member of the editorial board of *Journal of Moral Education*, he produced relatively little work on moral education as such. Much the same may be said in respect of religious education as such, since — as we have already noticed — his main published work on this topic was more directly focused on the pros and cons of faith schooling. That said, he was clearly much interested in both topics and this section aims to draw together those McLaughlin papers that afford key insights into his views on the moral dimensions of education and teaching, and on the vexed status of religious instruction in (particularly) common schools.

The first paper of this section, 'Philosophy, values and schooling' offers a particularly clear and elegant exploration of a problem in which McLaughlin was especially interested concerning the moral dimensions of education and teaching. Like many of his educational philosophical contemporaries, McLaughlin was deeply concerned about latter day political and professional tendencies to construe teaching as little more than a kind of technical expertise that anyone might master with the right training. Recognizing in this paper that education and teaching are inevitably implicated in moral influence and formation, he sets out to clarify the character and extent of teachers' responsibilities for the transmission of values and virtues in (particularly) common schools. In the course of this, McLaughlin pays particular attention to the view that insofar as teaching involves the exemplification of values and virtues to the young, it is difficult to draw the same sharp line between professional role and personal character that may be possible with other occupations.

The interest of educational policy makers and professionals in the idea of 'spiritual education' intensified in the mid-nineteen nineties in response to concerns about (inter alia) growing instrumental trends in education, declining standards of youth conduct and the problematic status of school religious education in conditions of encroaching secularity. Like many of his philosophical contemporaries, McLaughlin was concerned to ask some hard questions about the conceptual coherence of the new discourse of spiritual education – particularly, again, in contexts of common schooling. McLaughlin's fine paper 'Education, spirituality and the common good' directly addresses these concerns and is also one source of his well-known and influential distinction between (religiously) 'tethered' and 'untethered' conceptions of spirituality.

McLaughlin's paper 'Sex education, moral controversy and the common school' offers an equally pioneering exploration of another important issue of great moral educational significance. Thus, after emphasizing in the strongest terms that it is vain to look for any neutral conception of sex education that completely eschews wider value commitments or which avoids reference to more morally implicated aspects of human association, McLaughlin's careful exploration of the pitfalls to which discussion in this area is heir opens the way to a much clearer view of the possibilities of common school sex education.

The last two papers in this section, equally concerned to explore the ideas of other philosophers, both provide considerable insight into Terry McLaughlin's views on the nature of religion and the right direction for religious education in common schools. The first paper, originally an invited contribution to a special issue of *Studies in Philosophy and Education*, takes a hard but sympathetic look at the educational implications of the remarks on religion of Wittgenstein – as well as of those (such as Rush Rhees, D. Z. Phillips and Fergus Kerr) who have attempted to develop such remarks. In this place, McLaughlin expresses considerable reservations about the (especially confessional) implications of what might be called (perhaps for the want of better terms) 'non-realist' or 'non-cognitive' conceptions of religion for common school religious education.

The final paper of this section, whilst also an invited contribution to a special issue of *Studies in Philosophy and Education* in honour of Israel Scheffler, actually gives us Terry McLaughlin's perspectives on two founding fathers of post-war educational philosophy for the price of one – since his paper devotes as much space to his own mentor R. S. Peters as it does to Scheffler. In the event, however, the paper provides not just much interesting comparison and contrast between the ideas on religion and education of Peters and Scheffler, but also much insight into McLaughlin's own enduring personal preoccupations with possible tensions between reason and faith.

David Carr

Chapter 11

Philosophy, Values and Schooling

*Principles and predicaments
of teacher example*

Introduction

In recent years there has been a wide-ranging philosophical debate about the nature and justification of the forms of complex evaluative influence that schools in pluralist liberal democratic societies exert on their students. Schooling is not, of course, synonymous with education, but schools remain important institutional contexts in which education is made available to children and young people and the organisation and distribution of schooling gives rise to many issues which have philosophical aspects or dimensions, not least because schooling, like education itself, is inherently value laden. Central to much recent philosophical debate are issues relating to the respective mandates for educational influence claimed in pluralist democratic societies by 'common' schools on the one hand and by 'faith-based' (or religious) schools on the other (see, for example, Callan, 1997, 2000; Dwyer, 1998; Gutmann, 1987; Feinberg, 1998; Halstead and McLaughlin, 2005; Levinson, 1999; McDonough and Feinberg, 2003; McLaughlin, 1992, 2003a; Macedo, 2000; Reich, 2002; Salomone, 2000; Thiessen, 2001; and White, 1996).

As befits a discipline that has been described as pre-eminently concerned with a discussion of abstract matters in the abstract, much of this philosophical debate has been conducted at a distance from educational practice. It has become increasingly clear, however, that a philosophical approach of these matters 'from above' educational practice needs to be complemented by a philosophical approach 'from below' if pertinent questions are to be fully illuminated. In particular, contemporary debate has tended to neglect the point that the distinctive forms of educational influence that both 'common' and religious schools seek to achieve are pre-eminently exerted through teachers. I have argued elsewhere that many of the philosophically significant burdens and dilemmas of common schooling require resolution at classroom level via a form of pedagogic *phronesis* on the part of teachers (McLaughlin, 2003a) as do judgements about equivalent burdens and dilemmas in religious schools (McLaughlin, 1999).

One distinctive form of educational influence that teachers exert is through their example. Our expectations of teachers therefore extend to the example that they set to the children and young people in their charge. No adequate discussion of the nature and justification of the forms of educational influence exerted by different kinds of schools can ignore the different kinds of teacher example which these schools presuppose and require. In this chapter I shall seek to show that an exploration of the principles and predicaments of teacher example in different schooling contexts throws important light on our understanding of the principles and predicaments relating to 'common' and 'faith-based' schools respectively.

The chapter has four sections. In the first, as a background to the discussion, I shall outline in general terms the scope of the example of the teacher. In the second section, I indicate how all forms of teacher example can generate significant controversy. The third section addresses the nature of our expectations with respect to the moral example given by the teacher in a 'common' school. In the fourth section I turn specifically to expectations concerning the moral and religious example of the teacher in 'faith-based' or religious schools. Throughout the discussion I will be using the term 'school' in the British sense to refer institutions of learning for students up to the age of 18.

The Scope of Teacher Example

At the outset, it is useful to look in more detail at the range of expectations we have of teachers with respect to the example they set to students, regardless of the sort of schools in which teaching and learning is taking place. In what follows, I shall refer to three (interrelated) categories of teacher example.

The first of these relate to what is seen by many as the main function of a teacher: the teaching of a subject or area of study. These 'subject related' expectations cover a number of different aspects of teacher example. We expect a teacher to give a good example of subject-related competence, skill and flair. We would think little of an English teacher whose own handwriting was illegible, whose imaginative response to poetry was poor or who displayed little love for literature. Similarly, a Mathematics teacher whose own practice of the subject was bedevilled by inaccuracy or a PE teacher who was incapable of displaying effectively the skills being taught would rightly be thought to be giving a poor example to students. Our expectations of 'subject-related' teacher example extend beyond competence, skill and flair. We also expect, among other things, that teachers will give an example of enthusiastic involvement in their subject and in learning generally.

It is important to avoid an unduly narrow view of the significance of 'subject-related' teacher example and to appreciate why *example* is indispensible. In his essay 'Learning and Teaching' (Oakeshott, 1989), Michael Oakeshott illuminates the complexity of the 'inheritance' which teachers must pass on to their pupils. It is not, he claims, a kind of property which could be conveyed by lawyers, requiring on the part of pupils merely 'legal acknowledgement'. On the contrary, it is a wide ranging inheritance of

> feelings, emotions, images, visions, thoughts, beliefs, ideas, understandings, intellectual and practical enterprises, languages, relationships, organizations, canons and maxims of conduct, procedures, rituals, skills, works of art, books, musical compositions, tools, artefacts and utensils (p. 45).

To enter this inheritance, claims Oakeshott, involves both the acquisition of 'information', which can be communicated through 'instruction', and of 'judgement' which, in Oakeshott's view, cannot properly be communicated in such a direct way. For Oakeshott, 'judgement' involves the development of the intellectual virtues (such as disinterested curiosity, patience, exactness, industry and the like) and an awareness of 'style' (the detection of an 'individual intelligence' operating in every 'utterance'). 'Judgement' cannot be communicated by instruction but must be 'imparted' in everything which is taught. Oakeshott writes

> It is implanted unobtrusively in the manner in which information is conveyed, in a tone of voice, in the gesture which accompanies instruction, in asides and oblique utterances, and by example (p. 61).

With regard to the latter, Oakeshott acknowledges his debt to a particular teacher for giving him a recognition of certain important virtues

> ... I owed it to him, not on account of anything he ever said, but because he was a man of patience, accuracy, economy, elegance and style (p. 62).

The wide ranging sorts of influence over pupils that the teacher has to exert in the 'conversation between the generations' that constitutes education means that the teacher must be a *certain sort of person* who communicates not only knowledge and skill but also (parts of) him or herself.

The requirement that a teacher be a certain sort of person is apparent too in the second category of teacher example to which I shall refer. This category relates to our expectation that the teacher should act as a responsible adult. The kind of example being sought here embraces, and extends beyond, the duties of acting *in loco parentis*. We expect a teacher not only to set an example of prudence, care and common sense in relation to many matters, but also to exemplify broader personal qualities such as balance, wisdom and maturity.

The third category of teacher example is the specifically moral example that we expect a teacher to set. The slogan 'every teacher is a moral educator' captures the important point that a teacher cannot avoid moral responsibility. Education, teaching and schooling are inherently laden with moral values. Moral considerations are deeply implicated in all properly educational aims, relationships and processes. With regard to educational aims, we expect teachers to assume some responsibility for the moral education of pupils and to help (at least to some extent) to form their moral beliefs and character. Many other educational aims have strong moral overtones, such as the development of the 'critical independence' of pupils and the provision of 'equality of opportunity'. With regard to educational relationships, we expect teachers to control and discipline pupils not merely through the exercise of power, but through an appropriate form of authority, with its concern for reason, justification and fairness. We also look for morally resonant qualities such as integrity and respect in relationships between teachers and pupils. With regard to educational processes, we expect teachers to avoid intimidation, indoctrination, discrimination and the like, and to take account of morally significant considerations such as respect for the autonomy and dignity of the pupil.

The moral influence of the teacher is therefore wide-ranging and pervasive, and is inseparable from all other forms of teacher influence. As with these other forms, moral influence is exercised not only (or necessarily) through formally taught lessons, although moral questions can be directly handled in the classroom and arise in relation to aspects of many issues and subjects. A number of morally significant forms of learning, however, cannot take place simply through instruction or discussion. Morally significant qualities of the teacher such as integrity can only be detected in their exemplification. The forms of moral example that may be given by teachers are varied, and include not only actions but also less tangible ways in which attitudes and sensitivities can be expressed, including reactions and gestures. As with other aspects of teacher example, omissions can be highly significant. Teacher example is not confined to matters which are directly intended. The matters in relation to which moral example can be given are similarly varied, as are the contexts in which it can arise.

It is important to underscore the interrelatedness of the three categories of teacher example which I have identified. Moral considerations, for example, permeate both 'subject-related' and 'adult' teacher example. It is also important to note that within each of these categories, the expectations that arise vary as to their status and character. Some expectations have contractual or legal dimensions, in that a failure to satisfy them can involve the possibility of censure, dismissal or legal proceedings. One can readily imagine cases involving subject-related incompetence, lack of adult responsibility or moral failure which fall into this category. Other expectations in the categories relate to our broader expectations of the teacher as a professional, and several of these are matters which might feature in a professional code of ethics (on ethical codes of practice for teachers see, for example, Carr, 2000, Sockett, 1993, Ch 6, the Code of Professional Values and Practice for Teachers of the General Teaching Council for England <www.gtce.org.uk> and the Code of Ethical Practice for the Teaching Profession prepared by the Universities Council for the Education of Teachers <www.ucet.ac.uk>). A number of our expectations of teacher example, however, go beyond the contractually, legally or professionally significant and involve matters of personal preference, aspiration and style.

Controversiality and Teacher Example

As noted earlier, not all forms of teacher example are equally controversial. It might be thought, for instance, that in contrast to 'moral'
forms of teacher example, 'subject-related' and 'adult' examples are,
or should be, relatively uncontroversial. The qualifier 'relatively' is
important here, however, and we should not overlook the respects
in which all forms of teacher example can give rise to significant or
well-grounded controversy.

With regard to 'subject-related' teacher example, there is much
disagreement about what should be taught in schools (the 'inheritance' which teachers are responsible for passing on) and about
methods of teaching, and this can be expressed in terms of disagreement about related aspects of teacher example. Those who feel that
open critical discussion in the classroom of (say) sensitive political or
religious matters is inappropriate may regret a teacher's exemplification of Socratic questioning in relation to current political events
or the existence of God, and devotees of a particular author or play-
wright might criticise the example given by a teacher in dismissing
his or her work. Similarly, critics of 'progressive' teaching methods
may object to the failure of teachers to exemplify their favoured pedagogic virtues. There are, after all, different traditions of practice
within teaching, with different educational perspectives and commitments (McLaughlin, 2003b).

Disagreement about 'adult' teacher example can arise from differences of view on the nature of appropriate adult behaviour, and can
be expressed in terms of unease about (say) teachers' dress, linguistic style or demeanour (cf. Carr, 2000, ch. 6). Another source of possible controversy about 'adult' teacher example is the claim that, since
teachers 'model' adult life, women and members of ethnic minorities should be properly represented on the staff of a school, and in
positions of authority, so that pupils are not given a restricted set of
perceptions and aspirations. Such policies may give rise to controversy about the criteria that should appropriately govern the
appointment and promotion of teaching staff.

The moral example of the teacher, however, is particularly susceptible to controversy, in part because of the controversial character of
the moral domain as a whole in pluralist liberal democratic societies.
Controversy can focus upon the nature and extent of the moral
example which can be expected of a teacher. The issues involved
here differ according to particular schooling contexts. I shall there-

fore consider this matter first in relation to the 'common' school and then in relation to schools with a specifically religious character.

The Common School and the
Moral Example of the Teacher

A common school can be regarded as one in which all students are educated together regardless of differentiating characteristics such as religious and cultural background, and which aspires to offer a common conception of education which is seen as embodying an educational entitlement judged as appropriate for members of society as a whole. In the context of the value diversity of a pluralist democratic society, such a school is faced with a complex task with respect to moral influence. In aspiring to offer a common form of moral education for all pupils, such a school lacks a mandate to offer a specific form of moral influence which goes beyond that acceptable to society in general. The sort of moral influence which the common school can exert is illuminated by the familiar, albeit problematic, distinction between 'public' and 'non-public' morality in a pluralist democratic society, which can be accepted for the sake of the present argument. Roughly expressed, 'public' values can be regarded as those which, in virtue of their fundamentality or inescapability, can be insisted upon for all democratic citizens and for all reasonable and decent persons in general. It is in relation to common or 'public' values of this kind that the common school strives to exert a substantial and non-negotiable moral influence. It is therefore unhesitant in its advocacy of (say) kindness, toleration and honesty and its rejection of (say) cruelty, racism and deceit. In virtue of their strong commitment to the 'public' values, common schools cannot be accused of lacking a moral basis or of aspiring in any general way to value neutrality.

With regard, however, to values which are not 'public' or 'shared', the common school cannot exert a similarly strong and unambiguous moral influence. Such values are significantly controversial, often because of their connection with particular overall frameworks of belief which are themselves matters of disagreement and dispute. The moral significance of a canonically invalid marriage, for example, can only be appreciated within the broader framework of Catholic belief and practice. Such values can be described as 'non-public' not because they are, or can be, completely isolated in all respects from the 'public' domain, but because they cannot (either on principle or in practice) be imposed upon all citizens through the exercise of political power, or through a common form of education. In relation to such 'non-public' values the common school therefore lacks a mandate to shape either the beliefs or personal qualities of pupils in a way which assumes the truth or normative force of values of this kind. The common school must in these matters exert a principled forebearance from influence. It cannot, for example, express disapproval of (say) re-marriage after divorce on the religious ground that since divorce has only legal and not moral force, the couple in question is living in a state of permanent adultery. Nor can it exert a substantial and non-negotiable moral influence against cohabitation outside marriage on grounds which appeal to religious norms. In relation to religious matters, the common school has the role of developing the understanding of pupils and their capacity to make their own critical responses, judgements, and decisions. In important respects, the common school must regard questions of 'non-public' value as 'open', not in a sense which implies a relativistic view of them, but which insists that their public status inhibits the assumption and transmission of them in a definitive way.

The moral influence of the common school in a pluralist democratic society is therefore two-fold in character. On the one hand, it seeks a unifying and universalising influence, 'transmitting' the common and non-negotiable values, principles and procedures of such a society, and securing appropriate forms of respect for, and allegiance to, them on the part of pupils. On the other hand, the school seeks a diversifying and particularising influence with regard to significantly controversial moral questions where the demands of diversity and pluralism are acknowledged. In relation to such matters, the common school encourages on the part of pupils appropriate forms of understanding, open- mindedness, critical judgement and tolerance.

The moral role of the common school which has emerged in this sketch, together with the queries and difficulties to which it gives rise, requires much fuller elaboration and discussion, which I have attempted to provide elsewhere (McLaughlin, 2003a). For our present purposes, however, the sketch can serve as a basis on which the nature and extent of the moral example expected of the teacher in the common school can be brought into focus.

The two-fold character of the moral influence of the teacher in the common school is reflected in the nature and extent of the moral example which the teacher is expected to give. With regard to 'public' values such as kindness, care, fairness, impartiality, benevolence and the like, the teacher can be expected to offer a clear and unqualified example which mirrors the clarity and forthright commitment of the school to values of this kind. Teachers cannot opt out, for example, of providing an example of non-racist attitudes and behaviour. The claim that teachers in common schools should exemplify 'public' values is, however, more complicated than it may seem at first sight in the light of the fact that many of these values, properly understood, are themselves complex and morally textured. For example, the common school needs to achieve a fine-grained understanding of 'respect' on the part of its students. 'Respect' should not be presented as requiring the necessary approval of the choices which people make within the limits of their rights on (say) relativistic grounds, nor should 'civic' respect be presented as the only form of respect. Teachers therefore need to exemplify, particularly in the classroom, a form of respect which is sufficiently rich to satisfy the educational aims of the school. More generally, Callan's account of the nature and demands of the attitudes, habits and abilities required by public virtue (Callan, 1997), some of which are subtle and complicated, have their implications for teacher exemplification. A further complication for this task arises from the fact that the common school should be concerned with the *fit* between the public and the non- public views which students affirm.

With respect to 'non-public' values, the common school cannot *require* a teacher to 'model' an aspect of 'non-public' belief, such as a particular form of religious practice. It may not *forbid* a teacher providing such an example, providing that it is made clear that no processes are involved which suggest that pupils are being directly and unfairly persuaded to subscribe to the values involved. Thus many Christian teachers who work in common schools see themselves as having a vocation to provide a personal example of Christian commitment to pupils. The school may have no objection to the commitment of the teacher becoming clear to pupils in various contexts, as long as the teacher in question does not attempt to directly encourage his or her pupils to become religious believers in unacceptable ways. In general, therefore, where a teacher does offer an example related to 'non-public' moral value, the common school requires that that teacher offer an additional example of principled forebearance from influence and an encouragement of pupils to think for themselves on the matters at stake. The difficulties inherent in making a judgment about when 'undue influence' is being exerted, or when a proper encouragement to pupils to think for themselves is being given, highlights the complexity of the practical judgements needed in relation to matters of this kind. An interesting question concerning the 'non-public' domain and teacher exemplification concerns the extent to which a teacher's own views on controversial questions should be revealed in classroom discussions of such matters.

One important issue which arises in relation to the extent of the moral example which can be expected of the teacher in a common school is the relationship between the 'professional' and the 'personal' life of the teacher. In relation to the moral example of the teacher — and indeed the role of the teacher more broadly — the 'professional' and the 'personal' cannot be separated from each other in any very simple way. The professional responsibilities of a teacher cannot be isolated from the qualities which the teacher possesses as a person (on these matters see Carr, 2000, Hare, 1993). In contrast, in the case of some professions, it is possible to envisage a less strong connection between the personal characteristics of the professional and his or her professional competence. However, the strong connection between the 'professional' and the 'personal' in teaching needs to be understood carefully.

The issues involved are usefully illuminated by a recent discussion by David Carr. In his consideration of the close relationship between the moral role of teachers and their moral personhood, Carr insists that '… it is the normal expectation that decent or right values will be exhibited only by those who hold them' (Carr, 1993, p. 195). Although 'hold' is somewhat ambiguous (as between, say, 'believe in' and 'live by'), the general point here can be accepted. However, Carr goes on to claim that '… values are not the sort of qualities that a person assumes in one context and sheds in another; since they crucially define what or who a person *is* they can only be expected to assert themselves across the different contexts of life in which an individual operates' (Carr, 1993, p. 198). Further, Carr argues, '… an effective teacher of values can only be the individual who clearly exhibits them in his personal life' (Carr, 1993, p. 205). Whilst there is a good deal of truth in both of these observations, their interpretation in relation to the moral role of the teacher needs some care. There is a certain ambiguity in the notion of the 'personal life' of the teacher. A distinction needs to be drawn between the 'personal' and the 'private'. For reasons mentioned earlier, the 'personal' has wide ranging significance for the professional work of the teacher, but the significance of the 'private' is less easy to judge. Drawing a distinction between the 'personal' and the 'private' gives rise to the question: Are *all* the 'contexts of life' in which the teacher operates relevant to his or her professional role? Carr does point out that what a teacher is like as a 'private person' is a not a matter of indifference and he gives homosexuality and extra-marital cohabitation as examples of the sorts of aspects of the lives of teachers which parents are inclined to worry about (Carr, 1993, p. 195). He does not, however, give a full account of how these matters should be handled.

How might the domains of the 'professional' and the 'private' be distinguished with regard to the teacher in a common school? This is no easy task. A solution to the problem can, however, be developed along the following lines. First, the 'professional' role of the teacher can be seen as relating directly to his or her work in school in its various aspects. As indicated earlier, this role is inseparable from the personal qualities of the teacher, and for this reason it is impossible for the teacher's 'personal life' in this sense to remain wholly irrelevant to, or concealed from, pupils: the 'professional' includes significant aspects of the 'personal'. Underpinning the professional role of the teacher are the 'public' values described earlier, and the attitude toward 'non-public' values which was also described. Second, it is possible, and necessary, to delineate a 'private' domain of the 'personal' life of the teacher. This is the context in which the teacher lives his or her life in a fuller sense, including the living out of a personal vision of life as a whole governed by 'non-public' values. Teachers in common schools do not expect that their own religious faith (or lack of it), political beliefs or domestic arrangements will be seen as matters which have a bearing on their professional role, provided that these matters do not intrude inappropriately upon that role. A teacher's 'private' life cannot, however, escape some degree of moral assessment. This is particularly the case when an infringement of 'public' values is involved. Thus a teacher's conviction for theft, violence or child abuse could not be regarded as a 'private' matter, even though the offences may not have been committed in school. Many matters involving 'non-public' values relating to the teacher's life outside school might, however, be seen as of no concern to the professional role of the teacher in the common school. Therefore if teachers are living in a homosexual relationship or re-married after divorce, this should not be seen as relevant to their professional work. There has been in recent years an expansion of the 'private' domain of teacher's lives, compared to earlier times when teachers in common schools were expected to embody a much wider range of moral qualities and virtues than is now found acceptable, in part because of the complex part which religion has played in the development of public schooling in England and Wales (on this matter see, for example, Tropp, 1957).

The suggestion that matters involving 'non-public' values relating to the teacher's life outside school is of no relevance to the professional role of the teacher needs, however, to be handled with caution. Within the 'private' domain of the life of the teacher there is a 'public/private' area, where some aspect or aspects of the private life and belief of teachers may come into the public domain. This may be through the direct statements of teachers, or by the visibility of (say) their political activities or domestic arrangements in the vicinity of the school.

Kenneth Strike draws attention to a complex 'middle ground' between, on the one hand, matters which are clearly part of the teacher's private life and in relation to which interference is justifiable only on very strong evidence of their causing educational harm and, on the other, matters which either in virtue of their direct harm to students or their illegality do require interference. This 'middle ground' he argues contains

> ... activities that usually are not illegal and that may have some degree of legal protection as part of a right of privacy but that are found to be immoral or offensive by some part of the community (Strike, 1990, p. 196).

What is particularly difficult about such matters is that

> There is no moral consensus about them, they may be held to be part of the individual's private sphere regardless of whether they are thought to be immoral, and their effects on students are difficult to ascertain (p. 197).

The existence of this 'middle ground' is underscored by the fact that common schools exist in social, cultural and political contexts which are complex and changing. The evaluative basis of such schools cannot be solely derived from considerations of abstract principle. If it is accepted that a principled distinction between 'public' and 'non-public' values is broadly tenable, it is important to note that what is in fact regarded as signficantly controversial, and therefore as a public or a non-public matter, will vary in different contexts and over time. We do not enjoy a stable consensus about matters in the 'middle ground' to which Strike refers. It is therefore not possible to map a very clear distinction between the 'public' values (which might be thought to govern the 'professional' role of teachers including its 'personal' aspects) and the 'non-public' (governing their 'private' life). This will call for discretion about the extent to which matters in the 'private' domain are made public. These difficulties are reinforced by close attention to the mandate of the common school. Strictly speaking it is required to have an 'open' view on matters of non-public value. But it might be thought that a teacher known to have a certain position on a 'non-public' matter is jeopardising his capacity to teach in an even-handed way.

The demands upon the moral example of the teacher in the common school are therefore not straightforward. Complex practical judgement in relation to this matter is called for as it is in relation to the aspiration of the law to specify 'reasonable requirements' for the behaviour of teachers without unjustifiably restricting their liberty.

The Moral and Religious Example of the Teacher in the Faith School

The issues which arise concerning the moral example of the teacher in a faith or religious school are clearly different from those which arise in the common school as a result of the wider mandate for the exercise of educational influence which faith schools enjoy. In contrast to the common school, the educational influence of the faith school can be based on an overall philosophy of life. Thus, in the Catholic school, for example '. . . a specific concept of the world, of man, and of history is developed and conveyed' (Sacred Congregation for Catholic Education [1977] – hereinafter CS – para 8). Faith schools can be described as seeking to achieve non-common educational aims in a non-common educational environment (Halstead and McLaughlin, 2005). The non-common educational aims to which most faith schools aspire are to present a particular religion as true, together with a range of beliefs, values and attitudes (including those of a moral kind) which follow from this, including the aspiration to form the religious commitment of students in some way. Aims such as these are non-common in that, in pluralistic liberal democracies, they are not shared by society as a whole, although care should be taken to avoid giving the impression that there are no significant overlaps between aims of this kind and those of the common school. The educational environment of a faith school is non-common in that it is precisely intended for a particular group within society and not for society as a whole, even if, for various reasons, admissions to the school may extend beyond these boundaries. In virtue of these distinctive aims and environments, faith schools can expect a greater scope of moral example on the part of its teachers than can common schools, and this expectation can extend to religious example as well.

The centrality of the example of the teacher to the educational mission of faith schools is strongly emphasized. Thus the teacher in the Catholic school is seen as one who not only transmits knowledge but forms human persons by communicating Christ (Sacred Congregation for Catholic Education [1982] – hereinafter LWCF – para 16). He or she must provide a 'concrete example' of the Catholic concept of the human person (LWCF paras 18, 22), be a source of spiritual inspiration (LWCF para 23), extend horizons through their personal faith (LWCF para 28) and provide a wide ranging example of faith witness (LWCF paras 32–33; 40–41; 59). For reasons such as these the life of Catholic teachers is seen as involving not merely the exercise of professionalism but of a personal vocation (LCWF para 37) in which '… they reveal the Christian message not only by word but also by every gesture of their behaviour' (CS para 43).

It might be thought that these requirements of teacher example in the faith school are appropriate only for certain teachers in the school, such as those concerned with the teaching of religion and holders of key leadership roles. However, at least at the level of principle, this conclusion cannot be drawn so easily in the case of many faith schools. Catholic education, for example, aims to provide a holistic educational experience. This 'holistic dimension' is one of the major reasons why the church considers that separate Catholic *schools* are such an important part of its educational mission. Therefore it seeks to 'integrate … all the different aspects of human knowledge through the subjects taught, in the light of the Gospel' (CS para 37, see also paras 26, 33–43). What is involved in this wider Catholic influence on the general curriculum of the school is complex, as is the broader question of the distinctive character of the life and work of the Catholic school as a whole. The aspiration, however, to provide an integrated or holistic educational experience is clear. There is therefore a need for all teachers in the school to share a common purpose and commitment – so that 'unity in teaching' and the development of community can be achieved (CS paras 29, 59–61).

The range of things which teachers are expected to exemplify in the faith school is therefore wide ranging. If these expectations are to be construed non-platitudinously, they require, amongst other things, a formation for teaching which in its nature and scope goes far beyond what is currently envisaged by most faith communities.

In the case of Catholic schools, for example, there has been a tendency for Catholic teacher education to be seen as requiring no more than the addition of a few elements to teacher education generally conceived. It seems clear, however, that from the point of view of the expectations of exemplification, a much fuller kind of personal and spiritual formation is needed for teachers in Catholic schools (McLaughlin, 2003b). A focus on the expectations of exemplification also invite closer attention to what some of the expectations actually mean and imply. This is the case, for example, in relation to the integrative aspects of the Catholic school. What must a maths teacher exemplify, for example, in integrating mathematics with the light of the Gospel?

The requirements of faith schools with regard to the moral and religious example given by their teachers would seem to call into question the distinctions between the 'professional', 'personal' and 'private' lives of teachers which were drawn in the case of teachers in common schools. In the context of the common school it was argued that the 'private' life of the teacher (the context in which he or she lives out his fuller vision of life governed by 'non-public' values) can be seen as separable from his or her professional role, subject to compatibility with public values and sensitivity to 'middle ground' issues. It would seem, however, that the 'private' lives of teachers are inseparable from the moral and religious example which they are invited to give in the faith school. It is precisely this expanded expectation of teacher example which has led to criticism of faith schools, especially when such schools are supported to some extent by public funds.

The most obvious aspect of the private lives of teachers which is seen as part of the example they must give in the faith school is their own religious belief and practice. This example would seem to extend also to other aspects of lifestyle and behaviour relating to and required by religious belief and practice. Thus a Catholic school, for example, might be thought to have grounds for censuring or dismissing a teacher who is openly co-habitating in a sexual relationship outside of marriage (including homosexual relationships) or is living in a marriage which is canonically invalid on the grounds that their example in these matters is undermining the influence of the school by contradicting its teaching on important issues.

Two approaches to such cases which are designed to allay the difficulties they present are not wholly convincing. The first approach is to argue that compassion and forgiveness for individuals are more important Christian virtues to emphasize and exemplify than judgements of individual guilt. This approach is illustrated by cases such as the following: A teacher who is the Deputy Head of a Catholic school informs her headteacher that she is pregnant as the result of a casual, regretted affair, and offers her resignation on the ground that her position in the school is incompatible with her being an unmarried mother. The Head, supported by his governors, rejects the resignation because he sees compassion and forgiveness as prior Christian virtues to be exemplified to pupils. Further, the Head argues, in not having an abortion his colleague is specifically exemplifying for pupils the right thing to do in this situation from the point of view of Catholic teaching. Cases such as these are not, however, straightforward. The pedagogical impact of the decision of the Headteacher may indeed be to exemplify the virtue of compassion, but is also capable of exemplifying a justification of the original actions of the Deputy Head. The pedagogic influence arising from decisions such as these is ambiguous. The second approach is to argue that if there is a concern in such cases with scandal, then as a matter of contingent fact most people today are not in fact scandalised by such behaviour. This, however, is to construe 'scandal' as mere subjective offence rather than as a stumbling block to faith. The very fact that people are not subjectively offended may demonstrate that they are indeed scandalised in the sense of the term which concerns the church.

These considerations, however, do not remove a range of difficulties relating to wide ranging expectations of teacher example on the part of faith schools of the kind which has been indicated. A number of points are relevant to the further pursuit of these difficulties. First, as a matter of practical reality, many faith schools have to employ teachers who are themselves not members of the sponsoring faith of the school. Here, the most that the school can expect is that the teacher in question will be invited to support and aims and ethos of the school in some agreed and specified way and not to undermine them. Second, difficult judgements are called for in relation to the selection of the elements of exemplification which are judged worthy of emphasis by the faith school. Why matters of sexual morality, for example, rather than kindness or generosity? Third, the position in the school held by a particular teacher is highly relevant to expectations with respect to teacher example. The requirement to set an example of the appropriate kind is more stringent on holders of important posts. Fourth, the extent to which various forms of perceived counter-witness is in the public domain is a significant matter.

Conclusion

The current philosophical debate about the nature and justification of the evaluative influence exerted by common and faith schools respectively on their students specifies in the case of both types of school kinds of influence which are complex and subtle. In the case of common schools, for example, it is necessary for students to understand the nature, scope and significance of the distinction between 'public' and 'non-public' values and to achieve a proper grasp of notions such as 'respect'. In the case of faith schools, students are being formed in a faith tradition but also being invited to approach it critically and to relate it to the wider values and practices of the broader society. In both kinds of school, relevant forms of educative influence are exerted pre-eminently by teachers. In some quarters, the task is seen in an over-simple way as requiring, for example, the judicious selection by teachers of curriculum content and the adoption of forms of teaching which emphasize discussion.

However, a focus on the forms of teacher exemplification which the two kinds of school presuppose and require opens up a much richer perspective on the nature and coherence of the kinds of educative influence which they are invited to exert and upon what is involved in putting these into practice. The present chapter has sought to identify some of the principles which might be proposed in relation to the forms of teacher example expected in each context. In the process a range of predicaments has emerged which relate not only to the individuals involved, but are also significant in relation to the justification of the principles themselves, and of the forms of complex educative influence from which they arise.

Chapter 12

Education, Spirituality, and the Common School

The claim that education (and more specifically schooling) should be concerned with 'spirituality' and with 'spiritual development' invites immediate attention to two related questions which are fundamental, pressing and inescapable. These questions are: (i) How are 'spirituality' and 'spiritual development' to be properly understood? and (ii) What constitutes justifiable educational influence in relation to the spiritual domain? Progress in relation to both (i) and (ii) involves, amongst other things, the making of important distinctions. In relation to (i) I have argued elsewhere in work with Hanan Alexander that a useful distinction for educational purposes can be drawn between 'religiously tethered' and 'religiously untethered' conceptions of spirituality (Alexander and McLaughlin 2003: 359–60). In relation to (ii) I have argued in that work that distinctions between education in spirituality 'from the inside' and 'from the outside' respectively and between differing schooling contexts and mandates for the exercise of educational influence (separate religious schools and common schools) are also of significance (Alexander and McLaughlin 2003: 361–73).

This chapter seeks to explore central aspects of these two fundamental questions and the distinctions proposed in relation to them from a broadly philosophical perspective and in relation to a specific question: What form might 'education in spirituality' justifiably take in the common school? Three preliminary points can be usefully made at the outset of the discussion. First, the discussion is concerned with education and schooling in societies of a broadly liberal democratic kind, and although England is taken as a particular point of reference, the points which are made have broader application to other liberal democratic societies. Second, the various distinctions drawn in the discussion are rather stipulative and imprecise and are intended merely to provide a set of analytical tools based on discriminations which are seen as both intuitively plausible (at least in general terms) and useful in bringing into focus key issues in the educational debate. Third, it is acknowledged that the questions which arise in this discussion cannot be fully illuminated, let alone resolved, by philosophical considerations alone. Any merely philosophical approach to these questions is but necessarily incomplete. The chapter has three sections. The first section offers a brief outline of the notion of the common school and the specific mandate it enjoys for the exercise of educational influence. The second section explores two concerns which arise in relation to 'education in spirituality' in the context of the common school, which I shall describe as a concern for clarity and coherence and a concern for 'admissability for common educational influence' respectively. The third section addresses the forms which 'education in spirituality' might justifiably take in the common school.

The Common School and its Educational Mandate

The term 'common school' is not widely or unproblematically used in England (or, for that matter, in the United States). I use the term to refer to schools which are open to, and intended for, all students within a liberal democratic society regardless of specific differentiating characteristics of the students and their families such as spiritual belief and practice. Common schools can therefore be identified in broad terms with 'non-voluntary' or 'community' schools in England in the 'maintained', or publicly funded, sector, and with 'public' schools in the USA. Such schools are contrasted with separate schools of one kind and another in these contexts, such as religious schools, whether or not (as in England) such schools receive some measure of support from public funds. In confining itself to some of the central principles relating to common schools, this section is not unaware of the dangers of undue idealisation and abstraction inherent in appearing to ignore the fact that common schools take particular forms in particular societal contexts. The implications of the contextualised nature of common schools will be alluded to in due course. At this stage, attention to matters of general principle will help to bring important central points into focus for the purposes of our discussion.

The common school forms the major part, and in some cases the sole part, of the publicly funded schooling system in liberal democratic societies. The mandate for educative influence possessed by common schools emphasises the importance of influence which is broadly acceptable to society as a whole. The concept of 'broad acceptability to society as a whole' is, of course, in need of more precise definition. One familiar resource for providing such a definition is the political theory of liberalism in which the theory of common schooling in liberal democratic societies is frequently articulated. From this perspective, the ideal of the common school specifies not only a particular institutional arrangement for schooling but also a 'conception of common education' based on liberal democratic philosophical and educational ideals with which it is presumptively associated.[1] From the point of view of this ideal, common schools lack a mandate to assume the truth of, or promote, any particular, overall, 'thick' or 'comprehensive' vision of the good life as a whole, in virtue of the 'significantly controversial' character of these visions in contemporary liberal democratic societies. Such schools cannot, for example, assume the truth of any particular religious faith and seek to shape its students into religious believers, and nor can they shape the beliefs, values and practices of students in the light of any substantive conception of 'spirituality'. In this context, religious and spiritual beliefs, values and practices are seen as 'significantly controversial' and therefore as matters for the reflective evaluation, decision and response of individuals and families. On such controversial matters, the common school is required either to remain silent, or to open up the issues at stake for critical reflective discussion and consideration by students. In contrast, in relation to the 'common' or 'public' values which articulate a liberal democratic society, such as respect for the autonomy and dignity of individuals, and a concern for the demands of education for democratic citizenship and civic virtue (including the development of appropriate forms of empathy and tolerance), the common school seeks to achieve a substantial influence on the beliefs of students and on their wider development as persons. At the heart of the educational influence of the common school is therefore the need to achieve a balance between unifying and diversifying imperatives and forces which are characteristic of pluralist liberal societies themselves. The fact that

---

[1]   On the general conception of education associated with liberal democratic societies, see, for example, Callan 1997; Gutmann 1987; Levinson 1999; Macedo 2000; Reich 2002; Tomasi 2001: ch. 5; J. White 1990; P. White 1996.

the common school must exercise a form of forbearance from undue substantive influence on controversial matters means that the claim that we should 'educate the whole child' in the common school is problematic (McLaughlin 1996).[2]

An acceptance of these general principles outlining the educational mandate of the common school does not depend solely upon an acceptance of the theory of liberalism in which they have been articulated, but corresponds to widely held intuitions among educational professionals and the public at large in liberal democratic societies. In England, for example, there is little widespread general enthusiasm for developing (say) an explicitly Christian form of spiritual belief and practice in students in the common school, despite the non-neutrality towards religious faith in common schools in England which is reflected in the history of the development of these schools and the continuing requirement that they hold a daily act of collective religious worship.[3]

In contrast to the common school, 'separate' schools (such as 'religious' or 'faith' schools) enjoy a mandate to educate students in the context of a fuller view of life as a whole such as a religious faith and to include a formation in particular religious and spiritual belief and practice as part of their overall educational influence. (On such schools and their related conceptions of education, see, for example, McLaughlin 1992.)

The concept of the common school and its educational mandate which has emerged from this brief outline is not, of course, unproblematic. Challenges to this broad account of the concept and mandate arise from articulations of the common school which do not invoke the philosophical theory of liberalism and which point to the acceptability of such schools transmitting 'default norms' based on the dominant norms (including religious norms) prevalent in a society.[4] Even within the theory of philosophical liberalism there is dispute about precisely how the concept and mandate of the common school should be precisely characterised. In the light of this theory, for example, I have argued elsewhere that common schools face a series of complex and neglected burdens and dilemmas relat-

---

[2] On the concept of the common school see, for example, Callan 1997: especially ch. 7; Feinberg 1998; McLaughlin 1995a, 2003; Salomone 2000.

[3] On the relationship between Church and State in education in England, see, for example, Chadwick 1997.

[4] On this notion, see, for example, McLaughlin 1995a: 245-8. On the 'neutrality' or otherwise of the common school, see Sandsmark 2000.

ing to the public domain, the non-public domain and the interface between the two (McLaughlin 2003).

Leaving aside these complexities, however, it seems clear that two general concerns arise in relation to the claim that the common school should engage in 'education in spirituality', and that these concerns are experienced in general terms as much by educational practitioners and teachers on widely accessible grounds as by educational theorists. These concerns can be described respectively as a concern for clarity and coherence and a concern for 'admissibility for common educational influence'. The concern for clarity and coherence expresses an aversion to imprecision and vagueness in relation to central notions such as 'spirituality' and 'spiritual development'. The concern for 'admissibility for common educational influence' expresses a desire to ensure that the forms of 'education in spirituality' envisaged are genuinely acceptable as part of the 'conception of common education' being offered by the common school.

Two Concerns and their Implications

A concern for both clarity and coherence and for 'admissibility for common educational influence' have been a marked characteristic of the debate concerning 'education in spirituality' in common schools in England. With regard to clarity and coherence, it has long been acknowledged in this debate that the concepts of 'spirituality' and 'spiritual development' are resistant to easy clarification and definition and that educational policy and practice in relation to these notions have been underinformed by necessary forms of transparency and comprehensibility. The concern with 'spirituality' and 'spiritual development' in common schools in England and its discussion and implementation at the policy level have struggled, not always successfully, with these issues[5] and more general discussions of education in spirituality by educational theorists and philosophers of education have also been preoccupied with these questions.[6] Terence Copley describes the area as 'a beguiling mist' (Copley 2000: 11) and John Haldane observes that when educational

[5]   On the development of educational policy with respect to 'spirituality' and 'spiritual development' in England, see, for example, Copley 2000: Introduction and ch. 2; Erricker 2000; Wright 2000: ch. 6. On policy and discussion documents dealing with these matters, see, for example, Department of Education and Science 1977a, 1977b; National Curriculum Council 1993; Office for Standards in Education 1994; Schools Curriculum and Assessment Authority 1996.

[6]   For such discussions, see, for example, Best 1996; Blake 1996, 1997; Carr 1995, 1996; Copley 2000; Erricker 2000; Hull 1996; Thatcher 1999; Wright 1998, 2000.

theorists talk about 'spiritual development' 'they are usually either struggling to take a last dip in the shallows of the ebbing tide of faith, or engaged in the practice of aggrandising the ordinary, or else doing both at once' (Haldane 2000: 54). David Carr expresses a widely felt view in observing that notions of spirituality in an educational context often amount to little more than 'a hotchpotch of only vaguely connected items of cognition, intuition and feeling between which it is well nigh impossible to discern any coherent conceptual connections' (Carr 1995: 84).

This lack of clarity and coherence gives rise to several kinds of reaction. At one level, the lack of clarity and coherence is seen simply as undermining the prospect of intelligible educational practice. Terence Copley, for example, complains that schools 'neither know clearly what they are trying to do, how they are trying to do it, nor how they are going to evaluate their efforts' (Copley 2000: 136). The difficulty of being able to specify clear criteria for 'spiritual development' is one aspect of this phenomenon (on this, see, for example, J. White 1994). A different kind of reaction, however, expresses a concern with a range of actual or potential dangers which a lack of clarity and coherence is seen as leaving room for. A prominent concern is that 'spirituality' and 'spiritual development' in the common school may act as a Trojan horse for more specific religious influence seen as objectionable on various grounds (Beck 1998: ch. 3; J. White 1994, 1995) as well as for influence, seen as equally objectionable, of a more general, metaphysical, kind (Blake 1997; Flew 1997).

A further concern is that an emphasis on 'spirituality' and 'spiritual development' may act in various ways as a distortive influence on other areas of the work of the school, such as education for citizenship and social and moral development (P. White 1994). A different reaction to a lack of clarity and coherence can be seen in Copley's description of a 'tendency to sanitise and secularise spiritual development within the UK educational system, to render it a benign, consensus-driven, self-exploratory process, at pains to offend no one' (Copley 2000: 128; cf. Blake 1997). John Hull, for example, argues that 'spirituality' and 'spiritual development', properly conceived, have an important but neglected critical role to play in relation to contemporary materialism (Hull 1996). Another reaction to lack of clarity and coherence is a claim that defensible educational activities which may be conducted under the labels of 'spirituality' and 'spiritual development' would be better approached under labels which are more transparent and acceptable. John White, for example, writes: I would advocate an absolute embargo on the use of the terms "spirituality" or "spiritual development" in all official documents on education, all conferences on education, all in-service courses for teachers … The words simply get in the way of thinking' (J. White 1995: 16).[7]

It should be stressed that a concern with a lack of clarity and coherence in relation to 'spirituality' and 'spiritual development' does not depend upon an unreasonable demand that educational policy-making and practice should or could wait upon fully articulated and philosophically approved conceptualisations of these matters. (On the complex relationship between philosophy and educational policy, see McLaughlin 2000.) Nor does it depend on a claim that educational policy-makers and teachers in this area have been wholly insensitive to the demands of clarity and coherence.

The concern for clarity and coherence leads on to the second concern which has been identified: 'admissibility for common educational influence'. Here the concern is to specify forms of educational influence in relation to 'spirituality' and 'spiritual development' which can satisfy the kinds of criteria for common educational influence identified earlier. This task requires attention to the spiritual domain and to the possibility of making useful distinctions both within this domain and in relation to educative processes concerning it.

Education in Spirituality in the Common School

In the light of the foregoing discussion, what forms might education in spirituality justifiably take in the common school?[8] This question is brought into clearer focus by two sets of distinctions: between 'religiously tethered' and 'religiously untethered' forms of spirituality and between 'education in spirituality from the inside' and 'education in spirituality from the outside' respectively.

Before turning to these distinctions, however, it is necessary to explore why the area of the 'spiritual' broadly conceived should feature in the work of the common school at all. Perhaps the strongest line of argument in relation to this matter[9] concerns the need for any

[7]   See also Beck 1998: especially 63-5; Lambourn 1996.

[8]   For an extended discussion of this matter, see Mott-Thornton 1998.

[9]   Included among these perspectives by Peters are '[a] … sense of the beauty of the world … of man's strivings to give concrete embodiment to intimations about the human condition that he cannot explicitly articulate … the place of man in the natural and historical orders … the contingency, creation and continuance of the

education worthy of the name to address fundamental questions about the nature and context of human life which are open to responses of a 'spiritual' kind. Peters insists that education should include attention to attempts to 'make sense of and give sense to the human condition' (1981: 41), requiring students to be made aware of various perspectives on this matter which are acceptable within, if not demanded by, a democratic way of life — 'in the hope that many will develop insights and sensitivities that may become of increasing significance to them' (Peters 1981: 41). Also included in this process is attention to the 'predicaments' of life for which, in contrast to 'problems', there are, in principle, no solutions (Peters 1981: 45).

This last emphasis of Peters resonates with John Haldane's account of the 'quiet desperation and other non-eccentric conditions of the soul or psyche' (Haldane 2000: 66) which he sees as a starting point for reflections about the meaning of life associated with forms of spirituality not confined to the religious. John White argues that all students need to be introduced to a secular 'cosmic framework' within which their well-being can be conceived and pursued and which relates to 'the widest horizons of our being' (J. White 1995: 19).Whilst White imposes a strictly secular conception of these 'horizons' and resists talk of 'spirituality' in relation to them, Martha Nussbaum insists on a recognition of the difficulty, mysteriousness and continuing openness of ultimate questions relating to life and death, and our need to recognise the shortcomings of our current explanations (Nussbaum 2003). Charles Taylor explores the neglected dangers of an 'exclusive humanism' which excludes a transcendental vision altogether and which involves, in his view, a kind of 'spiritual lobotomy' (Taylor 1999). Nussbaum and Taylor can be read as calling for an openness in relation to the interpretation of questions of a fundamental or 'cosmic' kind to which the common school can be invited to respond.[10]

If a general justification along these lines for the involvement of the common school with 'spiritual' questions can be provided, how should 'spirituality' be understood? The spiritual domain involves a wide range of kinds of human sensitivity, experience, belief, judge-

---

world, which are beyond the power of man to comprehend ... [giving rise to] ... awe and wonder ... [T]he human condition ... viewed in a wider perspective, under "a certain aspect of eternity" ... [generating] ... ways of life ... that transcend and transform what is demanded by morality and truth' (Peters 1981: 41; cf. Peters 1972: especially Lecture 4; Elliott 1986).

[10] On the relationship between the cosmic imagination and specific beliefs and values, see Hepburn 2000.

ment, response, disposition, motivation, commitment, virtue and achievement.[11] The domain is in many cases related, by implicit presupposition and implication if not by explicit avowal, to a range of perspectives and beliefs concerning underlying fundamental questions such as the nature of reality, of persons and of the good. The resistance of the spiritual domain to easy clarification and definition consists in part in the inherently opaque nature of some of its elements, the wide variety of phenomena included under its name, and its close affinity with related areas such as the aesthetic. A central issue claiming attention is what can be said to be *distinctive* of the spiritual (see, for example, Carr 1995, 1996; Haldane 2000).

In previous work with Hanan Alexander, I have drawn a rough distinction between 'religiously tethered' and 'religiously untethered' forms of spirituality (Alexander and McLaughlin 2003: 359–60). In part, the aim of this distinction is to try to pin down 'spirituality' more clearly by marking out at least one general aspect of spirituality which it is relatively easy to bring into focus.

Religiously 'tethered' spirituality takes its shape and structure from various aspects of the religion with which it is associated and which makes it possible to identify the nature and shape of 'spirituality' within that context, including criteria for spiritual development. As John Haldane observes, within religious domains 'spirituality' has definite meanings (Haldane 2000: 54). In the Christian tradition, for example, 'developmental criteria' for spiritual development can be discerned in the life and work of figures such as Ignatius of Loyola, St John of the Cross, and St Francis de Sales, whose experiences and reflections are located within an extended and elaborated tradition of belief, practice and value and infused with its central tenets and commitments.[12] The theological, epistemological, ethical and collective aspects of religion all have their spiritual correlates. The theological aspects of religion provide an intentionality to spirituality by delineating the nature of a divine reality or favoured state of contemplation or consciousness seen as the object or goal of the spiritual quest. The epistemological aspects

[11]   For general treatments of the spiritual domain, see, for example, Alexander 2001; Hadot 1995; Haldane 2000; Hick 1999; McGhee 2000; Wright 1998, 2000. On the notion of the spirituality of childhood, see, for example, Coles 1992; Hay with Nye 1998.

[12]   On the Christian tradition in spirituality, see, for example, Jones et al. 1992; McGrath 1999. For an accessible appropriation of aspects of this tradition, see, for example, Norris 1993, 1996, 1998.

of religion underpin and give direction to the search for meaning which is such a marked feature of the spiritual domain and which is reflected in many religious traditions in the search to know God through prayer. The ethical aspects of religion infuse forms of spirituality which are part of, and support, a life configured to the acquisition, cultivation and maintenance of the virtues as part of a religiously inspired conception of the good and flourishing life. The collective aspects of religion are expressed in part in forms of spirituality developed and exercised in the different communal contexts of a faith community, especially in different forms of liturgy. 'Religiously tethered' spirituality therefore is typically both substantive and elaborated.

As is widely argued, spirituality extends beyond the religious domain, and much attention has been given to the question of how a non-religious form of spirituality can be characterised (on this, see, for example, Haldane 2000). Religiously 'untethered' spirituality involves beliefs and practices that are disconnected from, and may even be discomforting to, religions. Religiously untethered spirituality takes many forms. Some forms are substantive and elaborated in much the same way as some 'religiously tethered' forms of spirituality are. Other forms may lack a definite shape and structure and may be unconnected to any wider tradition of belief, practice and value, thereby making it difficult to specify criteria for spiritual development in relation to them.

The contrast between religiously 'tethered' and 'untethered' conceptions of spirituality can be illustrated by reference to five interrelated strands which often characterise the spiritual domain (a search for meaning, the cultivation of 'inner space', the manifestations of spirituality in life, distinctive responses to the natural and human world, and collective or communal aspects) (Alexander and McLaughlin 2003: 359–60).

The distinction between 'religiously tethered' and 'religiously untethered' conceptions of spirituality needs, of course, to be handled with considerable caution. The domain of religion is not itself one with clear features and boundaries. It is not always easy, therefore, to distinguish with any degree of rigour a religious from non-religious perspective, and the phenomenology of spirituality does not correspond to any rigid distinction of the sort that has been drawn. Nevertheless, despite its imprecision, the distinction may serve a useful purpose for the present discussion.

The second set of distinctions pertinent to the present discussion involves a distinction between 'education in spirituality from the inside' and 'education in spirituality from the outside',[13] which can also be brought to bear on education in religion (Alexander and McLaughlin 2003: 361–73). 'Education in spirituality from the inside' refers to forms of education in spirituality which are seen as appropriate for those *within* a particular spiritual tradition, or those who are being initiated into such a tradition. Central to these forms of education in spirituality is the attempt to *form* and *nourish* a commitment to the particular beliefs, values and practices of a specific spiritual tradition. The aim of such forms of education in spirituality is therefore not merely to bring about understanding of the spiritual domain but a particular form of spiritual belief and practice. This kind of education in spirituality, which need not necessarily involve indoctrination, is most appropriately located in separate religious schools, where it will be linked with 'religiously tethered' forms of spirituality. (For an example of education in spirituality of this kind, see Haldane 1999).[14]

'Education in spirituality from the outside' refers to forms of education in this domain in which no assumptions are made about the belief and involvement or otherwise of students in relation either to the spiritual domain as a whole or to particular spiritual traditions within it. Initiation into this domain and into these traditions does not constitute an aim of the enterprise. Spiritual belief, commitment and practice on the part of individuals are therefore neither presuppositions of, nor aims of, the process. The aim rather is to engage in exploration, discussion and critical assessment of the spiritual domain and issues of meaning, truth and value relating to it. For these reasons, education of this kind can be described as 'from the outside' of particular spiritual traditions. It is important to insist, however, that education of this form cannot remain 'on the outside' in the sense that no attempt is made to understand the spiritual domain from the insider's point of view. Such attempts are necessary if spiritual traditions and ideas are to be properly illuminated for the purposes of understanding and assessment.

In the light of these distinctions, what can be said about the nature of 'education in spirituality' in the common school? In relation to 're-

[13] For complexities in the meaning of the terms 'from the inside' and 'from the outside' in this context, see Alexander and McLaughlin 2003: 372, fn. 1.

[14] On the contribution which a Catholic philosophy of education might make to education in general in relation to spiritual matters, see Groome 1998.

ligiously tethered' spirituality, any form of 'education in spirituality from the inside' would amount to formation in a particular religious faith, and would thereby be incompatible with principles relating to 'admissibility for common educative influence' of the sort discussed earlier. 'Education in spirituality from the outside' in the case of 'religiously tethered' spirituality would seem to be justified on very much the same grounds as similar forms of Education in Religion in common schools and be subject to the same kinds of problems and dilemmas, particularly those relating to the achievement of an internal perspective on the domain for students.[15] Any exploration of the domain of spirituality in the common school cannot ignore 'religiously tethered' spirituality, and an examination of this form of spirituality 'from the outside' is therefore appropriate and necessary.

In the case of 'religiously untethered' spirituality, 'education from the outside' is in principle compatible with the requirements of 'admissibility for common educative influence'. A general difficulty encountered by 'education from the outside' in relation to spirituality of whatever kind is captured in David Carr's querying of the extent to which students can achieve a genuine understanding of spirituality short of 'a substantial examination of (even initiation into) the reflection, practices and achievements of some actual spiritual tradition or other' (Carr 1996: 173). The diffuse nature of 'religiously untethered' spirituality and a temptation to approach the area in an eclectic way might be thought to exacerbate the difficulty to which this remark draws attention. One dimension of this difficulty is that students may come to see the spiritual domain exclusively under the aspect of the kind of distorted 'consumerist' mentality associated with the culture of 'authenticity' or expressivist self-awareness in relation to spiritual things to which Charles Taylor has pointed (Taylor 2002).

'Education in spirituality from the inside' seems to be incompatible with the requirements in the case of 'religiously untethered' spirituality for much the same general reasons as in the case of its 'religiously tethered' counterpart. Whilst the form of influence here may not amount to formation in a religious faith, it may involve initiation into practices and perspectives which embody to a greater or lesser extent controversial assumptions and beliefs.

[15] For philosophical aspects of these problems and dilemmas, see, for example, Alexander and McLaughlin 2003: 363-9; McLaughlin 1995b; Hobson and Edwards 1999.

This aversion to 'education in spirituality from the inside' in the case of 'religiously untethered' spirituality is challenged by Clive Erricker, who argues that 'spiritual development involves — ... self-transformation through practice' (Erricker and Erricker 2001: 58). For Erricker, 'knowledge', 'the conceptual', 'rationality' and the like cannot achieve the necessary forms of understanding, and he insists that 'You actually have to carry out the practices, techniques or strategies that relate to spirituality and reflect upon the effects' (Erricker and Erricker 2001: 58). Erricker and others argue that students should be encouraged to engage in the practice of meditation in common schools. Included among the benefits claimed in relation to this activity are the alleviation of stress and other physical ailments, the enhancement of awareness and clarity, the facilitation of experiential learning, the promotion of calm, a sense of inner strength, self-reliance, well-being and the like (Erricker and Erricker 2001: especially chs 7–9). Whilst being alert to potential objections arising from a perception that engagement of students in this kind of activity may involve the imposition of controversial imbedded beliefs,[16] it has been claimed that 'Meditation does not presume a particular faith or non-faith stance but is a means to calming the mind and acquiring insight into the nature of experience and how the mind works' (Erricker and Erricker 2001: 21). Things may not, however, be this simple.[17] An alertness to the assumptions and beliefs which are imbedded in all spiritual practices is part of the responsibility of the

[16] One writer observes that such processes 'may be viewed only as something associated with new age thinking or religious belief which if imposed upon students could be harmful' (Erricker and Erricker 2001: 4).

[17] See the following passages in Erricker and Erricker (2001) which are selected from a range which give rise to questions about presupposed assumptions or beliefs: 'opportunities to balance the external and inner world' (p. 6); 'To learn how to simply be' (p. 7); 'the abstract needs of their inner being' (p. 7); 'the laws of polarity, positive and negative, impermanence and change' (p. 10); 'to allow things to be as they are' (p. 22); 'beyond thought and concept, a place of direct awareness' (p. 33); 'the investigation of experience without ultimately relying on conceptual thinking ... challenges conceptual maps of reality. It challenges and undermines doctrines, whether religious or secular, that say that this is how the world is, this is what we must do, and this is how we should behave. This challenge to authority comes from determining that there is higher authority, whether within one's own consciousness and conscience or beyond oneself, that cannot be denied. Meditative experience is a basis of that authority: a being true to oneself (p. 53); 'a path beyond thought and imagination into the indwelling presence within our hearts' (p. 129).

common school.[18] 'Education in spirituality from the inside' of whatever kind in the common school is inherently problematic.

Education in spirituality in the common school faces a range of difficulties and dilemmas, many of which have been indicated. It is important to note that many of these can be resolved only via a form of practical judgement by educational leaders and teachers at school level. Teachers who can realise the complex mandate of the common school must be *certain sorts of people* who possess not merely an abstract understanding of matters of principle relating to this mandate, but can also bring to bear the kind of pedagogic *phronesis* needed for its interpretation and application in practical contexts. Whilst this is a point of general application (McLaughlin 2003: 145–47) its significance in the case of 'education in spirituality' is manifest.

[18]   For a range of 'spiritual exercises' giving rise to the need for this kind of care, see, for example, Hadot 1995; cf. Haldane 2000.

Chapter 13

Sex Education, Moral Controversy and the Common School

It is widely agreed that schools should assume some responsibility for sex education.[1] Yet sex education in schools remains significantly controversial. The word 'significantly' here is important. There are different kinds of controversy. At one level, the mere existence of disagreement can be described as a controversy, even when the disagreement is based on ignorance, misunderstanding or ill-will. There is no doubt that some of the controversy about sex education in schools is of this kind, in part stimulated and sustained by sections of the media. However, there is a deeper sense of controversy which can be described as 'significant' in virtue of its grounding in serious disagreements of an epistemological and ethical kind.[2] In what follows, I shall be referring throughout to 'controversy' in this deeper, 'significant', sense. Understood in this way, controversy arises in relation to a number of aspects of sex education in school. In this essay, I shall be concerned with controversy relating to the values — especially moral values — that should guide and permeate this aspect of the work of one particular kind of school — the common

[1]   See, for example, Reiss 1993 p. 125.

[2]   Dearden, R.F. 1984, p. 86. Dearden mentions four kinds of epistemological disagreement: (a) where a matter is in principle one which could be settled by evidence, but that evidence is as yet unavailable; (b) where decision making criteria are agreed but there is disagreement about the weight to be given to different criteria; (c) where no decision making criteria are agreed; (d) where whole frameworks of understanding are in dispute. (Dearden, R.F. 1984, pp. 86–87). For wider grounds for serious disagreement see Rawls' notion of 'the burdens of judgement' (the sources of ineliminable rational disagreement) Rawls 1993, pp. 54–58. The precise delineation of the category of the 'significantly controversial' is itself, of course, significantly controversial.

school. Schools of all forms are, of course, only one of several contexts in which sex education takes place. Sex education in school — and, more specifically in the common school — is, however, the concern of this essay.

Controversy with regard to sex education should not surprise us. Schools, and educational processes more generally, exercise influence not only upon the thoughts and minds of students, but also upon their wider development as persons. In an important sense, schools shape persons and their lives. It is therefore both inevitable and necessary that educational influence should come up for careful assessment, not only by parents, but also by society as a whole. Such careful assessment does not always lead to controversy, and many aspects of educational influence are supported by a wide ranging consensus of view. However, controversy is likely to arise in relation to educational influence when (a) that influence concerns complex and sensitive matters which are not only of great significance for the personal well being and fulfilment of individuals but which also have important and many-sided implications for society as a whole, and when (b) the values seen as appropriate in determining the aims, content, processes and evaluation of the influence in question are disputed in the light of deep seated and well grounded differences of belief and judgement, some of them related to fundamental questions about the proper interpretation of human life itself. Few could doubt that (a) applies to sex education. Whilst the extent to which (b) applies to sex education is itself a matter of controversy, few could also doubt that, at least in important respects, (b) is applicable to sex education as well, especially in the context of the common school.

It would be wrong to claim that research and practice in sex education has ignored questions of value, and this is particularly true of recent work.[3] However, to date insufficient work of either a conceptual or an empirical sort has been conducted into the 'value dimension' of sex education and, in particular, into its moral dimension. We therefore lack a clear and detailed grasp of the principles which should govern the moral aspects of sex education, including those appropriate for the handling of moral controversy, and there are relatively few adequate and detailed guidelines and resources available to support the practical work of teachers in relation to these matters.

[3] See Health Education Authority 1994, Ray and Went (Ed.) 1995, Sex Education Forum 1993, Reiss (Ed.) 1997a, Thomson 1997.

In this essay, I shall explore a number of questions relating to moral aspects of the 'value dimension' of sex education in common schools. The essay has four sections. The first section offers a brief examination of the aims of sex education in school. The second section outlines a number of general considerations relating to education, values and the development of the person. In the following section, attention is focused briefly upon some general points relating to the common school as a distinctive context in which sex education may take place, in the light of the nature of the mandate common schools enjoy for the exercise of educational influence. In the final section, several moral aspects of sex education are explored in the context of the common school, and three major areas of concern about influence upon these matters in this context are identified and discussed.

My discussion throughout is philosophical in character. Many questions of great significance for the questions I address therefore fall outside the scope of this essay.[4]

The Aims of Sex Education in School

It is useful to begin the present discussion by bringing clearly into focus the general aims that are thought appropriate for sex education in school.

In his account of the general aims of school sex education, Michael Reiss indicates how, over time, schools have assumed increasingly wide and ambitious aims for this aspect of their work.[5] Reiss discusses a number of aims for sex education, ranging from stopping girls getting pregnant to providing an ethical framework for sexual expression. It is useful to attempt to categorise these aims. Although Reiss does not himself offer a categorisation of the kind attempted

[4]   It is important to note that whilst philosophical considerations have an indispensible part to play in illuminating the 'value dimension' of sex education, such considerations alone cannot settle all the questions relevant to this dimension, even questions of aim and principle. A full discussion of this dimension of sex education requires attention to a wide range of considerations of different kinds. These considerations include inter alia psychological, biological, sociological, historical, political and practical ones. For example, progress in addressing the moral aspects of sex education requires a sound understanding of the existing moral values held by students and parents and an insight into how in concrete terms educational influence with respect to these values can best be exercised in practice. On some of these matters, together with a discussion of recent initiatives in educational policy and practice with respect to the value dimension of sex education in England and Wales, see Thomson 1997.

[5]   Reiss 1993. On the aims of sex education see also Passmore 1980, Ch. 13.

here, it is easy to see how the aims he mentions can fit readily into the proposed categories. Thus we can distinguish between 'preventative' aims (stopping girls getting pregnant and reducing the incidence of sexually transmitted disease), 'informational' aims (decreasing ignorance), 'reassurance' aims (decreasing guilt, embarrassment and anxiety), 'sexual autonomy' aims (enabling students to make their own decisions about their sexuality, to develop assertiveness and to question the present role of women and of men in society) and 'value' aims (providing an ethical framework for the expression of sexuality). It is possible to add a number of categories additional to those derivable from Reiss's discussion. For example, Reynold Jones insists that sex education should help people '... to achieve as much sexual satisfaction and pleasure as is possible'.[6] This category can be interpreted (though not without further argument) as involving 'fulfilment' aims. Jones also claims that, as part of sex education, sex should be made the subject of disinterested enquiry.[7] This category can be described as involving 'study' aims. Re-ordering these categories of aim (though not in any strict order of priority), we therefore encounter 'preventative', 'informational', 're-assurance', 'fulfilment', 'study', 'sexual autonomy' and 'value' aims for sex education. Most of the aims which are articulated in discussions of sex education can be roughly located within categories of these general kinds.[8] This proposed categorisation of aims is therefore offered as widely acceptable at least in broad terms. It is, however, important to note the interrelatedness of the aims.[9] Highly significant for the present discussion is the point that the 'value' category of aim in sex education is indispensible for, and cannot be

[6]   Jones 1989, p. 57; 65–68.

[7]   Jones 1989, p. 57; 59–60.

[8]   See, for example, Ray and Went (Ed.) 1995. Some of the aims proposed by authors are difficult to categorise precisely. Passmore's claim that sex education should offer a 'preparation for love' is a case in point (Passmore 1980, Ch. 13).

[9]   'Preventative' and 'reassurance' aims both require 'informational' aims, and (arguably) 'fulfilment' aims require all (or almost all) of the other categories of aim. There are interesting structural aspects to the relationships within and between the categories. 'Sexual autonomy', for example, is a 'higher order' category of aim which embraces the other categories. Further, sex educators seek to achieve a number of categories of aim in their work, often simultaneously. It is very unlikely, for example, that any given teaching act will be aimed at the achievement of merely one category of aim. Sensitivity to differences between categories of aim and the relationships between them is, however, important.

excluded from, all the other categories of aim; it is both practically and logically all-pervasive across them.

Each of the categories of aim which have been mentioned can give rise to controversy of a philosophical kind.[10] Controversy may arise especially in relation to the interpretation of the categories, and to questions concerning their prioritisation and justification.

With regard to matters of interpretation, for example, how is a notion such as 'sexual autonomy' to be understood? What is the nature of the moral framework within which sexual autonomy is seen as legitimate? Which values and ethical framework are seen as appropriate for sex education? How, at the level of interpretation, are matters of ethical controversy to be identified?

Matters of prioritisation arise because, for various (and sometimes complex) reasons, not all the categories of aim can and should be pursued to an equal extent simultaneously. Given the need for choices to be made, which categories of aim should be favoured? Should some aims not be attempted at all? Should 'prevention' always be given priority, and what are the implications of such a policy for overall value influence? How much emphasis should be placed on 'reassurance' at the expense of reality? John Passmore, for example, insists on the importance of understanding '... the horrors and terrors of sexuality, the way in which sexual relationships can drive men and women to desperation'[11] and this is clearly in tension with the provision of reassurance. Another difficulty which arises in relation to the achievement of 'reassurance' is that sex education can increase regrets, since it may raise the expectations of people more than it improves their actual experiences.[12] Within the 'value' category of aim, to what extent should the transmission of a core set of basic moral values take pride of place over the illumination of moral complexity, even at the expense of oversimplification and a fair treatment of ethical diversity? Many questions of prioritisation are time-related in that a given aim might be thought to have particular salience at (say) a later rather than an earlier stage in the development of students. Not all the categories of aim mentioned involve time-neutral goods. Given this time-related character of many questions of prioritisation, how can matters of (say) time-suitability for

[10] On the various controversies of a more practical kind which arise see Ray and Went (Ed.) 1995. It should not, of course, be assumed that any rigid division between 'philosophical' and 'practical' controversies is tenable.

[11] Passmore 1980, p. 245.

[12] BMA Foundation for AIDS et al. 1997, p. 7.

the study of particular matters be assessed? Determining that topics of a certain sort are or are not suitable for students of a certain age involve judgements of more than a practical kind.

Questions of justification are clearly related to those of interpretation and prioritisation. The precise character and adequacy of the justification of an aim such as 'sexual autonomy', for example, depends crucially on the interpretation offered of the aim in question, and the priority it is given in relation to other aims.

The issues which arise from a detailed examination of the general aims of sex education in school are complex and wide ranging, and cannot all be addressed in this essay. For the purpose of the present discussion, it is important to note the centrality to all the educational aims which have been mentioned of the importance and inescapability of values and of the fact that the educational influence in question is aimed at the wide ranging development of the person.

Education, Values and the Development of the Person

It is appropriate to make some general points about each of these matters in turn.

(a) Education and values

A number of points are relevant here, some of which I have discussed in more detail elsewhere.[13]

First, education and schooling are inherently value-laden. The aims, content, processes and achievements of education and schooling are practically and logically saturated with value. There can be no value-free education and schooling. It is important to insist upon this point in the context of sex education, where there is a temptation in some quarters to invoke a distinction between, on the one hand, the supposedly value-free 'facts' of (say) sexual reproduction and, on the other, the values involved in (say) human choices with respect to sexual behaviour and life-style. Such a distinction, it is sometimes claimed, can allow at least part of the work of sex education to proceed without the involvement of value questions. In an educational context, however, 'facts' presented to students cannot be value-free. In the first place, 'facts' must be selected for presentation, and this presupposes judgements about what it is valuable for students to know. Nor can such judgements be avoided by appeal to (say) the notion of 'health', since properly understood, that notion, and its

---

[13] See especially McLaughlin 1994a, 1995a.

educational treatment, is not value-free.[14] Further, the way in which the 'facts' are presented in an educational context is inevitably value-laden. Teachers properly seek to make their teaching effective, and what counts as 'effectiveness' in an educational context requires interpretation in terms of educational values. Teachers, after all, seek forms of understanding on the part of their students, and not mere rote learning. Teachers are also concerned, as indicated above, with aims such as the provision of reassurance and the development of autonomy, and this will necessarily influence the way in which 'facts' are presented. Any suggestion that there can be value-free selection and presentation of 'facts' in sex education is therefore misleading.

A further temptation in sex education is to claim that, even with respect to the more explicitly 'value' aspects of the task, it is possible to proceed in a way which is significantly 'value-free'. This is seen in claims that, in matters of (say) sexual ethics, teachers should attempt to be 'neutral' or 'non-judgemental'. It is important to insist, however, that, properly conceived, such attempts involve not the absence of value judgements but the presence of complex ones. 'Teacher neutrality', whatever its merits, is a strategy which invites the teacher to refrain from the expression of judgements in the classroom about certain sorts of issues for specific pedagogic reasons. Both the sorts of issues seen as candidates for this approach, and the pedagogic reasons given for the forbearance of expression of judgement by the teacher, are laden with complex judgements of value.[15] The suggestion that a teacher adopt a 'non-judgemental' approach to matters of sexual ethics with students is also value-laden. A 'non-judgemental' attitude in a teacher is often best described as a 'non-censorious' one.[16] Avoiding censoriousness is not the same as avoiding all forms of moral guidance (or even instruction), especially in relation to basic or widely accepted moral values. A

---

[14] On this point see Reiss 1996.

[15] On the notion of the 'neutral teacher' in more detail see Bridges 1986.

[16] Teachers generally seek to avoid the danger of alienating particular individuals and families through (even implicit) criticism of their values and lifestyle. Further, teachers may judge that the best way of exerting some value influence on students (say on matters of basic sexual morality) is through avoiding the expression of prescriptive guidance and opinion, with its attendant dangers of rejection as 'preaching'. Whatever its merits, the strategy of 'non-judgementality' here clearly involves the making of judgements (viz: about the most effective way of exercising value influence). Further, the strategy, if educationally acceptable, cannot exclude the expression to students of judgements of every kind.

'non-judgemental' teaching strategy which is educationally appropriate cannot be value-free.

The inherently value-laden character of education is readily seen in the discussion of the general aims of sex education in the last section. All the general categories of aim referred to assume that what is aimed at is valuable in some sense (for example, that it is good that people should have relevant information about sexual matters and that they should achieve a form of 'sexual autonomy' in this domain).

It is important to note that a value-free education and schooling is not only practically impossible but, given the centrality of value to the very notion of education, a contradiction in terms. The most important value question for sex education, therefore, is not whether sex education can be value-free, but what sorts of values should be seen as appropriate for it.

This leads to a second general point about education and values: the values inherent in education and schooling are of many different kinds. Often 'values' in the context of education is interpreted to mean 'moral values', and this is particularly true in the case of sex education. It is important to note, however, that there are many different kinds of value, and of educational value.[17] Moral values constitute a part, albeit an important part, of the domain of educational value more generally.[18] Although the focus of this essay is on moral values, the broader domain of educational value should not be lost from view.

A third general point about education and values is the need for clarity. Since education is essentially a practical and not a theoretical enterprise, this clarity about educational values needs to extend beyond matters of general principle to specific value questions involved in the conceptualisation and realisation of particular courses of study, teaching strategies and institutional policies. In the past, critical discussions of the kind which are needed about matters of educational value have been inhibited by inadequate and unduly polarised rhetoric and debate, lack of appropriate theoretical resources and a failure of will on the part of political and educational leaders to face up to the complex issues involved. The recent consultation process on educational values launched by the School Curric-

---

[17] On this see Halstead and Taylor (Eds) 1996, Haydon 1997, Ch. 3.

[18] For further discussion of these and related points see McLaughlin 1994a, esp. pp. 455–457.

ulum and Assessment Authority (SCAA), involving the establishment of the National Forum for Values in Education and the Community, is a very welcome initiative in remedying these inhibitions and placing the matters at stake clearly on the political and educational agenda.[19]

A fourth general point about education and values is the controversial character of many educational values. The moral values seen as appropriate for sex education is a prominent example of this controversiality.

(b) Education and the development of the person

It is important to note that educational influence cannot be seen in narrow terms. This is apparent in relation not only to the aims of educational influence but also to its implications. With regard to educational aims, many of the achievements at which educators aim directly involve the wide ranging development of the person in ways which go beyond matters of knowledge and understanding. For example, this is true of the 'preventative', 'reassurance' and 'sexual autonomy' general categories of aim for sex education discussed earlier. 'Preventative' aims involve an aspiration to affect attitudes and behaviour as well as knowledge and understanding, and the development of virtues such as self-control and prudence are therefore required, together with the disposition on the part of the person to exercise them appropriately. 'Reassurance' aims seek the transformation of feelings and emotions. 'Sexual autonomy' also requires more than the development of knowledge and understanding. The virtues, skills and dispositions involved in the exercise of autonomy include courage to pursue a chosen course of action in the face of social pressure, skills to put what is decided into practice and the disposition to achieve and maintain autonomy of the appropriate kind. The broader transformation of the person is also involved in the aim of morally educating students in relation to sexual matters. It has long been realised that moral education requires more than the development of the understanding of students, as John Wilson's delineation of the 'components' of a morally educated person bears witness. Apart from knowledge and understanding of various kinds, these components involve *inter alia* concern and respect for others, relevant forms of emotional awareness, empathy, practical

[19] See School Curriculum and Assessment Authority (1996). Compare Marenbon 1996, p. 20.

262 Liberalism, Education and Schooling

skills in dealing with people and dispositions to act in principled and person-orientated ways.[20]

Aside from the fact that many educational aims directly seek the development of the person in a wider sense, such a development is an implication of all educational aims, including those which are apparently confined to the development of knowledge and understanding.[21]

In sum, in sex education, as in other areas of education, we want students not only to know and to understand but also to feel, to care and to do. This involves a transformation not only of the knowledge and understanding of persons but also of their emotions, motives, dispositions, virtues and other personal qualities.

The Common School

Any progress in determining the principles which should govern the treatment of the moral aspects of sex education in school requires attention to differing schooling contexts in which educational influence can be exercised. One important distinction is between the 'common' school and the 'separate' school.[22] Often this distinction is overlooked in discussions of the moral aspects of sex education, and the 'common' school is tacitly assumed as the context in which the discussion is taking place. However, it is important to attend to the

---

[20] Wilson 1990, Ch. 8.

[21] To transform a person's beliefs is, other things being equal, to transform the other aspects of personhood to which the beliefs are related. To introduce a child to a subject of study is to open up not only possibilities for cognitive or intellectual development but also for the development of new attitudes, emotions, feelings and motivations. This can be readily seen in the case of the 'information' and 'study' aims of sex education. With regard to the former, for example, information about the facts of menstruation is, other things being equal, likely to allieviate concern and anxiety in pubescent girls. With regard to the latter, the study of the phenomenon of sexuality is unlikely to leave attitudes and emotions untouched. Another respect in which the development of knowledge and understanding implies the development of wider aspects of the person arises from the fact that knowledge and understanding can often only be acquired though the development and exercise of personal qualities such as a concern for truth and a determination to work hard.

[22] On the common school and the separate school respectively see McLaughlin 1995b and 1992. As noted earlier, the present discussion is confined to sex education in the context of the school. Clearly, the home is an important context for sex education, with its own distinctive mandate for the exercising of influence. On parents educational rights see, for example, McLaughlin 1994b.

differing mandates for the exercise of educational influence which each kind of school possesses.[23]

The common school can be regarded as one which is open to, and intended for, all students regardless of religious, ethnic, class and cultural background, and which aspires not only to offer a form of common schooling but also a common conception of education. By a 'common conception of education' here is meant an educational entitlement which is appropriate for all members of a liberal democratic society and which stresses the significance of *inter alia* the development of a form of personal autonomy, critical reason and the ability to make the kinds of complex moral evaluations of the sort demanded by a diverse and plural liberal democracy.[24] The common school forms the major part, and in some cases the sole part, of the publicly funded schooling system in liberal democratic societies. The mandate for value influence possessed by common schools[25] emphasises the importance of influence which is broadly acceptable to society as a whole. Thus, common schools cannot assume the truth of, or promote, any particular, overall, 'thick' or 'comprehensive' vision of the good life as a whole, since such visions are significantly controversial.[26] Such schools cannot, for example, assume the truth of any particular religious faith and seek to shape its students into religious believers. In pluralist liberal democratic societies, religious faith is seen as significantly controversial and as a matter

[23] Moral influence in a school of whatever kind is, of course, exercised in a complex way. Such influence involves far more than the comments, injunctions or principles explicitly articulated by teachers and contained within study materials and programmes. What is not said and not referred to is equally significant in terms of moral influence. The wider organisation and structure of the school, including its 'ethos', is also important in the explicit and implicit moral influence it exerts.

[24] On these matters see McLaughlin 1995b, pp. 82–86.

[25] A full account of this matter requires attention to complexities arising from the claims to influence upon this mandate arising from (for example) the differing rights of parents, students and the state and arguments relating to the proper role of market forces in education. On the 'thickness' or otherwise of value influence relating to such schools see, for example, Haydon 1995.

[26] Michael Walzer notes that 'thick' values are associated with complexity and disagreement (Walzer 1994, p. 6). This is in part because of the inherent, and perhaps permanent, controversiality of 'thick' theories of the good. John Rawls, for example, holds that in the light of the 'burdens of judgement' (the sources of ineliminable rational disagreement) (on this notion see Rawls 1993, esp. Lecture II) significant controversy concerning competing reasonable theories of the good is '… the inevitable long-run result of the powers of human reason at work within the background of enduring free institutions'. (Rawls 1993, p. 4).

for individual and family evaluation, decision and response. Such matters fall into the 'non-public' domain in the sense that they may not be imposed on all through the use of political power, or through common schooling.[27] On such controversial matters, the common school is required either to remain silent, or to open up the issues at stake for critical reflective discussion and consideration by students. In contrast, in relation to the 'common' or 'public' values which articulate a liberal democratic society, such as respect for the autonomy and dignity of individuals, a concern for evidence and for reason and the importance of developing an appropriate form of tolerance, the common school seeks to achieve a substantial influence on the beliefs of students and on their wider development as persons.[28]

The philosophical underpinnings of this account of the mandate of the common school, including the view of the moral domain and the moral life which it contains, are far from unproblematic.[29] The difficulties involved cannot, however, be pursued here. If we assume, however, for the purposes of argument that the principles for the exercise of educational influence by the common school are

[27] The notion of the 'non-public' needs to be carefully understood. There is no suggestion, for example, that religious belief is non-social either in the sense that it can be practised non-socially, or that it will lack a perspective upon, or significance for, the 'public' domain. The crucial point is that 'non-public' values, in virtue of their significant controversiality, cannot have decisive bearing in the political sphere.

[28] There is much concern in liberal democratic societies about the lack of substantiality of these common values and the related notion of 'the common good'. On these matters see, for example, Etzioni 1993, Fukuyama 1996, Sacks 1991, 1995, 1997. Such concerns are frequently associated with the general perspective of 'communitarianism'. For critical discussion of this perspective see, for example, Bell 1993, Mulhall and Swift 1996. Such concerns may be underscored by a tendency of philosophers to describe such values as 'thin'. However, as Michael Walzer has pointed out, the description 'thin' here does not imply that the values in question are 'substantively minor' or 'emotionally shallow'. On the contrary, he claims, they are 'close to the bone' in that they concern fundamental values such as justice and truth, which can arouse passionate intensity when threatened. Thus Walzer insists that, in moral discourse, '… thinness and intensity go together …' (Walzer 1994, p. 6).

[29] Since a major source of these philosophical underpinnings is the philosophical theory of liberalism, both the varying positions within this tradition, and the tradition as a whole, requires assessment in any attempt to defend the underpinnings themselves. A specific difficulty which requires attention is the precise character and tenability of the division between 'thick' and 'thin' values which has been invoked.

broadly correct, it is clear that, in a number of important respects, this mandate differs from that enjoyed by 'separate' schools.[30]

In the light of this mandate, what are the principles which should govern the moral aspects of sex education in the common school?

Morality, Sex Education and the Development of the Person in the Common School

Concern about the moral aspects of sex education in common schools, which is by no means confined to defenders of 'traditional' sexual morality[31] can have a number of aspects.

(a) Difficulties in the determination of common values for moral influence in sex education

As we have seen earlier, the mandate for substantive and unqualified moral influence possessed by the common school relates strongly to the 'common' or 'public' values referred to earlier. In relation to these values, it will be recalled, the common school has a mandate to achieve a substantial influence on the beliefs of students and on their wider development as persons. What, however, are the common values which can be invoked in relation to the moral aspects of sex education?[32]

Abstract philosophical principles alone cannot provide us with a precise, uncontroversial, answer to this question. Beyond a number of basic and fundamental values relating to sexual matters[33] there is

---

[30] Separate schools can be of several kinds. One prominent general kind of separate school is religious in character. Such schools seek to educate their students within a particular or 'thick' view of the good life, and they claim a mandate to do so in the light of the exercise of parental rights. Such religious schools typically do not neglect the 'common' values which have been alluded to, and nor are they necessarily in conflict with liberal educational principles (On these matters see McLaughlin 1992, 1996b). Such schools can, however, exert an evaluative influence upon students which is much more wide ranging than that which can be justifiably attempted by the common school.

[31] For moral concerns about sex education in relation to gender bias and injustice see Morgan 1996.

[32] For an approach to this matter based on a broad framework of assumptions similar to those adopted in the present article see McKay 1997, pp. 292–298.

[33] The unacceptability of rape and other forms of sexual exploitation falls into this category, as do other forms of sexual exploitation. In these matters, there is no room for 'pluralism' or respected differences of view. Embodied in law and expressed in terms of rights, these values can be regarded as 'basic' and 'non-negotiable' for a civilised (and, in particular, democratic) society and as applicable to all. One reason why such values can command widespread assent is that acceptance of them does not require acceptance of any broader perspective

room for considerable disgreement about the common values which should inform sex education, which reflects the wider disagreement about sexual morality which is prevalent in contemporary liberal democratic societies.[34] Disagreement on the educational questions is exacerbated by the devolution to some extent of the moral aspects of sex education to the level of the local school.[35] Despite its merits, this devolutionary strategy may make it harder to produce general agreement about these matters across society as a whole, while at the same time perhaps making it easier for compromises to be made, pressures to be exerted and issues fudged at the local level.[36] Whilst acknowledging that complete agreement may elude us, there are good grounds for seeking a national consensus on the moral influence appropriate for sex education in the common school which goes beyond the vague and ambiguous to as much detail as possible.

One approach to the determination of this influence, which is often seen in documents and statements relating to sex education, is via the specification of general moral principles.[37] However, such principles, whilst not wholly uninformative or empty, are of their nature open to variable interpretation at the level of detail. This interpretative flexibility and lack of 'content', whilst valuable in the search for consensus, gives rise to two difficulties.

The first difficulty is that such principles may fail to satisfy those from several quarters[38] who take the view that specific moral guidance and prescription, and not merely the articulation of general moral principles, are necessary in sex education. The immorality of pre- and extra- marital sex, homosexual sex, and abortion are typically seen as matters for concern here, as is the character of marriage

on life as a whole, or subscription to any wider 'thick' or 'comprehensive' theory of the good. Muslims, for example, can join followers of other religions and with agnostics and atheists in finding child sexual abuse abhorrent. Such behaviour falls within an 'overlapping consensus' of evaluation which exists between wider moral views.

[34] One of the issues here is whether there is a distinctively sexual morality. On this see, for example, Jones 1989, pp. 61–64. On questions related to sexual morality in general see LaFollette 1996, Montefiore 1973, Vardy 1997.

[35] On this general matter, see Sex Education Forum 1993, pp. 8–9. Compare Thomson 1997, pp. 265–266.

[36] On the role of parents in relation to the exercise of influence see, for example, Christians in Education and The Order of Christian Unity 1988.

[37] See Health Education Authority 1994 Appendix C, Veasey 1994, pp. 20–21.

[38] See Christians in Education and The Order of Christian Unity 1988, esp. Ch. 3, 4, The Islamic Academy 1991, Riches 1986.

as a permanent and exclusive commitment. One reaction to such concerns is to claim that the specific values proposed fail the criterion which values must satisfy if they are to be promoted by the common school: acceptability to society as a whole, or at least a significant proportion of it. Thus it might be argued that, despite thoughtful and telling defences of aspects of 'traditional' sexual morality and their related social, cultural and political implications[39] the common school lacks a mandate for insisting upon (as distinct from presenting for consideration) such values, since they have been subjected to criticism and rejection on morally serious grounds.[40] Debate about the mandate of the common school in these matters is, however, more complex than is usually realised, especially when the inescapability of a particular cultural content for education, and the significance of the presentation to students of 'default' norms, is acknowledged.[41]

The second difficulty which arises in relation to the approach to the determination of common moral influence in sex education through the specification of general principles is that it may fail requirements which can be described as 'the demands of substantiality'. These 'demands' insist that a view of sexuality presented to students must satisfy a number of conditions which go beyond the procedural or the minimalistic.[42] Such a view, it is suggested, must stress the emotional depth and meaning of sexuality (as seen, for example, in healing, sustaining and affirming persons), illuminate the significance of deep personal bonds and of self-control and self-denial and offer to students more than a set of 'options' for 'choice' which imply an over-exaggerated and naive view of the ability of young people to make such 'choices' in the contemporary 'jungle of preferences'. Therefore, it is argued, a more substantial set

[39] See Almond 1988, Davies 1993, Dominian 1991, Morgan 1995, Sacks 1991, Ch. 3; 1995, Ch. 4; 1997, Ch. 16, Storkey 1995, Whelan 1995.

[40] For criticisms of traditional conceptions of the family, see, for example, Midgley and Hughes 1995, Wringe 1994.

[41] On these matters see McLaughlin 1995b, pp. 87–90. Relevant also to these matters are the attempts of the Islamic Academy to achieve a consensus among religious believers about common moral influence in sex education (The Islamic Academy 1991) and to transform in a more general way the moral basis of common schooling (The Islamic Academy 1990).

[42] On the limitations of the 'harm principle' (the view that sexual behaviour should be judged according to the extent to which it harms others) in relation to the moral aspects of sex education see Morgan 1996. One of the prominent difficulties here concerns how 'harm' should be understood.

of features of good human relationships should be identified and presented unequivocally to students not merely in terms of abstract principles but also in terms of concrete practices and responsibilities. These features, although substantial, are seen as formulable in a way which renders them capable of transcending value differences (including those of a cultural and ethnic kind) and therefore apt for embodiment in sex education programmes without accusations of unjustified value influence.[43] In the absence of the identification and formulation of such features, it is claimed, there is a real danger that hedonism, relativism, individualism and confusion will fill the vacuum.

The two difficulties which have been identified can be seen readily in relation to a widely invoked general principle for moral behaviour in relation to sexuality: 'love'.

The central question which arises here, well articulated in Plato's Symposium, is how 'love' should be understood. An initial task which arises here is the need to distinguish different senses of the concept.[44] A number of important ethical principles for sex education can be derived from an understanding of love which is linked closely to such notions as personhood, equality and respect,[45] but clearly a good deal of interpretation and argument is needed to articulate these fully for educational purposes. Although the concept of 'love' must clearly feature in some form in any adequate sex education programme, an uninterpreted notion of 'love' is inadequate with respect to both of the difficulties outlined above. It is, however, clearly an important part of sex education to encourage students to develop an understanding of what love is,[46] including the notion of 'being in love'.[47] The difficulties and complexities inherent in this task should not be underestimated.[48] Since the question of how a

[43] On this general line of argument see Ulanowsky (1998).

[44] On this matter see, for example, Lewis 1960, Giddens 1992, Ch. 3

[45] See, for example, Spiecker 1992, Wilson 1995.

[46] On the notion of love see Brown 1987, Gregory 1995, Newton Smith 1973, LaFollette 1996, Scruton 1986. On our knowledge of love see Nussbaum 1990, Ch. 11, 12. See also Passmore 1980, pp. 247–250.

[47] For a checklist of considerations relevant to determining whether one loves someone or not, see Wilson 1995, pp. 192–195.

[48] This is seen, for example, in Giddens's comment that couples embarking on romantic love are confronted with the creation of a 'mutual narrative biography' (Giddens 1992, p. 46). For an interpretation of the nature of love in relation to persons see Dominian 1991.

'person' should be understood is at the heart of this task, its complexity comes readily into focus.[49]

It might be thought that the 'demands of substantiality' might be met by the combination of several principles for moral influence in sex education. After all, sex education programmes are never articulated in terms of only one moral principle. However, can an invocation of a combination of underinterpreted principles meet 'the demands of substantiality' unless the combination overall has a clearly interpretable coherence? One obstacle to the achievement of this is the lack of a mandate for the common school to exert moral influence in the light of any overall vision of life as a whole.[50]

Rachel Thomson, who has acted as the co-ordinator of the Sex Education Forum, has proposed that a solution to the problem of establishing a consensus on moral influence in sex education lies in focusing attention upon — '… a practical consideration of the realities and contingencies of young people's lives and of educational practice …'[51] rather than on the context of abstract principle. She writes, '… if faced with the realities and challenges of young people's moral dilemmas, all parties tend to pool their educational and ethical resources in order to develop practical strategies of support and development.'[52] A full evaluation of this kind of strategy needs to address the question of whether it can adequately serve not merely as a short-term response to perceived practical needs but also as base from which appropriately balanced approaches to moral influence in sex education can develop.

(b) Inattention to the demands of moral texture and complexity

Questions of moral texture and complexity arise in relation to the lack of mandate of the common school to assume the truth of, or promote, any particular or 'thick' overall vision of the good life, and its corresponding duty in relation to controversial matters of value in the 'non-public' domain to either remain silent about them, or to open them up for critical reflective discussion.

---

[49] On the centrality of the notion of a person to a proper understanding of love, see Spiecker, 1992.

[50] For an attempt to articulate an emerging overall 'ethics of personal life' relevant to sexual and related matters and based on the changes in sexual attitudes and practices which have taken place in recent years see Giddens, 1992.

[51] Thomson 1997, p. 267.

[52] Thomson 1997, p. 267.

The lack of mandate of the common school to promote any 'thick' vision of sexual morality is widely recognised in general terms.[53] With regard to the duty of the common school in relation to controversial matters of value in the 'non-public' domain, it is also widely accepted that silence is an inadequate response. The task of opening up the controversial values for critical reflective discussion is therefore also widely acknowledged.[54]

This task of the common school in relation to controversial values is a challenging one, particularly in relation to the achievement of 'balance'[55] or fairness.

The task of opening up controversial issues for discussion by students is often presented in the literature on the moral aspects of sex education in a way which does not emphasise, or bring clearly into focus, matters of moral texture and complexity. A central tension which emerges here can be seen in the two rather different sorts of claims which are typically made about the kind of educational influence which is seen as required. On the one hand are claims which can be broadly described as 'inclusive' in character. Thus, the Sex Education Forum argues that—'Schools should ensure that the moral framework within which sex education is taught is inclusive of all young people including those whose rights and identities may be marginalised within a religious framework, for example lesbian and gay young people.'[56]

---

[53] Thus, the Sex Education Forum notes that 'Adherence to one set of prescriptive values will not only exclude some students, but it would also obscure the range of conflicting values that young people have to negotiate in their own lives. A more inclusive and appropriate approach would help young people develop the skills to deal with moral diversity and to develop their own opinions and values' (Sex Education Forum 1993, p. 12).

[54] Thus, the Sex Education Forum insists that sex education should be sensitive to the needs and identities of young people, including those shaped by religion and ethnicity, and should give attention to '... historical, social, cultural and credal differences in sexual norms and practices' (Sex Education Forum 1993, p. 1). This it is claimed, involves the sharing and exploration of a range of moral views and choices as part of a consideration of wider value systems relevant to the sexual domain. Students should be made aware '... of the diversity of moral opinion in society concerning sexual behaviour and personal relationships ... the range of cultural frameworks which exist in society for regulating sexual behaviour and relationships ... (and) ... the diversity of identities, practices and moral frameworks they experience in society.' (Sex Education Forum 1993, pp. 11–12).

[55] On complexities in the notion of balance in an educational context, see Dearden 1984, Ch. 5.

[56] Sex Education Forum 1993, p. 11. Emphasis in original.

On the other hand, however, are claims which can be described as 'identity-sustaining' in nature. Thus, the Sex Education Forum insists that young people should be supported and not undermined in their cultural identities.[57] However, it may be tempting to ease the tensions inherent in the simultaneous pursuit of these two sorts of aim by blunting the critical edge of moral disagreement.

The suspicion that moral texture and complexity may be blunted can be enhanced by the rather loose way in which some documents and guidelines relating to the moral aspects of sex education articulate the basic assumptions lying behind their work. For example, there is more than a hint of tacit relativism in the Health Education Authority's claim that differences in sexual value and behaviour (whether related to religious belief or cultural practice) should be 'accepted', 'celebrated' and seen as requiring 'equal respect.'[58] Indeed, 'non-judgemental openness' and 'unconditional positive respect' for diversity is urged.[59] Although these remarks are somewhat balanced by a number of others[60] one may doubt whether the conceptual articulation of the document is sophisticated enough to meet the demands of moral texture and complexity. A lack of nuance is also visible in the insistence of the Sex Education Forum that cultural diversity should be presented to students as the norm[61] and that 'difference' should be 'recognised', 'respected' and 'celebrated'.[62]

The primary duty of the common school with respect to moral texture and complexity is to do justice to the demands of informed moral judgement involved in the development of a form of 'moral bilingualism', where students are capable of distinguishing between, on the one hand, the demands of civic virtue and, on the

---

[57] Sex Education Forum 1993 p. 12. Schools must support '… the individual in their own identity in all its complexity' and care should be taken '… not to undermine beliefs and to leave pupils in isolation' (Sex Education Forum 1993, p. 10).

[58] Health Education Authority 1994, p. 5.

[59] Health Education Authority 1994, Appendix A.

[60] These balancing statements include a caution about the danger of overly general language obscuring differences of view (Health Education Authority 1994, p. 8) and about the significance and necessity of conflict, constructive forms of which can lead to '… ways of agreeing to differ, reaching a consensus, agreeing, or compromising' (Health Education Authority 1994, p. 9).

[61] Sex Education Forum 1993, p. 15.

[62] Sex Education Forum 1993, p. 10. On the distinction between 'toleration' and 'celebration' and its significance in the context of Muslim attitudes to sex education see Halstead 1997.

other, virtue (or moral goodness) seen from a fuller perspective.[63] These demands can be frustrated by a number of dangers. I shall consider seven here.

The first of these I shall describe as the danger of 'public' moral evaluation being given illicit salience by the school. An interesting illustration of this danger is found in Patricia White's recent discussion of the educational treatment of homosexuality.[64] Educational principles demand that this subject not be ignored as an educational issue. However, in her discussion of the values which should be brought to bear on this matter, White gives prominence to the question of whether homosexual relationships violate the basic moral principles (or 'public values') of a democratic society. Having concluded that, in principle, such relationships do not, she draws the conclusion that the school should not only present homosexuality as a morally acceptable lifestyle which pupils might adopt, but should also contribute to its flourishing.

This seems to go too far. Strong liberal arguments may support the moral acceptability, for political purposes, of homosexuality within the sphere of 'civic virtue'. In arguing that the school should present homosexuality as a morally acceptable lifestyle and should help it to flourish, White may be referring only to the civic sphere, and claiming that the moral influence of the school should be confined strictly to 'public' values. However, it seems more likely that White is arguing that the common school should present homosexuality as morally acceptable in a more wide ranging way. This position depends on the claim that there cannot be any 'non-public' moral criticism of homosexuality which is reasonable in according homosexual practice civic respect, but nevertheless withholding from it full moral approval on the basis of a wider 'comprehensive' theory of the good.[65]

---

[63] On the complexity of the ethical difficulties, attitudes and virtues that liberal democratic societies demand, including the role that certain forms of hypocrisy play in sustaining such societies see Shklar 1984, esp. Ch. 2, 6.

[64] White 1991.

[65] An example of such a view is contained in a recent statement of Cardinal Hume on the teaching of the Catholic church on homosexual people. The statement insists that all persons, including those of homosexual orientation, should be treated with dignity, respect and fairness, that the oppression and contempt which homosexual people have suffered should be combatted by the church and that homophobia and violence against homosexuals in speech or action should be condemned. (Hume 1995, paras 12, 14, 15). Further, the statement acknowledges that civil legislation relating to the elimination of injustice against homosexual

Without entering into further detailed discussion of this particular example, it illustrates the need of the common school to distinguish in any particular moral issue between what is (a) fully morally acceptable both civicly and from any reasonable non-public perspective and (b) what is morally acceptable civicly but, from at least some reasonable non-public perspectives, not fully. This brings with it the difficulty in determining what is to count as a *reasonable* non-public evaluation of a particular matter, and of assessing the current state of reasonable non-public evaluation of it. Failure to attend to these aspects of moral texture and complexity runs the risk of confusing students about the forms of value and respect which are due to the differing and possibly conflicting moral views found in the 'thick' or 'non-public' domain of value.[66]

A second danger which may frustrate the demands of complex moral judgement is the danger of relativism[67] where, for example, views in the non-public domain are presented as mere preferences. One aspect of this danger emerges where it is suggested that ele-

---

people requires practical judgement and the assessment of social consequences in relation to which Catholics may reach diverse conclusions (Hume 1995, para 13). These remarks indicate a form of valuing and respect for homosexuality. However, the value and respect which is accorded to homosexuality is restricted in an important respect. Drawing a distinction between homosexual orientation and homosexual acts (Hume 1995, paras 6,7) the statement re-iterates church teaching on the immorality of the latter. Thus, whilst it is suggested that it might be appropriate to acknowledge legal rights of some kind to engage in homosexual acts, it is insisted that '... there can be no moral right to homosexual acts, even though they are no longer held to be criminal in many secular legal systems' (Hume 1995, para 5 cf. para 12). For related discussions see Reiss 1997b and Halstead and Lewicka 1998.

[66] The notions of 'diversity' and 'pluralism' are capable of interpretation in a merely descriptive way. Understood descriptively, 'diversity' and 'pluralism' merely refer to (or describe) the differences of value which exist, without necessarily specifying any particular attitude thought appropriate towards them. However, understood evaluatively, 'diversity' and 'pluralism' standardly imply that differences in the 'non-public' domain of value, where they do not come into conflict in a significant way with the 'public' or common values, are valuable and worthy of respect in some sense. The qualification 'valuable and worthy of respect in some sense' is of crucial significance here and the educational implications of this qualification are often overlooked. The respects in which reasonable moral views in the 'non-public' domain are seen as valuable and worthy of respect in 'diversity' and 'pluralism' vary significantly. It is a consequence of taking seriously the claim that the non-public domain contains serious conflicts, as distinct from mere differences, of view about evaluative matters that a nuanced view about the forms of value and respect accorded to the non-public domain is needed (On pluralism see, for example, Kekes 1993).

[67] On moral relativism see Harman and Jarvis Thomson 1996.

ments of such views can be combined together without attention to their structural character. Some views are 'architectonic' in the sense that they establish a general framework or perspective which determines, at least to some extent, the 'lower level' values compatible with them and sets limits to the degree to which compatibility with alternative frameworks and perspectives can be achieved.[68]

A third danger relates to failures of inclusion with respect to moral views offered for consideration in sex education. The general principle of inclusion urges that a sufficiently broad range of views be considered. The range of choices about sexual lifestyle discussed must, for example, include the choice not to be sexually active.[69] Further, it is clear that religious perpectives must not only be included in relation to the moral dimension of sex education in the common school, but also treated seriously. As Michael Reiss points out, in the same way that health education can be racist or sexist, it can also be 'religionist' in that it indoctrinates its pupils into a primarily agnostic perspective.[70] The 'serious' treatment of religion requires that religious perspectives be presented without illicit preconceptions. For example, the impression should not be given that religious perspectives on sex are largely negative.[71] It is also important to ensure that the relationship between religious and cultural values is clearly conceptualised, and the two not illicitly conflated.[72] Further, the differences of view which exist within varying faiths about matters of sex should be acknowledged.[73] One difficulty in overemphasising heterogeneity within religious beliefs and traditions, however, is that traditional religious believers may feel that justice is not being done

[68]   On these general matters see McLaughlin 1994a, esp. pp. 456.

[69]   Sex Education Forum 1993, p. 1.

[70]   Reiss 1996, p. 101. For a related discussion see Haydon 1994. On the general point that religion should be included alongside (say) ethnicity and gender in categories relating to the equal opportunities and anti-discrimination agenda see Sex Education Forum 1993, p. 8.

[71]   Sex Education Forum 1993, pp. 4, 19.

[72]   Health Education Authority 1994, p. 9.

[73]   The Sex Education Forum, for example, whilst noting a degree of consensus among the religions about such matters as the prohibition of sex before marriage and the disapproval of sexually active homosexual relationships, also draws attention to the fact that religious views may develop and change and that there may be a gap between religious ideals and practice. (Sex Education Forum 1993, p. 10. See also p. 8 and Health Education Authority 1994, Appendix D). For a range of religious perspectives on sex, sexuality and sex education see Sex Education Forum 1993, pp. 17–98.

to their distinctive beliefs, especially if a relativistic tone is characteristic of the sex education programme as a whole.

It is important to note that the principle of inclusion gives rise not only to question about which viewpoints should be considered but when the alternatives in question are considered. Ray and Went are surely correct in insisting that sex education '… should be placed within a human context where values, emotions and beliefs are explored alongside biological and physiological explanations'.[74] The notion of 'alongside' is of significance here. Religious perspectives, for example, should not be confined to separate periods of religious studies, if they are not to be seen as merely hypthothetical or marginal. Some of the tensions and dilemmas to which a requirement of this kind may give rise are illustrated (for example) by a claim that, when 'safe sex' practices are discussed, they should not be only evaluated in terms of physical health; the moral unacceptability of many of the practices in question on religious grounds should also be mentioned.

A fourth danger concerns the possibility that courses or programmes of study as a whole may be articulated on biased value assumptions. A striking example of this can be seen in the programme 'Condoms across the curriculum.'[75] The programme offers twenty seven '… varied and interesting ways in which condoms can be introduced into almost every curricular area …'[76] in the school. Thus, for example, in Modern Languages the foreign vocabulary surrounding condoms and their use is studied, whilst in history the development of the condom up to the present day is given attention. The clear difficulty here is that the programme seems to prejudge the fundamental moral acceptability of contraception, a question which should be left open for discussion in a properly balanced programme. Where sex education is provided in different parts of the curriculum, and not under the label 'sex education', it may be difficult to make judgments about overall balance of value influence.[77]

A fifth danger involves neglect of the various sensitivities which arise in relation to illicitly value-laden language which can be used in programmes of sex education. The way in which sexual matters

[74] Ray and Went 1995, p. 27.
[75] Harvey (Ed.) 1993.
[76] Harvey (Ed.) 1993, p. 1.
[77] Ray and Went 1995, p. 20.

are described is not evaluatively neutral. As Anthony Giddens observes 'Once there is a new terminology for understanding sexuality, ideas, concepts and theories couched in these terms seep into social life itself, and help re-order it.'[78] So objections to certain forms of language do not just concern matters of offence; language changes perceptions and realities, and therefore has an impact upon power relations from a value point of view. This explains in part some of the objections to 'linguistic revisionism' which are found.[79] An example of the sorts of concern which arise here involves unguarded uses of the term 'homophobia'. An acceptable, focused, definition of this term is contained in a quotation reported by Ray and Went: '... an irrational dislike for individuals who identify as lesbian, gay or bisexual.'[80] However, sometimes the term is used to imply that all moral criticism of homosexual practice is ipso facto homophobic. Used in this way, the term 'homophobia' serves to pre-empt necessary moral debate. A related potential danger of illicitly value-laden language in sex education arises in relation to the terms used in the characterisation of various value positions, as seen, for example, in unguarded use of the terms 'restrictive' and 'permissive'[81] and in distinctions such as that drawn between 'prescriptive' and 'enabling' values.[82]

A sixth danger worthy of consideration concerns insensitivity to the offence which might be caused by the way in which sex education is conducted. For example, in Massachusetts students and their parents recently mounted a legal action in relation to a mandatory AIDS awareness presentation which was regarded, in virtue of its sexually explicit character, as offensive, humiliating and intimidating by several parents.[83] Michael Reiss is correct in insisting upon recognition of the distinction between embarrassment and modesty

[78] Giddens 1992, p. 28.

[79] For example, in an article in The Times on 27th December 1986, 'Only a moral revolution can contain this scourge', the former Chief Rabbi Sir Immanuel Jakobovits calls for the elimination from 'the common vocabulary' of 'euphemisms or misnomers that make perversions acceptable'. He gives as examples of these '... words like "gay" for homosexual, "heterosexual" for normal, "safe sex" for inadmissable indulgence, and "stable relationships" for unmarried couples'.

[80] Ray and Went 1995, p. 85.

[81] See McKay 1997, esp. pp. 286–292.

[82] See Thomson 1997, esp. pp. 263–271.

[83] Zirkel 1996.

in open discussion about sexual matters[84] and this is clearly relevant to cultural and religious differences.[85] Since the adoption of certain approaches in sex education can not only be offensive but also biased and pre-emptive from a value point of view, there is a clear need to discern strategies which can minimise these dangers.[86]

A seventh danger relates to the possibility that an unduly narrow range of skills may be proposed for development in students.[87] Skill development is potentially problematic in sex education because it assumes that the skills to be developed are, in moral terms, acceptable. For purposes of balance, therefore, the skills aimed at should include (for example) those '… to avoid and resist unwanted sexual experience'.[88]

In the light of the sorts of requirements which have been indicated, it is apparent that the project of aiming at a common school seeking to achieve a form of moral texture and balance is one which confronts significant difficulties.

One category of difficulty is practical in character. The demands on teachers are extensive, and there are as yet relatively few guidelines and resources of the relevant kind available, together with appropriate forms of training. A related practical difficulty is that of securing appropriate forms of agreement and approval for the work to proceed. Other kinds of difficulty are deeper in nature, however. It may be felt, for example, that there is a logical flavour to the difficulty, and perhaps impossibility, of illuminating perspectives in the 'non-public' domain. This may be due to the consequences for coherence and intelligibility of abstracting isolated principles and values from the wider frameworks of belief and practice in which they have their home. Another related difficulty with a logical flavour is determining the range of views to be considered, and the nature of balance.

[84] Reiss 1993, p. 129.

[85] On the need for sensitivity to the possibility of offence in relation to resources in sex education see Sex Education Forum 1993, p. 11.

[86] For an indication of a range of such strategies in relation to Muslim sensitivities concerning sex education see Halstead 1997, esp. p. 328. On Islamic attitudes in general to sex education see also Amer 1997.

[87] On the claim that the development of skills should not be neglected in sex education see BMA Foundation for AIDS et at. 1997, p. 6. On the advice about contraception which schools should give to students see Ray and Went 1995, pp. 20–22.

[88] Ray and Went 1995, p. 1.

It may also be felt that even if the demands of moral texture and complexity could be met both in principle and practice, it would be undesirable to meet them. This is because these demands may be in conflict with other, prior, educational aims and values, all of which may be threatened or undermined by an emphasis on moral texture and complexity. These other educational aims and values include the need to transmit common, civic values in a relatively unproblematic way, the practical need to encourage students to adopt health-related sexual practices and the need to achieve a number of 'reassurance' aims, including the reduction of guilt. For example, the aim of encouraging students to adopt 'safe sex' practices may be frustrated by drawing the attention of the students to the morally dubious character of many of these practices from some points of view.

Notwithstanding these difficulties and dilemmas, however, the demands of moral texture and complexity are central to the question of defensible moral influence in sex education in the common school.

(c) Inadequacy with respect to the development of the person

As insisted earlier, sex education, like education itself, involves the wide ranging transformation of the person.[89] In the common school, however, it will be recalled that the mandate for the exercise of such influence upon the person is problematic. Whilst we speak of 'education of the whole child' quite freely in common schools, it is not clear that this can in fact be attempted in any unqualified way in this context.[90]

There are, however, forms of personal development — of dispositions, virtues and qualities of character[91] which can be reasonably undertaken in the common school in virtue of their fundamentality or inescapability with respect both to the 'common' values of a liberal democratic society and to its associated conception of education.[92]

---

[89] On the wide ranging transformations of the person involved in education see, for example, Passmore 1980, Part II.

[90] On this see, McLaughlin 1996a.

[91] On virtues and qualities of character in relation to moral development see, for example, Peters 1974 Part Two; Carr 1991.

[92] One category here relates to the basic common values of the society, whose development in students need not necessarily be seen in terms of the controversial notion of 'character training'. (On the notion of character training see Lickona 1996, Etzioni 1993, Ch. 3). There can be little objection from any

What qualities of personhood and character can be developed in the common school in the context of sex education? A full answer to this question requires attention to generally neglected questions concerning the nature of specific virtues, such as self-control[93] and the relationship between judgement and action.[94] In the light of the foregoing discussion about the lack of mandate for the common school to develop in students any overall view of life it is clear that the common school lacks a mandate to develop in students any very specific virtues associated with views such as chastity.[95] A crucial question relating to the virtues and qualities of character which the common school is licensed to develop concerns the possibility of its formulating an adequate response to 'the demands of substantiality' of the sort outlined in the last section.

Some of the most well-grounded of the forms of development which the common school may have a mandate to promote in sex education are those relating to basic sexual morality and to sexual autonomy. There are certain kinds of virtues related to basic sexual morality (such as caring for the feelings of others and avoiding sexual exploitation and violence) which could scarcely be objected to by any reasonable person. They are presupposed to anything which might be regarded as morality in this sphere. The concept of sexual autonomy brings with it a range of associated virtues and qualities of

quarter, for example, to the development in students of the disposition to care for the feelings of others and to avoid hatred and violence. Other forms of personal development which should in principle be relatively unproblematic in common schools relate to the requirements of learning. Hugh Sockett, for example, discusses a range of personal qualities of will related to these requirements which are manifest as habits or character traits or virtues: determination, carefulness, concentration, self-restraint and forbearance, patience, conscientiousness, and endurance, which he categorises under the headings of endeavour, heed and control (Sockett 1988). All of these virtues, it is claimed, properly conceived and sensitively attuned to cultural difference (Sockett 1988 pp. 208-209) can be confidently developed in the common school. If this were not so, indeed, it would be hard to see how the school could invite its students to engage in any kind of sustained learning. A further category of personal quality is that relating to the leading of a flourishing life as a citizen, and as a person more generally, in a liberal democratic society. Some of these qualities are discussed by Patricia White in 'Civic Virtues and Public Schooling' (White 1996). For a general discussion of the virtues relevant to a liberal form of life see Macedo 1990.

[93]   On this see Steutel 1988.

[94]   On this see Straughan 1982, 1989.

[95]   On the notion of chastity see, for example, Carr 1986. For an example of an overall view of life and of sexual morality within which a specific notion of chastity might be housed see Catechism of the Catholic Church 1994 esp. paras 2352, 2353, 2357, 2366, 2368–2370, 2380–2381, 2382, 2390, 2391. Compare Kelly 1998.

character. Personal autonomy in general, after all, involves not merely (an appropriate degree of) self-directedness in thinking, but also in disposition and action. It therefore follows that the school must be concerned with those qualities of personhood which enable autonomy to be achieved. An example of the sort of virtues and qualities of character which might be involved here relate to forms of empowerment for young women in relation to sexual matters in general and to sexual encounters in particular.[96] A further prominent example of general significance here involves the virtues and qualities of character required for the achievement of an uncontroversial notion of 'sexual health'.

One of the interesting questions which arises here is whether the virtues and qualities of character seen as presupposed to the exercise of sexual autonomy can be seen to include a general emphasis upon virtues and qualities of prudence and hesitation. Here an emphasis on 'abstinence' would be justified not because of its connection with a specific overall view of life, but because of its aptness with respect to the development and exercise of sexual autonomy. Such an emphasis may well achieve the support of parents of rather different overall views of life and of sexuality, including those who seek to put their children into a position where they might adopt a religious life.[97] Such questions give rise to complex considerations about what is involved generally in putting a student into a position where he or she can make decisions which are as objective as possible about sex-

[96] Holland *et al*. 1991. Mere knowledge of risk, it is argued, is insufficient to ensure the avoidance of risk-taking behaviour. Therefore, women with an interest in their safety and well being in sexual matters '... have to be socially assertive and so to be prepared to challenge, to some extent at least, the conventions of feminity' (Holland *et al*. 1991, p. 2) and to be prepared to face the resultant consequences, which may involve losing a partner or a potential partner. Young women, it is claimed, must not only have a positive conception of feminine sexuality, but must also be able to put that conception into practice against the male sexual pressure which is often seen as part of the conventions of 'normal' heterosexuality (Holland *et al*. 1991, p. 3). Since sexual autonomy, like autonomy more generally, demands more than understanding, a model of education which stresses merely the hypothetical consideration of possibilities and options is inadequate for its development (On the gap between 'intellectual empowerment' and 'experiential empowerment' see the five case studies outlined in Holland, *et al*. 1991, pp. 10–23).

[97] On the related matter of possible common ground between radical feminists and Muslims on similar issues see Halstead 1991.

ual matters, and about the role of practices of modesty and sexual hesitation in the promotion of autonomy.[98]

One limitation of the common school with respect to the development of the person is its inability to shape the person in any overall way, and, in particular, to base its work on any overarching view of the proper structure of the virtues derived from any specific normative vision of the nature of the human person and of human flourishing. Virtues and qualities of character do, after all, have a structural character to them[99] and the moral life generally is significantly informed by narrative considerations.[100] This may lead some parents to seek a context for the sex education of their children, such as the 'separate' school, which enables this much fuller development to be aimed at.[101]

Conclusion

Despite all the complex problems which have been identified, it may nevertheless be felt that the common school is a context in which the moral aspects of sex education can be dealt with fairly and effectively. If this is to happen, however, sharply focused and wide ranging discussion and debate is needed on the matters to which attention has been drawn here. This discussion needs to extend beyond matters of general principle to the detailed implications of, and requirements for, particular programmes, teaching strategies and contexts.

Acknowledgements

Earlier versions of this essay were presented to a seminar at the Faculty of Psychology and Education at the Free University, Amsterdam in December 1994 and at the twenty-fifth anniversary conference of the Journal of Moral Education on 'Morals for the Millennium: Educational Challenges in a Changing World' at the University College of St Martin, Lancaster in July 1996. I am very grateful to the participants in the discussions on these occasions for their comments and criticisms.

[98] On these matters, and for a defence of a 'traditional sexual education', see Scruton 1986, esp. Ch 11.

[99] On this see Dent 1984; McDermott 1989; Sherman 1989.

[100] On this see Hansen 1996, Hauerwas 1981.

[101] On the fuller kind of sexual education and formation which can be attempted in the 'separate' school see Foundation for the Family 1996, Isaacs 1984, Pierson 1994, Sacred Congregation for Catholic Education 1983.

Chapter 14

Wittgenstein, Education and Religion

Wittgenstein's remarks about religion are neither systematic, complete nor wholly transparent. Nevertheless, they interestingly illuminate a number of central philosophical issues relating to the religious domain and to education in religion.

Any exploration of this illumination confronts the difficulty of establishing a reliable account of what Wittgenstein's views on religion actually were. This is a task of no mean complexity (see, for example, Barrett, 1991; Hudson, 1975; Keightley, 1976; Kerr, 1986; Malcolm, 1993; Phillips, 1993; Sherry, 1977; Shields, 1993; Rhees, 1969, Ch. 13; Winch, 1987, Ch. 6, 8, 9; 1993). One aspect of this task is the need to distinguish the views of Wittgenstein himself from those of philosophers who have developed a more fully worked out philosophy of religion influenced by him (e.g. Phillips, 1965, 1970a, 1971, 1976, 1986, 1988, 1993). Another problem which arises is the need to select from among a wide range of potential issues for discussion.

In this paper I shall confine myself to exploring the educational significance of a number of central themes relating to religion which are recognisably Wittgensteinian in the sense that they are to be found in, or as plausible developments of, Wittgenstein's work. My discussion will tend to focus upon elements found in Wittgenstein's later philosophy, although it should be noted that the sections of the Tractates concerned with 'the inexpressible' are of significance for religious questions, as is the issue of the continuity of Wittgenstein's thought on religious matters between his earlier and later work (on Wittgenstein's early thought in relation to religion and the question of continuity see, for example, Barrett, 1991, Chs. 1–5, 12–13; Hudson, 1975, Ch. 3, pp. 151–152). For reasons of space, the selection and the characterisation of the themes with which I deal, and the extent to which they can properly be ascribed to Wittgenstein himself, will receive less discussion than they deserve. Nor will I be able to consider in detail the extensive criticism to which this general perspective has been subjected (on this see, for example, Cook, 1988; Mackie, 1982, Ch. 12; O'Hear, 1984, Ch. 1; Trigg, 1973, Ch. 2). However, in the discussion of its educational significance, a number of considerations relevant to the evaluation of the perspective will become apparent.

An interesting preliminary indication of this significance can be gained by reference to a general view concerning education in religion which is currently very influential, and which can be briefly sketched.

Education in Religion: A Contemporary View

It is widely agreed among contemporary philosophers of education, and educationalists more generally, that education in religion, at least in the common schools of a pluralistic liberal democracy, should aim not at the fostering of religious belief and practice in students but at their achievement of *understanding* in this domain. Education qua education is seen as unconcerned with whether students are, or become, religious believers or unbelievers, or, more broadly, religious persons. The forms of commitment it seeks to bring about are those of the educated, rather than the religious, person. It is therefore seen as quite wrong for educators to present or teach a particular religion *as if it were true*. Or, to put the point more precisely, it is insisted that students must be made aware that the domain of religion, though one worthy of engaged attention, involves uncertainty and controversy and the question of religious faith and practice is therefore a matter for personal reflective evaluation, decision and response.

Although the precise arguments articulating such a perspective are varied, one general conception of education in religion in which it is embodied is very familiar (cf. Hirst, 1972, 1974a, esp., Ch. 3, 1974b, 1981, 1984, 1985; Hull, 1984; Schools Council, 1971; Sealey, 1985; Smart, 1968; Great Britain Parliament House of Commons, 1985, Ch. 8). This conception is supported by a range of equally familiar arguments concerning the uncertain and controversial epistemological and ethical status of religious beliefs, the distinction between public and private values in a pluralistic liberal democratic society and the requirements of a conception of education which has as its heart the crucial importance of critical, reflective and appropriately independent judgement by individuals as part of their achievement of a form of personal autonomy (McLaughlin, 1992 including footnotes 4, 5, 7, 9, 15, 18, 25, 47). Although this view is explicitly addressed to the form of education in religion appropriate for the common schools of a pluralistic liberal democratic society, it also calls into question the character and legitimacy of education in religion in religious schools (ibid.).

This general view of education in religion needs to be properly understood. In ruling out the teaching of any particular religion as if it were true, for example, the view is not expressing hostility to religious faith as such, but seeking to achieve for individuals an appropriate degree of objectivity of judgement and scope for self-determination. In stressing the need for personal reasoning and decision in religion, neither a paradigm of reasoning alien to the domain, nor a Utopian conception of the autonomy of the individual need be assumed. Nor need the complexity involved in achieving understanding in the religious domain be overlooked or oversimplified. The significance of the 'internal' perspective, for example, is typically acknowledged. This is seen, for example, in a well known passage from a Schools Council report: 'Religion cannot be understood simply from the outside. It is like stained-glass windows in the cathedrals. You see them from the outside, and they are nothing, grey and colourless. You see them from the inside, and they are wonderful, full of life and colour. Unless they are understood as seen from the inside religious dogmas and rituals seem grey and sapless, if not absurd' (Schools Council, 1976, p. 49). Since this general view rules out the formation and maintenance of faith, attempts are made to satisfy the requirements of this 'internal' perspective through such strategies as sympathetic imaginative participation (Smart, 1973).

For ease of reference, I shall describe this general view of education in religion as an LR — Liberal Rational — one, without entering into discussion of the complexities inherent in the use of such a label. The extent to which this view actually underpins contemporary educational policy and practice is unclear (on this issue in relation to England and Wales see, for example, Jackson, 1992). However, at the theoretical level, even when properly understood, the view gives rise to a number of prominent questions and difficulties which are rich in implication for educational practice. What is involved in achieving objectivity of judgement in religious matters? To what extent can understanding in religion be achieved by those who do not have religious beliefs and live a religious life? Can the demands of the 'internal' perspective be adequately satisfied by strategies such as 'sympathetic imaginative participation'? Is religious understanding essentially particular rather than general in character? How are 'understanding' and 'truth' to be understood in the religious domain? In presenting religion as an uncertain and controversial matter calling for personal reflective decision and response are central elements of the life of religious faith misrepresented?

These are all matters on which Wittgenstein's discussion of religion throws some light. As is obvious, the Wittgensteinian perspective offers a challenge to many of the underlying philosophical assumptions (e.g. Hirst, 1985; Cooper, 1993) on which the view which has just been sketched depends, not least, perhaps, its conception of the rational human agent (cf. Kerr, 1986, Chs. 1, 3–6). The nature of this challenge can be seen in the themes considered below.

Wittgenstein on Religion

There has been much speculation about Wittgenstein's own religious beliefs, attitudes and commitments (Malcolm, 1993, esp. Ch. 1; McGuinness, 1988; Monk, 1990) occasioned in part by remarks of his such as: 'I am not a religious man but I cannot help seeing every problem from a religious point of view' (quoted in Rhees 1984, p. 79), and the nature and significance of characteristically religious perspectives in Wittgenstein's general approach to philosophy have been explored in a number of recent studies (Malcolm, 1993, esp. Ch. 2–7; Shields, 1993; Winch, 1993).

Wittgenstein's remarks about religious belief are not confined to his rather brief academic discussions of the matter (e.g. LA). References to religion are scattered throughout his work (see especially CV) and much of interest can be gleaned from his diaries (McGuinness, 1988; Monk, 1990) and from the recollections and reports of those who knew him (e.g. Rhees, 1984, esp. the conversations reported by M.O'C. Drury, pp. 76–171).

From this wide range of material, varying in significance and complexity, a number of distinctively Wittgensteinian themes can be identified which illuminate the LR view of education in religion.

(I) The status of religious faith and practice

One of the starting points for the LR view is an anxiety about the uncertain epistemological status of religious beliefs. This is seen in Hirst's claim that: '... as there is no agreement in our society on the truth of any body of religious claims, nor even how we might in principle judge such beliefs to be true, we have no justification for teaching any body of such claims *as a body of established knowledge*' (Hirst, 1970, p. 213).

Leaving to one side at this point the issue of what it is appropriate to teach, it is clear that, for various reasons, this description of the status of religious faith and practice is uncongenial to a Wittgensteinian perspective.

That this is so is seen in the reaction of D.Z. Phillips to Hirst's claim that there are (at present) no public criteria in religion to distinguish the true from the false. Accusing Hirst of a 'misplaced scepticism', Phillips points to the criteria within religious traditions which do exist. Anticipating Hirst's response that such tests constitute tests merely for orthodoxy and not for truth (Hirst, 1970, p. 214), Phillips accuses Hirst of making demands which arise from inattention to the actual character of religious beliefs. Although Phillips misunderstands Hirst in interpreting him as seeking criteria of truth external to the religious domain (Phillips, 1970b, p. 12), his accusation stands in relation to the demands which Hirst in fact does make, which insist *inter alia* upon a distinction between 'accepted public rules' for the use of religious language and 'tests for truth' making possible the objective adjudication of alternative religious claims (Hirst, 1970, p. 214; 1985). For on Phillips' view religious beliefs are not conjectures or hypotheses at all; much less ones which can be objectively adjudicated or about which believers and non-believers can share a common understanding and disagree. Rather they are distinctive ways in which life can be seen and lived out in the light of commitments which have an absolute character. 'Truth' in the religious domain is concerned with the possibility of commitment to the religious life. Thus Phillips insists: '... religious beliefs are not a class of second-best statements, hypotheses awaiting confirmation or conjectures longing to be borne out. They are a body of truths, in the sense I have been talking about, which have played an important part in the history of mankind, and by which many people still regulate or attempt to regulate their lives' (Phillips, 1970b, p. 12).

Aside from the question of the extent to which Phillips' general position can be regarded as similar to that of Wittgenstein himself, contained in this statement are a number of central Wittgensteinian themes which require exploration (for a brief general overview of such themes from Phillips' perspective see Phillips, 1993, Introduction).

(II) The distinctiveness of religious commitment

In the notes of Wittgenstein's 'Lectures and Conversations on Aesthetics, Psychology and Religious Belief' (LA) taken down by his students, we find a number of remarks about the distinctiveness of religious commitment: To hold a religious belief is not to hold a (mere) opinion, for example about whether there is a German aeroplane overhead (LA, p. 53) but to have an unshakeable belief, which will show in the believer: '… not by reasoning or by appeal to ordinary grounds for belief, but rather by regulating for all in his life' (ibid., p. 54), involving sacrifices and risks which would not be made for beliefs which are better established. Wittgenstein comments: '… there is this extraordinary use of the word "believe". One talks of believing and at the same time one doesn't use "believe" as one does ordinarily. You might say (in the normal use): "You only believe — oh well." Here it is used entirely differently; on the other hand it is not used as we generally use the word "know"' (LA, pp. 59-60). Hilary Putnam makes the point that Wittgenstein cannot be supposed here to be claiming that religious belief is always free from doubt, but that, whilst belief may alternate with doubt, it 'regulates for all' in the believer's life (Putnam, 1992, p. 145).

Wittgenstein points out that religious commitment is not based on reason and evidence in a normal way. 'Reasons look entirely different from normal reasons. They are, in a way, quite inconclusive. The point is that if there were evidence, this would in fact destroy the whole business' (LA, p. 56).[1] Religious beliefs involve the use of 'pictures' with their associated 'technique of usage', which rules out as inappropriate talk of (say) 'eyebrows' in relation to 'the eye of God' (LA, p. 71). In religious belief: 'The expression of belief may play an absolutely minor role' (LA, p. 55) in contrast to the way it is embedded in the believer's thoughts and life. Religious belief is unique in that, in contrast to other kinds of belief, failure to believe is seen as something bad (LA, p. 59). Further, religious believers and unbelievers are not involved in clear-cut disagreement and contradiction. Of a person who thinks of illness in terms of punishment, Wittgenstein remarks: 'If I'm ill, I don't think of punishment at all. If you say: "Do

[1] cf. Wittgenstein's remarks about Father O'Hara, who claimed that religious beliefs could be made reasonable: LA, pp. 58-59. See also LA, pp. 60-63.

you believe the opposite?" — you can call it believing the opposite, but it is entirely different from what we would normally call believing the opposite. I think differently, in a different way. I say different things to myself. I have different pictures' (LA, p. 55; see also LA, pp. 55–59).

In his recent discussion of these lectures, Hilary Putnam takes them to exemplify in a powerful way the need for us: '… to take our lives and our practice seriously in philosophical discussion' (Putnam, 1992, p. 135), and cautions against a too hasty classification of Wittgenstein's conception of religious belief as incommensurable, 'non-cognitive', relativist or (given that there is no 'essence of reference') non referential (ibid., Ch. 7, 8). Nor should Wittgenstein too hastily be described as providing a reductionist account of religious belief. Of the notion of a 'picture' Wittgenstein says: 'It says what is says. Why should you be able to substitute anything else? … If I say he used a picture, I don't want to say anything he himself wouldn't say. I want to say that he draws these conclusions' (LA, p. 71). Although this matter is difficult to interpret, Cyril Barrett claims that, however unorthodox they may appear, Wittgenstein's views on religion are rooted in a traditional theology and philosophy of religion (Barrett, 1991, p. xiii. On the application of Wittgenstein's ideas to theological questions see, for example, Kerr, 1986, Ch. 8).

(III) Religion and practice

In a remark published in 'Culture and Value' Wittgenstein claims that: 'Christianity is not a doctrine, not, I mean, a theory about what has happened and will happen to the human soul, but a description of something that actually takes place in human life' (CV, p. 28), which is echoed in his remark that '… the words you utter or what you think as you utter them are not what matters, so much as the difference they make at various points in your life. How do I know that two people mean the same when each says he believes in God? … *Practice* gives the words their sense' (CV, p. 85, cf. C, #229). For Wittgenstein, what matters in Christianity is not 'sound doctrines' but a change of life (CV, p. 53). Considerations such as these lead into the familiar Wittgensteinian emphasis upon religion as a 'language game' and 'form of life'.

Wittgenstein's conception of these notions needs no detailed recapitulation here (on their application to religion see, for example, Barrett, 1991, Ch. 6–10; Hudson, 1975, Ch. 2 II, 5) nor the related account of Wittgenstein's move from his earlier abstract, static and uniform theory of the nature of language in the Tractatus to a conception of it as a 'set of tools' for use in various contexts and for various purposes, meaning being connected to use. 'Language games', consisting of language and (crucially): '... the actions into which it is woven ...' (PI, I, #7) 'forms of life', make possible (among other things) agreement in judgements, and are significantly distinct in virtue of their own rules or 'logical grammar' (PI, I, # 373; cf. PI, I, #664) and their own activities.

A number of issues arise in relation to these notions. Those of particular significance to religion include the nature of the grounding of the religious language game and form of life, the question of the 'reality' with which these are concerned and the relationship between religious understanding and religious practice.

(IV) The grounds of religious belief

On the grounding of language games and forms of life in general, Wittgenstein writes: 'The origin and the primitive form of the language game is a reaction; only from this can more complicated forms develop. Language — I want to say — is a refinement, "in the beginning was the deed"' (CV, p. 31) — '... it is our acting, which lies at the bottom of our language-game' (C, # 204). Language games, and their related forms of life, are not based on 'grounds' but are rather entrenched in our life and thinking, held fast by surrounding beliefs (C, # 144; cf. C, ## 140, 141, 225) and supported by such attitudes as 'acknowledgement' (C, # 378), acceptance (PI, II, xi, p. 226; CV, p. 16; C, # 559), respect (appropriate for a picture which is at the root of our thinking: CV, p. 83), 'observance' (for Wittgenstein, culture is, or presupposes, an observance: CV, p. 83) and trust. 'If I have exhausted the justifications I have reached bedrock, and my spade is turned. Then I am inclined to say: "This is simply what I do"' (PI, I, #217).

Consistent with this perspective, Wittgenstein holds that the religious form of life is not concerned with empirical hypotheses (see LA; cf. Phillips, 1976) or grounded in evidence (cf. C, #336) or metaphysical theories about the nature of the world, but on certain basic or primitive reactions to our 'natural-historical setting'. As Fergus Kerr puts it: 'The very idea of God depends on such brute facts as that, in certain circumstances, people cannot help shuddering with awe or shame, and so on' (Kerr, 1986, p. 183). Wittgenstein's account of how religious faith may become possible for a person echoes his account of religious faith as a form of trusting not superstitious fear

(CV, p. 72; cf. C, # 509). He writes: 'Life can educate one to a belief in God. And *experiences* too are what bring this about; but I don't mean visions and other forms of sense experience which show us the "existence of this being", but e.g., sufferings of various sorts. These neither show us God in a way a sense impression shows us an object, nor do they give rise to *conjectures* about him. Experiences, thoughts, — life can force this concept on us' (CV, p. 86) (cf. '... faith is faith in what is needed by my *heart*, my *soul*, not my speculative intelligence ... What combats doubt is, at it were *redemption*' (CV, p. 33)).

Given that standards of explanation, intelligibility and justification are internal to particular language games and forms of life, the search for external standards, including 'grounds' is, in Wittgenstein's view, illusory (Brown, 1969; cf. Barrett, 1991, Ch. 9; cf. in contrast, Hepburn, 1987). The extent to which Wittgenstein's perspective on these matters can properly be described as relativistic has given rise to considerable discussion (Barrett, 1991, Ch. 7; Putnam, 1992, Ch. 8; Smeyers, 1992).

(V) Religious truth and reality

Rush Rhees claims that if people come to love God: '... this has to do with the life they lead and in which they take part' (Rhees, 1969, p. 122). It is in a religious life, including activities such as worship, that the reality of God can be found. But what is the nature of this reality? As we saw earlier, Wittgenstein holds that this is something very distinctive. 'If the question arises as to the existence of a god or God, it plays an entirely different role to that of the existence of any person or object I ever heard of' (LA, p. 59). One of the distinctive features of the use of religious pictures to which Wittgenstein draws attention is the absence of a 'technique of comparison' in the case (say) of a picture of God creating Adam, in contrast to that available in the case of a picture of a tropical plant, where the thing depicted can be compared to the depiction (LA, p. 64).

For D.Z. Phillips, coming to see that there is a God does not amount to discovering that an additional being exists; it is *seeing the point of* or *discovering* the religious way of life. For Phillips, the reality of God is embodied and lived out in the religious attitude. To participate in the love of God, he argues, is to adopt the perspective of 'the eternal'. A central feature of such an attitude is an independence of the believer from 'the way things go': no empirical event can affect his or her love of God. This is part of the 'grammar' of the concept 'God', a feature which Wittgenstein associated with 'being safe whatever happens' (cf. Malcolm, 1993, p. 7) on the part of the religious believer. Phillips seems to equate believing in God with participating in the religious attitude, 'the eternal', and living according to it. He writes: 'The God-given ability to give thanks in all things is the goodness of God' (Phillips, 1970a, p. 209); 'To *use* this language is to worship, to believe in God' (ibid., p. 69). Thus, for Phillips, a man who finds God has not found an object but: '... he has found God in a praise, a thanksgiving, a confessing and an asking which were not his before' (Phillips, 1976, p. 181).

On this view, religious beliefs are neither metaphysical theories nor factual hypotheses; they do not postulate 'transcendental' reality of an ontological or metaphysical kind. The language is not *referential* in the sense that it is about an *object*: God, but expressive of the values contained in the religious attitude to life '... it is a grammatical confusion to think that this language is referential or descriptive. It is an expression of value. If one asks what it says, the answer is what it says itself' (Phillips, 1976, p. 147). Phillips rejects the 'exclusive simple choice' implicit in the suggestion that talk of God must either literally refer to a fact or object or be metaphorical (cf. Phillips, 1988, pp. 317–325) and has delineated in considerable detail the character of the religious life that emerges on his view. (For an application of this approach to the notion of prayer see Phillips, 1965 and to the concept of immortality see Phillips, 1971; see also Moore, 1988.)

Phillips has vigorously rejected the charge that his approach reduces religion to either morality (he opposes Braithwaite's reduction of religion to an adjunct of moral behaviour: Phillips, 1993, Ch. 4, esp. pp. 45–46) or to language games. For Phillips, '... the meaning of God's reality is to be found in His divinity, which is expressed in the role worship plays in people's lives. This does not imply that God's reality, divinity or worship, can be equated with language-games; that is not what they *mean*!' (Phillips, 1970a, p. 130).

To think otherwise, claims Phillips, is to confuse '... a linguistic context with what is said' (ibid.). An exploration of the 'depth grammar' of religious beliefs, at least 'non-superstitious' ones, reveals their non-metaphysical character. Phillips' position is illuminated by the contrasts he draws between it and the views of the proponents of 'Reformed epistemology' (Phillips, 1988) and recent 'non-realist' theorists of religion (Cupitt, 1980, 1984; see also Dawes, 1992; Freeman, 1993; D. Hart, 1993).[2]

[2]   For assessment and criticism of non-realism and religion and some of its proponents see Cowdell, 1988; Hebblethwaithe, 1988; Runzo, 1993; Ward, 1982;

Whether Phillips' approach does justice to Wittgenstein's own views on the matter, and is acceptable in itself, has invited considerable debate. WD. Hudson, for example, although influenced by Wittgenstein, holds that the object of religious belief is constituted by the concept of 'transcendent consciousness and agency'. In relation to the reality of this concept, he stresses, against Phillips, the need and possibility of a perspective and a status which is, in important respects, 'external' to the religious form of life (Hudson, 1975, pp. 164; 175–193). Similarly, Cyril Barrett finds fault with Phillips' account of the 'something' to which religious life, on the Wittgensteinian view, refers (Barrett, 1991, Ch. 13; see also Brummer, 1993).

(VI) Religious understanding and religious practice

A central element in Wittgenstein's approach to religion is the close connection, which emerges in all that has been outlined above, between understanding in religion and religious practice. As D.Z. Phillips puts it: '... there is no theoretical knowledge of God' (Phillips, 1970a, p. 32).

Two related questions which arise here are whether religious understanding is *impossible* without religious practice and whether the believer and unbeliever understand each other. On the former question, Phillips has rejected claims that he holds such a view. Whilst certain forms of religious understanding presuppose belief, other forms of religious understanding do not, and the possibility of elucidating religious belief to non-believers is open (Phillips, 1986, pp. 10–12). On the question of whether the believer and the unbeliever understand each other, Wittgenstein's comments may serve to discourage a dogmatic answer to the question: 'You might say "well if you can't contradict him, that means you don't understand him. If you did understand him, then you might". That again is Greek to me. My normal technique of language leaves me. I don't know whether to say that they understand one another or not' (LA, p. 55; see also Bambrough, 1991; Barrett, 1991, Ch. 8,9; Brown, 1969; Putnam, 1992).

Wittgenstein and Education in Religion

A considerable task of exegesis and interpretation is required for the achievement of a full critical understanding of Wittgenstein's views on religion. The precise meaning and import of these views are

White, 1994. For Phillips' reaction to this general position see his papers in Runzo, 1993.

unclear and disputed, and there is much that is puzzling and unresolved. In the absence of a much more extended discussion, only general lines and directions of implication for education in religion can be indicated. On the basis of the elements of those general views which have been outlined, however, a number of significant implications for education in religion and, in particular, the LR conception of that task, can be discerned.

Educational practice in general, and therefore education in religion, is not, of course, and cannot be, determined solely by philosophical considerations. The LR conception of education in religion, for example, is articulated as much by social and cultural realities as by philosophical argument, and the implications of this point will be returned to in due course. However, Wittgenstein's perspective on religion, through its capacity to influence the way in which education in religion is conceptualised, is potentially one rich in implication for the way in which education in religion is conducted.

(I) Wittgenstein and the LR conception of education in religion: some preliminary points

Wittgenstein's general approach clearly calls into question a number of the major features and philosophical underpinnings of the LR conception. From a Wittgensteinian perspective, it is no longer possible (for example) to maintain a sharp distinction for educational purposes between fostering religious belief and practice and developing religious understanding; the presentation of religion as uncertain and requiring rational assessment, decision and commitment misrepresents some of the central distinctive features of the domain; religious truth and reality are seen as requiring a much more subtle and nuanced elucidation, and so forth (for general implications for the general 'Liberal Rational' view of education of a broadly Wittgensteinian critique see Lloyd, 1980). Hirst's recent work stressing the significance for education of initiation into certain substantive social practices (Hirst, 1993) can be regarded as a step in the right direction from the Wittgensteinian point of view, although its evaluation from that perspective depends heavily on how Hirst's continuing, though modified, commitment to the notion of rational critical assessment is to be understood. One issue which has emerged is the question of whether, on a Wittgensteinian view, education in religion in a recognisably LR sense is impossible (Marples, 1978). Proponents of such a view neglect, however, the possibility of kinds and degrees of understanding and the significance of the religious imagination (cf. Hepburn, 1992).

At the very least, however, Wittgenstein's view of the nature of religious belief and practice inhibits an over-confident articulation of the LR view, and places it squarely in the context of the engaged persuasive discussion referred to by Marshall and Smeyers in their introduction to this volume.

(II) Some general requirements of a Wittgensteinian approach to education in religion

A number of requirements for education in religion can be plausibly deduced from the Wittgensteinian point of view.

The most basic requirement is to accurately portray the distinctive character of religious belief as understood from the perspective. Wittgenstein writes: 'An honest religious thinker is like a tightrope walker. He almost looks as though he were walking on nothing but air. His support is the slenderest imaginable. And yet it really is possible to walk on it' (CV, p. 73). What is involved in illuminating this sort of perception for pupils is complex and underexamined. One aspect of this complexity arises from the fact that, because of the nature of the development of the understanding of pupils, many religious notions in their characteristically Wittgensteinian form will need to be presented to pupils initially in straightforwardly realist and literal terms (Astley, 1993, 1994, pp. 170–185).

A related requirement from the Wittgensteinian perspective is the need to avoid the treatment of religion in an unduly abstract or context-free way (Phillips, 1970b, p. 16), although there is a tension between an acknowledgement by the perspective on the one hand of the general salience of particularity and on the other of its acceptance that there is no 'essence' or single normative form of religion.

Another conclusion that can be safely drawn from the Wittgensteinian perspective is that education in general has an obligation to combat our tendency to: '... remain unconscious of the prodigious diversity of all every-day language-games because the clothing of our language makes everything alike' (PI, II, xi, p. 224). Education must 'teach us differences' (cf. Malcolm, 1993 pp. 43–47). One interesting task here is that of helping students to distinguish between religious and scientific beliefs, and to come to an understanding of the proper relationship between them (cf. Winch, 1987, Ch. 9).

(III) Confessionalism

One requirement that might be deduced from Wittgenstein's general view of religion is to see education in this domain as requiring a confessional approach viz. one which proceeds from, and seeks to develop and sustain commitment to, a (particular) religious faith.

There are elements in Wittgenstein's position which lend strong support to this conclusion. Wittgenstein writes: 'It strikes me that a religious belief could only be something like a passionate commitment to a system of reference. Hence, although it's *belief*, it's really a way of living, or a way of assessing life. It's passionately seizing hold of *this* interpretation. Instruction in a religious faith, therefore, would have to take the form of a portrayal, a description, of that system of reference, while at the same time being an appeal to conscience. And this combination would have to result in the pupil himself, of his own accord, passionately taking hold of the system of reference. It would be as though someone were first to let me see the hopelessness of my situation and then show me the means of rescue until, of my own accord, or not at any rate led to it by my *instructor*, I ran to it and grasped it' (CV, p. 64). Given that religious believers do not come to believe on the basis of reasons and proofs, Wittgenstein comments: 'Perhaps one could "convince someone that God exists" by means of a certain kind of upbringing, by shaping his life in such and such a way' (CV, p. 85, cf. C, # 107).

In addition to statements such as these, support for a confessional approach to education in religion can be derived from a number of other central elements in Wittgenstein's position. For example, Wittgenstein observes: 'Religion says: *Do this! — Think like that!* — but it cannot justify this and once it even tries to, it becomes repellent; because for every reason it offers there is a valid counter-reason. It is more convincing to say: "Think like this! however strangely it may strike you"' (CV, p. 29). Further: 'Christianity is not based on a historical truth; rather, it offers us a (historical) narrative and says: now believe! But not, believe this narrative with the belief appropriate to a historical narrative, rather: believe, through thick and thin, which you can only do as the result of a life. *Here you have a narrative, don't take the same attitude to it as you take to other historical narratives!* Make a *quite different* place in your life for it' (CV, p. 32).

Another element is the close connection between religious understanding and religious practice. One aspect of this is the complexity involved in learning religious pictures, including the theology which articulates the grammar implicit in the pictures. 'The word

"God" is amongst the earliest learnt — pictures and catechisms, etc. But not the same consequences as with pictures of aunts. I wasn't shown [that which the picture pictured]... "Being shown all these things, did you understand what this word meant?" I'd say: "Yes and no. I did learn what it didn't mean. I made myself understand. I could answer questions, understand questions when they were put in different ways — and in that sense could be said to understand"' (LA, p. 59, cf. p. 63). This process is illuminated by Phillips' remark that 'mystery' '... is an integral part of concept-formation in faith and worship' (Phillips, 1988, p. 278).

Given Wittgenstein's general perspective, it is easy to conclude that the most natural way in which people develop the sorts of understanding to which he has been alluding is by being brought up in, and leading, a religious life. This finds some echo in Hamlyn's remark that capability for understanding depends upon how what is being taught fits into the life of the individual (Hamlyn, 1989, p. 221), a remark which, although not originally used in relation to religion, is relevant here.

A number of other elements in Wittgenstein's view lend support to a confessional interpretation of what is required in terms of education in religion. A general theme which can be given application here is the general role of certainty over doubt in upbringing (cf. e.g. C ##106, 107, 115, 128, 129, 143, 144, 152, 153, 159, 160, 166, 310–317, 476–480; cf. Bambrough, 1993; O'Hear, 1991; Kazepides 1991a).

In his article *Confession and Reason*, Ieuan Lloyd (Lloyd, 1986) develops a case for a confessional approach to education in religion from a broadly Wittgensteinian perspective. Lloyd is suspicious of the claims of 'rationality' in education and bemoans the fact that demands concerning it are often couched: '... in the language of the abstract not tempered by example or an understanding of the past' (ibid., p. 140). In an earlier article, Lloyd develops telling criticisms of John White's aim of maximising the choice of pupils, and accuses him of being in danger of picturing school: '... as being like a sweet shop in which a child has been given money to spend' (Lloyd, 1980, p. 334), and of conceiving the child as: '... without roots, without attachments and without love, concerned only with choosing ...' (ibid., p. 341). In view of this danger, and in the absence of abstract standards of rational judgement in religion, Lloyd holds that it is appropriate, by an extension of the general need for the child to have unshakeable beliefs of a basic sort (Lloyd, 1986, p. 142), to initiate pupils into religion as a precondition of their achievement of understanding in this domain. In arguing for this initiation, Lloyd makes a somewhat un-Wittgensteinian distinction between the 'foundations' of religion and its 'superstructure', (ibid., p. 143), initiation being justified into the former.

It is unclear quite what Lloyd intends in this distinction. His overall philosophical position seems to debar him from referring to a general 'external' foundation for religion (cf. Peters, 1972; cf. Elliott, 1986) and his recognition of the significance of the particular and his concern that a child's 'confession of a faith' might be brought about: '... in an educational institution' (Lloyd, 1986, p. 143) points to his having in mind the confession of a particular faith.

In the absence of any indication to the contrary, Lloyd seems to be referring in his argument to education in religion in the common schools of a pluralist democratic society. In this context, however, his view encounters inescapable contemporary social and cultural obstacles. Although Lloyd makes some reference to the heterogeneity of attitudes to religious belief now prevalent (ibid., pp. 142, 144), he does not address the difficulties that this presents for his advocacy of confessionalism.

There are good Wittgensteinian grounds, in addition to practical ones and those emanating from the LR view, for rejecting a confessional approach in common schools. The most basic Wittgensteinian point here is that the relevant forms of life are not (generally) flourishing in the lives of the pupils and their families in the school. The grounding for the educative task in confessional terms is therefore missing. Such considerations call into question Lloyd's attempt to argue that the need for the child to have unshakeable beliefs can be extended from basic beliefs to religious beliefs in an unproblematic and wide ranging way.[3] Here Hirst's point that religious beliefs have an uncertain epistemological status can be transposed into the point, telling for the Wittgensteinian, that the religious form of life has an uncertain existence.

However, what does emerge from such a line of argument is a more modest and nuanced case for the confessional approach to be acknowledged as having some significance in particular contexts, where the relevant 'forms of life' are in place or under development, as in religious upbringing in the family and religious teaching in religious schools (McLaughlin, 1984, 1992). A form of confessional

[3] On such basic beliefs see Gardner, 1988; McLaughlin, 1990. For arguments that religious doctrines are not on the same level as 'epistemically primordial' or 'river-bed' propositions see Kazepides, 1991b.

approach in these contexts has certain distinctive benefits (cf. Nichols, 1992) over the LR approach, which has Wittgensteinian overtones (see also Martin, 1987). This does not mean that the form of confessionalism at issue is non-rational or (from an LR perspective) indoctrinatory given that Wittgenstein allows for a kind of assessment of religious beliefs (for Wittgenstein on free will and religious belief see Barrett, 1991, Ch. 11). Although it is likely, however, to lead to charges of indoctrination being seen in a more nuanced way (cf. Thiessen, 1993), Wittgenstein's point of view does not lead to wide ranging rehabilitation of the confessional approach.

The existence of heterogenous moral beliefs and forms of life in common schools also calls into question the view of moral education developed by D.Z. Phillips (Phillips, 1979, 1980), which in its desire to avoid a focus on abstract moral principles stresses the transmission of substantial values which are tacit and implicit in school life and school subjects. This might be thought to presuppose a stability and homogeneity of moral practice which does not exist.

(IV) Advocacy and elucidation

Can an approach to education in religion based on Wittgensteinian insights be conducted in non-confessional context? A crucial distinction relevant to this possibility is made by Phillips, who distinguishes 'advocacy' from 'elucidation' (Phillips, 1970b, p. 13). Elucidation involves: '… unpacking the significance of values, ideals, different conceptions of worship and love, and the roles they play in people's lives' (ibid., p. 17). Phillips's appeal to Simone Weil's analogy of the display of a thing of beauty underscores the requirement that teachers have a 'sympathetic relation' to religion; they must 'take religion seriously', 'see something in it' and respect it. But, considers Phillips, the teacher need not be a religious believer. An acceptable teacher could: '… include someone who had come to the conclusion that religious beliefs were false in that he had a regard in his own life for conflicting beliefs, but thought a great deal needed to be said to appreciate the nature of religious beliefs' (ibid., p. 17). So the connection that Phillips is making here is not between understanding and belief, but understanding and sympathy. Since Phillips acknowledges that the reactions of children to such elucidation, like that of adults, is likely to be varied, the approach is significantly 'open'.

This is seen in the reaction of Weil to the question: 'Is it true?' which Phillips reports as follows: 'It is so beautiful that it must certainly contain a lot of truth. As for knowing whether it is, or is not, absolutely true, try to become capable of deciding that for yourselves when you grow up' (ibid., pp. 14–15). Indeed, an attitude of significant neutrality is explicitly attributed to Weil in her remark that: 'It would be strictly forbidden to add, by way of commentary, anything implying either a negation of dogma or an affirmation of it' (ibid., p. 15) and Phillips leaves open whether the child will actually regulate his or her life by this conception of beauty in later years (ibid., p. 15).

These are, however, many complex questions which arise in relation to this notion of 'elucidation'. Wittgenstein's concept of religious belief as a kind of 'tightrope' walk has been alluded to earlier. From such a perspective, a religious educator in a common school must achieve a balance in the understanding of students between a crude realism or literalism about religion on the one hand, and an equally crude reductionism on the other.

The Wittgensteinian conception of the nature of religion is intellectually and spiritually sophisticated. (For an example of a set of considerations from this perspective which might confront students see Moore, 1988, p. 67.) But how is an understanding of this kind to be brought about in a common school, in the absence of a stable tradition of religious belief and practice? Such a tradition seems crucial for religious understanding for the reasons already mentioned. These include the need to present religious notions in initially literal and realist terms if they are to be grasped. This is relevant to the presentation of the prophetic demands of the religion which were indicated in the last section. Another problem facing the 'elucidation' is the difficulty of illuminating the nature and force of orthodoxy and orthopraxis in religion, in the face of a temptation to eclecticism on the part of students, without invoking realist considerations.

The notion of elucidation from a Wittgensteinian perspective is therefore underexplored. Another of the underexplored notions is the distinctively Wittgensteinian notion of a 'limit to questioning'.

(V) The limits to questioning

The Wittgensteinian approach is suspicious of the corrosive and distortive effect of questioning upon a proper understanding of the religious domain. Too much questioning of the wrong kind could lead to religious beliefs being seen as hypothetical metaphysical beliefs. This point is developed by W.D. Hudson who claims that education in religion is only logically possible if the 'constitutive concept' of the religious form of life (god: a distinctive concept in Hudson's hands) (Hudson, 1973, pp. 169–177) is not called into question. Given that religious education is not merely education *about* religion, but education in it, Hudson holds that it requires initiation into 'devotion': '… engaging in those ways of committing oneself in trust and obedience to god, which are characteristic of the expression of religious belief' (ibid., pp. 177-178). Referring to the 'scope for reasoning' in religion he writes: 'There is however a limit to this reasoning. Within religious belief … god's existence cannot be questioned because this whole universe of discourse presupposes it. Therefore, one must not say that religious education is not education unless it allows, as part of the process of such education, for the abandonment of religious belief' (ibid., p. 185). Hudson makes a distinction between independence of mind *about* religion and independence of mind *within* it (ibid., p. 187). Religious education is concerned only with the latter and not the former (since Hudson concedes that education more generally should be concerned with independence *about* religion it is not clear how much his point is a definitional one). Although Hudson makes it clear that the religiously educated person is not necessarily a religious believer (Hudson, 1987, p. 111) a form of religious formation seems to be envisaged. Hudson claims in a rather un-Wittgensteinian way that: '… the object of the exercise is not to get one's pupils to accept any particular content, but to initiate them into theology and devotion as such, the content of these being open to change or development as the pupil begins to think for himself in terms of god' (ibid., p. 191) (for further discussion of this argument see Kazepides, 1982; Hudson, 1982). Regardless of the merits of this argument, it seems to be significantly in tension with a Wittgensteinian perspective.

A second way in which limits to questioning arise on this perspective concerns the philosophical interpretation of religion. It is clear that Phillips brings to bear a particular philosophical theory to his account of religious education, which is, in an important sense, non-negotiable. How would Phillips react to a child in the classroom who advocated a non-Wittgensteinian point of view? Phillips regards, for example, a philosophical defence of immortality in terms of survival after death as 'bad philosophy' (ibid., p. 265) (on the general relationship between faith and philosophy see Phillips, 1970a, Ch. 13; 1993, Ch. 14). Any one claiming, contra Phillips, that foundationalism and evidentialism are appropriate ways in which religion ought to be philosophically discussed would be ruled out of court. Phillips claims that he has reached his conclusion by philosophical reflection: 'It is not a presumption with which I begin ... But there is a risk involved in philosophical enquiry. The conclusions I have come to cannot be guaranteed in advance, and one may not arrive at them. But the man who is genuinely philosophically puzzled has no choice. He has to go where the argument takes him.' (Phillips, 1993, p. 235. For criticisms of this conception of philosophy see, for example, Nielsen, 1971). Phillips is articulating a notion of philosophy as 'disinterested enquiry', but there is no evidence that he would allow other philosophical views in the classroom as other than mistakes to be corrected. He allows (as in the last section) for religious belief (properly understood) to be rejected as unattractive. But it is important to note the very character of the philosophical understanding of religious belief seems non-negotiable. Those unpersuaded by the Wittgensteinian perspective will find this a troubling aspect of its implications for education in religion. A.C. Grayling holds that, for all its importance and interest, Wittgenstein's general approach to philosophy has generally failed to convince (Grayling, 1991, p. 64). It is an interesting question how far the Wittgensteinian perspective can hold its own philosophical presuppositions open to enquiry in the classroom.

Questioning is a crucial element in any genuinely educative process. Questioning, of course, must be within limits. It might be argued, however, that the limits drawn by the Wittgenstein perspective are too tight.

Such an argument, however, leaves open the issue of how questioning, and the 'elucidation' to which it is related, is properly to be conceived and conducted in education in religion in common schools.

Conclusion

Wittgenstein's approach to religion is an important part of any assessment of the significance of his thought as a whole for educational thinking and practice. As we have seen, although his view of religion is elusive and stands in need of definitive evaluation, it offers a number of insights and challenges.

Whilst Wittgenstein's approach conflicts in important respects with the LR view of education in religion, because that view is based on important social and cultural realities which are significant for Wittgensteinian principles, it is not supplanted. The Wittgensteinian approach both supplies important perspectives which will enrich the LR view, whilst giving support to a greater pluralism in the way in which education in religion is conceived, including forms of substantial religious upbringing and schooling.

Acknowledgements

An earlier version of this paper was presented to a meeting at the Faculty of Psychology and Educational Sciences, Catholic University of Leuven, Belgium, in November 1992. I am very grateful to Professor Dr. Paul Smeyers for the invitation to present the paper, and to him and the participants in the discussion for their helpful comments. I am also grateful to Dr Jeff Astley for allowing me to see unpublished material of his relevant to the matters raised in the paper.

Wittgenstein References

All references to works of Wittgenstein are to the following publications and with the use of the indicated abbreviations:

Wittgenstein, L.: 1922, *Tractatus logico-philosophicus*, trans. D. Pears & B.F. McGuinness, Routledge and Kegan Paul, London. **TLP**

Wittgenstein, L.: 1953, *Philosophical investigations/Philosophische Untersuchungen*, trans. G.E.M. Anscombe, Basil Blackwell, Oxford. **PI**

Wittgenstein, L.: 1961, in G.H. von Wright & G.E.M. Anscombe (eds.), *Notebooks, 1914-1916*, trans. G.E.M. Anscombe, Basil Blackwell, Oxford. **NB**

Wittgenstein, L.: 1964, in G.H. von Wright, R. Rhees, & G.E.M. Anscombe (eds.), *Remarks on the foundations of mathematics/Bemerkungen über die Grundlagen der Mathematik*, trans. G.E.M. Anscombe, Basil Blackwell, Oxford. **RFM**

Wittgenstein, L.: 1965, A lecture on ethics, *Philosophical Review* 74, 3-12. **LE**

Wittgenstein, L.: 1966, in C. Barrett (ed.), *Lectures and conversations on aesthetics, psychology and religious belief*, Basil Blackwell, Oxford. **LA**

Wittgenstein, L.: 1967, in G.E.M. Anscombe & G.H. von Wright (eds.), *Zettel*, trans. G.E.M. Anscombe, Basil Blackwell, Oxford. **Z**

Wittgenstein, L.: 1968, *The blue and brown books*, Basil Blackwell, Oxford. **BB**

Wittgenstein, L.: 1969, in G.E.M. Anscombe & G. H. von Wright (eds.), *On certainty/Über Gewissheit*, trans. D. Paul & G.E.M. Anscombe, Basil Blackwell, Oxford. **C**

Wittgenstein, L.: 1974, in R. Rhees & A. Kenny (eds.), *Philosophical grammar*, Basil Blackwell, Oxford. **PG**

Wittgenstein, L.: 1977, in G.E.M. Anscombe (ed.), *Remarks on colour/Bemerkungen über die Farben*, trans. L.L. MacAlister, Basil Blackwell, Oxford. **ROC**

Wittgenstein, L.: 1979, 'Remarks on Frazer's Golden Bough', in C. Luckhardt (ed.), *Wittgenstein: Sources and perspectives*, pp. 61-81, The Harvester Press, Hassocks, Sussex. **GB**

Wittgenstein, L.: 1980, in G.H. von Wright & H. Nyman (eds.), *Remarks on the philosophy of psychology/Bemerkungen über die Philosophic der Psychologie, vol. 1*, trans. C.G. Luckhardt & M. Aue, Basil Blackwell, Oxford. **RPP I**

Wittgenstein, L.: 1980, in G.H. von Wright & H. Nyman (eds.), *Remarks on the philosophy of psychology/Bemerkungen über die Philosophie der Psychologie, vol. 2*, trans. C.G. Luckhardt & M. Aue, Basil Blackwell, Oxford. **RPP II**

Wittgenstein, L.: 1980, in G.H. von Wright (ed.), *Culture and value/Vermischte Bemerkungen*, trans. P. Winch, Basil Blackwell, Oxford. **CV**

Chapter 15

Israel Scheffler on Religion, Reason and Education

No assessment and celebration of Israel Scheffler's overall contribution to philosophy of education can neglect the significance of his attitude to religion and to education in religion. This is both for general and for specific reasons. In general, it is illuminating to gain a sense of the fundamental overall framework of thought in which the particular views of any thinker are located[1] and religion can often be an important guide to this. Further, religious questions are important in themselves, and no complete philosophy of education can neglect them. More specifically, Scheffler is known to be personally influenced by, and concerned with, religion, and attention to this somewhat neglected aspect of his thought is therefore particularly appropriate.

Scheffler's philosophy of education, and his thinking more generally, has often been compared to, and seen as having considerable affinity with, that of R.S. Peters. The extent of this affinity with respect to their views on religion and education in religion is interesting, and it is instructive to begin a consideration of Scheffler's views on these matters with some reference to those of Peters.

Both men report that a fascination with religious questions was closely linked to the growth of their interest in philosophy.[2] Whilst the central elements of the overall framework of thought of both thinkers are independent of religious presuppositions and considerations, Scheffler and Peters have each sought to make a religious dimension of a certain sort compatible with, although not directly

[1] On this point in relation to R.S. Peters see Elliott, 1986.
[2] Peters, 1974, Ch. 23; Scheffler, 1995.

required by, their general perspective. Further, they have both been personally involved in religious faith and practice, Scheffler as a Jew and Peters as a member of the Society of Friends (Quakers), albeit one who, on his own account, is 'on the fringe' of that society.[3]

Both Scheffler and Peters share a markedly similar view about the central importance of the role of reason (properly understood) in education and in human life generally, together with an insistence upon the significance of objectivity. Since the demands of reason and objectivity are particularly challenging for religious belief and practice, the way in which Scheffler and Peters seek to reconcile these demands with a religious perspective is worth exploring. Neither Scheffler nor Peters has developed a detailed and comprehensive approach to religious questions, and these matters do not figure prominently in their thought. Although Scheffler's studies of ritual[4] and of ambiguity, vagueness and metaphor in language[5] are of significance for religious questions, it is only relatively recently that he has written directly about the religious domain.[6] Peters' remarks about religion are for the most part confined to his 1972 Swarthmore Lecture,[7] which, though often overlooked, has been described as one of the least dispensable expressions of his thought.[8]

I

Peters considers and rejects the view that a rational person must necessarily be hostile to religion since it involves a dependence upon authority or revelation, both of which are 'anathema' to a man or woman committed to reason. To be rational in the sphere of religion, claims Peters, is not to face a choice between two stark alternatives: rejection of religion on the one hand or faith in an authority or in some kind of personal revelation on the other. There is, he suggests, a third possibility '… it is possible to proceed in religion in the same sort of way as one proceeds in science or in a rational morality.'[9] Conceding that most religions and religious believers do not seem to proceed in this experimental kind of way, Peters claims that it was

[3]   Peters, 1972, p. 1.
[4]   Scheffler, 1986, Ch. 6,7, 8.
[5]   Scheffler, 1979.
[6]   Scheffler, 1992a, 1992b, 1992c, 1995.
[7]   Peters, 1972. See also Peters, 1974, Ch. 19.
[8]   Elliott, 1986, p. 43.
[9]   Peters, 1972, p. 76.

because Quakerism seemed to permit this kind of approach that he joined the Society. He notes that Quakerism is allergic to detailed credal or dogmatic content and authority, and it makes reference and appeal to the equivalent of 'fundamental principles' in the moral sphere: a range of religious considerations or principles shared by members of the Society – such as those implicit in the Quaker notion that there is 'that of God in every-man' – which bind the group together and provide the framework for agreement and disagreement. Thus a religious figure such as Jesus is, in the light of these principles, valued for his personal insight into religious truths rather than as an authoritative and binding source of them. Further, Quakerism emphasises individual spiritual insight – 'the inner light' – which Peters regards as the corollary of individual autonomy in the moral sphere. Peters writes – 'Just as autonomy in morals has to be understood in terms of a critical authenticity informed by sensitivity to fundamental principles, so too the "inner light" presupposes a shared sensitivity to religious considerations.'[10] In this way, 'cranks' and 'fanatics' whose individual insights lack a basis in public experience are coped with. These features of Quakerism[11] make it for Peters a form of religion which is 'not alien' to the person who believes in the use of reason.[12]

As indicated earlier, Peters emphasises that objectivity is crucial to the use of reason A rational engagement with religion therefore invites the question:- 'In virtue of what kinds of shared experiences do human beings come to agree about religious judgements?'[13] Peters suggests, somewhat tentatively, that religion is grounded in an experience accessible in principle to any reflective person: awe. This he characterises as '… an emotion to which human beings are subject when they are confronted with events, objects or people which are of overwhelming significance to them but which seem, in

[10] Ibid., 1972, p. 78.
[11] For an overall perspective on Quakerism see, for example, Religious Society of Friends (Quakers) in Britain 1995.
[12] For Peters account of 'the life of reason' see, for example, Peters, 1972, Lecture III.
[13] Peters, 1972, p. 80. Relevant here is Peters' reaction to 'some modern approaches to the Philosophy of Religion' – 'Awkward questions about the truth of religious beliefs are side-tracked by combining a study of comparative religion with an analysis of the role of religious belief in a way of life. Indeed if one asks questions about the truth of such beliefs one is sometimes made to feel a very crude fellow indeed. I have always thought that, both in morals and in religion, the questions that matter most relate to the grounds of belief. In both these spheres I remain unrepentantly a crude fellow' (Peters, 1974, p. 21).

some important respect or other, inexplicable and shot through with contingency. Things are momentously thus, and not otherwise - but for no discernible reason.'[14] Peters gives as an example here the way in which the Hebrew religion developed from a feeling of awe evoked by volcanoes in the consciousness of the followers of the cult of Jahveh. The 'appropriate' response to such feelings of awe is for a person to '... express how he feels in some symbolic form ...'[15] Such forms, which include prostrating oneself, praying or singing, Peters describes as worship, central to which '... is the attempt to express the sense of the impressiveness and significance of the object of awe.'[16] Worship not only *expresses* such feelings, claims Peters, but *endorses* them, particularly if it takes the form of public rituals. Public mourning, for example, endorses the feeling of grief and loss experienced by those close to the deceased.

Crucial to a proper understanding and assessment of Peters' position on these matters is his account of the nature of the *object* or *objects* of awe and worship. In primitive religions, Peters notes, these tended to be 'powers of nature', 'exceptional people', 'impressive events' and the like, and worship sought through petition and magic to placate and manipulate the mysterious beings or forces thought responsible for them. The development of science has provided more adequate means of explanation and manipulation, but has not dispelled the feelings of awe which are at the root of worship. They are now attached to more general phenomena. These include the 'ultimate contingency' of the universe itself and man's situation within it, and 'the limits of human reason'. Peters writes – '... it comes to be appreciated, as it was preeminently by Kant, that in thinking about the universe we reach the "limits of human reason." If we ask questions about its creation, or about its continuance, or about why there should be this type of system rather than some other we grasp that we are posing questions which admit no answer in terms of the type of equipment that we have for answering questions'.[17] A 'new level of awe' is opened up to a rational person who appreciates the limits of reason and man's unique position in the natural world. On the one hand, the universe is merely a physical system exhibiting 'the order described by Newton's Laws'. But on the other hand, human beings,

[14] Peters, 1972, p. 81.
[15] Ibid., p. 81.
[16] Ibid., p. 81.
[17] Ibid., p. 82.

whilst part of this physical system, seem to be so much more than it; members of a Kantian 'kingdom of ends' as well as of a 'kingdom of nature'. In Peters' view, such reactions lie behind Biblical passages such as 'When I consider the heavens, the work of thy fingers, the sun and moon which thou has ordained, what is man that thou art mindful of him, and the son of man that thou considereth him?'

Peters' more precise understanding of 'man's situation in the world' emerges in the interpretation he offers of a number of aspects of religious belief and practice by reference to it. For Peters, Christian love is an 'intensified' and 'particularised' form of respect for the individual and awe that arises as a result of an awareness of the fact that - 'We are born. We grow up and gradually our predicament dawns on us. We have to make something of the brief span of years that is our lot, with the variable and partly alterable equipment with which we are blessed. To view another trying to make something of himself in this context, and to be intensely concerned about him is to love him in the Christian sense.'[18] Religious experience is not unique and distinctive (Peters explains that he can make little of the mystical tradition within Quakerism) but a different 'level' at which we might experience our everyday lives, whether it be our experience of love[19] or of activities such as gardening.[20] Religious experience is not seen as superseding rational morality, but as enhancing our conviction of the objectivity of values by situating them within a context of universal significance which awakens awe[21] and by giving an emphasis to certain particular values. The Quaker belief that 'there is that of God in every man' is the principle of respect for persons seen in religious terms — '... respect passes into reverence and love when the perspectives and purposes of a particular man are viewed in the

[18] Ibid., p. 84.

[19] 'Love will appear not just as a joyous, transforming type of experience, but as an all pervading bond between individuals that helps them to share their predicament in the world — the inescapable cycle of the human condition, birth, youth, reproduction, bringing up children, death, together with its contrasts such as joy and suffering, hope and despair, good and evil' (Peters, 1972, p. 86).

[20] Peters, 1972 p. 85– 86. For discussion of the significance of a religious perspective for the question of how a person should spend his or her time see pp. 98–101.

[21] 'Religion, by placing the fact of suffering in a cosmic context, objectifies the particular response to it that is thought appropriate. It elevates some response to the badness of suffering, or to the importance of truth, which feature in any developed ethical system, to a more substantive status. Human beings are thought of as co-operating with, or surrendering themselves to a permanent response to the human condition' (Peters, 1972, p. 90).

broader context of human life on earth.'[22] Further, religion 'endorses' and 'objectifies' the autonomy of the individual.[23]

What place do more specifically religious concepts, such as those of a theistic kind, have in Peters' argument? He claims that to use the word 'God' in connection with the reactions he describes is '... to suggest that it is this general situation which calls forth awe.'[24] The 'general situation' here is the 'ultimate contingency of the world' and man's situation within it together with the various aspects and implications which Peters delineates.[25] For him, 'God' is a symbolic label. Peters notes that for some people the word has associations of 'a theism which they have outgrown', and they are therefore unwilling to use 'God' in describing the experiences they have as they explore the limits of human understanding in the way he describes. Peters is relaxed about this. Invoking Wisdom's famous 'parable of the gardener,'[26] he asks of such people – '... in what ways does their religious response differ from that of the theist? ... What extra work does the postulation of a spirit behind the phenomena do? Is it really necessary to express the awe one feels about the contingency, creation and continuance of the world in these personal terms?'[27] Peters is fully aware that many people do indeed describe their religious experiences in more specifically theistic terms – speaking, for example, of being 'called' or of witnessing or participating in 'acts of God'. However, he notes – '... these types of conviction are somewhat idiosyncratic, especially amongst more reflective people.'[28]

Peters therefore does not see religion as concerned with an objectively existing transcendent theistic entity of the sort involved in the major monotheistic faiths.[29] For him, the focus and object of the reli-

[22] Peters, 1972, p. 96.

[23] Ibid., pp. 94-98.

[24] Ibid., p. 82.

[25] See, for example, footnote 37. On Peters' account of 'the human predicament' see also Peters, 1974, Ch. 19; Elliott, 1986.

[26] Wisdom, I. 1962.

[27] Peters, 1972, p. 83.

[28] Ibid., p. 83.

[29] In his paper 'Subjectivity and Standards', Peters commente 'Most of theology, frankly, I would deal with like FR Tennant dealt with the doctrine of the trinity – in a footnote' (Peters, 1974, Ch. 19, p. 422). Relevant to this is Peters' comment in 'Ethics and Education' – 'Many have, perhaps mistakenly, given up using religious language ... because they have been brought to see what its use commits

gious sense, and its attitudes and reactions, is (roughly) the human 'situation' and 'predicament' in relation to the contingency of the world. Neither human beings, nor the world itself, has any inbuilt teleological structure[30] and there is no 'spirit behind the scenes.'

A number of questions arise in relation to this position, not least its adequacy as an account of what Quakers typically believe, an issue which does not trouble Peters unduly.[31] Leaving aside questions about the adequacy of Peters' position from the perspective of orthodox Christianity, there are a number of elements internal to it which are strained. The most prominent of these concerns Peters' account of worship. Does not worship as distinct from (say) meditation, require an object with attributes of the sort which theism has emphasised? Ninian Smart, for example, argues that the activity of worship requires an object or focus which is invested with qualities of personhood. Worship is a relational activity which involves the acknowledgement by the worshipper of the superiority (in an appropriate sense) of the object of worship.[32] In the light of considerations such as these, in what sense can 'man's situation in the world' be an object of worship! For Peters, what converts an activity such as gardening into worship is a '... tendency to view it in a certain light, to connect it with some very general view of the natural world, which ... (vests) ... this activity with a very different type of significance.'[33] More specifically, Peters claims that worship involves a '... concentration of consciousness in the face of the world'[34] motivated by the awe he describes and by a concern to '... see more under a cer-

them to, e.g. saying things which purport to be true for which the truth conditions can never be produced' (Peters, 1966, p. 115).

[30]   Compare, for example, Carr, *et al.*, 1995.

[31]   'These views about religion ... are not put forward ... as being in any way representative of the views of members of the Society. Indeed they are probably shared more widely by people who are not members of any organized religion. But that they can be held by a member of the Society of Friends, without causing undue offence to its more orthodox members, is an important fact about the Society of friends which should be of significance to many who are religious but who feel thai there is no place for them in any organized religion.' (Peters, 1972, p. 4). Compare MacMurray, 1965.

[32]   Smart, N 1972. On Quaker worship see, for example, Otto, R 1958 Appendix VIII, pp. 210–214.

[33]   Peters, 1972, p. 85-86.

[34]   Ibid., p. 86.

tain aspect of eternity.'[35] Worship, he continues, '... provides a context in which a man can express, especially in a receptive silence, his acceptance of and awe before the numinous',[36] where 'numinous' has a strictly this-worldly interpretation.[37] Further, it represents an attempt to counter the 'massive momentum of the mundane' by schooling ourselves to see life '... under a certain aspect of eternity'[38] with certain transformative effects.[39]

Since my aim in referring to Peters' view of religion has been to illuminate it sufficiently for purposes of comparison with Scheffler, further exploration of Peters' view is out of place here. Peters' account, related strongly to his view of the world and of life as a whole, with its strong Stoic emphases,[40] is, as he himself notes, a view of religion of a person who is something of an 'outsider' to religious faith and practice. Peters is aware that his account is likely to be judged 'gravely deficient' by most religious people for what it leaves out, although it may, he suggests, be acceptable 'as a beginning' for what it puts in.[41] Peters offers a foundation for the religious sense and for religious attitudes and reactions, but there is no detailed treatment of more developed religious beliefs, rituals, and practices of the sort which might be found in a 'thicker' religious tradition such as Judaism. Nor does Peters discuss how the elements of such 'thicker' traditions could be related to the kinds of 'foundational' experiences and elements which he specifics. From the perspective of such traditions, Peters may be seen as offering an unduly 'thin' account of religion. A judgement about the 'thinness' or otherwise of the specifically religious elements in Peters' account can be

---

[35]   Ibid., p. 87. Peters is influenced here by Spinoza, whom he interprets as emphasising in his remarks about the significance of viewing things under "a certain aspect of eternity' that it is important for a person '... to connect, to grasp the pattern.', and relationships which structure his life' (Peters, 1972, p. 68).

[36]   Peters, 1972. p. 87.

[37]   'There is the contingency of the world without which there could be neither the motion of the planets, nor earthquakes and famine. There is the awesome spectacle of human beings trying to make some sort of sense of the world and trying to sustain and cultivate a crust of civilization over a volcanic core of atavisitic emotions. And there is the loving awareness of other individuals, which draws us to them and encourages us to share with them our flickering perspective on this awesome predicament' (Peters, 1972, p. 87).

[38]   Peters, 1972, p. 87.

[39]   Ibid., pp. 87–88; 98–101.

[40]   See, for example, Elliott, 1986, pp. 46-47.

[41]   Peters, 1972, p. 80.

usefully advanced by exploring the precise differences between it and John White's recent argument claiming that personal well being should be seen in a 'cosmic context' — in relation to 'the widest horizons of our being' — but where what is involved is seen in explicitly secular terms.[42]

Peters has not explored the educational implications of his view of religion in any detail, although in his paper 'Democratic Values and Educational Aims'[43] he argues that room should be made for sensitising pupils to 'the human condition' viewed, broadly in the way outlined in the Swarthmore Lecture, under 'a certain aspect of eternity.'[44] We can safely read into Peters' argument here the context the common school in a pluralistic, democratic society, with the ethical and other principles associated with it, not least those enjoining forebearance of influence in relation to significantly controversial matters.[45] Applied to Peters' argument this context yields worries about undue religious influence upon pupils. Such worries might involve the fear, not of religious indoctrination in any full-blown sense, but of illicit pressure on pupils to adopt Peters' general perspective on 'the human condition'. It is not difficult to envisage a successful line of defence which Peters could adopt in relation to such concerns. He could insist, for example, that pupils should merely be given an opportunity to reflect upon the issues at stake, not that they should come to share his own perspective on them. He notes, for example, that some people are unmoved by the sort of perspective he outlines and are content in their lives to '... operate within the limits of human understanding.'[46] However, he insists — '... both types of reaction are available only for those who have had their awareness extended in this dimension by education.'[47] The claim that education in the common school should encourage pupils to engage in a significantly open way with such fundamental mat-

[42]   White, 1995.

[43]   Peters, 1981, Ch. 3.

[44]   Ibid., pp. 34; 41-46. Compare the following remarks of Iris Murdoch - '...someone may say, what can we do now that there is no God? This does not affect what is mystical. The loss of prayer, through the loss of belief in God, is a great loss. However, a general answer is a practice of meditation: a withdrawl, though some disciplined quietness, into the great chamber of the soul. Just sitting quiet will help. Teach it to children.' (Murdoch, 1992, p. 73).

[45]   On this see, for example, McLaughlin, 1995a.

[46]   Peters, 1981, p. 41.

[47]   Ibid., p. 41.

ters is a plausible one. Peters has nothing directly to say about more specific forms of religious formation and schooling.

At this point it is appropriate to turn to Scheffler, whose involvement in a 'thicker' religious tradition can be expected to shed light on a number of the issues which Peters does not address.

II

Unlike Peters, Scheffler has provided us with an extended, intriguing and rich 'educational memoir'[48] which, in its attention to aspects of his early Jewish upbringing and education, reveals something about Scheffler's religious attitudes and thought in some detail.

Scheffler reports himself as an 'intellectual bilingualist' in that he 'belongs to both sides' of a divide that has separated most Jewish academics and intellectuals of his generation.[49] He has been committed fully to both the 'universalistic' character of philosophy, with its emphasis upon scepticism, rationality, objectivity and the like[50] and to religious belief and practice. He writes —'… I have always supposed that the universal and the particular are compatible, that grounding in a particular historical and cultural matrix is inevitable and could not conceivably be in conflict with universal principles.[51] Scheffler's intention in his memoir is not to address philosophical matters relating to these issues in any direct and sustained way,[52] but what he does have to say is of considerable interest in relation to them.

[48] Scheffler, 1995.

[49] Ibid., pp. 14–15.

[50] Scheffler writes —'My own philosophical inclinations have … been in total agreement with such emphases. I have been formed philosophically by pragmatism with its emphasis on problem solving, by positivism with its stress on verification, by logic and semantics, with their focus on rigorous inference and attention to meanings, by philosophy of science with its concern for objective methods and testable hypotheses. I have, further, championed the cause of objectivity, promoted the emphasis on reasons, and upheld the need for economy of assumptions and clarity of concepts in systematic thinking. Not only do I understand the appeal of universalism in modem thought, I agree with it and have promoted it in the respects above outlined' (Scheffler, 1995, p. 14). See Scheffler, 1960, 1965, 1973, 1974, 1979, 1982, 1986,1991. Compare Hanson. 1993; Neiman and Siegel, 1993.

[51] Scheffler. 1995, p. 14.

[52] Scheffler, writes 'My aim is not to … address "the God of the philosophers" but rather to see how faith in "the God of Abraham, Isaac and Jacob" was reflected in the schooling I received in my youth' (Scheffler, 1995, p. 15).

Scheffler's general attitude to religion is conveyed well in the following passage: 'Religion is too important to be ceded either to the total believers or the total disbelievers – to be romanticized by its dogmatic faithful or distorted by its dogmatic foes. It needs to be seen from various distances, from afar as well as close up.'[53] It cannot, in Scheffler's view, be ignored.[54]

Scheffler notes that he is one of the few members of his generation who did receive a strong Jewish religious education which formed in a fundamental way his 'character and existence.'[55] One motive for writing his memoir is to give a 'positive glimpse' of the religious generation he describes and to render it not merely comprehensible but worthy of admiration[56] by outlining how Jewish faith and life was embodied in the work of his teachers. Another motive for writing the memoir which Scheffler reports is his desire to achieve an 'integrated understanding' of himself.[57] The question of integration arises naturally for a person with Scheffler's twin loyalties, although it is not always one that philosophers in a similar position face up to. Hilary Putnam, for example, reports that in his early career he simply kept the two parts of himself (the scientific materialist and the Jewish believer) separate from each other.[58]

Scheffler notes that the 'cultural treasures' brought to the New World by his parents cannot be '... wholly captured in code, reduced to formulas of belief and custom'[59] but are embodied in complex human, social and cultural realities which cannot be adequately articulated in an abstract way.[60] Nor can they be rendered immune from inevitable transformation by successive generations.[61] Scheffler notes the way in which the religious elements of their heritage came to be rejected by successive generations of Jewish immigrants to America in the light of several pressures, including in the

[53] Scheffler, 1995, p. 10.

[54] Ibid., p. 10.

[55] Ibid., p. 13.

[56] Ibid., pp. 13–14.

[57] Ibid., pp. 4–5.

[58] Putnam. 1992. p. 1.

[59] Scheffler, 1995, p. 9.

[60] "They live as well in the actions and style of action exemplified, the habits of thought and attitude, the climate of home, school, synagogue and community, the responses of the heart'. (Scheffler, 1995, p. 10).

[61] Scheffler. 1995. pp. 9–10. See also p. 172.

case of Jewish students and intellectuals, the appeal of universalism and scientific method, and the lack of an adequate Jewish education.[62] One of the aims of Scheffler's memoir is to delineate a form of Jewish education which is '... both informed and warm, authentic and sophisticated, rooted and universal.'[63] The concern that parents have to secure a religious education and formation for their children is therefore given recognition in Scheffler's discussion.[64]

Scheffler indicates how, brought up in an orthodox Jewish family and environment, his religious background was all embracing, with every aspect of life being put in perspective by the 'grand panorama' of religion.[65] What emerges in Scheffler's account of this background is a far cry from the repressive and indoctrinatory visions of religious upbringing conjured up in many contemporary discussions. As well as sustained religious practice and study related to Judaism and its linguistic, literary, musical and religious resources, we encounter much warmth, humour, wisdom and open-mindedness. Scheffler brings to life the 'human, social and cultural realities' involved in being brought up in a substantial tradition of belief, practice and value, and illuminates the nuances, tacit understandings, solidarities and human idiosyncracies that escape from a more abstract account.

Two aspects of Scheffler's discussion are particularly relevant to an understanding of his views on religion. The first concerns the relationship between his religious faith and the secular world in its various dimensions. Throughout his upbringing and education, the secular world was not excluded, and secular study was given its due. Scheffler spent his years from the age of six to fourteen at public school, which his parents regarded as complementary to, and not in conflict with, the Jewish education he was receiving at the hands of tutors and in supplementary classes. They felt no conflict between the overarching American culture of the public school and the particular cultural heritage offered by the family.[66] In the Rabbi Jacob

[62]   Ibid., pp. 10–12.

[63]   Ibid., p. 17.

[64]   See, for example, Scheffler, 1995, pp. 28–30.

[65]   Scheffler, 1995, pp. 17–25.

[66]   '... the education offered by the public school was not, after all, aimed at what they deemed of ultimate and supreme value, that is, a life of righteousness and charity, of study and worship in accord with the Divine commandments of the Torah. It was not a matter of considering public schooling to be in conflict with a Jewish religious education; it was rather a matter of considering them as

Joseph School, an all-day religious school which Scheffler attended for a year from the age of fourteen, there was a unified, though not oppressive religious atmosphere[67] and religious instruction was offered in the morning and secular instruction in the afternoon, reflecting the division between the two kinds of knowledge. Scheffler spent the next three years at the Rabbi Isaac Elchanan Yeshiva, whose Talmudical Academy was a High School with the same 'two worlds' division of kinds of study. Scheffler's father wanted his Jewish studies to be pursued in a 'modernist' manner, and placed within a modern context, so he insisted that Scheffler attend the City College of New York rather than a Jewish college, whilst also attending the Seminary College of Jewish studies, thereby providing a grounding for both the secular and religious worlds within which Scheffler was moving.[68] When he later returned to the Yeshiva, Scheffler continued his College education in the evenings at Brooklyn College. His father never feared the potentially corrosive effects of a general secular education upon Jewish identity and faith.[69]

This experience inevitably led Scheffler to reflect on the relationship between the 'two worlds'. Initially, he simply encountered them alongside each other. Scheffler notes that in the Rabbi Jacob Joseph School there was no attempt to reconcile or integrate them: it offered an 'education by juxtaposition'. Of the attitude of the school Scheffler comments — 'it simply incorporated these two worlds within itself and, by offering them both to us as our daily fare, it built them both into our consciousness, bequeathing to us at the same time the ragged boundaries and the gnawing conflicts between them.'[70] He continues — 'Surely, neither the school nor its faculties had any philosophy to offer capable of resolving the two-world tensions they inculcated. They had only the conviction that both worlds

occupying different levels on an absolute scale of value, even though both were indispensable for an effective and full life' (Scheffler, 1995, p. 60). See pp. 62–63 for acceptance of the predominantly Christian atmosphere of the school and the refusal to seek parity of religious expression.

[67]   Scheffler, 1995, pp. 84-85.

[68]   Ibid., p. 126.

[69]   Ibid., pp. 127-129. 'America for him was the opportunity to be free, to be yourself, to learn whatever you wanted to without fear. The idea of a synthesis of Jewish and secular studies was, for him, not a threat, nothing to be afraid of, no more problematic than the chance America offered him of being Jewish in a blessed country of political equality and cultural diversity' (p. 128).

[70]   Scheffler. 1995, pp. 85–86.

were vital. To choose one over the other would be worse than holding on, however uncomfortably, to both. So they left to us the task of working out in the future how to manage what they themselves could not control or foresee. They educated us by juxtaposing the incongruous realms rather than smoothing out the incongruities or offering phony reconciliations.'[71] And whilst the Yeshiva which he later attended attempted more than a mere juxtaposition, there was nothing behind the notion of 'synthesis' which it vaunted.[72] Working out a satisfactory personal synthesis was therefore a practical and piecemeal matter.[73] Scheffler reports that it was the Seminary College of Jewish Studies which shook his protected two-worlds upbringing. 'It ... for the first time, and in a fundamental way, awoke me from my unphilosophical slumber, at once satisfying my latent thirst for philosophical discussion of Judaism and at the same time challenging the naive orthodoxy I had imbibed in growing up.'[74]

This leads on to the second aspect of Scheffler's discussion which is of particular interest: the gradual sophistication of his religious faith. Scheffler's 'naive orthodoxy' was no intellectual straightjacket. Of it he writes — '(It) ... is hard for me to reconstruct now. It was less a matter of fierce positive beliefs than an acquiescence in traditional religious culture, its practices, formulations, lore and idioms. Practice was the key rather than creed; the study of texts was required and not professions of belief. No one pressed us to decide what we believed on theological topics. Skeptical doubts were not denied or disapproved as sinful, and allegorical readings of religious fundamentals were available and persuasive. The great homileticists and commentators had already demonstrated how far one could depart from literal readings of the Scriptures in search of a persuasive truth. And the Biblical prophets, even earlier, had shown that one could argue with God, question the Divine order, and demand that such order be justified within the bounds of human reason and moral

[71] Ibid, p. 86.

[72] Ibid., pp. 120-121.

[73] 'For most of us ... the figuring out did not come en bloc, as a global answer or a stroke of insight. It was a matter of living with the problem over an extended period, testing this aspect and then that, trying this direction and then changing course, monitoring the feel of one hypothetical solution and comparing it to that of another, all the while alert and listening, receptive to the various messages beamed at us from all points in life's compass' (Scheffler. 1995. p. 121). See, however, pp. 122–123.

[74] Scheffler, 1995, p. 132.

Liberalism, Education and Schooling

intuition. In all of my prior Jewish education, the texts were seen from within and viewed with a positive glow; somehow they could be rationally interpreted, whether in literal or metaphorical terms, so as to yield profound riches. General criticisms of the authority of texts or of the bases of religion were not raised. The result was a kind of dreamlike complacency, a state of trance-like piety in which the details of the religious life were embedded.'[75] At an early stage Scheffler became aware of the distinction between Jewish culture and religious faith through his gradual realisation that his early Talmudic teacher Mr Savage, was, despite his immersion in the teaching of the Jewish faith and culture, not himself a believer in religious doctrine literally conceived.[76] For Scheffler, this gave rise to questions, very significant for his mature thought, about how a lack of literal theological belief and an engagement in Jewish religious culture can be rendered compatible with each other.[77] From his encounter with Mr Savage, Scheffler came to a number of realisations central to a non-dogmatic attitude to religious questions — '... axiomatic creeds cannot encompass human diversity... ultimate loyalties have complex roots ... the private realm of belief is to be respected... the common treasury of religious lore demands active devotion but not conformity of doctrine or singleness of spirit ... '[78]

Scheffler reports how his 'naive orthodoxy' was painfully shattered by Professor Kaplan at the Seminary College, with his developmental and historical approach to the Bible and his critical approach to cosmological and theological conceptions inherent within it. The Biblical text was subjected to assessment by, and reinterpretation in the light of, 'independent conceptions of truth and morals' and with an insistence upon intellectual honesty.[79] In a long and painful struggle, and in an engagement with the philosophical questions to which Kaplan had introduced him, Scheffler achieved 'a new and freer sense' of his Jewish heritage. He writes - 'Liberated from the need to see it all as one seamless web to be defended in every detail, I could view it as a changing and evolving plant, differentiating its roots from its fruits, recognizing the continual need for pruning and shaping, for feeding and watering it. I could view the

[75] Ibid., p. 132.
[76] Ibid., pp. 38–41.
[77] Ibid., pp. 40–41.
[78] Ibid., p. 41.
[79] Ibid., pp. 133–136.

literary product of a given period in its historical context, appreciating its achievements while recognizing its inadequacies to the present. These two attitudes were no longer incompatible, no more so here than in the history of science, where appreciation of a past theory does not imply its current acceptance, nor docs current rejection of a theory imply that past proponents were not worthy of praise.'[80] In his later study of philosophy at Brooklyn College, Scheffler's 'half muffled quest for a rational account of fundamentals'[81] was answered. In contrast to his religious education, where he had encounted '... continual resistance to a free philosophical discussion of foundations'[82] he found a 'satisfyingly comprehensive' critical attitude.

Scheffler draws his memoir to a conclusion before the beginning of the later, postgraduate, stages of his educational career, which included advanced studies at the. Jewish Theological Seminary, as well as Graduate study in philosophy. However, as he indicates, we have in the memoir an outline of the foundations on which his mature thought rests.

III

One of the central elements in Scheffler's mature thought about religion and Jewish education is his sympathy to a historical and naturalistic approach — '... which eschews apologetics and builds on the. firmest views available in general scholarship, rational philosophy and scientific research.'[83] Thus, 'our independent conceptions of truth, logic and evidence' take precedence over the inherited text and religious practice as they stand, and require that their epistemic and moral authority be reassessed and reinterpreted. The basis of Jewish life must be philosophically re-thought, and contemporary interpretations on the one hand and the beliefs of earlier generations on the other must be clearly differentiated.[84]

On his own position in the light of such re-thinking, Scheffler writes — 'I reject the view that religious authority derives from some occult source, obliging us to deny our ordinary powers of observation, logical judgment, funded scientific information or moral intu-

[80] Ibid., p. 137.
[81] Ibid., p. 143. See pp. 140–156.
[82] Ibid., p. 144.
[83] Ibid., p. 176.
[84] Compare Sacks, 1991, 1995.

ition. On the contrary, I hold that religion, insofar as worthwhile, is harmonious with all of these and provides a commentary on our human life rather than a report of never lands beyond.'[85] It '... does not report on an occult world ... break the continuity of nature or extend mortal life.'[86] For Scheffler, 'a stronger metaphysical view' of the significance of religious practice is 'intellecually impossible.'[87]

Although Scheffler does not put the matter in this way, he seems to be committed to the view that the texts, doctrines and rituals of Judaism, to the extent that they refer to, or imply, transcendent and metaphysically significant realities and claims, are literally false. Scheffler's view on the meaningfulness or otherwise of these texts, doctrines and rituals in their unreinterpreted state is less easy to discern. Presumably they cannot he wholly meaningless, otherwise it would be impossible to judge them false or to engage in reinterpretation. However, properly reinterpreted, Scheffler insists, such texts, doctrines and rituals embody 'categories' of understanding and value, which are otherwise not prevalent—'... providing a commentary on life not abstractly available in the mere functioning of observation or judgment, in the mere concept of scientific method or information.'[88]

The similarity between Scheffler's position on these matters and that of Peters is worth noting. Both are sensitive to the riches contained in the religious domain, but offer a 'this worldly' interpretation of their meaning and significance. Peters could readily agree with Scheffler's insistence that religious traditions are important '... not because they report on another world but because, and to the extent that, they give us a new purchase on this, not because they illuminate the afterlife but because they reveal the hidden depths of this. To live in the presence of ultimate questions, whether of religion or philosophy, is to live a different life, here and now. To live with constant symbolic reminders that sensitize one to the categories

[85]   Ibid., p. 176.

[86]   Ibid., p. 178.

[87]   Ibid., p. 182.

[88]   Ibid., p. 178. Compare Atkins 1995, who argues for the omnicompetence of science. 'Scientists liberate truth from prejudice, and through their work lend wings to society's aspirations. While poetry titillates and theology obfuscates, science liberates.' (Atkins, 1995, p. 123); 'There is no reason to suppose that science cannot deal with every aspect of existence. Only the religious—among whom I include not merely the prejudiced but also the underinformed—hope that there is a dark comer of the physical Universe, or of the universe of experience, that science can never hope to illuminate' (Atkins, 1995, p. 125).

of justice, compassion, holiness, truth, duty, conscience, is to acquire a particular character.'[89] For Scheffler, such 'symbolic reminders' include 'exemplars' in the Jewish tradition of traits such as modesty, which can be transformed into 'compelling general criteria' of human value.[90] As might be expected, Scheffler gives a much more extended place to religious tradition in his account than does Peters, offering in particular a much fuller treatment of the nature of ritual. For Scheffler, ritual has an educative 'reflexive symbolic impact' in helping to '... relate its participants to higher values and more exalted purposes'[91] through its denotative, expressive and reenactive functions[92] and is in consequence an important resource in Jewish education.

Scheffler's position on both religion and on education in religion invite a number of questions and criticisms.

With regard to religion, a major issue concerns the character and coherence of Scheffler's reinterpretive approach. Clearly Scheffler, with his involvement in a substantial and complex religious tradition, has a much more extensive reinterpretive task than Peters. Questions concerning the adequacy of his reinterpretive approach arise both within Judaism, and more generally. The questions internal to Judaism concern whether Scheffler's reinterpretation offers a recognisable and adequate account of the Jewish religion, and the Jewish tradition more generally, preserving significant continuity. Scheffler insists that reinterpretation is a constant feature of religion and points to a number of features of Judaism which render it less resistant than some other religious traditions to reinterpretive influences. These include the perception of the Torah not as a fixed written text which can be mastered and possessed but as requiring dialectical discussion and interpretation.[93] Further, Scheffler relevantly draws attention to '... the traditional Rabbinic favoring of

[89]   Scheffler, 1995, p. 178.

[90]   Ibid., p. 177.

[91]   Ibid., p. 180. Of ritual, Scheffler writes — 'It is not a piece of magic, superstition, rational theory, cosmic technology or outmoded theology. It constitutes a language which organizes a world, structuring time and space, orienting Jews in history, binding them in community, and sensitizing them to those features of life in which their forebears have found the highest value and deepest meanings -freedom, responsibility, sincerity, humility, care, loyalty, righteousness, compassion.' (p. 182)

[92]   Scheffler 1995, pp. 180–182. For fuller discussion of ritunl sec Schcfflcr, 1986, Chs. 6–8, 1993a. Compare Matthews, 1980.

[93]   Scheffler, 1995, pp. 182–186.

conduct over creed, of consensus in practice over concordance in metaphysical belief.'[94] However, Scheffler is fully aware of the gap between his position and that of more orthodox Jewish believers, as revealed in his indication of the lack of agreement about the 'philosophical basis' of contemporary Jewish life and in his acknowledgement that his account of ritual, for example, is remote from that of his Jewish teachers – '... for whom the symbolic interpretation of ritual was only part of the story.'[95] Such interpretive disputes within religious traditions are far from unknown, and Scheffler's reinterpretive project is mirrored by a number of similar contemporary lines of argument in a Christian context.[96] Although these matters 'internal' to Judaism cannot be explored here, Scheffler, as he himself acknowledges, can anticipate a detailed debate within Judaism over such reinterpretive proposals. Some elements of the Jewish religious tradition are notably more resistant than others to reinterpretation in a Schefflerian way. For example, Scheffler may share in common with Peters a difficulty in rendering the concept of worship compatible with his overall interpretive perspective. Scheffler does not offer a detailed account of his understanding of the notion of God, although it seems reasonable to interpret him as sharing with Peters a conception of God as a (complex) symbolic label. Another kind of question 'internal' to Judaism is whether a reinterpretive account of the tradition such as Scheffler's can sufficiently account for its 'normative' or authoritative character for Jews. This matter will be returned to shortly.

The more general questions which arise concerning Scheffler's reinterpretation of religion are wide ranging. His position can be located within the developing contemporary philosophical debate concerning 'non-realism' in religion.[97] Religious realism can be briefly characterised as the view that there exists a transcendent divine reality which is at least in part independent of human thought, action or attitudes. Religious non-realism, which is not necessarily anti-religious, denies this.[98] One way in which this dispute is

[94]   Ibid., p. 116.

[95]   Ibid., p. 182.

[96]   See, for example, Cupitt, 1980, 1984, 1995. Freeman, 1993.

[97]   For proponents of (broadly) 'non-realist' approaches to religious faith see, for example, Cupitt, 1980, 1984, 1995; Freeman, 1993. For critical assessments see, for example, Cowdell, 1988; Hebblethwaite. 1988; Martin Soskice, 1985; Chs. 6–8, 1987; Runzo (Ed), 1993; Ward, 1992; White, 1994.

[98]   Runzo (Ed), 1993, p. xiii.

sometimes characterised is in terms of the enduring question: 'Did God create us, or we God?' The issues involved in the articulation of this general dispute, let alone its resolution, are complex and wide ranging, as can readily be seen by even a brief reflection on the varying ways in which 'realism' and 'non-realism' can be understood. The central issues involved with regard to 'realism' in the dispute include the meaning and ontological status of a reality such as 'God', its significance and necessity for religious faith and practice, and the possibility of reconciling claims about such a reality with the demands of reason and objectivity. With regard to 'non-realism', central issues include how the nature and 'point' of a religious form of life seen in terms of 'non-realism' are to be understood, and the character of the precise grounds on which such a perspective might be favoured. With regard to the latter issue, a number of contrasting grounds are invoked, which in turn are related to wider philosophical considerations and disputes[99] Since Scheffler does not offer a detailed philosophical articulation of his religious views, I will not pursue these philosophical matters at length at this point, although a number of the central matters at stake will emerge shortly. We can expect Scheffler to react to the concepts of 'realism' and 'non-realism' with his characteristic incisive caution, and to locate his own position in a nuanced way within the general debate.

It is important to re-iterate that 'non-realism' in religion is not necessarily anti-religious. There can be strong spiritual motives for a reinterpretive project such as Scheffler's. Iris Murdoch, for example, articulates the vital need for the insights and resources of religion to be liberated from literalist theology and doctrine.[100] A related point is that there is subtle affinity between sophisticated 'realist' views of religious faith and certain emphases of 'non-realism'. Even from the perspective of orthodox theism, for example, there is no suggestion that great clarity and confidence about the objects of belief are possible.[101] However, it should be noted that what is involved in a 'non-realist' view of religious faith and practice is by no means clear.

---

[99] For a distinction between 'descriptive' and 'prescriptive' non-realism in religion see Runzo (Ed), 1993, p. xviii. Compare Chs. 3 & 5.

[100] Murdoch, 1992.

[101] Iris Murdoch writes—'... religion can console at any level, but also contains a self-transcending imperative, a continuous iconoclastic urge to move beyond false consolation, suggesting a magnetic end-point where there is no more illusion, only truth, where consolation and explanation vanish' (Murdoch, 1992, p. 124). See also Steiner, 1989.

Murdoch strikes an important cautionary note in her observation that there may come a point when a 'demythologised' religion may become intolerable, losing its identity and coherence in the mind of the believer.[102]

It is appropriate to pursue a number of the central issues which arise in relation to Scheffler's reinterpretive project in the context of his discussion of Jewish education. In part this is because this is the context in which Scheffler himself largely discusses them, and in part because in any case it is a context in which the issues at stake are brought powerfully to life.

Scheffler emphasises the challenges which confront Jewish education today arising from the wide ranging intellectual and social developments of recent times.[103] Contemporary Jewish education therefore requires re-interpretation.[104] One difficulty which arises is that, given the collapse of Jewish community life, it faces the task of - '... creating the very society of which it should be the reflection.'[105] An important general question here, which has a significant philosophical dimension, is whether a Jewish community can flourish on the basis of a reinterpretive account of the Jewish tradition of the sort developed by Scheffler, or whether such a community requires a tradition with a metaphysical dimension, albeit a muted one, of the sort discernible in the Jewish communities described in his memoir.

Scheffler sees the reinterpreted Jewish education he supports as supplementary to, and not a substitute for, the sort of general education he has regularly delineated.[106] It has its own distinctive philosophy[107] and aims.[108] Although Scheffler does not directly address the

[102] Murdoch. 1992, pp. 126–127.

[103] Scheffler, 1992b, pp. 21–22.

[104] On the need, for example, for texts to be reinterpreted for contemporary pupils see Scheffler, 1992b, p. 25.

[105] Scheffler, 1992b, p. 22.

[106] Ibid., p. 20.

[107] For Scheffter's discussion of Judaism's philosophy of education see Scheffler, 1992a.

[108] Regarding these aims Scheffler writes — 'Viewed in relation to the pupil, they are: to initiate the Jewish child into the culture, history, and spiritual heritage of the Jewish people, to help the child to learn and face the truth about Jewish history, identity, and existence, to enhance his or her dignity as a Jewish person, and to enable the child to accept, and to be creative in, the Jewish dimension of its life. Viewed rather in its relation to the Jewish people, the purposes of Jewish education are: to promote Jewish survival and welfare, to interpret and communicate authentic Jewish experience, to sustain and defend Jewish honor

matter, it is interesting to speculate on the compatibility or otherwise of these features of Jewish education with the principles embodied in Scheffler's more general educational vision. As a central part of this general vision, Scheffler holds that, in the light of the relationship between democracy and reason,[109] education for all in a democratic society, must '... surrender the idea of shaping or molding the mind of the pupil. The function of education in a democracy is rather to liberate the mind, strengthen its critical powers, inform it with knowledge and the capacity for independent inquiry, engage its human sympathies, and illuminate its moral and practical choices,'[110] a requirement that finds expression in Scheffler's well known account of the requirements of teaching.[111] A number of queries can be raised about the compatibility of elements of Scheffler's educational vision of this kind with his vision of Jewish education, and these are rich in implication for his general views concerning religion.

One query arises from the fact that, in contrast to general education, Jewish education seeks to nourish, support (and perhaps in a sense mold) the child in membership of a distinctive cultural community. Why is this considered to be valuable and justifiable? What is involved seems to go beyond the emphasis on the significance of traditions which is found in Scheffler's general educational perspective. In this reply to this question, Scheffler stresses the particular and unique contributions to human life and flourishing which the Jewish tradition contains and offers. We can infer that Scheffler is sympathetic to arguments about the value of distinctive cultural membership of the sort developed by Will Kymlicka.[112] Such cultural membership can, in Kymlicka's view, be regarded as a 'primary good' compatible (at least in principle) with liberal values because individuals need a secure 'context of choice' in which they become aware of meaningful options and develop the capacity to seriously evaluate them. There are resonances here with Scheffler's

and loyalties, to create living links with the Jewish past, preserving and extending its heritage for future generations. Ideally, Jewish education should be a natural reflection of the inner dignity of the Jewish people, and of its ethical, spiritual and cultural resources, as well as a response to current social and intellectual realities' (Scheffler, 1992b, pp. 20–21).

[109] Scheffler, 1973, p. 142.

[110] Ibid., p. 139.

[111] Scheffler, 1960, Chs. 4, 5, 1973, Ch. 6.

[112] Kymlicka, 1989, 1995.

remarks about the need for 'grounding in a particular historical and cultural matrix.'[113] As mentioned earlier, Scheffler considers that such a grounding is 'inevitable' and '… could not conceivably be in conflict with universal principles.'[114] As it stands, however, this point seems overstated. As Kymlicka points out, some forms of cultural membership are incompatible with universal principles of a liberal kind because, for example, those forms of membership frustrate the rights and opportunities for individuals to achieve appropriate forms of critical autonomy. Perhaps Scheffler should be interpreted as meaning that in general a conflict between cultural specificity and universal principles is inconceivable. In any case one can discern within his account of Jewish culture and education, resources which can be deployed to argue against a conflict arising in this case.

Can Jewish education adequately embody the strong emphases on reason, criticism and the like which are contained within Scheffler's general views on education? The scope of Jewish education on Scheffler's view is wide ranging. It amounts to nothing less than the formation of the whole person viewed from a Jewish perspective,[115] in which a form of significant religious formation is involved. This is because of the '… intimate historical dependence of Jewish civilization upon its religious core,'[116] the indissoluble combination of religion, morality and good manners in Jewish life and the role of the teacher in offering both religious guidance and religious doctrine.[117] Apart from insisting that central elements in the Jewish tradition and its attitude to education are harmonious with reason and autonomy, Scheffler seeks to embody a critical perspective in the process of Jewish education by insisting that pupils must be encouraged from its early stages to engage in philosophical reflection.[118] This, however, gives rise to some interesting tensions and problems.

[113] Scheffler, 1995, p. 14.

[114] Ibid., p. 14.

[115] Scheffler, 1992a, pp. 8–10.

[116] Scheffler, 1992b, p. 25.

[117] Scheffler, 1992a, p. 13.

[118] '… the mind abhors a philosophical vacuum. No philosophy means bad philosophy. Sacred texts taught without a philosophical attitude are in danger of being received either as literal but incredible dogma, or as mere fairy tale, or as nonsense to be repeated with a pious incomprehension that will nor survive adult reflection. Certainly there are degrees of sophistication which must be

Of philosophers in general, Scheffler writes — 'The Philosopher wants to see things in perspective and he wants to see things sharp and clear. He strives for a maximum of vision and a minimum of mystery.'[119] If this is true too of the philosopher-pupils in Jewish education, a tension emerges with Scheffler's stress upon ritual in the Jewish educative process.

The engagement of pupils with rituals on Scheffler's view of Jewish education would seem to require the achievement on their part of a judicious mixture of 'acceptance' on the one hand and 'a critical search for clarity' on the other.[120] 'Acceptance', in the sense of a willingness of pupils to participate in a ritual and to let it 'speak' to them through its various modes without an undue concern about clarity of meaning, seems necessary if the ritual is to have any authority, force and stability, and if it is to exercise its distinctive educative effect. The complex significance of ritual is well illustrated by Scheffler's observation that ritual can be at one and the same time 'multiply symbolic.'[121] Ritual elements may symbolise many things, and through many processes and modes, often simultaneously.[122] This feature of ritual accounts for its flexibility with respect to doctrinal interpretations. The same ritual can survive interpretive changes. Ritual is '... anchored by multiple referential bonds to objects. When one or more are cut, the others meanwhile hold fast. When one requires relocation under a new interpretive idea, the untying and retying process docs not destroy the whole linkage.[123] Ritual has 'priority over dogma', surviving changes and developments in it and entering new 'interpretive contexts'. It is this feature of ritual which renders it open to the sort of reinterpretation

apportioned suitably to the levels of maturity of the pupils. But adult teachers need to be philosophically prepared to provide at least tentative explanations upon demand, to respond to serious questions as to how this or that text is to be taken, even if such response consists only in further questions. Philosophy is in this sense no luxury but a vital necessity for cultural survival.' (Scheffler, 1995, p. 174).

[119] Scheffler. 1960, p. 5.

[120] On the general question of the relationship between 'acceptance' and 'critical questioning' in religious schools see McLaughlin, 1992.

[121] Scheffler, 1986, p. 50

[122] 'Whatever a given rite may in fact portray, it may simultaneously exemplify, literally or metaphorically, quite different things. Explicitly representing episodes of a sacred story, it may at the same time express, rather than represent, dependence or victory, atonement, or thirst for redemption' (Scheffler, 1986, p. 59).

[123] Scheffler, 1986, p. 50. On change in relation to ritual see Scheffler, 1993a.

attempted by Scheffler, capable of providing a common focus of shared practice for those with differing interpretations, and as flexibly educative in the way Scheffler suggests. However, despite its interpretive flexibility, ritual requires an attitude of 'acceptance' if it is to yield its multiple meanings and not to disintegrate, suffer abandonment or be replaced by new capriciously invented rituals lacking the same depth and range of symbolic significance. Scheffler emphasises the point that there are constraints of different kinds upon rituals. Every ritual act has 'firm specifications' or 'prescriptions' which it must satisfy. 'These may be transmitted orally or written down or understood in context, but that there is a right and a wrong way of execution is normally evident.'[124] A correct performance of a rite constitutes a sample or exemplification of it. Without an attitude of 'acceptance' on the part of participants these features of rituals, and indeed rituals themselves, would disappear.

There are, however, a number of forces emphasising the need for the pupil to achieve a critical clarity of understanding with respect to ritual. Some of these arise simply from the nature of ritual itself. Scheffler holds that intent is not necessary for ritual performance,[125] but this seems somewhat in conflict with his later observation that rituals are intended to affect the sensibilities of participants. Thus Scheffler notes — 'The question "Does he truly believe what he is saying?" is relevant to the ritual performer alone, while artful simulation of belief is a feat valued only in the actor.[126] Thus there is a 'certain expected linkage' between the properties expressed in rituals and the mentality and sensibility of participants. A ritual participant is one whose character is affected by the role he or she performs[127] and this is achieved at least in part by clarity of understanding. Further, Scheffler insists, '... ritual performance typically needs to carry its specifications on its face ... participants passive as well as active need to comprehend the specifications of the actions being carried out ... in order to grasp the point of the performance.[128] Such requirements might be met by factual or procedural information of the sort: 'This means x, and we do a,b,c'. However, this sort of response is inadequate for Scheffler, who in order to make the connection with

[124] Ibid., p. 53.
[125] Ibid., p. 58.
[126] Ibid., p. 59.
[127] Ibid., p. 60.
[128] Scheffler, 1993, pp. 159–160.

his reinterpretative view of religion and his wider educational values, insists that philosophical questions be raised for and by pupils from the early stages of Jewish education, and a questioning attitude of a philosophical kind encouraged.

However, a number of difficulties arise with too extensive a preoccupation with critical clarity of understanding on the part of pupils in this context. Such a preoccupation may inhibit the participation of the pupils in rituals and may destabilise the rituals themselves. As indicated earlier, the. educative, value of rituals consists in part in their stability and 'givenness' and these may be undermined by too great a preoccupation with critical clarity of meaning, where every ritual engagement becomes the occasion of a seminar. This danger is perhaps exacerbated by the fact that, in Scheffler's case, the encouragement of philosophical reflection is associated with a reinterpretive attitude to religion. This exacerbation may occur for at least three, reasons

First, reinterpretation invites fundamental reflection and has an impulse to push pupils to consider *inter alia* the 'independent beliefs'[129] relevant to interpreting the reference of any ritual and the worth of the values and insights it embodies. This may draw attention away from the rituals themselves and to lead to them being seen merely as material for reflection of a more general kind. Second, engagement in ritual with a reinterpretive perspective of the sort delineated by Scheffler involves an attitude of some complexity and sophistication. The precise character of this attitude stands in need of further philosophical elucidation. Presumably pupils will need to encounter rituals initially in their 'realist' or 'surface meaning' form, and it may be hard to convey the meaning and point of continuing to engage in them from a reinterpreted perspective. Scheffler seeks to identify a form of continuing post-reinterpretive involvement with ritual which is neither (mere) nostalgic formalism nor a crudely instrumental view of the tradition as a resource to be mined for general insights, perhaps in an eclectic way. Both of these attitudes run the risk of underplaying the. authoritativeness of the Jewish tradition, and the seriousness and tenacity of engagement with the tradition which Scheffler is anxious to retain and emphasise. Some pupils may ask, for example, why, once the reinterpreted insights have been gained in the shape of some 'general exemplars', their ritualised embodiment continues to have any value and force. Scheffler's

[129] Scheffler, 1986, p. 70.

330 *Liberalism, Education and Schooling*

insistence that the received texts and practices are not dispensable once they have yielded their reinterpreted meanings, or that they are not straightforwardly translatable into other terms without remainder may not be easy to convey.[130] Scheffler may agree with the general character of Dewey's claim in 'A Common Faith' that religion is relevant to '... the attitudes that lend deep and enduring support to the processes of living'[131] but we can safety speculate that he is suspicious of Dewey's vision of how religion, shorn of the 'encumbrances' of the. supernatural and of tradition and history, can enable many people to realise a religious potential through commitment to certain inclusive ideal ends presented to us by the imagination. For Scheffler, religious tradition is important. The third factor relates to the reply which Scheffler is likely to make to these difficulties. In his remark that teachers need to adopt degrees of sophistication of response to the philosophical questioning of pupils in the light of the pupils' level of maturity[132] Scheffler seems to imply that the relevant judgements (about, for example, the right balance to be struck between the requirements of 'acceptance' and 'critical clarity') require the exercise of a form of Jewish practical wisdom The notion of 'practical wisdom' in this context may be undermined, however, by Scheffler's acknowledgement of the need for Jewish education to have plural philosophical underpinnings. Scheffler writes — 'Pluralism is the prospect I foresee and welcome, a pluralism of doctrines compatible with a common seriousness of reflection and search, a pluralism of ideological approaches to Jewish life, consistent as well with common efforts to preserve common values, memories, institutions and practices.'[133] Can, however, these elements of plurality and commonality be coherently held together in an established way of life in the light of a reinterpretive approach to the religious elements of the tradition of the sort which Scheffler outlines? This is a central question not only for the possibility of a form of Jewish practical wisdom but also for his view in general.

Whilst these difficulties relating to Scheffler's concept of Jewish education clearly have practical aspects to them, they also have important connections with the deeper philosophical questions which arise concerning his overall reinterpretative position, and act

[130] Scheffler, 1995, pp. 176–178.
[131] Dewey, 1934, p. 15. See Scheffler, 1974, pp. 240–242.
[132] Scheffler, 1995, p. 174.
[133] Ibid., p. 175.

as a lens through which they can be viewed. Although the points mentioned here do not by any means encompass all those which are relevant to Scheffler's position, they hopefully indicate a range of educationally significant questions which open up the broader range of issues.

Education, and indeed life itself, cannot take place in a vacuum. They require tradition and substance, and traditions cannot easily be invented or reinvented from scratch. Scheffler's memoir, and his view of religion and education in religion more generally, is a powerful reminder of these central truths. The significance of formation and education in a substantial tradition of belief, practice and value — a culturally specific identity — is widely recognised and acknowledged. Scheffler brings this significance to life in a vivid way. Much current debate among philosophers of education, and educators more generally, concerns the relationship between the formation of such culturally specific identities and the general and civic demands of 'public' education and its more universalist principles and aspirations in the context of a pluralist liberal democracy. Unlike Peters, Scheffler's discussion makes no reference to the form that education in religion might take in the common school. It would, however, be interesting to learn whether he considers that Peters' approach to this matter might form the basis on which an approach to religious issues in the common school can be made which might satisfy sensibilities relating to this matter in the United States. Scheffler's discussion of Jewish education illuminates a number of questions relating to forms of religious education and schooling which seek to achieve compatibility with 'public' educational principles and values. Central among these questions is the nature of what is involved in achieving a genuinely educative understanding of the religious tradition from a perspective internal to the faith on the one hand which also does justice to the various demands arising from the civic or public domain on the other.[134] Scheffler's distinctive approach to these matters is far from unproblematic and gives rise to many intriguing and underexplored questions. It will, however, considerably enrich our debate about the relationships between religion, reason and education.

[134] On these matters see, for example, McLaughlin, 1992, 1995b.

Publications by Professor Terence H. McLaughlin

1. Books, Monographs and Guest Editorships

2007 *Higher Education and National Development: universities and societies in transition,* co-edited with David Bridges, Palmira Juceviciene, Robertas Jucevicius and Jolanta Stankeviciute (Abingdon, Routledge).

2004 'Philosophy, Education and Comparative Education', co-edited with J. Mark Halstead, Special Issue of *Comparative Education,* Vol 40, No 4

2000 'Philosophy and Moral Education: the contribution of John Wilson', co-edited with J. Mark Halstead, Special Issue of *Journal of Moral Education,* Vol 29, No 3

1999 *Education in Morality,* co-edited with J. Mark Halstead (London and New York, Routledge) Reprinted 2001.

1997 *Siuolaikine Ugdymo Filosofija: Demokratiskumas, Vertybes, Ivairove (Contemporary Philosophy of Education: Democracy, Values, Diversity)* (Kaunas Lithuania, Technologija, in association with the Open Society Fund) (A collection of articles re-published in Lithuanian translation).

1996 *The Contemporary Catholic School: Context, Identity and Diversity,* co-edited with Joseph O'Keefe SJ and Bernadette O'Keeffe (London, The Falmer Press) Reprinted 2000.

1995 *Values, Education and Responsibility,* a monograph co-authored with Elizabeth Pybus (St Andrews, Centre for Philosophy and Public Affairs, University of St Andrews).

1994 *Education and the Market Place,* co-edited with David Bridges (London, Falmer Press).

1994 'Values and the School: Contexts, Principles and Strategies', co-edited with Bernard Barker and Sylvia West, Special Issue of *Cambridge Journal of Education,* Vol 24, No 3.

2. Chapters in Books

2007 'Universities and societies: traditions, transitions and tensions' in David Bridges, Palmira Juceviciene, Roberta Jucevicius, Terence H McLaughlin and Jolanta Stankeviciute (Eds) *Higher Education and National Development: universities and societies in transition* (Abingdon, Routledge).

2005a 'What is Controversy?' in William Hare and John P. Portelli (Eds.) *Key Questions for Educators* (Halifax Nova Scotia, Edphil Books), pp. 61-64,

2005b 'Are Faith Schools Divisive?' (with J. Mark Halstead) in Roy Gardner, Jo Cairns and Denis Lawton (Eds.) *Faith Schools: Consensus or Conflict?* (Abingdon, RoutledgeFalmer), pp. 61-73.

2005c 'Citizenship and Higher Education in the UK' (with John Annette) in James Arthur with Karen E. Bohlin (Eds.) *Citizenship and Higher Education. The Role of Universities in Communities and Society* (London, RoutledgeFalmer), pp. 74- 95.

2004a 'Philosophy, Values and Schooling: Principles and Predicaments of Teacher Example' in William Aiken and John Haldane (Eds.) *Philosophy and its Public Role. Essays in Ethics, Politics, Society and Culture*, St Andrews Studies in Philosophy and Public Affairs (Exeter, UK and Charlottesville, USA, Imprint Academic), pp. 69-83.

2004b 'Nicholas Burbules on Jesus as Teacher' in Hanan Alexander (Ed.) *Spirituality and Ethics in Education. Philosophical, Theological and Radical Perspectives* (Brighton, Sussex Academic Press, pp. 21-33.

2003a 'Teaching Controversial Issues in Citizenship Education' in Andrew Lockyer, Bernard Crick and John Annette (Eds.) *Education for Democratic Citizenship. Issues of Theory and Practice* (Aldershot, Ashgate), pp. 149-160.

2003b 'Education, Spirituality and the Common School' in David Carr and John Haldane (Eds.) *Spirituality, Philosophy and Education* (London, RoutledgeFalmer), pp. 185-199.

2003c 'The Burdens and Dilemmas of Common Schooling' in Kevin McDonough and Walter Feinberg (Eds.) *Citizenship and Education in Liberal-Democratic Societies. Teaching for Cosmopolitan Values and Collective Identities* (Oxford, University Press), pp. 121-156.

2003d 'Education in Religion and Spirituality' (with Hanan Alexander) in Nigel Blake,Paul Smeyers, Richard Smith and Paul Standish (Eds.) *The Blackwell Guide to the Philosophy of Education* (Oxford, Blackwell Publishing), pp. 356-373.

2002   'Education for European Identity and European Citizenship' (with KatarzynaLewicka-Grisdale) in Jose Antonio Ibanez-Martin and Gonzalo Jover (Eds.) *Education in Europe: Policies and Politics* (Dordrecht, Kluwer Academic Publishers), pp. 53-81.

2001   'Paul H Hirst' in Joy A. Palmer (Ed.) *Fifty Modern Thinkers on Education. From Piaget to the Present* (London, Routledge), pp. 193-199.

2000a   'The European Dimension of Higher Education: Neglected Claims and Concepts' in Francis Crawley, Paul Smeyers and Paul Standish (Eds.) *Universities Remembering Europe. Nations, Culture, and Higher Education* (Oxford, Berghahn Books), pp. 3-25.

2000b   'Values in Education' in John Beck and Mary Earl (Eds.) *Key Issues in Secondary Education. Introductory Readings* (London, Cassell), pp. 109-117.

2000c   'Schools, Parents and the Community' in John Beck and Mary Earl (Eds.) *Key Issues in Secondary Education. Introductory Readings* (London, Cassell), pp. 86-95.

1999a   'Education in Character and Virtue' (with J. Mark Halstead) in J. Mark Halstead and Terence H McLaughlin (Eds.) *Education in Morality* (London and New York, Routledge), pp. 132-163.

1999b   'Distinctiveness and the Catholic School: Balanced Judgement and the Temptations of Commonality' in James C. Conroy (Ed.) *Catholic Education: Inside-Out Outside-In* (Dublin, Veritas), pp. 65-87.

1998   'Diversity, identity and education: some principles and dilemmas' in Adalberto Dias de Carvallo (Ed.) *Diversidade E Identdade* (Instituto de Folosofia, Faculdade de Letras, da Universidade do Porto).

1997a   'Education, Democracy and the Formation of National Identity' (with Palmira Juceviciene) in David Bridges (Ed.) *Education, Autonomy and Democratic Citizenship: Philosophy in a Changing World* (London, Routledge), pp. 23-35.

1997b   'La Identidad Nacional y la Educacion'/'National Identity and Education' in Miguel Anxo Santos Rego (Ed.) *Politica Educativa En La Union Europea Despue De Maastricht/Educational Policy in the European Union After Maastricht* (Santiago de Compostela, Coleccion Monografias, Escola Galega de Administracion Publica), pp. 45 - 68 (publication side-by-side on the page in Spanish and English).

1996a   'Educating Responsible Citizens' in Henry Tam (Ed.) *Punishment, Excuses and Moral Development* (Aldershot, Avebury), pp. 181-195.

1996b 'Education, Multiculturalism and the Demands of Recognition' in Maria G. Amilburu (Ed.) *Education, the State and the Multicultural Challenge* (Pamplona, Ediciones Universidad de Navarra SA: EUNSA), pp. 135-158.

1996c 'Education of the Whole Child?' in Ron Best (Ed.) *Education, Spirituality and the Whole Child* (London, Cassell), pp. 9-19.

1996d 'The Distinctiveness of Catholic Education' in Terence H. McLaughlin, Joseph O'Keefe and Bernadette O'Keeffe (Eds.) *The Contemporary Catholic School: Context, Identity and Diversity* (London, Falmer Press), pp. 136-154.

1996e 'Setting the Scene: Current Realities and Historical Perspectives' (with Joseph O'Keefe and Bernadette O'Keeffe) in Terence H. McLaughlin, Joseph O'Keefe and Bernadette O'Keeffe (Eds.) *The Contemporary Catholic School: Context, Identity and Diversity* (London, Falmer Press), pp. 1-21.

1995 'Public Values, Private Values and Educational Responsibility', in Elizabeth Pybus and Terence H McLaughlin *Values, Education and Responsibility* (St Andrews, Centre for Philosophy and Public Affairs, University of St Andrews), pp. 19-32.

1994a 'The Scope of Parents' Educational Rights' in J. Mark Halstead (Ed.) *Parental Choice and Education. Principles, Policy and Practice* (London, Kogan Page), pp. 94-107.

1994b 'Mentoring and the Demands of Reflection' in Margaret Wilkin and Derek Sankey (Eds.) *Collaboration and Transition in Initial Teacher Training* (London, Kogan Page), pp. 151-160.

1994c 'Politics, Markets and Schools: The Central Issues' in David Bridges and Terence H. McLaughlin (Eds.) *Education and the Market Place* (London, Falmer Press), pp. 153-168.

[Reprinted in Paul H Hirst and Patricia White (Eds.) (1998) *Philosophy of Education: Major Themes in the Analytical Tradition. Volume 3* (London, Routledge), pp. 442-456].

1992 'The Ethics of Separate Schools' in Mal Leicester and Monica Taylor (Eds.) *Ethics, Ethnicity and Education* (London, Kogan Page), pp. 114-136.

1987 '"Education for All" and Religious Schools' in Graham Haydon (Ed.) *Education for a Pluralist Society: Philosophical Perspectives on the Swann Report* (Bedford Way Paper No 30 University of London Institute of Education), pp. 67-83.

Introductions

1999   'Introduction' (with J. Mark Halstead) in J. Mark Halstead and
        Terence H. McLaughlin (Eds.) *Education in Morality* (London and
        New York, Routledge), pp. 1-4.

1997   'Pratarme' (Introduction) (in Lithuanian) in Terence H.
        McLaughlin *Siuolaikine Ugdymo Filosofija: Demokratiskumas,
        Vertybes, Ivairove (Contemporary Philosophy of Education: Democ-
        racy, Values, Diversity)* (Kaunas Lithuania, Technologija), pp. 5-6.

1994   'Education and the Market Place: An Introduction' (with David
        Bridges) in David Bridges and Terence H. McLaughlin (Eds.)
        Education and the Market Place (London, Falmer Press), pp. 1-8.

3. Articles in Refereed Journals

2005a   'The Educative Importance of Ethos', *British Journal of Educational
        Studies,* Vol 53, No 3, pp. 306-325.

2005b   'School Choice and Public Education in a Liberal Democratic
        Society', *American Journal of Education,* Vol 111, No 4, pp. 442-463.

2004   'Education, Philosophy and the Comparative Perspective', *Com-
        parative Education,* Vol 40, No 4, pp. 471-483.

2003a   'Open-Mindedness as an Aim in Moral Education', *Journal of
        Thought,* Vol 38, No 2, pp. 21-32.

2003b   'Teaching as a Practice and a Community of Practice: The Limits
        of Commonality and the Demands of Diversity', *Journal of Philos-
        ophy of Education,* Vol 37, No 2, pp. 339-352. [Also published in
        Joseph Dunne and Padraig Hogan (Eds.) (2004) *Education and
        Practice. Upholding the Integrity of Teaching and Learning* (Oxford,
        Blackwell Publishing), pp. 48-60].

2003c   'An Extra-Liberal (?) Stance to Philosophy of Education: Adding
        to, or Going Beyond, Liberalism?', *Journal of Philosophy of Educa-
        tion,* Vol 37, No 1, pp. 174-184.

2002   'A Catholic Perspective on Education', *Journal of Education and
        Christian Belief,* Vol 6, No 2, pp. 121-134.

2001a   'Four Philosophical Perspectives on School Inspection: An Intro-
        duction', *Journal of Philosophy of Education,* Vol 35, No 4, pp.
        647-654.

2001b   'A Spiritual Dimension to Sex Education?' *International Journal of
        Children's Spirituality,* Vol 6, No 2, pp. 223-232.

2000a   'Citizenship Education in England: The Crick Report and
        Beyond', *Journal of Philosophy of Education,* Vol 34, No 4, pp.
        541-570.

2000b 'Philosophy and Educational Policy: Possibilities, Tensions and Tasks'. *Journal of Educational Policy,* Vol 15, No 4, pp. 441-457.

[Reprinted in Wilfred Carr (Ed.) (2005) *The RoutledgeFalmer Reader in Philosophy of Education* (Abingdon, RoutledgeFalmer), pp. 17-33].

[Reprinted in *Kwartalnik Pedagogiczny* Vol XLIX, No 1-2, 2004, pp. 239-264 (Warsaw, Warsaw University)] .

[Published in Polish translation as 'Filozofia a Polityka Oswiatowa — Mozliwosci, Napiecia i Zadania' *Kwartalnik Pedagogiczny,* Vol XLIX, No 1-2, 2004, pp. 265-291 (Warsaw, Warsaw University).

2000c 'John Wilson on Moral Education', (with J. Mark Halstead) *Journal of Moral Education*, Vol 29, No 3, pp. 247-268.

2000d 'An Interview with John Wilson', (with J. Mark Halstead) *Journal of Moral Education,* Vol 29, No 3, pp. 269-283.

1999 'Beyond the Reflective Teacher', *Educational Philosophy and Theory,* Vol 31, No 1, pp. 9-25.

1998a 'Kenneth Strike on Liberalism, Citizenship and the Private Interest in Schooling', *Studies in Philosophy and Education,* Vol 17, No 4, pp. 231-241.

1998b 'Sex Education, Moral Controversy and the Common School', *Muslim Education Quarterly,* Vol 15, No 3, pp. 28-52.

[Also published in Michael J Reiss and Shaikh Abdul Mabud (Eds.) (1998) *Sex Education and Religion* (Cambridge, The Islamic Academy), pp. 186-224].

1998c 'Four Anxieties about Open-Mindedness: Reassuring Peter Gardner' (with William Hare), *Journal of Philosophy of Education,* Vol 32, No 2, pp. 283-292.

1997 'Israel Scheffler on Religion, Reason and Education', *Studies in Philosophy and Education,* Vol 16, Nos 1-2, pp. 201-223.

[Also published in Harvey Siegel (Ed.) (1997) *Reason and Education: Essays in Honor of Israel Scheffler* (Dordrecht, Kluwer Academic Publishers), pp. 201-223].

1996 'National Identity and the Aims of Education', *Socialiniai Mokslai: dukologija,* Vol 5, No 1 (Kaunas Lithuania, Faculty of Administration, Kaunas University of Technology), pp. 7-14.

1995a 'Wittgenstein, Education and Religion', *Studies in Philosophy and Education,* Vol 14, Nos 2-3, pp. 295-311.

[Also published in Paul Smeyers and James D Marshall (Eds.) (1995) *Philosophy and Education: Accepting Wittgenstein's Challenge* (Dordrecht, Kluwer Academic Publishers) pp. 171-187].

1995b 'Liberalism, Education and the Common School', *Journal of Philosophy of Education,* Vol 29, No 2, pp. 239-255.

[Also published in Yael Tamir (Ed.) (1995) *Democratic Education in a Multicultural State* (Oxford, Blackwell Publishers), pp. 81-97].

1995c 'Return to the Crossroads: Maritain Fifty Years On' (with David Carr, John Haldane and Richard Pring), *British Journal of Educational Studies,* Vol XXXXIII, No 2, pp. 162-178.

1994a 'Values, Coherence and the School', *Cambridge Journal of Education,* Vol 24, No 3, pp. 453-470.

1994b 'Open-mindedness, Commitment and Peter Gardner' (with William Hare), *Journal of Philosophy of Education,* Vol 28, No 2, pp. 239-244.

1992a 'Citizenship, Diversity and Education: a philosophical perspective', *Journal of Moral Education,* Vol 21, No 3, pp. 235-250.

[Reprinted in *The School Field. International Journal of Theory and Research in Education,* Vol X, Nos 1/2, 1999, pp. 37-56].

1992b 'Fairness, Controversiality and the Common School', *Spectrum,* Vol 24, No 2, pp. 105-118.

[Reprinted in Jeff Astley and Leslie J Francis (Eds.) (1994) *Critical Perspectives on Christian Education: a reader on the aims, principles and philosophy of Christian education* (Leominster, Gracewing), pp. 331-342].

1990   'Peter Gardner on Religious Upbringing and the Liberal Ideal of Religious Autonomy', *Journal of Philosophy of Education,* Vol 24, No 1, pp. 107-125.

[Reprinted in Paul H Hirst and Patricia White (Eds.) (1998) *Philosophy of Education: Major Themes in the Analytical Tradition. Volume 4* (London, Routledge), pp. 119-142].

1985   'Religion, Upbringing and Liberal Values: a rejoinder to Eamonn Callan', *Journal of Philosophy of Education,* Vol 19, No 1, pp. 119-127.

1984   'Parental Rights and the Religious Upbringing of Children', *Journal of Philosophy of Education,* Vol 18, No 1, pp. 75-83.

[Reprinted in Jeff Astley and Leslie J Francis (Eds.) (1994) *Critical Perspectives on Christian Education: a reader on the aims, principles and philosophy of Christian education* (Leominster, Gracewing), pp. 171-183].

1983 'The Pastoral Curriculum: concept and principles', *Educational Analysis,* Vol 5, No 1, pp. 91-99.

1982 'The idea of a Pastoral Curriculum', *Cambridge Journal of Education,* Vol 12, No 1, pp. 34-52.

Editorials

2004 'Editorial: Philosophy, Education and Comparative Education' (with J. Mark Halstead), *Comparative Education,* Vol 40, No 4, pp. 467-470.

2001 'Editorial', *Cambridge Journal of Education,* Vol 31, No 2, pp. 133-134.

2000 'Editorial' (with J. Mark Halstead), *Journal of Moral Education,* Vol 29, No 3, p. 245.

1999 'Editorial', *Cambridge Journal of Education,* Vol 29, No 1, pp. 5-6.

1994 'Editorial' (with Bernard Barker and Sylvia West), *Cambridge Journal of Education,* Vol 24, No 3, pp. 355-359.

1993 'Editorial', *Cambridge Journal of Education,* Vol 23, No 2, pp. 123-124.

4. Published Conference Papers

2000 'Diversity, Identity and Education: Some Principles and Dilemmas' in Adalberto Dias de Carvalho , Eugenia Vilela, Isabel Baptista, Maria Joao Couto , Paula Cristina Pereira and Zelia Almeida (Eds.) *Diversidade e Identidade. Actas da 1a Conferencia Internacional de Filosofia da Educacao* (Porto Portugal, Gabinate de Filosofia da Educacao, Instituto de Filosofia, Faculdade de Letras da Universidade do Porto), pp. 123-140.

1999a 'A Response to Professor Bridges' in David Carr (Ed.) *Values in the Curriculum. Proceedings of the Gordon Cook Foundation Conference Edinburgh 1997* (Aberdeen, Gordon Cook Foundation), pp. 36-46.

1999b 'Challenges and Opportunities for Education in the Next Millennium: A Philosophical Perspective' in Palmira Juceviciene (Ed.) *The Role of Social Science in the Development of Education, Business and Government Entering the 21st Century: International Conference Selected Papers Volume 1* (Kaunas Lithuania, Technologija), pp. 17-23.

5. Other Output

Articles in Periodicals

2006   'Spiritual Learning Curve', *The Tablet,* Vol 260, No 8625, 4 February, pp. 20-21.

1999a   'Does this Vision Work?' *The Tablet,* Vol 253, No 8303, 9 October, p. 1357.

1999b   'Teachers Behaving Badly', *The Tablet,* Vol 253, No 8282, 15 May, pp. 662-663.

1998   'The three Rs are just the start', *The Tablet,* Vol 252, No 8219, 14 February, pp. 200- 202 .

1995   'Values East and West', *The Tablet,* Vol 249, No 8076, 27 May, pp. 666-667.

1993a   'Learning for life: An interview with Dominic Milroy', *The Tablet,* Vol 247, No 7993, 16 October, pp. 1334-1336.

1993b   'A man for this season', *The Tablet,* Vol 247, No 7958, 13 February, pp. 198-200.

1992   'Beyond the edu-babble', *The Tablet,* Vol 246, No 7940, 10 October, pp. 1259-1260.

Book Reviews

2004   'Higher Learning and Catholic Traditions', edited by Robert E Sullivan (Notre Dame IN, University of Notre Dame Press), *Theory and Research in Education,* Vol 2, No 1, pp. 87-92.

2002   'Religious Schools: The Case Against' (Humanist Philosophers' Group, British Humanist Association), *British Journal of Religious Education,* Vol 25, No 1, pp. 82-84.

1995   'Freedom and Indoctrination in Education: International Perspectives', edited by Ben Spiecker and Roger Straughan (Cassell), *Journal of Philosophy of Education,* Vol 29, No 1, pp. 155-157.

1992a   'The Teaching of Values: Caring and appreciation' by James L. Jarrett (Routledge), *The Curriculum Journal,* Vol 3, No 2, pp. 205-206.

1992b   'The Morality of the School: The Theory and Practice of Values in Education' by Mike Bottery (Cassell), *Journal of Philosophy of Education,* Vol 26, No 2, pp. 278-280.

1992c   'In Praise of the Cognitive Emotions and Other Essays in the Philosophy of Education' by Israel Scheffler (Routledge), *The Philosophical Quarterly,* Vol 42, No 168, pp. 382-383.

List of References

Ackerman, B. A. (1980) *Social Justice in the Liberal State* (Yale University Press, New Haven and London).

Aiken, W. and LaFollette, H. (eds) (1980) *Whose Child? Children's Rights, Parental Authority, and Stale Power* (Littlefield, Adams & Co, Totowa, New Jersey).

Akhtar, S. (1990) *A Faith for All Seasons. Islam and Western Modernity* (Bellew Publishing, London).

Albertini, T. (1997) 'Islamic philosophy: an overview', in: E. Deutsch & R. Bontekoe (Eds) *A companion to world philosophies* (Oxford, Blackwell), 93-133.

Aldrich, R. and White, J. (1998) *The National Curriculum beyond 2000: the QCA and the aims of education* (University of London: Institute of Education).

Alexander, H. A. (2001) *Reclaiming Goodness: Education and the Spiritual Quest* (Notre Dame: University of Notre Dame Press).

Alexander, H. A. and McLaughlin, T. H. (2003) 'Education in religion and spirituality', in N. Blake, P. Smeyers, R. Smith and P. Standish (eds), *The Blackwell Guide to the Philosophy of Education* (Oxford: Blackwell).

Alexander, R. J. (2001) 'Border crossings: towards a comparative pedagogy', *Comparative Education*, 37(4), 507-523.

Almond, B. (1987) *Moral Concerns* (Atlantic Highlands NJ: Humanities Press International).

Almond, B. (1988) 'Conflict or Compromise? Religious and moral education in a plural context', in McClelland, V A (ed) (1988).

Almond, B. (1988) 'Human Bonds', *Journal of Applied Philosophy* 5, 1 pp. 3-16.

Almond, B. (1990) 'Alasdair MacIntyre: the virtue of tradition', *Journal of Applied Philosophy* 7, 1, 99-103.

Almond, B. (1995) 'Introduction: Ethical Theory and Ethical Practice', in B. Almond (ed.), *Introducing Applied Ethics* (Oxford: Blackwell).

Amer, F. (1997) 'The Problems of Sex Education within the Context of Islamic Teachings — Towards a Clearer Vision of the British Case', *Muslim Education Quarterly*, 14, 2, pp. 16-36.

Anderson, B. (1983) *Imagined Communities* (London: Verso).

Ashraf, S. (1988) 'A view of Education — an Islamic Perspective', in O'Keeffe, B (ed) *Schools for Tomorrow: Building Walls or Building Bridges* (Falmer Press, Lewes).

Astley, J. (1993) (September), *Faith on the level? On teaching a Christian spirituality without God*, Paper presented at a National Conference on

Moral and Spiritual Education at the University of Plymouth, Exmouth Campus, UK.

Atkins, P.W. (1995) 'The Limitless Tower of Science', in Cornwell, J. (Ed) *Nature's Imagination. The frontiers of scientific vision* (Oxford, Oxford University Press).

Bailey, C. (1984) *Beyond the Present and the Particular. A Theory of Liberal Education* (London: Routledge and Kegan Paul).

Ball, S. (1988) 'A comprehensive school in a pluralist world — division and inequalities', in O'Keeffe, B (ed) *Schools for Tomorrow: Building Walls or Building Bridges* (Falmer Press, Lewes).

Ball, W. and Troyna, B. (1987) 'Resistance, rights and rituals: denominational schools and multi-cultural education', *Journal of Educational Policy*, 2, 1, pp 15-25.

Bambrough, R. (1987) 'The roots of moral reason', in Straughan, R and Wilson J (eds) *Philosophers on Education* (Macmillan, London).

Bambrough, R. (1991) 'Fools and heretics', in A. Phillips Griffiths (ed.), *Wittgenstein centenary essays*, pp. 239-250 (Cambridge University Press, Cambridge).

Bambrough, R. (1993) 'Invincible knowledge', in A. Phillips Griffiths (ed.), *Ethics*, pp. 51-62 (Cambridge University Press, Cambridge).

Bantock, G. H. (1984) *Studies in the History of Educational Theory. Volume II. The Minds and the Masses 1760-1980* (London: George Allen & Unwin).

Barr, J. (1977) *Fundamentalism* (SCM Press, London).

Barrett, C. (1991) *Wittgenstein on ethics and religious belief* (Basil Blackwell, Oxford).

Barrow, R. (1974) *Plato, Utilitarianism and Education* (Routledge and Regan Paul, London).

Barrow, R. (1976) 'Competence and the Head', in R.S. Peters (ed.), *The Role of the Head* (London: Routledge and Kegan Paul).

Batho, G. (1990) 'The history of the teaching of civics and citizenship in English schools', *The Curriculum Journal*, 1(1), pp. 91-107.

Beck, C. (1994) 'Postmodernism, Pedagogy and Philosophy of Education', in A. Thompson (ed.), *Philosophy of Education 1993* (Urbana Illinois: Philosophy of Education Society).

Beck, J. (1998) *Morality and Citizenship in Education* (London: Cassell).

Bell, D. (1993) *Communitarianism and its Critics* (Oxford, Clarendon Press).

Bellah, R. N., Madsen, R., Sullivan, W. M., Swidler, A. & Tipton, S. M. (1985) *Habits of the Heart. Individualism and Commitment in American Life* (Berkeley, University of California Press).

Bellah, R. N., Madsen, R., Sullivan, W. M., Swidler, A. & Tipton, S. M. (1991) *The Good Society* (New York, Alfred A. Knopf).

Benn, S. I. & Gaus, G. F. (Eds) (1983) *Public and Private in Social Life* (London, St Martin's Press).

Benton, P. (Ed) (1990) *The Oxford Internship Scheme: Integration and Partnership in Initial Teacher Education* (London, Calouste Gulbenkenian Foundation).

Best, R. (ed.) (1996) *Education, Spirituality, and the Whole Child* (London: Cassell).

Bigelow, H., Campbell, J., Dodds, S. M., Pargetter, R., Prior, E. W. and Young, R. (1988) 'Parental autonomy', *Journal of Applied Philosophy*, 5, 2, pp 183-96.

Bishop, S. (1980) 'Children, autonomy, and the right to self-determination', in Aiken, W. and LaFollette H. (eds) *Whose Child? Children's Rights, Parental Authority, and Stale Power* (Littlefield, Adams & Co, Totowa, NJ).

Blackburn, S. (1999) *Think. A compelling introduction to philosophy* (Oxford, Oxford University Press).

Blake, N. (1996) 'Against Spiritual Education', *Oxford Review of Education* 22, 4: 443-56.

Blake, N. (1996) 'Between Postmodernism and Anti-Modernism: The Predicament of Educational Studies'. *British Journal of Educational Studies*, 44(1), 42 − 65.

Blake, N. (1997) 'Spirituality, anti-intellectualism, and the end of civilisation as we know it', in R. Smith and P. Standish (eds), *Teaching Right and Wrong. Moral Education in the Balance* (Stoke-on-Trent: Trentham Books).

Blake, N., Smeyers, P., Smith, R. & Standish, P. (1998a) *Thinking again. Education after postmodernism* (Westport, CT, Bergin & Harvey).

Blake, N., Smith, R. and Standish, P. (1998b) *The Universities We Need. Higher Education After Dearing* (London: Kogan Page).

BMA Foundation for AIDS, Health Education Authority and Sex Education Forum (1997) *Using effectiveness research to guide the development of school sex education* (BMA Foundation for AIDS, London).

Bonnett, M. (1986) 'Personal authenticity and public standards: towards the transcendence of a dualism', in Cooper, D E (ed) *Education, Values and Mind. Essays for R S Peters* (Routledge and Kegan Paul, London).

Bonnett, M. (1994) *Children's Thinking. Promoting Understanding in the Primary School* (London: Cassell).

Bridges, D. (1986) 'Dealing with controversy in the school curriculum; a philosophical perspective', in Wellington, J J (ed) *Controversial Issues in the Curriculum* (Basil Blackwell, Oxford).

Bridges, D. (1997) 'Philosophy and Educational Research: a reconsideration of epistemological boundaries', *Cambridge Journal of Education*, 27(2), 177 − 189.

Bridges, D. (1998a) 'Educational Research: Re-establishing the Philosophical Terrain', in G. Haydon(ed.), 50Years of Philosophy of Education. Progress and Prospects. Bedford Way Papers (London: Institute of Education, University of London).

Bridges, D. (1998b) 'On Conceptual Analysis and Educational Research: a response to John Wilson'. *Cambridge Journal of Education*, 28(2), 239-241.

Bridges, D. (Ed.) (1997) *Education, autonomy and democratic citizenship. Philosophy in a changing world* (London, Routledge).

Bridges, D. and R. Jonathan (2003) 'Education and the Market', in *The Blackwell Guide to the Philosophy of Education*, ed. Nigel Blake, Paul Smeyers, Richard Smith, and Paul Standish (Oxford: Blackwell).

Brighouse, H. (2000) *Educational Equality and the New Selective Schooling* IMPACT No 3 (Philosophy of Education Society of Great Britain).

Brighouse, H. (2000) *School Choice and Social Justice* (Oxford: Oxford University Press).

Brighouse, H. (2004) *Justice* (Cambridge: Polity).

Brighouse, H. (2004) 'What's Wrong with Privatising Schools?', *Journal of Philosophy of Education* 38 (4): 617-31.

Brighouse, H. (2005) 'Faith-Based Schools in the United Kingdom: An Unenthusiastic Defense of a Slightly Reformed Status Quo', in *Faith Schools: Consensus or Conflict?* ed. Roy Gardner, Jo Cairns, and Denis Lawton (Abingdon: Routledge Falmer).

Broadfoot, P. (2000) 'Comparative education for the 21st century: retrospect and prospect', *Comparative Education*, 36(3), 357-371.

Brown, A. (1986) *Modern Political Philosophy: Theories of the Just Society* (Penguin, Harmondsworth).

Brown, R. (1987) *Analyzing Love*, Cambridge, Cambridge University Press.

Brown, S. & McIntyre, D. (1993) *Making Sense of Teaching* (Buckingham, Open University Press).

Brown, S. C. (1969) *Do religious claims make sense?* (SCM Press, London).

Brummer, V. (1993) 'Wittgenstein and the irrationality of rational theology', in J.M. Byrne (ed.), *The Christian understanding of God today*, pp. 88-102 (Columba Press, Dublin).

Burbules, N. (1996) 'Postmodern Doubt and Philosophy of Education', in A. Neiman (ed.), *Philosophy of Education* 1995 (Urbana Illinois: Philosophy of Education Society).

Burbules, N. C. & Warnick, B. R. (2004) 'Philosophical inquiry'. Available online at: www.cedu.nui.edu/epffoundations/CMRE_(final).htm (accessed 28 July 2004).

Burtt, S. (2003) 'Comprehensive Educations and the Liberal Understanding of Autonomy', in McDonough and Feinberg, *Citizenship and Education in Liberal-Democratic Societies*.

Calderhead, J. & Gates, P. (Eds) (1993) *Conceptualizing Reflection in Teacher Development* (London, The Falmer Press).

Calderhead, J. (1989) 'Reflective teaching and teacher education', *Teaching and Teacher Education* 5(1) pp. 43-51.

Callan, E. (1985) 'McLaughlin on parental rights', *Journal of Philosophy of Education*, 19, 1, pp 111-18.

Callan, E. (1988) 'Justice and denominational schooling', *Canadian Journal of Education*, 13, 3, pp 367-83.

Callan, E. (1989) 'Godless moral education and liberal tolerance', *Journal of Philosophy of Education*, 23, 2, pp 267-81.

Callan, E. (1991) 'Pluralism and civic education', *Studies in Philosophy and Education*, 11, 1, pp 65-87.

Callan, E. (1994) 'Beyond Sentimental Civic Education', *American Journal of Education* 102

Callan, E. (1997) *Creating Citizens. Political Education and Liberal Democracy* (Oxford: Clarendon Press).

Carlgren, I., Handal, G. & Vaage, S. (Eds) (1994) *Teachers', Minds and Actions. Research on Teachers' Thinking and Practice* (London, The Falmer Press).

Carr, D. (1986) 'Chastity and Adultery', *American Philosophical Quarterly* 23, 4.

Carr, D. (1991) *Educating the Virtues. An Essay on the Philosophical Psychology of Moral Development and Education* (London, Routledge).

Carr, D. (1995) 'Towards a distinctive conception of spiritual education', *Oxford Review of Education* 21, 1: 83-98.

Carr, D. (1996) 'Rival conceptions of spiritual education', *Journal of Philosophy of Education* 30, 2: 159-78.

Carr, D. (1998) 'Introduction: The Post-War Rise and Fall of Educational Epistemology', in D. Carr (ed.), *Education, Knowledge and Truth. Beyond the Postmodern Impasse* (London: Routledge)

Carr, D. (ed.) (1998) *Education, Knowledge and Truth. Beyond the Postmodern Impasse* (London: Routledge).

Carr, D., Haldane, J., McLaughlin, T., Pring, R. (1995) 'Return to the Crossroads: Maritain Fifty Years On', *British Journal of Educational Studies* XXXXIII, 2, 162-178.

Carr, W. & Kemmis, S. (1986) *Becoming Critical. Education, Knowledge and Action Research* (London, The Falmer Press).

Carr, W. (1991) 'Education for Citizenship', *British Journal of Educational Studies*, XXXIX(4), pp; 373-385.

Carr, W. (1991) 'Education for Democracy? A Philosophical Analysis of the National Curriculum', *Journal of Philosophy of Education*, 25(2), pp. 183-191.

Carr, W. (1995) *For Education. Towards Critical Educational Inquiry* (Buckingham, Open University Press).

Carr, W. (1995) 'Education and democracy: confronting the postmodernist challenge', *Journal of Philosophy of Education* 29(1) pp. 75-91.

Carr, W. (1997) 'Philosophy and Method in Educational Research'. *Cambridge Journal of Education,* 27(2), 203 – 209.

Catechism of the Catholic Church (1994) (London, Geoffrey Chapman).

Cave, P. (2001) 'Educational reform in Japan in the 1990's: "individuality" and other uncertainties', *Comparative Education*, 37(2), 173-191.

Chadwick, P. (1997) *Shifting Alliances. Church and State in English Education* (London: Cassell).

Chamberlin, R. (1989) *Free Children and Democratic Schools: A Philosophical Study of Liberty and Education* (Falmer Press, Lewes).

Christians in Education and The Order of Christian Unity (1988) *Towards a New Sexual Revolution. Guidance for Governors and Parents on Sex Education in Schools* (Cambridge and London, CIE and OCU).

Chubb, J. E., and T. M. Moe (1990) *Politics, Markets and America's Schools* (Washington, DC: Brookings).

Cochran, C. E. (1990) *Religion in Public and Private Life* (London, Routledge).

Codd, J. A. (1995) 'Educational Policy as a Field of Philosophical Enquiry'. Paper presented to the Annual Conference of the Philosophy of Education Society of Great Britain, Oxford.

Cohen, B. (1981) *Education and the Individual* (George Allen and Unwin, London).

Coles, R. (1992) *The Spiritual Life of Children*, London: HarperCollins.

Commission for Racial Equality (1990) *Schools of Faith. Religious Schools in a Multicultural Society* (CRE, London).

Cook, J. W. (1988) 'Wittgenstein and religious belief', *Philosophy* 63,427-452.

Coons, J. E. and Sugarman, S. D. (1978) *Education by Choice: the Case for Family Control* (University of California Press, Berkeley).

Cooper, D. E. (1986) 'Introduction', in: D. E. Cooper (Ed.) *Education, values and mind. Essays for R. S. Peters* (London, Routledge and Kegan Paul), 1-7.

Cooper, D. E. (1987) 'Multi-cultural education', in North, J (ed), *The GCSE: An Examination* (The Claridge Press, London).

Cooper, D. E. (1993) 'Truth and liberal education', in R. Barrow & P. White (eds.), *Beyond liberal education. Essays in honour of Paul H. Hirst*, pp. 30-48 (Routledge, London).

Cooper, D. E. (2003a) *World philosophies. An historical introduction* (2nd edn) (Oxford, Blackwell Publishing).

Cooper, D. E. (2003b) 'Postmodernism', in: R. Curren (Ed.) *A companion to the philosophy of education* (Oxford, Blackwell Publishing), 206-217.

Cooper, D. E. (ed) (1986) *Education, Values and Mind. Essays for R S Peters* (Routledge and Kegan Paul, London).

Copley, T. (2000) *Spiritual Development in the State School. A Perspective on Worship and Spirituality in the Education System of England and Wales* (Exeter: University of Exeter Press).

Cowdell, S. (1988) *Atheist Priest? Don Cupitt and Christianity* (London, SCM Press).

Cowen, R. (2000) 'Comparing futures or comparing pasts?', *Comparative Education*, 36(3), 333-342.

Cox, C, Douglas-Home, J., Marks, J., Norcross, L. & Scruton, R. (1986) *Whose Schools? A Radical Manifesto* (London, The Hillgate Group).

Cox, E. and Cairns, J. M. (1989) *Reforming Religious Education: The Religious Clauses of the 1988 Education Reform Act* (Kogan Page, London).

Crick, B. & Porter, A. (1978) *Political Education and Political Literacy* (London, Longman).

Crittenden, B. (1982) *Cultural Pluralism and Common Curriculum* (University Press, Melbourne).

Crittenden, B. (1988) *Parents, the State and the Right to Educate* (Melbourne University Press, Victoria).

Crossley, M. & Jarvis, P. (Eds) (2000) Special Issue. Comparative education for the twenty-first century, *Comparative Education*, 36(3).

Crossley, M. & Jarvis, P. (Eds) (2001) Special Issue. Comparative education for the twenty-first century: an international response, *Comparative Education*, 37(4).

Crossley, M. & Tikly, L. (Eds) (2004) Special Issue. Postcolonialism and comparative education, *Comparative Education*, 40(2).

Cupitt, D. (1980) *Taking Leave of God* (London, SCM Press).

Cupitt, D. (1984) *The Sea of Faith* (London, British Broadcasting Corporation).

Cupitt, D. (1995) *The Last Philosophy* (London. SCM Press).

Curren, R. (Ed.) (2003) *A companion to the philosophy of education* (Oxford, Blackwell Publishing).

Curren, R., Robertson, E. & Hager, P. (2003) 'The analytical movement', in: R. Curren (Ed.) A companion to the philosophy of education (Oxford, Blackwell Publishing), 176-191.

D'Agostino, F. (1998) 'Expertise, Democracy and Applied Ethics'. *Journal, of Applied Philosophy*, 15(1), 49-55.

Davies, J. (Ed.) (1993) *The Family: Is it Just Another Lifestyle Choice?* (London, IEA Health and Welfare Unit).

Davies, L., Harber, C. & Schweisfurth, M. (Eds) (2002) Special Issue. Democracy and authoritarianism in education, *Comparative Education*, 38(3).

Davis, A. (1999) *Educational Assessment: a critique of current policy* IMPACT No 1 (Philosophy of Education Society of Great Britain).

Dawes, H. (1992) *Freeing the faith. A credible Christianity for today* (SPCK, London).

Day, C. (1993) 'Reflection: a necessary but not sufficient condition for professional development', *British Educational Research Journal* 19(1) pp. 83-93.

De Marneff, P. (2002) 'Liberalism, Neutrality, and Education', in Macedo and Tamir, *Moral and Political Education*.

Deakin, R. (1989) *New Christian Schools: The Case for Public Funding* (Regius Press, Bristol).

Dearden, R. F. (1984) *Theory and Practice in Education* (London: Routledge and Kegan Paul).

DeMarco, J. P. (1997) 'Coherence and Applied Ethics', *Journal of Applied Philosophy*, 14(3), 289-300.

Dent, N. J. H. (1984) *The Moral Psychology of the Virtues* (Cambridge, Cambridge University Press).

Department of Education and Science (1977) *The Curriculum 11-16* (London: HMSO).

Deutsch, E. & Bontekoe, R. (Eds) (1997) *A companion to world philosophies* (Oxford, Blackwell).

Deutsch, E. (1997) Preface, in: E. Deutsch & R. Bontekoe (Eds) *A companion to world philosophies* (Oxford, Blackwell), xii-xiv.

Dewey, J. (1933) *How We Think. A Restatement of the Relation of Reflective Thinking To The Educative Process* (New York, D. C. Heath).

Dewey, J. (1934) *A Common Faith* (New Haven and London, Yale University Press).

Dominion, J. (1991) *Passionate and Compassionate Love. A Vision for Christian Marriage* (London, Darton, Longman and Todd).

Duncan, G. (1988) 'Church schools in service to the community', in O'Keeffe, B (ed) *Schools for Tomorrow: Building Walls or Building Bridges* (Falmer Press, Lewes).

Dunlop, F. (1996) 'Democratic Values and the Foundations of Political Education', in Halstead J. M. & Taylor M. J. (Eds) *Values in Education and Education in Values* (London: The Falmer Press).

Dunne, J. (1993) *Back to the Rough Ground: 'Phronesis' and 'Techne' in Modern Philosophy and in Aristotle* (Notre Dame IN, University of Notre Dame Press).

Dworkin, G. (1988) *The Theory and Practice of Autonomy* (University Press, Cambridge).

Dwyer, J. G. (2002) 'Changing the Conversation about Children's Education', in Macedo and Tamir, *Moral and Political Education*.

Edwards, J. & Fogelman, K. (1991) 'Active citizenship and young people', in: Ken Fogelman (Ed.) *Citizenship in Schools* (London, David Fulton).

Eisgruber, C. L. (2002) 'How Do Liberal Democracies Teach Values?', in Macedo and Tamir, *Moral and Political Education*.

Elliott, J. (1991) 'Competency-based training and the education of the professions: is a happy marriage possible?', in: J. Elliott (Ed.) *Action Research for Educational Change*(Open University Press: Milton Keynes)

Elliott, J. (1993) 'Three perspectives on coherence and continuity in teacher education', in: J. Elliott (Ed.) *Reconstructing Teacher Education: Teacher Development* (London, The Falmer Press).

Elliott, J. (1994) 'Clarifying Values in Schools'. *Cambridge Journal of Education*, 24(3), 413-422.

Elliott, R. K. (1986) 'Richard Peters: a philosopher in the older style', in: D. E. Cooper (Ed.) *Education, values and mind. Essays for R. S. Peters* (London, Routledge and Kegan Paul), 41-68.

Enslin, P. (1993/94) 'Education for Nation-building: Feminist Critique', *Perspectives in Education* 15, 1

Eraut, M. (1994) *Developing Professional Knowledge and Competence* (London, The Falmer Press).

Erricker, C. (2000) 'A critical review of spiritual education', in C. Erricker and J. Erricker (eds), *Reconstructing Religious, Spiritual and Moral Education* (London: Routledge Falmer).

Erricker, C. and Erricker, J. (eds) (2001) *Meditation in Schools. A Practical Guide to Calmer Classrooms* (London: Continuum).

Etzioni, A. (1993) *The Spirit of Community. Rights, Responsibilities and the Communitarian Agenda* (New York, Crown Publishers).

Evers, C. W. (1993) 'Analytic and Post-Analytic Philosophy of Education: Methodological Reflections', *Discourse: The Australian Journal of Educational Studies*, 13(2), 35–45.

Farnham, D. (1992) 'The Citizen's Charter: improving the quality of the public services or furthering market values?', *Talking Politics*, 4(2), pp. 75-80.

Feinberg, J. (1980) 'The child's right to an open future', in Aiken, W. and LaFollette, H. (eds) *Whose Child? Children's Rights, Parental Authority, and Stale Power* (Littlefield, Adams & Co, Totowa, New Jersey).

Feinberg, W. (1983) *Understanding Education. Toward a Reconstruction of Educational Inquiry* (Cambridge: Cambridge University Press).

Feinberg, W. (1993) *Japan and the pursuit of a new American identity. Work and education in a multicultural age* (New York, Routledge).

Feinberg, W. (1998) *Common Schools/Uncommon Identities. National Unity and Cultural Difference* (New Haven and London: Yale University Press).

Fielding, M. (1988) 'Democracy and fraternity: towards a new paradigm for the comprehensive school', in: Hugh Lauder & Phillip Brown (Eds) *Education: in search of a future* (London, The Falmer Press).

Fielding, M. (1999) 'Editorial: Taking Education Really Seriously: two years of hard labour'. *Cambridge Journal of Education*, 29(2), 173-181.

Fisher, D. (1982) 'Family choice and education: privatizing a public good', in Manley-Casimir, M E (ed) *Family Choice in Schooling: Issues and Dilemmas* (D C Heath, Lexington, Massachusetts).

Fitzmaurice, D. (1992) 'Liberal neutrality, religious minorities and education', in Horton, J (ed) *Liberalism, Multiculturalism and Toleration* (Macmillan, London).

Flew, A. (1968) 'Against indoctrination', in Ayer, A J (ed) *The Humanist Outlook* (Pemberton, London).

Flew, A. (1987) *Power to the Parents: Reversing Educational Decline* (The Sherwood Press, London).

Flew, A. (1997) 'What is 'spirituality'?', in L. Brown, B.C. Farr and R.J. Hoffman (eds), *Modern Spiritualities. An Inquiry* (Oxford: Prometheus Books).

Fogelman, K. (Ed.) (1991) *Citizenship in Schools* (London, David Fulton).

Foundation for the Family (1996) *The New Corinthians Curriculum* (Cincinatti, Ohio, Foundation for the Family).

Freeman, A. (1993) *God in us. A case for Christian humanism* (SCM Press, London).

Froebel, F. (1888) *The Education of Man*. Trans. W. N. Hailmann (New York: D. Appleton and Company).

Fukuyama, F. (1996) *Trust. The Social Virtues and the Creation of Prosperity* (Harmondsworth, Penguin Books).

Furlong, J. & Maynard, T. (1995) *Mentoring Student Teachers. The Growth of Professional Knowledge* (London, Routledge).

Furlong, J. (1992) 'Reconstructing professionalism: ideological struggle in initial teacher education', in: M. Arnot & L. Barton (Eds) *Voicing Concerns: Sociological Perspectives on Contemporary Education Reforms* (Wallingford, Triangle Books).

Furlong, V. J., Hirst, P. H., Pocklington, K. & Miles, S. (1988) *Initial Teacher Training and the Role of the School* (Milton Keynes, Open University Press).

Galston, W. (1989) 'Civic education in the liberal state', in: Nancy L. Rosenblum (Ed.) *Liberalism and the Moral Life* (Cambridge, MA, Harvard University Press).

Galston, W. (1991) *Liberal Purposes. Goods, Virtues, and Diversity in the Liberal State* (Cambridge, University Press).

Galston, W. A. (2002) *Liberal Pluralism: The Implications of Value Pluralism for Political Theory and Practice* (Cambridge: Cambridge University Press).

Gardner, P (1988) 'Religious upbringing and the liberal ideal of religious autonomy', *Journal of Philosophy of Education*, 22, 1, pp 89-105.

Gardner, P (1991) 'Personal autonomy and religious upbringing: the "problem"', *Journal of Philosophy of Education*, 25, 1, pp 69-81.

Geuss, R. (2001) *Public Goods, Private Goods* (Princeton, NJ: Princeton University Press).

Gibson, R. (ed) (1986) *Liberal Education Today?* (Institute of Education, Cambridge).

Giddens, A. (1992) *The Transformation of Intimacy. Sexuality, Love and Eroticism in Modern Societies* (Cambridge, Polity Press).

Gilroy, P. (1993) 'Reflections on Schön: an epistemological critique and a practical alternative', in: P. Gilroy & M. Smith (Eds.) *International Analyses of Teacher Education*, JET Papers One (Oxford, Carfax).

Glenn, C. L. (2003) 'Protecting and Limiting School Distinctiveness: How Much of Each?', in Wolfe, *School Choice*.

Godfrey, R. (1984) 'John White and the imposition of autonomy', *Journal of Philosophy of Education*, 18, 1, pp 115-18.

Gordon, P. and White, J. (1979) *Philosophers as Educational Reformers. The Influence of Idealism on British Educational Thought and Practice* (London: Routledge and Kegan Paul).

Grace, G. (1994) 'Education Is a Public Good: On the Need to Resist the Domination of Economic Science', in *Education and the Market Place*, ed. David Bridges and Terence H. McLaughlin (London: Falmer).

Grant, N. (2000) 'Tasks for comparative education in the new millennium', *Comparative Education*, 36(3), 309-317.

Great Britain Parliament House of Commons (1985) *Education for All: The Report of the Committee of Inquiry into the Education of Children from Ethnic Minority Groups* (The Swann Report) Cmnd 9453 (London, HMSO).

Great Britain Parliament House of Commons (1990) *Encouraging Citizenship. Report of the Commission on Citizenship* (London, HMSO).

Green, A. (2000) 'Converging paths or ships passing in the night? An "English" critique of Japanese school reform', *Comparative Education*, 36(4), 417-435.

Gregory, P. (1995) 'Love and Personal Relationships', in Almond, B. (Ed.) *Introducing Applied Ethics* (Oxford, Blackwell).

Griffiths, M. & Tann, S. (1992) 'Using reflective practice to link personal and public theories', *Journal of Education for Teaching*, 18(1) pp. 69-84.

Griffiths, M. (1997) 'Why Teachers and Philosophers Need Each Other: philosophy and educational research', *Cambridge Journal of Education*, 27(2), 191 – 202.

Griffiths, M. (1999) 'Aiming for a Fair Education: What Use is Philosophy?', in R. Marples (ed.), *The Aims of Education* (London: Routledge).

Groome, T. H. (1998) *Educating for Life. A Spiritual Vision for Every Teacher and Parent* (Allen, Texas: Thomas More).

Gutmann, A. (1985) 'Communitarian critics of liberalism', *Philosophy and Public Affairs*, 14, 3, pp 308-22.

Gutmann, A. (1987) *Democratic Education* (Princeton NJ, Princeton University Press)

Gutmann, A. (1989) 'Undemocratic education', in: Nancy L. Rosenblum (Ed.) *Liberalism and the Moral Life* (Cambridge, MA, Harvard University Press).

Gutmann, A. (1992) 'Introduction', in Taylor, C *Multiculturalism and 'The Politics of Recognition'* (Princeton NJ, Princeton University Press)

Gutmann, A. (1993) 'Democracy & Democratic Education', *Studies in Philosophy and Education* 12, 1

Gutmann, A. (1995) 'Civic Education and Social Diversity', *Ethics* 105: 557-79.

Gutmann, A. (2002) 'Can Publicly Funded Schools Legitimately Teach Values in a Constitutional Democracy? A Reply to McConnell and Eisgruber', in Macedo and Tamir, *Moral and Political Education*.

Gutmann, A. (2002) 'Civic Minimalism, Cosmopolitanism, and Patriotism: Where Does Democratic Education Stand in Relation to Each?', in Macedo and Tamir, *Moral and Political Education*.

Gutmann, A. (2003) 'Assessing Arguments for School Choice: Pluralism, Parental Rights or Educational Results?', in Wolfe, *School Choice*.

Hadot, P. (1995) *Philosophy as a Way of Life. Spiritual Exercises from Socrates to Foucault* (Oxford: Blackwell).

Halbertal, M. & Halbertal, T. H. (1998) 'The Yeshiva', in: A. Oksenberg Rorty (Ed.) *Philosophers on education: New historical perspectives* (London, Routledge), 458-469.

Haldane, J (1985) 'Individuals and the theory of justice', *Ratio*, XXVII, pp 189-96.

Haldane, J (1991) 'Political theory and the nature of persons: an ineliminable metaphysical presupposition', *Philosophical Papers*, XX, 2, pp 77-95.

Haldane, J (1991) 'Identity, community and the limits of multiculture', paper presented to meeting on 'Identity, Community and Culture', Centre for Philosophy and Public Affairs, University of St Andrews, December 1991.

Haldane, J. (1999) 'The need of spirituality in Catholic education', in J.C. Conroy (ed.), *Catholic Education: Inside-Out/Outside-In* (Dublin: Veritas).

Haldane, J. (2000) 'On the very idea of spiritual values', in A. O'Hear (ed.), *Philosophy, the Good and the Beautiful* (Cambridge: Cambridge University Press).

Haller, E. J. and Strike, K. A. (1997) *An Introduction to Educational Administration. Social, Legal and Ethical Perspectives* (Troy NY: Educator's International Press).

Halstead, . M. (1991) 'Radical feminism, Islam and the single-sex school debate', *Gender and Education*, 3, 3, pp 263-78.

Halstead, J. M. (1986) *The Case for Muslim Voluntary-Aided Schools. Some Philosophical Reflections* (The Islamic Academy, Cambridge).

Halstead, J. M. (1988) *Education, Justice and Cultural Diversity: An Examination of the Honeyford Affair, 1984-85* (Falmer Press, Lewes).

Halstead, J. M. (1994) 'Moral and Spiritual Education in Russia', *Cambridge Journal of Education* 24, 3

Halstead, J. M. (1997) 'Muslims and Sex Education', *Journal of Moral Education* 26, 3, pp. 317-330.

Halstead, J. M. and Lewicka, K. (1998) 'Should Homosexuality be Taught as an Acceptable Alternative Lifestyle? A Muslim Perspective', *Cambridge Journal of Education* 28, 1, pp. 49-64.

Halstead, J. M. and T. McLaughlin (2005) 'Are Faith Schools Divisive?', in *Faith Schools: Consensus or Conflict?* ed. Roy Gardner, Jo Cairns, and Denis Lavrton (Abingdon: Routledge Falmer).

Halstead, J. M. and Taylor, M. J. (Ed.) (1996) *Values in Education and Education in Values* (London, The Falmer Press).

Hamilton, H. A. (1952) 'The religious roots of Froebel's philosophy'. In E. Lawrence (ed.), *Friedrich Froebel and English Education* (London: University of London Press).

Hamlyn, D. (1989) 'Education and Wittgenstein's philosophy', *Journal of Philosophy of Education* 23, 213-222.

Hamm, C. (1982) 'Constraints on parents' rights concerning the education of their children', in Manley-Casimir M E (ed) *Family Choice in Schooling: Issues and Dilemmas* (D C Heath, Lexington, Massachusetts).

Hammersley, M. (1997) 'Educational Research and Teaching: a response to David Hargreaves' TTA Lecture', *British Educational Research Journal*, 23(2), 141-161.

Hampshire, S. (1983) *Morality and Conflict* (Basil Blackwell, Oxford).

Hampshire, S. (Ed.) (1978) *Public and Private Morality* (Cambridge, University Press).

Hannon, P. (1992) *Church, State, Morality and Law* (Dublin, Gill and Macmillan).

Hansen, D. T. (1996) 'Finding One's Way Home: Notes on the Texture of Moral Experience', *Studies in Philosophy and Education* 15, 3, pp. 221-233.

Hanson, K. (1993) 'Reconstruction in Pragmatism', *Synthese* 94, 13-23.

Harber, C. (2002) 'Education, democracy and poverty reduction in Africa', *Comparative Education*, 38(3), 267-276.

Hare, W. (1993) *What Makes a Good Teacher. Reflections on Some Characteristics Central to the Educational Enterprise* (London Ontario, The Althouse Press).

Hargreaves, D. H. (1993) 'A common-sense model of the professional development of teachers', in: J. Elliott (Ed.) *Reconstructing Teacher Education: Teacher Development* (London, The Falmer Press).

Hargreaves, D. H. (1996) *Teaching as a Research-based Profession: Possibilities and Prospects. Teacher Training Agency Annual Lecture 1996* (London: Teacher Training Agency).

Hargreaves, D. H. (1997) 'In Defence of Research for Evidence-based teaching: a rejoinder to Martyn Hammersley'. *British Educational Research*, 23(4), 405-419.

Hargreaves, D. H. (1999) 'The Knowledge-Creating School'. *British Journal of Educational Studies*, 47(2), 122-144.

Harman, G. and Jarvis Thomson, J. (1996) *Moral Relativism and Moral Objectivity* (Oxford, Blackwell).

Harris, J. (1982) 'A paradox of multicultural societies', *Journal of Philosophy of Education*, 16, 2, pp 223-33.

Hart, D. A. (1993) *Faith in doubt. Non-realism and Christian belief* (Mowbray, London).

Hartnett, A. and Naish, M. (1986) '"The Values of a Free Society" and the Politics of Educational Studies', in A. Hartnett and M. Naish (eds), *Education and Society Today* (Lewes: Falmer Press).

Harvey, I. (Ed.) (1993) *Condoms Across the Curriculum* (Cambridge, Daniels Publishing).

Hauerwas, S. (1981) *A Community of Character. Toward a Constructive Christian Social Ethic* (Notre Dame, University of Notre Dame Press).

Haworth, L. (1986) *Autonomy: An Essay in Philosophical Psychology and Ethics* (Yale University Press, New Haven and London).

Hay, D. with Nye, R. (1998) *The Spirit of the Child* (London: Fount).

aydon, G. (1986) 'Collective moral philosophy and education for pluralism', *Journal of Philosophy of Education*, 20(1), pp. 97-106.

Haydon, G. (Ed.) (1987) *Education for a Pluralist Society. Philosophical Perspectives on the Swann Report*, Bedford Way Papers 30 (London, Institute of Education, University of London).

Haydon, G. (1987) 'Towards a framework of commonly accepted values', in: Graham Haydon (Ed.) *Education for a Pluralist Society. Philosophical Perspectives on the Swann Report*, Bedford Way Papers 30 (London, Institute of Education, University of London).

Haydon, G. (1994) 'Conceptions of the Secular in Society, Polity and Schools', *Journal of Philosophy of Education* 28, 1, pp. 65-75.

Haydon, G. (1995) 'Thick or Thin? The Cognitive Content of Moral Education in a Plural Democracy', *Journal of Moral Education* 24, 1, pp. 53-64.

Haydon, G. (1997) *Teaching about Values: A New Approach* (London, Cassell).

Haydon, G. (Ed.) (1998) *50 years of philosophy of education. Progress and prospects*, Bedford Way Papers (London, University of London Institute of Education).

Health Education Authority (1994) *Sex Education, Values and Morality* (London, Health Education Authority).

Heater, D. (1990) *Citizenship: the civic ideal in world history, politics and education* (London, Longman).

Hebblethwaite, B. (1988) *The Ocean of Truth. A Defence of Objective Theism* (Cambridge, Cambridge University Press).

Henley, K. (1979) 'The authority to educate', in O'Neill and Ruddick (eds) *Having Children: Philosophical and Legal Reflections on Parenthood* (University Press, Oxford).

Hepburn, R. W. (1987) 'Attitudes to evidence and argument in the field of religion', in R. Straughan & J. Wilson (eds.), *Philosophers on education*, pp. 127-146 (Macmillan, London).

Hepburn, R.W. (1992) 'Religious imagination', in M. McGhee (ed.), *Philosophy, religion and the spiritual life*, pp. 127-144 (Cambridge University Press, Cambridge).

Hepburn, R. (2000) 'Values and cosmic imagination', in A. O'Hear (ed.), *Philosophy, the Good and the Beautiful* (Cambridge: Cambridge University Press).

Her Majesty's Chief Inspector of Schools in England (1992) *Framework for the Inspection of Schools: Paper for Consultation* (London, Department for Education).

Heyting, F., Lenzen, D. & White, J. (Eds) (2001) *Methods in philosophy of education* (London, Routledge).

Hick, J. (1999) *The Fifth Dimension. An Exploration of the Spiritual Realm* (Oxford: Oneworld Publications).

Hirst, P. H. (1970) 'Philosophy and religious education: A reply to D.Z. Phillips', *British Journal of Educational Studies* 18,213-215.

Hirst, P. H. (1972) 'Christian education: A contradiction in terms?', *Learning for Living* 11,4,6-11.

Hirst, P. H. (1974) *Knowledge and the Curriculum. A collection of philosophical papers* (Routledge and Kegan Paul, London).

Hirst, P. H. (1974) *Moral Education in a Secular Society* (Hodder and Stoughton, London).

Hirst, P. H. (1979) 'Professional studies in initial teacher education', in: R. Alexander & E. Wormald (Eds) *Professional Studies for Teaching* (Guildford, Society for Research in Higher Education).

Hirst, P. H. (1981) 'Education, catechesis and the church school', *British Journal of Religious Education*, Spring, pp 85-93, 101.

Hirst, P. H. (1983) 'Educational theory', in: P. H. Hirst (Ed.) *Educational Theory and its Foundation Disciplines* (London, Routledge & Kegan Paul).

Hirst, P. H. (1984) 'Philosophy of education', in Sutcliffe J M (ed) *A Dictionary of Religious Education* (SCM Press, London).

Hirst, P. H. (1985) 'Education and diversity of belief', in Felderhof, M C (ed) *Religious Education in a Pluralistic Society* (Hodder and Stoughton, London).

Hirst, P. H. (1986) 'Richard Peters's contribution to the philosophy of education', in: D. E. Cooper (Ed.) *Education, values and mind. Essays for R. S. Peters* (London, Routledge and Kegan Paul), 8-40.

Hirst, P. H. (1990) 'The theory-practice relationship in teacher training', in: M. Booth, J. Furlong & M. Wilkin (Eds) *Partnership in Initial Teacher Training* (London, Cassell).

Hirst, P. H. (1990) 'Internship: a view from outside', in: P. Benton (Ed.) *The Oxford Internship Scheme: Integration and Partnership in Initial Teacher Education* (London, Calouste Gulbenkenian Foundation).

Hirst, P. H. (1993a) 'Education, Knowledge And Practices', in R. Barrow And P. White (Eds), *Beyond Liberal Education. Essays In Honour Of Paul H. Hirst* (London: Routledge).

Hirst, P. H. (1993) 'The Foundations Of The National Curriculum: Why Subjects?', in P. O'hear And J. White (Eds,) *Assessing The National Curriculum* (London: Paul Chapman).

Hirst, P. H. (1998) 'Philosophy of education: the evolution of a discipline', in: G. Haydon (Ed.) *50 years of philosophy of education. Progress and prospects*, Bedford Way Papers (London, Institute of Education, University of London), 1-22.

Hirst, P. H. and White, P. (1998a) 'The Analytic Tradition and Philosophy of Education: An Historical Perspective', in P. H. Hirst and P. White (eds), (1998) *Philosophy of Education: Major Themes in the Analytic Tradition. Volume 1* (London: Routledge).

Hirst, P. H. and White, P. (eds) (1998b) *Philosophy of Education: Major Themes in the Analytic Tradition* (4 volumes) (London: Routledge).

Hobson, P. (1984) 'Some reflections on parents' rights in the upbringing of their children', *Journal of Philosophy of Education*, 18, 1, pp 63-74.

Hobson, P. R. and Edwards, J. S. (1999) *Religious Education in a Pluralist Society. The Key Philosophical Issues* (London: Woburn Press).

Hogan, P. (1995) *Partnership and the Benefits of Learning. A Symposium on Philosophical Issues in Educational Policy* (Maynooth: Educational Studies Association of Ireland).

Holland, J., Ramazanoglu, C, Scott, S., Sharpe, S. and Thomson, R. (1991) *Pressure, Resistance, Empowerment: Young Women and the Negotiation of Safer Sex*, WRAP, Women, Risk and AIDS Project, Paper 6 (London, The Tufnell Press).

Hollis, M. (1977) 'The self in action', in: R. S. Peters (Ed.) *John Dewey Reconsidered* (London, Routledge & Kegan Paul).

Hollis, M. (1989) 'Atomic energy and moral glue', *Journal of Philosophy of Education*, 23(2), pp. 185-193.

Hollis, M. (1992) 'Friends, Romans and consumers', in: David Milligan & William Watts Miller (Eds) *Liberalism, Citizenship and Autonomy* (Aldershot, Avebury).

Hudson, W. D. (1973) 'Is religious education possible?', in G. Langford & D.J. O'Connor (eds.), *New essays in the philosophy of education*, pp. 167-196 (Routledge and Kegan Paul, London).

Hudson, W. D. (1975) *Wittgenstein and religious belief* (Macmillan, London).

Hudson, W. D. (1982) 'Educating, socialising and indoctrination: A reply to Tasos Kazepides', *Journal of Philosophy of Education* 16, 167-172.

Hudson, W. D. (1987) 'Two questions about religious education', in R. Straughan & J. Wilson (eds.) *Philosophers on education*, pp. 109-126, Macmillan, London.

Hull, J. (1984) *Studies in Religion and Education* (Falmer Press, Lewes).

Hull, J. (1996) 'The ambiguity of spiritual values', in J.M. Halstead and M.J. Taylor (eds), *Values in Education and Education in Values* (London: Falmer Press).

Hume, B. (1995) 'A Note on the Teaching of the Catholic Church Concerning Homosexual People', *Briefing*, 16 March, pp. 3-5.

Ichilov, O. (Ed.) (1988) *Citizenship and citizenship education in a changing world* (London, Woburn Press).

Ignatieff, M. (1994) *Blood and Belonging. Journeys into the New Nationalism* (London, Vintage)

Isaacs, D. (1984) *Character Building. A Guide for Parents and Teachers* (Blackrock, Four Courts Press).

Jackson, R. (1992) 'The misrepresentation of religious education', in M. Leicester & M. Taylor (eds.), *Ethics, ethnicity and education*, pp. 100-113 (Kogan Page, London).

Johnson, D. (1990) *Parental Choice in Education* (Unwin Hyman, London).

Jonathan, R. (1985) 'Education, Philosophy of Education and Context', *Journal of Philosophy of Education*, 19(1), 13-25.

Jonathan, R. (1997) *Illusory Freedoms: Liberalism, Education and the Market* (Oxford: Blackwell).

Jones, A. (2002) Politics and history curriculum reform in post-Mao China, *International Journal of Educational Research*, 37, 545-566.

Jones, C., Wainwright, G. and Yarnold, E. (eds) (1992) *The Study of Spirituality* (London: SPCK).

Jones, R. (1989) 'Sex Education in Personal and Social Education', in White, P. (Ed.), *Personal and Social Education: Philosophical Perspectives* (The Bedford Way Series, London, Kogan Page in association with The Institute of Education, University of London).

Jover, G. (2001) 'Philosophy of education in Spain at the threshold of the 21st century — origins, political contexts and prospects', *Studies in Philosophy and Education*, 20(4), 361-385.

Karjohn, L. (1989) 'Annotated bibliography', in White, P (ed) *Personal and Social Education: Philosophical Perspectives* (Kogan Page, London).

Kazepides, T. (1982) 'Educating, socialising and indoctrinating', *Journal of Philosophy of Education* 16, 155-165.

Kazepides, T. (1991) 'On the prerequisites of moral education: A Wittgensteinian perspective', *Journal of Philosophy of Education* 25, 259-272.

Kazepides, T. (1991) 'Religious indoctrination and freedom', in B. Spiecker & R. Straughan (eds.), *Freedom and indoctrination in education. International perspectives*, pp. 5-15 (Cassell, London).

Keightley, A. (1976) *Wittgenstein, grammar and God* (Epworth Press, London).

Kekes, J. (1988) *The Examined Life* (Associated University Presses, London).

Kekes, J. (1989) *Moral Tradition and Individuality* (University Press, Princeton, New Jersey).

Kekes, J. (1993) *The Morality of Pluralism* (Princeton, Princeton University Press).

Kelly, K. T. (1998) *New Directions in Sexual Ethics. Moral Theology and the Challenge of AIDS* (London, Geoffrey Chapman).

Kemmis, S. (1995) 'Some ambiguities in Stenhouse's notion of "the teacher as researcher": towards a new resolution', in: J. Rudduck (Ed.) *An Education That Empowers. A Collection of Lectures in Memory of Lawrence Stenhouse* (Clevedon, Multilingual Matters).

Kerr, F. (1986) *Theology after Wittgenstein* (Basil Blackwell, Oxford).

Kohli, W. (1991) 'Humanizing Education in the Soviet Union: A Plea for Caution in 'These Postmodern Times', *Studies in Philosophy and Education* 11, 1

Kohli, W. (Ed.) (1995) *Critical conversations in philosophy of education* (London, Routledge).

Kymlicka, W. (1989) *Liberalism, Community, and Culture* (Clarendon Press, Oxford).

Kymlicka, W. (1990) *Contemporary Political Philosophy: An Introduction* (Clarendon Press, Oxford).

LaBoskey, V. K. (1994) *Development of Reflective Practice. A Study of Preservice Teachers* (New York, Teachers College Press).

LaFollette, H. (1996) *Personal Relationships. Love, Identity, and Morality* (Oxford, Blackwell).

Lambourn, D. (1996) '"Spiritual" minus "personal-social" = ?: a critical note on an "empty" category', in R. Best (ed.), *Education, Spirituality and the Whole Child* (London: Cassell).

Langford, G. (1979) 'Education is of the whole man', *Journal of Philosophy of Education*, **13**, 65-72.

Langford, G. (1985) *Education, Persons and Society: A Philosophical Enquiry* (London: Macmillan).

Leicester, M. & Taylor, M. (Eds) (1992) *Ethics, Ethnicity and Education* (London, Kogan Page).

Leicester, M. (1986) 'Collective moral philosophy and education for pluralism: a reply to Graham Haydon', *Journal of Philosophy of Education*, 20(2), pp. 251-255.

Lencz, L. (1994) 'The Slovak Ethical Education Project', *Cambridge Journal of Education* 24, 3

Levin, H. M. (2001) 'Studying Privatization in Education', in *Privatizing Education: Can the Marketplace Deliver Choice, Efficiency, Equity and Social Cohesion?* ed. Henry M. Levin (Boulder, CO: Westview).

Levin, M. A. (1985) 'Ways of life, citizenship education, and the culture of schooling', in: David Nyberg (Ed.) *Philosophy of Education 1985: Proceedings of the forty-first annual meeting of the Philosophy of Education Society* (Normal, Illinois, Philosophy of Education Society, Illinois State University).

Levinson, M. (1999) *The Demands of Liberal Education* (Oxford: Oxford University Press).

Levinson, M. and S. Levinson (2003) '"Getting religion": Religion, Diversity, and Community in Public and Private Schools', in Wolfe, *School Choice*.

Lewis, C. S. (1960) *The Four Loves* (London, Geoffrey Bles).

Li, B. (1993) 'Moral Education in Transition: The Values Conflict in China', *Studies in Philosophy and Education* 12, 1

Lickona, T. (1996) 'Eleven Principles of Effective Character Education', *Journal of Moral Education* 25, 1, pp. 93-100.

Lloyd, D. I. (1980) 'The rational curriculum: a critique', *Journal of Curriculum Studies*, 12, 4, pp 331-42.

Lloyd, I. (1986) 'Confession and reason', *British Journal of Religious Education*, 8, pp 140-5.

Luntley, M. (2000) *Performance, Pay and Professionals* IMPACT No 2 (Philosophy of Education Society of Great Britain).

Macedo, S. (1990) *Liberal Virtues: citizenship, virtue, and community in liberal constitutionalism* (Oxford, Clarendon Press).

Macedo, S. (2000) *Diversity and Distrust. Civic Education in a Multicultural Democracy* (Cambridge, MA and London: Harvard University Press).

Macedo, S. (2003) 'Equity and School Choice: How Can We Bridge the Gap between ideals and Realities?', in Wolfe, cd., *School Choice*.

Macedo, S. and Y. Tamir, eds. (2002) *Moral and Political Education*. Nomos 43 (New York: New York University Press).

MacIntyre, A. (1981) *After Virtue: a Study in Moral Theory* (Duckworth, London).

MacIntyre, A. (1987) 'The idea of an educated public', in Haydon, G (ed) *Education and Values: The Richard Peters Lectures* (Institute of Education, University of London, London).

MacIntyre, A. (1988) *Whose Justice? Which Rationality?* (London, Duckworth).

MacIntyre, A. (1990) *Three Rival Versions of Moral Enquiry: Encyclopaedia, Genealogy and Tradition* (Duckworth, London).

MacIntyre, A. (1998) 'Aquinas's critique of education: against his own age, against ours', in: A. Oksenberg Rorty (Ed.) *Philosophers on education. New historical perspectives* (London, Routledge), 95-108.

Mackie, J. L. (1965) 'Causes and conditions', *American Philosophical Quarterly* 2,245-264.

Mackie, J. L. (1982) *The miracle of theism. Arguments for and against the existence of God* (Clarendon Press, Oxford).

MacMurray, J. (1965) *Search for Reality in Religion. The Swarthmore Lecture 1965* (London, Friends Home Service Committee).

Malcolm, N. (1993) *Wittgenstein: A religious point of view?* (Routledge, London).

Manley-Casimir, M. E. (ed) (1982) *Family Choice in Schooling: Issues and Dilemmas* (D C Heath, Lexington, Massachusetts).

Marenbon, J. (1996) *A Moral Maze: government values in education* (London, Politeia).

Marples, R. (1978) 'Is religious education possible?', *Journal of Philosophy of Education* 12, 81-91.

Marshall, J. D. (Ed.) (2000) Special Issue. Education and cultural difference, *Educational Philosophy and Theory*, 32(1).

Marshall, T. H. (1950) *Citizenship and Social Class and Other Essays* (Cambridge, University Press).

358 *Liberalism, Education and Schooling*

Martin Soskice, J. (1985), *Metaphor and Religious Language* (Oxford, Clarendon Press).

Martin Soskice, J. (1987) 'Theological Realism', in Abraham, W.J. & Holtzer, S.W. (Eds), *The Rationality of Religious Belief. Essays in Honour of Basil Mitchell* (Oxford, Clarendon Press).

Martin, D. M. (1987) 'Learning to become a Christian', *Religious Education* 82, 94-114.

Martin, T. J. (2003) 'Divergent ontologies with converging conclusions: a case study comparison of comparative methodologies', *Comparative Education*, 39(1), 105-117.

Masolo, D. A. (1997) 'African philosophy: an overview', in: E. Deutsch & R. Bontekoe (Eds) *A companion to world philosophies* (Oxford, Blackwell), 63-77.

Matthews, U. (1980) 'Ritual and the Religious Feelings', in Rorty, A.O. (Ed), *Explaining Emotions* (Berkeley, University of California Press).

May, S. & Aikman, S. (Eds) (2003) Special Issue. Indigenous education: new possibilities, ongoing constraints, *Comparative Education*, 39(2).

McClelland, V. A. (ed) (1988) *Christian Education in a Pluralist Society* (Routledge, London).

McConnell, M. W. (2002) 'Educational Disestablishment: Why Democratic Values Are Served by Democratic Control of Schooling', in Macedo and Tamir, eds., *Moral and Political Education.*

McDermott, T. (Ed.) (1989) *St Thomas Aquinas. Summa Theologiae. A Concise Translation* (London, Methuen).

McDonough, K. and Feinberg, W., eds. (2003) *Citizenship and Education in Liberal-Democratic Societies: Teaching for Cosmopolitan Values and Collective Identities* (Oxford: Oxford University Press).

McGhee, M. (2000) *Transformations of Mind. Philosophy as Spiritual Practice* (Cambridge: Cambridge University Press).

McGrath, A. E. (1999) *Christian Spirituality. An Introduction* (Oxford: Blackwell).

McGuinness, B. (1988) *Wittgenstein: A life. Young Ludwig 1889-1921* (Duckworth, London).

McIntyre, D. (1990) 'The Oxford Internship scheme and the Cambridge Analytical Framework: models of partnership in initial teacher education', in: M. Booth, J. Furlong & M. Wilkin (Eds) *Partnership in Initial Teacher Training* (London, Cassell).

McIntyre, D. (1993) 'Theory, theorizing and reflection in initial teacher education', in: J. Calderhead & P. Gates (Eds) *Conceptualizing Reflection in Teacher Development* (London, The Falmer Press).

McKay, A. (1997) 'Accommodating Ideological Pluralism in Sexuality Education', *Journal of Moral Education* 26, 3, pp. 285-300.

McLaughlin, T. H. (1984) 'Parental rights and the religious upbringing of children', *Journal of Philosophy of Education,* 18, 1 pp 75-83.

McLaughlin, T. H. (1985) 'Religion, upbringing and liberal values: a rejoinder to Eamonn Callan', *Journal of Philosophy of Education,* 19, 1, pp 119-27.

McLaughlin, T. H. (1987) '"Education for All" and religious schools', in Haydon, G (ed) *Education for a Pluralist Society. Philosophical Perspectives on the Swann Report*, Bedford Way Papers 30 (London, Institute of Education, University of London).

McLaughlin, T. H. (1990) 'Peter Gardner on religious upbringing and the liberal ideal of religious autonomy', *Journal of Philosophy of Education*, 24, 1, pp 107-25.

McLaughlin, T. H. (1991) 'Ethos, community and the school', paper presented to meeting on 'Identity, Community and Culture', Centre for Philosophy and Public Affairs, University of St Andrews, December 1991.

McLaughlin, T. H. (1992) 'Citizenship, Diversity and Education: a philosophical perspective', *Journal of Moral Education* 21, 3

McLaughlin, T. H. (1992) 'The Ethics of Separate Schools', in Leicester, M. and Taylor, M.J. (Ed.) *Ethics, Ethnicity and Education* (London, Kogan Page).

McLaughlin, T. H. (1994a) 'The scope of parents' educational rights', in J. M. Halstead (ed.), *Parental Choice and Education. Principles, Policy and Practice* (London: Kogan Page).

McLaughlin, T. H. (1994b) 'Values, coherence and the school'. *Cambridge Journal of Education*, **24** (3), 453-70.

McLaughlin, T. H. (1994c) 'Politics, Markets and School: The Central Issues', in *Education and the Market Place*, ed. David Bridges and Terence H. McLaughlin (London: Falmer).

McLaughlin, T. H. (1994d) Mentoring and the demands of reflection, in: M. Wilkin & D. Sankey (Eds) *Collaboration and Transition in Initial Teacher Training* (London, Kogan Page).

McLaughlin, T. H. (1995a) 'Public values, private values and educational responsibility'. In E. Pybus and T. H. McLaughlin (eds), *Values, Education and Responsibility* (Centre for Philosophy and Public Affairs, Department of Moral Philosophy, University of St Andrews).

McLaughlin, T. H. (1995b) 'Liberalism, education and the common school'. In Y. Tamir (ed.), *Democratic Education in a Multicultural State* (Oxford: Blackwell).

McLaughlin, T. H. (1995c) 'Wittgenstein, education and religion', in P. Smeyers and J. Marshall (eds), *Philosophy and Education: Accepting Wittgenstein's Challenge* (Dordrecht: Kluwer Academic Publishers).

McLaughlin, T. H. (1996) 'Education of the Whole Child?', in Best, R. (Ed.) *Education, Spirituality and the Whole Child* (London, Cassell).

McLaughlin, T. H. (1996) 'The Distinctiveness of Catholic Education', in McLaughlin, T.H., O'Keefe, J. and O'Keeffe, B. (Ed.) *The Contemporary Catholic School: Context, Identity and Diversity* (London, The Falmer Press).

McLaughlin, T. H. (1999) 'A Response to Professor Bridges', in D. Carr (ed.), *Values in the Curriculum* (Aberdeen: Gordon Cook Foundation).

McLaughlin, T. H. (1999a) 'Beyond the Reflective Teacher'. *Educational Philosophy and Theory*, 31(1), 9-25.

McLaughlin, T. H. (2000) 'Philosophy and educational policy: Possibilities, tensions and tasks', *Journal of Educational Policy*, 15(4), 441-457.

McLaughlin, T. H. (2003) 'The Burdens and Dilemmas of Common Schooling', in McDonough and Feinberg, *Citizenship and Education in Liberal-Democratic Societies.*

360   *Liberalism, Education and Schooling*

McLaughlin, T. H. (2003) 'Teaching Controversial Issues in Citizenship Education', in *Education for Democratic Citizenship: Issues of Theory and Practice*, ed. 'Andrew Lockyer, Bernard Crick, and John Annette (Aldershot: Ashgate).

McLaughlin, T. H. (2004) 'Philosophy, Values and Schooling: Principles and Predicaments of Teacher Example', in *Philosophy and Its Public Role: Essays in Ethics*, Politics, Society and Culture, ed. William Aiken and John Haldane. St. Andrews Studies in Philosophy and Public Affairs (Exeter, UK & Charlottesville, VA: Imprint Academic).

McLaughlin, T. H. (2004) 'Teaching as a Practice and a Community of Practice: The Limits of Diversity and the Demands of Diversity', in *Education and Practice: Upholding the Integrity of Teaching and Learning*, ed. Joseph Dunne and Padraig Hogan (Oxford: Blackwell).

McLaughlin, T. H. and Halstead, J. M. (2000) 'John Wilson on Moral Education', *Journal of Moral Education*.

Mendus, S. (1989) *Toleration and the Limits of Liberalism* (Macmillan, London).

Mendus, S. (1992) 'Strangers and brothers: liberalism, socialism and the concept of autonomy', in: David Milligan & William Watts Miller (Eds) *Liberalism, Citizenship and Autonomy* (Aldershot, Avebury).

Midgley, M. (1980) *Beast and Man: The Roots of Human Nature* (London: Methuen).

Midgley, M. (1994) *The Ethical Primate: Humans, Freedom and Morality* (London: Routledge).

Midgley, M. and Hughes, J. (1995) 'Trouble with Families?', in Almond. B. (Ed.) *Introducing Applied Ethics* (Oxford, Blackwell).

Mill, J. S. (1859) *On Liberty* (Pelican, Harmondsworth).

Miller, D. (1993) 'In Defence of Nationality', *Journal of Applied Philosophy*, 10, 1

Milligan, D. & Watts Miller, W. (Eds) (1992) *Liberalism, Citizenship and Autonomy* (Aldershot, Avebury).

Monk, R. (1990) *Ludwig Wittgenstein: The duty of genius*, Vintage, London.

Montefiore, A. (Ed.) (1973) *Philosophy and Personal Relations. An Anglo-French Study* (London, Routledge and Kegan Paul).

Moore, G. (1988) *Believing in God. A philosophical essay* (T and T Clark, Edinburgh).

Morgan, K. P. (1996) 'The Moral Politics of Sex Education', in Diller A., Houston B., Morgan K.P. and Ayim M. (Ed.), *The Gender Question in Education. Theory, Pedagogy and Politics* (Boulder Colorado and Oxford, Westview Press).

Morgan, P. (1995) *Farewell to the Family? Public Policy and Family Breakdown in Britain and the USA* (London, IEA Health and Welfare Unit).

Morrell, F. (1991) 'The work of the Speaker's commission and its definition of citizenship', in: Ken Fogelman (Ed.) *Citizenship in Schools* (London, David Fulton).

Mottahedeh, R. P. (1998) 'Traditional Shi'ite education in Qom', in: A. Oksenberg Rorty (Ed.) *Philosophers on education. New historical perspectives* (London, Routledge), 451-457.

Mott-Thornton, K. (1998) *Common Faith. Education, Spirituality and the State* (Aldershot: Ashgate).

Mulhall, S. and Swift A. (1996) *Liberals and Communitarians Second edition* (Oxford, Basil Blackwell).

Mulhall, S. and Swift, A. (1992) *Liberals and Communitarians* (Oxford: Blackwell).

Murdoch, I. (1992) *Metaphysics as a Guide to Morals* (London, Chatto and Windus).

Nagel, T. (1979) *Mortal Questions* (University Press, Cambridge).

National Curriculum Council (1990) *Curriculum Guidance 8: Education for Citizenship* (York, NCC).

National Curriculum Council (1990) *Curriculum Guidance 3: The Whole Curriculum* (York, NCC).

National Curriculum Council (1993) *Spiritual and Moral Development: A Discussion Paper* (London: National Curriculum Council).

Neilsen, K. (1971) *Contemporary critiques of religion* (Macmillan, London).

Neiman, A. and Siegel, H. (1993) 'Objectivity and Rationality in Epistemology and Education: Scheffler's Middle Road', *Synthese* 94, 55-83.

Newton-Smith, W. (1973) 'A Conceptual Investigation of Love', in Montefiore, A. (Ed.) *Philosophy and Personal Relations. An Anglo-French Study* (London, Routledge and Kegan Paul).

Nichols, K. (1992) 'Roots in religious education', in B. Watson (ed.), *Priorities in religious education. A model for the 1990s and beyond*, pp. 113-123 (Falmer, Lewes).

Ninnes, P. & Burnett, G. (2003) 'Comparative education research: poststructuralist possibilities', *Comparative Education*, 39(3), 279-297.

Norman, R. (1992) 'Citizenship, politics and autonomy', in: David Milligan & William Watts Miller (Eds) *Liberalism, Citizenship and Autonomy* (Aldershot, Avebury).

Norris, K. (1993) *Dakota. A Spiritual Geography* (New York: Houghton Mifflin).

Norris, K. (1996) *The Cloister Walk* (New York: Riverhead Books).

Norris, K. (1998) *Amazing Grace. A Vocabulary of Faith* (New York: Riverhead Books).

Nussbaum, M. C. (1997) *Cultivating Humanity: A Classical Defense of Reform in Liberal Education* (Cambridge, MA: Harvard University Press).

Nussbaum, M.C. (1990) *Love's Knowledge. Essays on Philosophy and Literature* (New York and Oxford, Oxford University Press).

Nussbaum, M.C. (2003) 'Judaism and the love of reason', in M. Bower and R. Groenhout (eds), *Philosophy, Feminism and Faith* (Bloomington: Indiana University Press).

Nyberg, D. (Ed.) (1985) *Philosophy of Education 1985: Proceedings of the forty-first annual meeting of the Philosophy of Education Society* (Normal, Illinois, Philosophy of Education Society, Illinois State University).

O'Hear, A. (1981) *Education, Society and Human Nature: an Introduction to the Philosophy of Education* (Routledge and Kegan Paul, London).

O'Hear, A. (1984) *Experience, explanation and faith. An introduction to the philosophy of religion* (Routledge and Kegan Paul, London).

O'Hear, A. (1985) 'Book Review: Charles Bailey: "Beyond the Present and the Particular"', *Journal of Philosophy of Education*, 9, 1, pp 146-51.

O'Hear, A. (1986) 'Education and rationality', in Cooper, D E (ed) *Education, Values and Mind. Essays for R S Peters* (Routledge and Kegan Paul, London).

O'Hear, A. (1987) 'Taking liberties', *Times Educational Supplement*, 16 January; p 4.

O'Hear, A. (1988) *The element of Fire. Science, Art and the Human World* (Routledge, London).

O'Hear, A. (1991) 'Wittgenstein and the transmission of traditions', in A. Phillips Griffiths (ed.), *Wittgenstein centenary essays*, pp. 41-60 (Cambridge University Press, Cambridge).

O'Keefe, Joseph M. (2003) 'Catholic Schools and Vouchers: How the Empirical Reality Should Ground the Debate', in Wolfe, *School Choice*.

O'Keeffe, B. (1988) 'On the margins of education: finding a dimension for belief', in Green, A G, and Ball, S J (eds) *Progress and Inequality in Comprehensive Education* (Routledge, London).

O'Keeffe, B. (1988) 'The Churches and educational provision in England and Wales', in McClelland, V A (ed) *Christian Education in a Pluralist Society* (Routledge, London).

O'Keeffe, B. (ed) (1986) *Faith, Culture and the Dual System: A Comparative Study of Church and County Schools* (Falmer Press, Lewes).

O'Keeffe, B. (ed) (1988) *Schools for Tomorrow: Building Walls or Building Bridges* (Falmer Press, Lewes).

O'Neill, J. (1994) 'Should Communitarians be Nationalists?', *Journal of Applied Philosophy* 11, 2.

O'Neill, O. (2003) 'Autonomy: The Emperor's New Clothes', *Proceedings of the Aristotelian Society* 77 (1): S1-S2I.

O'Neill, O. and Ruddick, W. (eds) (1979) *Having Children: Philosophical and Legal Reflections on Parenthood* (University Press, Oxford).

Oakeshott, M. (1962) *Rationalism in Politics and Other Essays* (Methuen, London).

Oakeshott, M. (1989) 'Learning and teaching', in: T. Fuller (Ed.) *The Voice of Liberal Learning. Michael Oakeshott on Education* (New Haven, Yale University Press).

Office for Standards in Education (1994) *Spiritual, Moral, Social and Cultural Development. An OFSTED Discussion Paper* (London: OFSTED).

Oksenberg Rorty, A. (1998a) 'The ruling history of education', in: A. Oksenberg Rorty (Ed.) *Philosophers on education. New historical perspectives* (London, Routledge), 1-13.

Oksenberg Rorty, A. (Ed.) (1998b) *Philosophers on education. New historical perspectives* (London, Routledge).

Otto, R. (1958) *The Idea of the Holy* (Oxford, Oxford University Press).

arfit, D. (1984) *Reasons and Persons* (Oxford University Press).

Passmore, J. (1980) *The Philosophy of Teaching* (London, Duckworth).

Pateman, C. (1983) 'Feminist Critiques of the public/private dichotomy', in: S. I. Benn & G F Gaus (Eds) *Public and Private in Social Life* (London, St Martin's Press).

Pendlebury, S. (1990) 'Practical reasoning and situational appreciation in teaching', *Educational Theory* 40, pp. 171-179.

Pendlebury, S. (1994) *Striking a Balance: practical wisdom and agency stances in teaching*. Paper presented to the Cambridge Branch of the Philosophy of Education Society of Great Britain.

Peters, R. S . (ed.) (1969) *Perspectives on Plowden* (London: Routledge and Kegan Paul).

Peters, R. S . (ed.) (1976) *The Role of the Head* (London: Routledge and Kegan Paul).

Peters, R. S. (1966) *Ethics and Education* (London: George Allen and Unwin).

Peters, R. S. (1972) *Reason, Morality and Religion. The Swarthmore Lecture 1972* (London, Friends Home Service Committee).

Peters, R. S. (1974) *Psychology and Ethical Development* (London, George Allen and Unwin).

Peters, R. S. (1977) 'John Dewey's philosophy of education', in: R. S. Peters (Ed.) *John Dewey Reconsidered* (London, Routledge and Kegan Paul).

Peters, R. S. (1981) 'Democratic values and educational aims', in Peters, R S, *Essays on Educators* (George Allen & Unwin, London).

Peters, R. S. (1983) 'Philosophy of education', in: P. H. Hirst (Ed.) *Educational theory and its foundation disciplines* (London, Routledge and Kegan Paul), 30-61.

Peters. R. S. (1981) *Essays on Educators* (London, Allen and Unwin).

Phillips, D. (2000) 'Learning from elsewhere in education: some perennial problems re-visited with reference to British interest in Germany', *Comparative Education*, 36(3), 297-307.

Phillips, D. C. (1975) 'The anatomy of autonomy', *Educational Philosophy and Theory*, 7, 2, pp 1-12.

Phillips, D. Z. (1965) *The concept of prayer* (Routledge and Kegan Paul, London).

Phillips, D. Z. (1970) *Faith and philosophical enquiry* (Routledge and Kegan Paul, London).

Phillips, D. Z. (1970) 'Philosophy and religious education', *British Journal of Educational Studies* 18,5-17.

Phillips, D. Z. (1971) *Death and immortality* (Macmillan, London).

Phillips, D.Z. (1976), *Religion without explanation* (Basil Blackwell, Oxford).

Phillips, D. Z. (1986) *Belief, change and forms of life* (Macmillan, London).

Phillips, D. Z. (1988) *Faith after foundationalism* (Routledge, London).

Phillips, D. Z. (1993) *Wittgenstein and religion* (Macmillan, London).

Pierson, V. (1994) 'The Teen Star Programme. Sexuality Teaching in the Context of Adult Responsibility', *The Sower* 15, 2, pp. 15-16.

Pring, R. (1984) *Personal and Social Education in the Curriculum* (Hodder and Stoughton, London).

Pring, R. (1985) 'In defence of TVEI', *Forum for the Discussion of New Trends in Education*, 28, 1, pp 14-17.

Pring, R. (1992) 'Education for a pluralist society', in: M. Leicester & M. Taylor (Eds) *Ethic Ethnicity and Education* (London, Kogan Page).

Pring, R. (1995a) 'The Community of Educated People'. *British Journal of Educational Studies*, 43(2), 125-145.

Pring, R. (1995b) 'Educating Persons: Putting *Education* Back into Educational Research'. The 1995 SERA Lecture. *Scottish Educational Review*, 27(2), 101-112.

364   *Liberalism, Education and Schooling*

Putnam, H. (1992) *Renewing Philosophy* (Cambridge MA, Harvard University Press).

Qualifications and Curriculum Authority (1998) *Education for Citizenship and the Teaching of Democracy in Schools. Final Report of the Advisory Group on Citizenship* (London: QCA).

Quinton, A. M. (1971) 'Authority and autonomy in knowledge', *Proceedings of the Philosophy of Education Society of Great Britain*, 5, 2, pp 201-15.

Rasmussen, D. (1990) *Universalism vs Communitarianism. Contemporary Debates in Ethics* (The MIT Press, Cambridge MA).

Rawls, J. (1971) *A Theory of Justice* (University Press, Oxford).

Rawls, J. (1985) 'Justice as fairness: political not metaphysical', *Philosophy and Public Affairs*, 14, 3, pp 223-51.

Rawls, J. (1987) 'The idea of an overlapping consensus', *Oxford Journal of Legal Studies*, 7, 1, pp 1-25.

Rawls, J. (1988) 'The priority of the right and ideas of the good', *Philosophy and Public Affairs*, 17, 4, pp 251-76.

Rawls, J. (1993) *Political Liberalism* (New York Columbia University Press)

Ray, C. and Went, D. (Eds.), (1995) *Good Practice in Sex Education: a sourcebook for schools* (London, National Children's Bureau/Sex Education Forum).

Raz, J. (1986) *The Morality of Freedom* (Clarendon Press, Oxford).

Reich, R. (2002) 'Testing the Boundaries of Parental Authority over Education: The Case of Homeschooling', in Macedo and Tamir, *Moral and Political Education.*

Reich, R. (2002) *Bridging Liberalism and Multiculturalism in American Education* (Chicago: Chicago University Press).

Reich, R. (2003) 'Common Schooling and Educational Choice', in *A Companion to the Philosophy of Education*, ed. Randall Curren (Oxford: Blackwell).

Reiss, M. (1993) 'What are the Aims of School Sex Education?', *Cambridge Journal of Education* 23, 2, pp. 125-136.

Reiss, M. J. (1996) 'Food, Smoking and Sex: Values in Health Education', in Halstead, J.M. and Taylor, M.J. (Ed.) *Values in Education and Education in Values* (London, The Falmer Press).

Reiss, M. J. (1997) 'Teaching about Homosexuality and Heterosexuality', *Journal of Moral Education* 26, 3, pp. 343-352.

Reiss, M. J. (Ed.) (1997) 'Moral Values and Sex Education', Special Issue of *Journal of Moral Education* 26, 3.

Religious Society of Friends (Quakers) in Britain (1995) *Quaker Faith and Practice* (London. The Yearly Meeting of the Religious Society of Friends [Quakers] in Britain).

Reynolds, C. H. & Norman, R. (Eds) (1988) *Community in America: the challenge of 'Habits of the Heart'* (Berkeley, University of California Press).

Rhees, R. (1969) *Without answers* (Routledge and Kegan Paul, London).

Rhees, R. (ed.) (1984) *Recollections of Wittgenstein* (Oxford University Press, Oxford).

Rich, J. M. (1985) 'Perfectionism, liberalism and citizenship education', in: D. Nyberg (Ed.) Philosophy of Education 1985: *Proceedings of the forty-first annual meeting of the Philosophy of Education Society* (Normal, Illinois, Philosophy of Education Society, Illinois State University).

Riches, V. (1986) *Sex and Social Engineering* (Milton Keynes, Family and Youth Concern).

Rosenblum, N. L. (2002) 'Pluralism and Democratic Education: Stopping Short by Stopping with Schools', in Macedo and Tamir, *Moral and Political Education*.

Rosenblum, N. L. (ed) (1989) *Liberalism and the Moral Life* (Harvard University Press, Cambridge MA).

Rudduck, J. & Hopkins, D. (Eds) (1985) *Research as a Basis for Teaching. Readings from the work of Lawrence Stenhouse* (London, Heinemann).

Runzo, J. (Ed) (1993) *Is God Real?* (London, Macmillan).

Russell, T. & Munby, H. (Eds) (1992) *Teachers and Teaching. From Classroom to Reflection* (London, The Falmer Press).

Russell, T. (1993) 'Critical attributes of a reflective teacher: is agreement possible?', in: J. Calderhead & P. Gates (Eds) *Conceptualizing Reflection in Teacher Development* (London, The Falmer Press).

Sacks, J. (1991) *The Persistence of Faith, Religion, Morality & Society in a Secular Age, The Reith Lectures 1990* (Weidenfeld and Nicolson, London).

Sacks, J. (1995) *Faith in the Future* (London, Darton, Longman and Todd).

Sacks, J. (1997) *The Politics of Hope* (London, Jonathan Cape).

Sacred Congregation for Catholic Education (1983) *Educational Guidance in Human Love. Outlines for Sex Education* (London, Catholic Truth Society).

Salomone, R. C. (2000) *Visions of Schooling. Conscience, Community and Common Education* (New Haven and London: Yale University Press).

Salomone, R. C. (2003) 'Charting a Constitutional Course between Private Values and Public Commitments: The Case of School Vouchers', in Wolfe, *School Choice*.

Sandel, M. J. (1982) *Liberalism and the Limits of Justice* (University Press, Cambridge).

Sandsmark, S. (2000) *Is World View Neutral Education Possible and Desirable? A Christian Response to Liberal Arguments* (Carlisle: Paternoster Press).

Scheffler, I, (1974) *Four Pragmatists. A Critical Introduction to Peirce, James, Mead, and Dewey* (London, Routledge and Kegan Paul).

Scheffler, I. (1960) *The Language of Education* (Springfield IL, Charles C Thomas).

Scheffler, I. (1973) *Reason and Teaching* (London, Routledge and Kegan Paul).

Scheffler, I. (1979) *Beyond the Letter. A Philosophical Inquiry into Ambiguity, Vagueness and Metaphor in Language* (London, Routledge and Kogan Paul).

Scheffler, I. (1982) *Science and Subjectivity* Second edition (Indianapolis, Hackett Publishing).

Scheffler, I. (1986) *Inquiries. Philosophical Studies of Language, Science and Learning* (Indianapolis, Hackett Publishing Company).

Scheffler, I. (1991) *In Praise of the Cognitive Emotions and Other Essays in the Philosophy of Education* (London, Routledge).

Scheffler, I. (1992) 'Judaism's Philosophy of Education. An Interpretation of Classical Sources', in Margolis. D.J. & Schoenberg, E.S. (Eds), *Curriculum, Community, Commitment. Views on the American Jewish Day School in Memory of Bennett I Solomon* (West Orange NJ. Behrman House Inc.).

Scheffler, I. (1992) 'Jewish Education, Purposes, Problems, and Possibilities', in Margolis, D.J. and Schoenberg, E.S. (Eds): *Curriculum, Community, Commitment. Views on the American Jewish Day School in Memory of Bennett I Solomon* (West Orange NJ, Behrman House Inc.).

Scheffler, I. (1992) 'Art, Science et Religion', *Les Cahiers du Musee National d'art Moderne* 41, 45-53.

Scheffler, I. (1993) 'Ritual Change', *Revue Internationale de Philosophie* 46, 185, 151-160.

Scheffler, I. (1993) 'Responses', *Synthese* 94, 127-137.

Scheffler, I. (1995) *Teachers of My Youth. An American Jewish Experience* (Dordrecht, Kluwer Academic Publishers).

Scheffler. I. (1965) *Conditions of Knowledge. An Introduction to Epistemology and Education* (Chicago, The University of Chicago Press).

Schön, D. (1983) *The Reflective Practitioner. How Professionals Think in Action* (New York, Basic Books).

Schön, D. (1987) *Educating the Reflective Practitioner* (San Francisco CA, Jossey-Bass Publishers).

School Curriculum and Assessment Authority (1996) *Education for Adult Life: The Spiritual and Moral Development of Young People*, SCAA Discussion Papers No. 6 (London: SCAA).

School Curriculum and Assessment Authority (1996) *National Forum for Values in Education and the Community. Consultation on Values in Education and the Community* (London, SCAA).

Schools Council (1971) *Working Paper 36: Religious Education in Secondary Schools* (Evans/Methuen, London).

Scruton, R. (1980) *The Meaning of Conservatism* (Penguin, Harmondsworth).

Scruton, R. (1980) 'Emotion, practical knowledge and common culture', in Rorty, A O (ed) *Explaining Emotions* (University of California Press, Berkeley).

Scruton, R. (1983) 'Freedom and custom', in Phillips Griffiths A (ed) *Of Liberty, Royal Institute of Philosophy Lecture Series 15* (University Press, Cambridge).

Scruton, R. (1986) *Sexual Desire. A Philosophical Investigation* (London, Weidenfeld and Nicolson).

Sealey, J. (1985) *Religious Education: Philosophical Perspectives* (George Allen & Unwin, London).

Sex Education Forum (1993) *Religion, Ethnicity and Sex Education: Exploring the Issues* (London, National Children's Bureau).

Sher, G. (1989) 'Educating citizens', *Philosophy and Public Affairs*, 18(1), pp. 68-80.

Sherman, N. (1989) *The Fabric of Character. Aristotle's Theory of Virtue* (Oxford, Clarendon).

Sherry, P. (1977) *Religion, truth and language games* (Macmillan, London).

Shields, P. R. (1993) *Logic and sin in the writings of Ludwig Wittgenstein* (University of Chicago Press, Chicago).

Shklar, J. (1984) *Ordinary Vices* (Cambridge, MA, Belknap Press of Harvard University Press).

Siegel, H. (1988) 'On the Obligations of the Professional Philosopher of Education', in W. Hare and J. P. Portelli (eds), *Philosophy of Education. Introductory Readings* (Calgary: Detselig Enterprises).

Smart, N. (1968) *Secular Education and the Logic of Religion* (Faber, London).

Smart, N. (1972) *The Concept of Worship* (London, Macmillan).

Smart, N. (1973) *The science of religion and the sociology of knowledge. Some methodological questions* (Princeton University Press, Princeton).

Smart, N. (2000) *World philosophies* (London, Routledge).

Smeyers, P. (1992) 'The necessity for particularity in education and child-rearing: The moral issue', *Journal of Philosophy of Education* 26, 63-73.

Smith, R. & Alred, G. (1993) The impersonation of wisdom in: D. McIntyre, H. Hagger & M. Wilkin (Eds) *Mentoring. Perspectives on School-Based Teacher Education* (London, Kogan Page).

Smith, R. (1987) 'Teaching on stilts: a critique of classroom skills', in M. Holt (Ed.) *Skills and Vocationalism. The Easy Answer* (Milton Keynes, Open University Press).

Smith, R. (1999) 'Paths of Judgment: The Revival of Practical Wisdom', *Educational Philosophy and Theory* 31 (3): 327-10.

Socialist Educational Association (1981) *The Dual System of Voluntary and County Schools* (SEA, Manchester).

Socialist Educational Association (1986) *All Faiths in All Schools: The Second Report of the Socialist Educational Association on Voluntary Schools and Religious Education* (SEA, London).

Sockett, H. (1973) 'Curriculum planning: taking a means to an end', in Peters, R S (ed) *Philosophy of Education* (University Press, Oxford).

Sockett, H. (1988) 'Education and Will: Aspects of Personal Capability', *American Journal of Education* 96, 2, pp. 195-214.

Soltis, J. F. (1988) 'Perspectives on philosophy of education', in: W. Hare & J. P. Portelli (Eds) *Philosophy of education. Introductory readings* (Calgary, Detselig Enterprises), 7-14.

Spiecker, B. (1992) 'Sexual Education and Morality', *Journal of Moral Education* 21, 1, pp. 67-76.

Standish, P. (1995) 'Post-modernism and the education of the whole person'. *Journal of Philosophy of Education*, **29** (1), 121-35.

Steiner, G. (1989) *Real Presences. Is there anything in what we say?* (London, Faber and Faber).

Steutel, J. (1988) 'Learning the Virtue of Self-Control', in Spiecker, B. and Straughan, R. (Eds.) *Philosophical Issues in Moral Education and Development* (Milton Keynes, Open University Press).

Storkey, E. (1995) *The Search for Intimacy* (London, Hodder and Stoughton).

Stout, J. (1988) 'Liberal society and the language of morals', in: Charles H. Reynolds & Ralph V. Norman (Eds) *Community in America: the challenge of 'Habits of the Heart'* (Berkeley, University of California Press).

Straughan, R. (1982) *I ought to, But...A Philosophical Approach to the Problem of Weakness of Will in Education*, Windsor, NFER-Nelson.

Straughan, R. (1989) *Beliefs, Behaviour and Education* (London, Cassell).

Straw, J. (1989) 'Islam, women and Muslim schools', *Muslim Educational Quarterly*, 6, 4, pp 7-9.

Liberalism, Education and Schooling

368   *Liberalism, Education and Schooling*

Strike, K. A. (1981) 'Toward a Moral Theory of Desegregation', in J. F. Soltis (ed.), *Philosophy and Education. Eightieth Yearbook of the National Society for the Study of Education.* Part 1 (Chicago: NS SE).

Strike, K. A. (1982) *Educational Policy and the Just Society* (University of Illinois Press, Urbana).

Strike, K. A. (1991) 'Humanizing education: subjective and objective aspects', *Studies in Philosophy and Education*, 11, 1, pp 17-30.

Strike, K. A. (1995) 'Discourse Ethics and Restructuring', in M. Katz (ed.), *Philosophy of Education 1994* (Urbana Illinois: Philosophy of Education Society).

Strike, K. A., Haller, E. J. and Soltis, J. F. (1988) *The Ethics of School Administration* (New York: Teachers College Press).

Swift, A. (2003) *How Not to Be a Hypocrite: School Choice for the Morally Perplexed Parent* (London: Routledge).

Tabachnich, B. R. & Zeichner, K. (Eds) (1991) *Issues and Practices in Inquiry-Oriented Teacher Education* (London, The Falmer Press).

Talbot, M. and Tate, N. (1997) 'Shared values in a Pluralist Society?', in R. Smith and P. Standish (eds), *Teaching Right and Wrong. Moral Education in the Balance* (Stoke on Trent: Trentham Books).

Tamir, Y. (1992) 'Democracy, Nationalism, and Education', *Educational Philosophy and Theory* 24, 1

Tamir, Y. (1993) *Liberal Nationalism* (Princeton NJ, Princeton University Press)

Tamir, Y., ed. (1995) *Democratic Education in a Multicultural State* (Oxford: Blackwell).

Taylor, C. (1992) *Multiculturalism and the 'The Politics of Recognition'* (Princeton NJ, Princeton University Press)

Taylor, C. (1999) 'A Catholic modernity?', in J. Heft (ed.), *A Catholic Modernity? Charles Taylor's Marianist Award Lecture* (New York and Oxford: Oxford University Press).

Taylor, C. (2002) *Varieties of Religion Today: . William James Revisited* (Cambridge, MA and London: Harvard University Press).

Thatcher, A. (ed.) (1999) *Spirituality and the Curriculum* (London: Cassell).

The Islamic Academy (1990) *Faith as the Basis of Education in a Multi-Faith, Multi-Cultural Country* (Cambridge, The Islamic Academy).

The Islamic Academy (1991), *Sex Education in the School Curriculum: The Religious Perspective – An Agreed Statement* (Cambridge, The Islamic Academy).

Thiessen, E. J. (1987) 'Two concepts or two phases of liberal education?', *Journal of Philosophy of Education*, 21, 2, pp 223-34.

Thiessen, E. J. (1993) *Teaching for commitment. Liberal education, indoctrination and Christian nurture* (McGill-Queen's University Press, Montreal & Kingston).

Thomson, R. (1997) 'Diversity, Values and Social Change: renegotiating a consensus on sex education', *Journal of Moral Education* 26, 3, pp. 257-271.

Tiles, J. E. (1988) *Dewey* (London, Routledge).

Tomasi, J. (2001) *Liberalism Beyond Justice. Citizens, Society, and the Boundaries of Political Theory* (Princeton and Oxford: Princeton University Press).

Tomasi, J. (2002) 'Civic Education and Ethical Subservience: From Mozert to Santa Fe and Beyond', in Macedo and Tamir, *Moral and Political Education*.

Tomiak, J. J. (2000) 'Polish education facing the twenty-first century: dilemmas and difficulties', *Comparative Education*, 36(2), 177-186.

Tooley, J. (1994) 'In Defense of Markets in Educational Provision', in *Education and the Market Place*, ed. David Bridges and Terence H. McLaughlin (London: Falmer).

Tooley, J. (1996) *Education without the State. Studies in Education No. 1* (London: Institute for Economic Affairs Education and Training Unit).

Tooley, J. (2000) *Reclaiming Education* (New York: Cassell).

Tooley, J. (2003) 'Why Harry Brighouse Is Nearly Right about the Privatisation of Education', *Journal of Philosophy of Education* 37 (3): 427-47.

Trigg, R. (1973) *Reason and commitment* (Cambridge University Press, Cambridge).

Ulanowsky, C. (1998) 'Sex Education: beyond Information to Values', in Michael J. Reiss and Shaikh Abdul Mabud (Eds) *Sex, Education and Religion* (Cambridge: The Islamic Academy, 1998).

Vardy, P. (1997) *The Puzzle of Sex* (London, Fount).

Veasey, D. (1994) 'Sex Education: Is Its Act Together? Christian and Secular Morality in School', *Pastoral Care in Education* 12, 2, pp. 13-22.

Wain, K. (1995) 'Richard Rorty, Education and Politics', *Educational Theory*, 45(3), 395-409.

Walford, G. (1990) *Privatization and Privilege in Education* (Routledge, London).

Wallace, R. (1986) 'TVEI as liberal education', in Gibson, R (ed) *Liberal Education Today?* (Institute of Education, Cambridge).

Walzer, M. (1983) *Spheres of Justice: A Defence of Pluralism and Equality* (Basil Blackwell, Oxford).

Walzer, M. (1994) *Thick and Thin. Moral Argument at Home and Abroad* (Notre Dame and London, University of Notre Dame Press).

Ward, K. (1982) *Holding Fast to God. A Reply to Don Cupitt* (London, SPCK).

Ward, K. (1983) 'Is autonomy an educational ideal?', *Educational Analysis*, 5, 1, pp 47-55.

Warren, B. (1992) 'Back to Basics: Problems and Prospects for Applied Philosophy'. *Journal of Applied Philosophy*, 9(1), 13-19.

Watts Miller, W. (1992) 'Liberal vegetarianism: moderation versus strong sentiments of morals', in: David Milligan & William Watts Miller (Eds) *Liberalism, Citizenship and Autonomy* (Aldershot, Avebury).

Weil, S. (1952) *The Need for Roots*, Routledge & Kegan Paul, London.

Weiming, T. (1997) 'Chinese philosophy: a synoptic view', in: E. Deutsch & R. Bontekoe (Eds) *A companion to world philosophies* (Oxford, Blackwell), 3-23.

Whelan, R. (Ed.) (1995) *Just a Piece of Paper? Divorce Reform and the Undermining of Marriage* (London, IE A Health and Welfare Unit).

White, J. (1973) *Towards a Compulsory Curriculum* (London: Routledge and Kegan Paul).

White, J. (1982) *The Aims of Education Re-Stated* (London: Routledge and Kegan Paul).

White, J. (1987) 'The quest for common values', in: Graham Haydon (Ed.) *Education for a Pluralist Society. Philosophical perspectives on the Swann Report*, Bedford Way Papers 30 (London, Institute of Education, University of London).

White, J. (1987a) The medical condition of philosophy of education, *Journal of Philosophy of Education*, 21(2), 155-162.

White, J. (1987b) 'Book Review: Philosophers on Education edited by Roger Straughan and John Wilson', *Journal of Philosophy of Education*, 21(2), 297-302.

White, J. (1990) *Education and the Good Life. Beyond the National Curriculum* (Kogan Page, London).

White, J. (1990) *Education and the Good Life. Beyond the National Curriculum* (London, Kogan Page).

White, J. (1992) 'Can education for democratic citizenship rest on socialist foundations?', *Journal of Philosophy of Education*, 26(1), pp. 19-27.

White, J. (1994) 'Education and the Limits of the Market', in *Education and the Market Place*, ed. David Bridges and Terence H. McLaughlin (London: Falmer).

White, J. (1994) 'Instead of OFSTED: a critical discussion of OFSTED on "spiritual, moral, social and cultural development"', *Cambridge Journal of Education* 24, 3: 369-77.

White, J. (1994) 'Liberalism, Nationality and Education'. Paper presented to conference of International Network of Philosophers of Education on 'Identity, Culture and Education'. Leuven.

White, J. (1995) 'Education and Nationality'. Paper presented to the Annual Conference of the Philosophy of Education Society of Great Britain, Oxford.

White, J. (1995) *Education and Well Being in a Secular Universe* (London: Institute of Education, University of London).

White, J. (1995) 'Problems of the philosophy of education', in: T. Honderich (Ed.) *The Oxford companion to philosophy* (Oxford, Oxford University Press), 216-219.

White, J. (2000) 'Editorial Introduction', in M. Luntley, *Performance, Pay and Professionals* IMPACT No 2 (Philosophy of Education Society of Great Britain).

White, J. (2003) 'Five critical stances towards liberal philosophy of education in Britain' (with responses by Wilfred Carr, Richard Smith, Paul Standish and Terence H. McLaughlin), *Journal of Philosophy of Education*, 37(1), 147-184.

White, J. and O'Hear, P. (1991) *A National Curriculum for All: Laying the Foundations for Success* (Institute for Public Policy Research, London).

White, J. and White, P. (1986) 'Education, liberalism and human good', in Cooper, D E (ed) *Education, values and mind. Essays for R. S. Peters* (London, Routledge and Kegan Paul).

White, J. and White, P. (1997) 'The Analytic Tradition in British Philosophy of Education' (unpublished).

White, J. & White, P. (2001) 'An analytic perspective on education and children's rights', in: F. Heyting, D. Lenzen & J. White (Eds) *Methods in philosophy of education* (London, Routledge), 13-29.

White, P. (1988) 'The New Right and Parental Choice', *Journal of Philosophy of Education*, 22, 2, pp 195-9.

White, P. (1988) 'The playground project; a democratic learning experience', in Lauder, H and Brown, P (eds) *Education: In Search of a Future* (Falmer Press, Lewes).

White, P. (1983) *Beyond Domination* (Routledge and Kegan Paul, London).

White, P. (1987) 'Self-respect, self-esteem and the "management" of schools and colleges', *Journal of Philosophy of Education*, 21, 1, pp 85-92.

White, P. (1987) 'Racism, self-esteem and the school', in Haydon, G (ed) *Education for a Pluralist Society. Philosophical Perspectives on the Swann Report*, Bedford Way Papers 30 (London, Institute of Education, University of London).

White, P. (1989) 'Educating courageous citizens', in White, P (ed) *Personal and Social Education: Philosophical Perspectives* (Kogan Page, London).

White, P. (1990) 'Friendship and education', *Journal of Philosophy of Education*, 24, 1, pp 81-91.

White, P. (1991) 'Humanisation, democracy and trust: the democratisation of the school ethos', *Studies in Philosophy and Education*, 11, 1, pp 11-16.

White, P. (1991) 'Hope, confidence and democracy', *Journal of Philosophy of Education*, 25, 2, pp 203-8.

White, P. (1991) 'Parents' rights, homosexuality and education', *British Journal of Educational Studies*, XXXIX, 4, pp 398-408.

White, P. (1994) 'Citizenship and spiritual and moral development', *Citizenship. The Journal of the Citizenship Foundation* 3, 2: 7-8.

White, P. (1996) *Civic Virtues and Public Schooling. Educating Citizens for a Democratic Society* (New York and London: Teachers College Press).

White, S. R. (1994) *Don Cupitt and the Future of Christian Doctrine* (London, SCM Press).

Whitty, G., Barrett, E., Barton, L, Furlong, J., Galvin, C. & Miles, S. (1992) 'Initial teacher education in England and Wales: a survey of current practices and concerns', *Cambridge Journal of Education*, 22(3) pp. 293-306.

Wilkin, M. (1993) I'nitial training as a case of postmodern development: some implications for mentoring', in: D. McIntyre, H. Hagger & M. Wilkin (Eds) *Mentoring. Perspectives on School-Based Teacher Education* (London, Kogan Page).

Williams, K. (1993) 'Civic Education, Nationhood and The "New Europe"'. Paper presented to the Cambridge branch of the Philosophy of Education Society of Great Britain, September

Williams, K. (1994) 'Education for European Citizenship: philosophical critique'. Paper presented to conference of International Network of Philosophers of Education on 'Identity, Culture and Education', Leuven

Williams, K. (1995) National Sentiment in Civic Education', *Journal of Philosophy of Education* 29, 3

Williams, M. S. (2003) 'Citizenship as Identity, Citizenship as Shared Fate, and the Functions of Multicultural Education', in McDonough and Feinberg, *Citizenship and Education in Liberal-Democratic Societies.*

Wilson, J. (1979) *Preface to the philosophy of education* (London, Routledge).

Wilson, J. (1986) *What Philosophy Can Do* (London: Macmillan).

Wilson, J. (1990) *A New Introduction to Moral Education* (London, Cassell).

Wilson, J. (1993) *Reflection and Practice. Teacher education and the teaching profession* (London, Ontario, The Althouse Press).

Wilson, J. (1995) *Love Between Equals. A Philosophical Study Of Love And Sexual Relationships* (London, Macmillan).

Wilson, J. (1996) 'First Steps In Moral Education', *Journal Of Moral Education*, 25(1), 85-91.

Wilson, J. (1998) 'Philosophy and Educational Research: a reply to David Bridges *et al*', *Cambridge Journal of Education*, 28(1), 129-133.

Wilson, J., Williams, N. and Sugarman, B. (1967) *Introduction to Moral Education* (Harmondsworth: Penguin).

Winch, C. (2000) *New Labour and the Future of Training* IMPACT No 4 (Philosophy of Education Society of Great Britain).

Winch, P. (1987) *Trying to make sense* (Basil Blackwell, Oxford).

Winch, P. (1993) 'Discussion of Malcolm's essay', in N. Malcolm (ed.), *Wittgenstein: A religious point of view?*, pp. 95-135 (Routledge, London).

Wisdom, J. (1962) 'Gods', in Flew A.G.N. (Ed), *Logic and Language* (Oxford, Blackwell).

Wolfe, A. (2003) 'Introduction', in Wolfe, *School Choice*.

Wolfe, A., ed. (2003) *School Choice: The Moral Debate* (Princeton, NJ: Princeton University Press).

Wright, A. (1998) *Spiritual Pedagogy. A Survey, Critique and Reconstruction of Contemporary Spiritual Education in England and Wales* (Abingdon: Culham College Institute).

Wright, A. (2000) *Spirituality and Education* (London: Routledge Falmer).

Wringe, C. (1984) *Democracy, Schooling and Political Education* (London, George Allen & Unwin).

Wringe, C. (1992) 'The ambiguities of education for active citizenship', *Journal of Philosophy of Education*, 26(1), pp. 29-38.

Wringe, C. (1994) 'Family Values and the Value of the Family'. *Journal of Philosophy of Education* 28, 1, pp. 77-88.

Yamashita, H. & Williams, C. (2002) 'A vote for consensus: democracy and difference in Japan', *Comparative Education*, 38(3), 277-289.

Young, R. (1980) 'In the interests of children and adolescents', in Aiken, W. and LaFollette, H. (eds) *Whose Child? Children's Rights, Parental Authority, and State Power* (Littlefield, Adams & Co, Totowa, New Jersey).

Young, R. (1986) *Personal Autonomy: Beyond Negative and Positive Liberty* (St Martin's Press, New York).

Zeichner, K. (1994) 'Research on teacher thinking and different views of reflective practice in teaching and teacher education', in: I. Carlgren, G. Handal & S. Vaage (Eds) (1994) *Teachers' Minds and Actions. Research on Teachers' Thinking and Practice* (London, The Falmer Press).

Zirkel, P. A. (1996) 'Courtside: Hot, Sexy—and Safer?', *Phi Delta Kappan*, September, pp. 93-94.

Index